No. 3101
$29.95

THE HANDBOOK OF
MICROCOMPUTER
INTERFACING
2nd Edition

STEVE LEIBSON

TAB BOOKS Inc.
Blue Ridge Summit, PA

SECOND EDITION
FIRST PRINTING

Library of Congress Cataloging in Publication Data

Leibson, Steve.
The handbook of microcomputer interfacing.

Includes index.
1. Computer interfaces. 2. Microcomputers.
I. Title.
TK7887.5.L44 1989   621.398′1   88-38011
ISBN 0-8306-9101-4
ISBN 0-8306-3101-1 (pbk.)

TAB BOOKS Inc. offers software for
sale. For information and a catalog,
please contact TAB Software Department,
Blue Ridge Summit, PA 17294-0850.

Questions regarding the content of this book
should be addressed to:

Reader Inquiry Branch
TAB BOOKS Inc.
Blue Ridge Summit, PA 17294-0214

Contents

Acknowledgments

Several companies contributed illustrations and a great deal of technical information to this book, all of which is greatly appreciated. In addition the help of their Denver, Colorado, representatives is greatly appreciated. These companies are:

General Instrument Corporation
Intel Corporation
Motorola Incorporated
National Semiconductor
OKI Semiconductor
Texas Instruments, Incorporated
Zilog, Inc.

To Pat and Shaina

To Professor Harry Mergler at Case Western Reserve University who taught
me that the written word was just as important
as the electron and the logic gate.
To Mike Kolesar and John Nairn at Hewlett-Packard who started me down the
I/O road.

Introduction

Welcome to the world of microcomputer interfacing! It is a place full of mysteries much like a computerized Adventure game. Those of us in the interfacing field are constantly trying to decode how to communicate with products from different manufacturers. Printers, plotters, terminals, tape readers, keyboards and many other peripherals are routinely connected to computers. Have you wondered how this is done? What are the standards involved in interfacing computers to other equipment?

This book was written to answer these questions and more. It is about how to get information out of (output) and into (input) computers. You will find out that the subject of interfacing (also called I/O for input/output) covers many fields. Both hardware and software are involved, but so are history, corporate conflicts and economics. The methods used in interfacing today have roots in the previous century, even before digital electronic computers were even imagined.

For those of you who are new to digital electronics, Chapter 1 serves as an introduction. In it, I introduce some basic terminology, digital circuits, gates and integrated circuits. Then you will look at codes, the language of interfacing. Basic microprocessor concepts are covered as are the basic types of interfaces. Though Chapter 1 is introductory, you may want to skim over it even if you have some experience in these areas. You never can tell what you might pick up.

In Chapter 2 you will look more closely at microprocessor structure and architecture. Since this is a book about interfacing to microprocessors, it is appropriate that we first study microprocessors and how they have been designed to talk to other devices. If you have ever wondered what the difference between memory-mapped and plain-vanilla I/O is, you'll find out in Chapters 2 and 3.

Finally you get down to the business of interfacing in Chapter 4, which is about parallel I/O. This can be the simplest type of interface, and that is why it is first. On the other hand, some variations of the parallel interface are quite complex. Integrated circuit manufacturers have spent the last few years making ever more complex parallel-interface chips. They, too, are in this chapter.

Chapter 5 is about serial interfacing and a paradox. The serial interface is the oldest type of electrical communication, with many years of experience and standards behind it. The fact is, however, that you can rarely plug two devices with "standard serial interfaces" together and get them to communicate the first time you try. This chapter explores why this is so and how you can increase your chances of getting the computer and a serial peripheral on speaking terms.

You leave the all-digital world in Chapter 6 to look at analog interfaces. Analog devices are concerned with "how much" signal is present while digital devices such as microprocessors only care about the presence or absence of a signal. Analog interfacing creates a bridge between the two worlds allowing the microprocessor to sense and control analog equipment.

In Chapter 7 you will enter the fourth dimension: time. Microprocessors, which control processes, are increasingly concerned about time: how long to run a heater, when to turn on the lights. This chapter divides time into two types: real and absolute. We then look at how to give both types of time

sense to a microprocessor, how to interface to time.

Chapter 8 looks at advanced interfacing concepts: It is about interrupts. Interrupts are advanced because we are diverting the computer from what it was doing. If you aren't careful, the processor may forget what it was doing before the interruption and lose itself entirely. Also in this chapter, you will look at the various interrupt systems that microprocessor manufacturers have devised and discuss the differences between hardware and software interrupts.

Chapter 9 looks at one of the most complex concepts in interfacing: direct memory access, or DMA. A microprocessor cannot perform DMA by itself; special hardware is needed. Sometimes this hardware is more complex than the processor!

I have already compared microcomputer interfacing to an Adventure game. This book is a set of guidelines on how to play the Interfacing game. A complete map of the game is not possible. Extra rooms are always being added to the dungeons by the computer, peripheral and integrated-circuit manufacturers. What I have provided, however, are several partial maps and helpful playing hints. These tell you about rules that don't change and techniques that work. They also warn you about rules that *almost* never change, and when they might. Armed with the knowledge in this book, you can start winning the Interfacing game.

Chapter 1

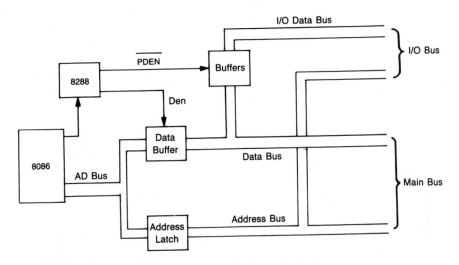

Bits, Bytes, and Busses

Interfacing circuits are based on digital electronics, as are all microprocessor-based systems. The roots of digital circuitry trace back to a nineteenth century mathematician, George Boole. In 1854 Boole published *An Investigation of the Laws of Thought on Which Are Founded the Mathematical Theories of Logic and Probabilities*. What Boole had done was to create an algebra of logic. Thus, the mathematics of computers was devised over 100 years before the logic circuits were developed that would allow wide use of Boole's theories.

Boole's work, and digital electronics, is based on binary numbers. The binary number system is based on the numerals zero (0) and one (1) unlike the familiar decimal number system we normally use every day, which is based on the numerals zero (0) through nine (9). Binary numbers are particularly useful in electronics. A single binary digit, called a *bit*, can be used to represent true or false, as in Boole's logic. Binary numbers are also used to represent numeric quantities, just as in the decimal number system. Several bits taken together can also be used to represent codes, such as character codes for transmitting text. Many such codes use eight bits, called a *byte*, which allow representation of up to 256 different characters.

This chapter introduces the ways in which binary numbers are used in digital electronics. It is an introductory chapter, but it is also very important. The use of binary numbers is fundamental to understanding microprocessors and how to talk to them.

BOOLEAN ALGEBRA

George Boole's intention in creating what is now called Boolean algebra was to allow problems in logic to be precisely stated. This was not seen at the time as a mathematics useful for electronics because no such field as electronics existed. Boolean algebra was devised for philosophy.

Philosophic logic is concerned with the truth or falsehood of statements derived from other statements. For example, the statement, "If it is light outside and the time is before noon, then it must

1

be morning," is a statement in logic. The substatement "If it is light outside" may be either true or false. This can also be said of the substatement "the time is before noon." The word "and" is a logic operation much like addition and subtraction are mathematical operations in algebra. if you call the statements "If it is light outside" and "the time is before noon" arguments, then the "and" operation requires that both arguments of the statement must be true for the conclusion "it must be morning" to be true.

These arguments can be either true or false. There is no "maybe" possible. These arguments are called Boolean variables because they may only have one of two values: true or false. Boole decided that true and false were too clumsy for use in an algebra of logic and reassigned the numeral 1 to true and the numeral 0 to represent false. In doing so, he forged an unbreakable link between Boolean algebra and the binary number system which only has the numerals 1 and 0.

BOOLEAN OPERATIONS

We are all familiar with the usual mathematical operations of addition, subtraction, multiplication, and division. Simple arithmetic is part of the public-school curriculum. Boolean algebra also has fundamental operations. They are called *and, or,* and *not*. These three operations are quite simple but can be combined into complex structures.

Computers are built of circuits that do little more than *and, or,* and *not*. The reason computers can become so powerful is that electronic technology has developed techniques that place thousands of Boolean-operation circuits on a single integrated circuit or chip. Let's look at these three basic Boolean operations and see what they do.

NOT

The *not* operation is the most simple. The Boolean variable operated on by *not* is inverted. Thus *not true* is false and *not false* is true. Since a Boolean variable may only have one of two values, if it does not have one value, it must have the other.

Putting it in Boolean terms:

$$\text{Not } 0 = 1 \qquad \text{Not } 1 = 0$$

In philosophical logic, the *not* operation is shown as a bar over the variable. For example, if we have a variable called A, then we represent "NOT A" as $\overline{A}$.

The electrical device that performs the NOT operation is called a NOT gate, or inverter. A symbol for an inverter with a truth table is shown in **Fig. 1-1**. The input to the inverter is on the left side of the symbol and the output is on the right. A logic signal applied to the inverter's input is transformed by the device and the inverse of the signal is available at the output.

The truth table in **Fig. 1-1** shows the output as a function of all possible inputs. An inverter has a single input which may only have one of two values; 0 or 1. Thus there are only two entries in the truth table of an inverter.

AND

The AND operator takes two or more arguments. We will first look at the two-argument AND.

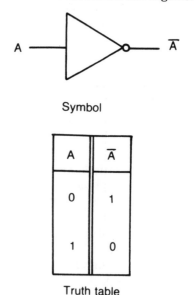

Symbol

A	$\overline{A}$
0	1
1	0

Truth table

Fig. 1-1. A NOT gate (inverter) and truth table.

In order for a statement using the AND operation to be true, both arguments must be true. Thus TRUE AND TRUE is TRUE while TRUE AND FALSE, FALSE AND TRUE, and FALSE AND FALSE are all FALSE. In Boolean terms:

$$0 \text{ AND } 0 = 0$$
$$0 \text{ AND } 1 = 0$$
$$1 \text{ AND } 0 = 0$$
$$1 \text{ AND } 1 = 1$$

The symbol for the AND operation is a centered dot (•), which is the same symbol used in arithmetic for multiplication. If we have two arguments called A and B, then the AND operation on those two arguments is written as A•B. Sometimes the AND operator is left out, so that AB is also the AND of A and B.

An AND gate is the electrical device which performs the AND operation. The symbol for a two-input AND gate is shown in Fig. 1-2, along with the AND truth table. The two inputs are shown on the left side of the gate and the output is on the right. Since this AND gate has two inputs, each of which can have one of two values applied to them, there are four entries in the truth table.

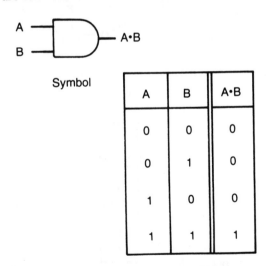

Symbol

A	B	A•B
0	0	0
0	1	0
1	0	0
1	1	1

Truth table

Fig. 1-2. A two-input AND gate and truth table.

A three-input AND gate and truth table are shown in Fig. 1-3. It has three inputs labeled A, B, and C. The truth table has eight entries. This is because each of the three inputs can have one of two values, resulting in eight input possibilities.

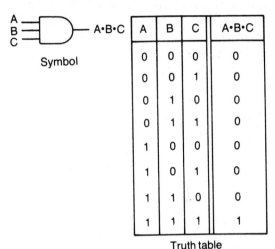

Symbol

A	B	C	A•B•C
0	0	0	0
0	0	1	0
0	1	0	0
0	1	1	0
1	0	0	0
1	0	1	0
1	1	0	0
1	1	1	1

Truth table

Fig. 1-3. A three-input AND gate and truth table.

By now, you should see a pattern to how many entries in the truth table a Boolean operation may have. The single-input inverter has two, a two-input AND gate has four and a three-input AND gate has eight. The number of entries in a truth table is equal to two raised to the power of the number of inputs. Thus:

Number of Inputs	Number of Entries
1	$2\ (2^1)$
2	$4\ (2^2)$
3	$8\ (2^3)$
4	$16\ (2^4)$
and so on	

OR

The OR operation also takes two or more arguments. In order for a statement using the OR operator to be true, only one of the arguments has to be true. Thus for a two-argument OR statement, TRUE OR FALSE, FALSE OR TRUE and TRUE

OR FALSE are all true statements. Only FALSE OR FALSE is FALSE. In Boolean terms:

$$0 \text{ OR } 0 = 0$$
$$0 \text{ OR } 1 = 1$$
$$1 \text{ OR } 0 = 1$$
$$1 \text{ OR } 1 = 1$$

The symbol for the OR operation is a plus sign (+), the same symbol used for arithmetic addition. This symbol is used in both philosophic and electric logic statements.

Figure 1-4 shows the symbol for a two-input OR gate with its truth table. The two inputs to the gate are on the left and the output is on the right. A three-input OR gate and truth table are shown in Fig. 1-5.

Symbol

A	B	C	A+B+C
0	0	0	0
0	0	1	1
0	1	0	1
0	1	1	1
1	0	0	1
1	0	1	1
1	1	0	1
1	1	1	1

Truth table

Fig. 1-5. A three-input OR gate and truth table.

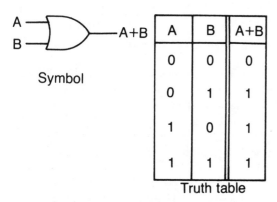

Symbol

A	B	A+B
0	0	0
0	1	1
1	0	1
1	1	1

Truth table

Fig. 1-4. A two-input OR gate and truth table.

MORE COMPLEX BOOLEAN OPERATORS

Although all logic functions can be built from the AND, OR, and NOT operations, it is much easier to develop a few slightly more complex operations. These new operations are a kind of shorthand schematic notation. For example, we will use four more Boolean operations in this book. They are NAND, NOR, Exclusive OR, and Exclusive NOR. Also, we will need a signal amplifier called a noninverting buffer which could also be called an IS gate.

NAND

The NAND operation is formed by following the AND operation with a NOT operation. NAND is a contraction of NOT and AND. Remember that in the AND operation, TRUE AND TRUE is TRUE while FALSE AND FALSE, FALSE AND TRUE, and TRUE AND FALSE are all FALSE. Following the AND function with a NOT produces opposite results. TRUE NAND TRUE is FALSE while FALSE NAND FALSE, FALSE NAND TRUE, and TRUE NAND FALSE are all TRUE. In Boolean terms:

$$0 \text{ NAND } 0 = 1$$
$$0 \text{ NAND } 1 = 1$$
$$1 \text{ NAND } 0 = 1$$
$$1 \text{ NAND } 1 = 0$$

The symbol for a two-input NAND gate with its truth table is shown in Fig. 1-6. Note the similarity to the AND gate. What has been added is the bubble at the output. This bubble has been taken from the output of the inverter and is used to represent the NOT operation. There is no written symbol for the NAND operation. It is written as the inverted AND of the arguments.

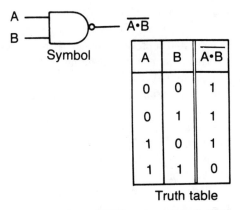

Truth table

Fig. 1-6. A two-input NAND gate and truth table.

A	B	$\overline{A \cdot B}$
0	0	1
0	1	1
1	0	1
1	1	0

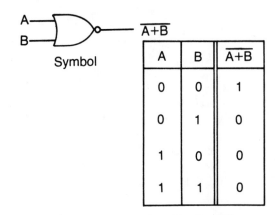

Truth table

Fig. 1-7. A two-input NOR gate and truth table.

A	B	$\overline{A+B}$
0	0	1
0	1	0
1	0	0
1	1	0

NOR

The NOR operation is formed by following the OR operation with a NOT operation. NOR is a contraction of NOT and OR. Remember that in the OR operation, FALSE OR FALSE is FALSE while FALSE OR TRUE, TRUE OR FALSE, and TRUE OR TRUE are all TRUE. Following the OR with a NOT produces opposite results. FALSE NOR FALSE is TRUE while FALSE NOR TRUE, TRUE NOR FALSE, and TRUE NOR TRUE are all FALSE. In Boolean terms:

$$0 \text{ NOR } 0 = 1$$
$$0 \text{ NOR } 1 = 0$$
$$1 \text{ NOR } 0 = 0$$
$$1 \text{ NOR } 1 = 0$$

The symbol for a two-input NOR gate with its truth table is shown in Fig. 1-7. Note the similarity between the NOR gate and the OR gate. A NOR gate is an OR gate with an inversion bubble on the output. There is no written symbol for the NOR operation, it is written as the inverted OR of the two arguments.

Exclusive OR

An Exclusive OR gate differs from an OR gate in that the operation produces a true result if only one of the inputs is true. If all inputs are false or more than one input is true, then the output is false.

Thus FALSE EXCLUSIVE-OR FALSE and TRUE EXCLUSIVE-OR TRUE are both FALSE while TRUE EXCLUSIVE-OR FALSE and FALSE EXCLUSIVE-OR TRUE are both TRUE. In Boolean terms:

$$0 \text{ EXCLUSIVE-OR } 0 = 0$$
$$0 \text{ EXCLUSIVE-OR } 1 = 1$$
$$1 \text{ EXCLUSIVE-OR } 0 = 1$$
$$1 \text{ EXCLUSIVE-OR } 1 = 0$$

The written symbol for Exclusive OR is "$\oplus$" which is the symbol for OR with a circle around it. The symbol for a two-input Exclusive-OR gate and its truth table is shown in Fig. 1-8. Note the similar-

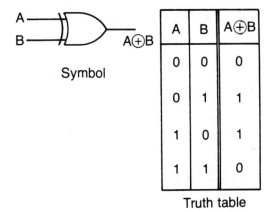

Symbol

Truth table

A	B	A$\oplus$B
0	0	0
0	1	1
1	0	1
1	1	0

Fig. 1-8. A two-input exclusive-OR gate and truth table.

ity between this symbol and that of the two-input OR gate. An extra line has been added on the input to indicate the "exclusiveness" of the gate.

Exclusive NOR

An Exclusive NOR gate differs from a NOR gate in that the operation produces a true result if the inputs match each other. Thus FALSE EXCLUSIVE-NOR FALSE and TRUE EXCLUSIVE-NOR TRUE are both FALSE. In Boolean terms:

$$0 \text{ EXCLUSIVE-NOR } 0 = 1$$
$$0 \text{ EXCLUSIVE-NOR } 1 = 0$$
$$1 \text{ EXCLUSIVE-NOR } 0 = 0$$
$$1 \text{ EXCLUSIVE-NOR } 1 = 1$$

There is no written symbol for the Exclusive NOR operation. It is shown as the inversion of the Exclusive OR of the arguments. The symbol for a two-input Exclusive NOR gate and its truth table is shown in **Fig. 1-9**. Note the similarity between this symbol and that of the two-input NOR gate. An extra line has been added on the input to indicate the "exclusiveness" of the gate. Exclusive NOR gates are useful for comparisons because the output is true if the inputs match.

Noninverting Buffer (IS)

It may seem strange to have a device that takes an input and reproduces it exactly at the output, but that is what a noninventing buffer does. Since FALSE IS FALSE and TRUE IS TRUE, you might think that a simple piece of wire would do the trick.

The usefulness of a noninverting buffer is not in the paper equations of philosophy but in the reality of circuitry. Real logic gates can provide only a certain amount of signal. If the output of the gate is overloaded, the signal will be distorted and the difference between a 0 and a 1 may not be detectable.

Noninverting buffers are like repeaters in telephone cables. They can take a 0 or 1 and amplify it so that the inputs of many gates can be driven with the same signal. Noninverting buffers are usually built so that they can drive many more inputs than regular gates.

The symbol and truth table for the noninverting buffer are shown in **Fig. 1-10**. Note the similarity with the symbol for an inverter. Only the inversion bubble on the output is missing.

FLIP-FLOPS

Logic gates allow us to create an output signal with a state determined by any logical combination

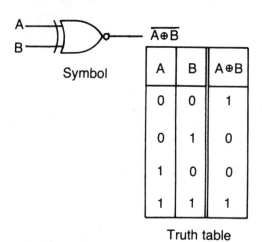

Fig. 1-9. A two-input exclusive-NOR gate and truth table.

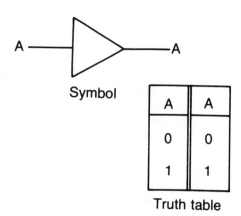

Fig. 1-10. A non-inverting buffer gate and truth table.

of inputs. They cannot remember anything however. The output states of logic gates are only dependent on the current state of the gate's inputs. Circuits built from gates are said to be made from combinatorial logic.

Frequently, we need to remember that an event has happened so that when a future event happens, the two events taken together can cause a third event to occur. A familiar example of this is dialing the telephone. Each digit we dial has to be remembered by the circuit so that when we have dialed the complete number, the proper telephone is rung.

Logic devices that remember are called flip-flops. The output of a flip-flop can be either a 0 or a 1 but that does not necessarily depend on what the inputs are at the present time. The output of the flip-flop can be either set (logic 1) or cleared (logic 0) and it will stay that way until changed.

There are several types of flip-flop. Each type has memory, the difference being how the output is set or cleared. The flip-flops we will discuss are the RS (reset-set), the D-type, and the JK.

RS Flip-Flop

This is the simplest of all flip-flops. An RS flip-flop symbol is shown in **Fig. 1-11**. Normally, both the S and R inputs are at 0. If a 1 is applied to the S input, the flip-flop will be set and the Q output will assume a 1 state. The Q output will stay in the 1 state even if the 1 applied to the S input is removed. The flip-flop is reset by applying a 1 to the R input. Resetting the flip-flop causes the Q output to assume A0 state. It is not valid to apply 1 states to both the S and R inputs at the same time—the results of doing this are supposed to be unpredictable. Note that the flip-flop has a second output, marked $\overline{Q}$. This

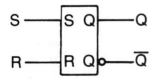

Fig. 1-11. An RS flip-flop.

output has an inversion bubble on it and is called the "inverted-Q," "Q-bar," or "not Q" output. It always assumes a state opposite that of the Q output.

Figure 1-12 shows one way to build an RS flip-flop using two NOR gates. To understand its operation we will assume both S and R inputs are in the 0 state. We will also assume that the flip-flop is in the reset state, so that the Q output is in a 0 state. This means both inputs to the top NOR gate are in a 0 state, so the output of the top NOR gate must be in a 1 state. That state is applied to one of the inputs of the bottom NOR gate. Since one input of the bottom NOR gate is a 1, the output of that gate must be in the 0 state. That brings us back to our initial assumption. Since the conclusion is consistent with our initial assumption, the assumption must have been correct in the first place.

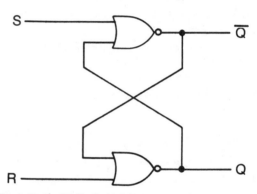

Fig. 1-12. An RS flip-flop implemented with cross-coupled NOR gates.

This is one stable state for the flip-flop. As long as both S and R inputs are in the 0 state, the flip-flop will stay in the reset state. We could also have assumed that the flip-flop was in the set state, so that the Q output was in a 1 state. This assumption also produces a consistent conclusion, and is the other stable state of the flip-flop. (As an exercise, see if you can produce the logical sequence of statements that produces this conclusion.)

If the flip-flop is in the reset state, the Q output is in the 0 state and the $\overline{Q}$ output is in the 1 state. If we apply a 1 to the R input, nothing happens because one input to the bottom NOR gate was already in the 1 state. The output of the bottom NOR gate will be 0 whether one or both inputs is a 1. However if we apply a 1 to the S input, the output of the top NOR gate will change from a 1 to 0. This will cause the output of the bottom NOR gate to change from a 0 to 1 and the flip-flop will have been set. Removing the 1 from the S input will not change the outputs because the 1 at the output of the bottom NOR gate maintains the 0 at the output of the top NOR gate. The state of the flip-flop has been flipped from reset to set.

The set flip-flop is cleared by applying a 1 to the R input. This produces an action similar to setting the flip-flop but with the two NOR gates changing places. You might wish to try writing down the sequence of events that cause the flip-flop to flop back into the reset state.

Notice that if we applied a 1 to both the S and the R inputs, both the Q and $\overline{Q}$ outputs would be 0. Since Q and $\overline{Q}$ are always supposed to have opposite values, we have produced an inconsistency in the circuit. The flip-flop is neither set nor reset. The input that is last returned to a 0 will determine which state the flip-flop is left in.

D Flip-Flop

This type of flip-flop has the same outputs as the RS flip-flop but different inputs. There are actually two types of D flip-flops: the positive-edge-triggered D and the transparent D.

The symbol for a positive-edge-triggered D flip-flop is shown in Fig. 1-13. It has Q and $\overline{Q}$ outputs like the RS flip-flop but the inputs are different. The D input is the D(ata) input and the C input is the C(lock) input.

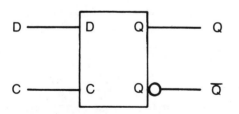

Fig. 1-13. A D-type flip-flop with an edge-triggered clock input.

Edge-triggered flip-flops are sensitive to transitions on the C input. The Q output will assume the same state as that applied to the D input at the instant that the signal applied to the C input changes from 0 to 1. After that 0-to-1 transition, the Q output will not change, even if the signal applied to the D input changes. The Q output will not change until the next 0-to-1 transition on the C input, when it will again assume the same state present on the D input.

A transparent-D flip-flop looks and works a little differently. **Figure 1-14** shows the symbol for a transparent-D flip-flop. It has a D input for D(ata) and an E input for E(nable).

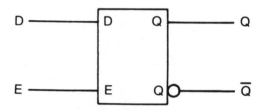

Fig. 1-14. A D-type flip-flop with an enable input.

While a 1 is applied to the E input, the Q output will assume the same state as that applied to the D input. If the signal applied to the D input changes while a 1 is applied to the E input, the Q output will follow along. Changing the signal applied to the E input to a 0 will freeze the Q output and it will not follow the level applied to the D input anymore.

Putting it another way, as long as the E input has a 1 applied to it, the flip-flop is transparent and will pass the state of the D input along to the Q output. When the E input has a 0 applied to it, the flip-flop is no longer transparent and the Q output will have the same state as the D input had just before the E input was changed from 1 to 0.

JK Flip-Flop

This type of flip-flop has three inputs and the familiar Q and $\overline{Q}$ outputs. **Figure 1-15** shows the symbol for the JK flip-flop. The three inputs are J, K, and C for C(lock).

JK flip-flops are edge triggered, like the edge-triggered D flip-flop above. Both positive and nega-

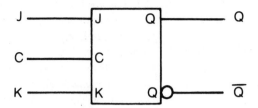

Fig. 1-15. A JK flip-flop.

tive edge-triggered JK flip-flops are available. The J and K inputs specify what the flip-flop will do when the appropriate transition is applied to the C input. If both J and K have zeroes applied to them when the transition occurs, the flip-flop does not change state, whether it is set or reset. If 1 is applied to J and 0 to K when the transition occurs, the flip-flop will be set. If 1 is applied to K and 0 to J when the transition occurs, the flip-flop will be reset.

If 1 is applied to both J and K when the transition on the clock input occurs, the flip-flop will toggle. That means if it was set before the transition, it will be reset. If the flip-flop was reset before the transition, it will be set.

DIGITAL CIRCUITS IN THE REAL WORLD

So far, we have been talking about "applying a 1" and "applying a 0" without defining what those terms really mean. There is no physical 1 or 0 to apply. In practice, some physical quantity is used to represent the logic ones and zeroes. This quantity may be a voltage or current or might be a magnetic spot on a piece of recording tape. Some systems use air or water pressures.

TTL LOGIC LEVELS

In this book, we will concentrate on one representation system, the so-called TTL logic levels. The term TTL stands for Transistor-Transistor Logic, an extremely successful family of integrated logic circuits.

TTL circuits were introduced in the late 1960s for military and space hardware. As manufacturers gained experience in making these circuits, the prices dropped so low that commercial products

could use them. TTL is a five-volt logic family. That means the power supply that powers the circuitry is specified to be five volts.

Since we are working with binary-valued signals, we need one voltage level to represent logic 0 and another for logic 1. For TTL circuits, there is actually a range of permissible voltage levels. The low logic-level is defined as a voltage between 0.0 and 0.8 volts. The high logic-level is defined as a voltage between 2.0 and 5.0 volts. **Figure 1-16** illustrates these levels.

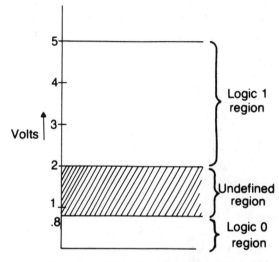

Fig. 1-16. The TTL logic levels. A valid low logic level is between zero and .8 volts. A valid high logic level is between 2.00 and 5.00 volts. The region between .8 volts and 2 volts is the undefined region. If the input to a TTL gate is in the undefined region, the output of the gate is not guaranteed to be at a valid logic level.

The region between 0.8 and 2.0 volts is not defined. Since we are working with binary signals, voltages in this region should not be allowed except for extremely short periods of time, when a signal is changing from high to low or low to high. If a logic gate has an undefined voltage applied to one of its inputs continuously, unpredictable behavior will result.

Voltages below 0.0 or above 5.0 volts should not be applied to TTL circuits. Some improved TTL families can withstand slightly higher or lower voltages, but it's still poor practice to apply such voltages.

Input and Output
Current Requirements

Logic gates have definite limitations as to how much load can be applied to their outputs. Each logic gate input requires a certain amount of current at the specified voltages. Each logic gate output can supply a certain amount of current at the specified voltages.

There are several subfamilies in the TTL family. First there was standard TTL. Then came the low-power and high-speed TTL subfamilies. Later, Schottky and low-power Schottky subfamilies were introduced. Recently, even more advanced subfamilies have been brought to the market. However the most successful series of TTL parts is the 7400 series, originally manufactured by Texas Instruments.

There is a simple numbering system which allows you to determine which subfamily a part is from. For example; a package containing four, 2-input NAND gates is a 7400 (called a quad 2-input NAND). The low-power version is the 74L00, the high-speed version is the 74H00, the Schottky version is the 74S00, the low-power Schottky version is the 74LS00, the advanced Schottky version is the 74AS00 and the advanced, low-powered Schottky version is the 74ALS00. Each of these subfamilies

has different input current requirements and output drive capabilities.

In order to bring a TTL input down to a low logic level, you must *sink* (consume) current out of it. To take a TTL input to a high logic level, you must *source* (supply) current into it. How much current you need to sink or source depends on the subfamily the circuit belongs to. **Table 1-1** is a list of the high- and low-level input currents for the above families. At the same time, each logic subfamily has certain output drive capabilities. These are listed in **Table 1-2**. Note that the output capabilities of the various gates in a logic family vary quite a bit. Some gates are designed for greater output capability. The data sheets will tell you the actual output current capability.

Notice that each logic family can drive ten inputs from its own subfamily. The low-power subfamily can drive eleven. Gates from different families can be mixed, as long as the gate outputs are not overloaded. For example, a low-power output can only drive one Schottky input. Generally, you don't need to worry too much about loading within a single subfamily until you get near a load of ten inputs.

Many of the interfacing circuits we will be dealing with in this book are not fabricated with TTL technology. However, the TTL levels have become such a standard that these circuits have been designed to be compatible with TTL levels. You still

SUBFAMILY	INPUT CURRENT	
	MAXIMUM HIGH-LEVEL (in microamps)	MAXIMUM LOW-LEVEL (in milliamps)
Standard (7400)	40	1.6
High Speed (74H)	50	2.0
Low Power (74L) type 1	10	0.18
type 2	20	0.8
Low-power Schottky (74LS)	20	0.4
Schottky (74S)	50	2.0

Table 1-1. Input Current Requirements for Common Logic Families.

	OUTPUT CURRENT	
SUBFAMILY	MAXIMUM HIGH-LEVEL (in microamps)	MAXIMUM LOW-LEVEL (in milliamps)
Standard (7400)	400	16
High Speed (74H)	500	20
Low-Power (74L)	100	2
Low-power Schottky (74LS)	400	4
Schottky (74S)	1000	20

Table 1-2. Output-current (drive) Capabilities of Common Logic Families.

need to check loading and drive requirements. Sometimes "TTL compatibility" means that the outputs can drive one and only one low-power TTL input.

POSITIVE- AND NEGATIVE- TRUE LOGIC

Now that we have defined the two signal levels we will use to represent logic levels, we have to decide which we will use to represent a logic 0 and which a logic 1. You may have assumed that the lower voltage level (0 to 0.8 volts) would represent logic 0. That would mean the higher voltage level (2.0 to 5.0 volts) would represent logic 1.

There is certainly nothing wrong with these assignments. Such an assignment system is called *positive-true logic* because the more positive voltage represents the logic 1 or TRUE state. We don't *have* to make that assignment, however. It is just as easy to assign the lower voltage level to represent logic 1 and the higher voltage level as logic 0. This is called *negative-true logic*. The more negative voltage represents the logic 1 or TRUE state.

Figure 1-17 is the logic symbol and truth table for one gate of a 7400 quad 2-input positive-NAND gate as it is drawn in the manufacturer's data book. The truth table has been filled in with H and L instead of zero and one because H and L represent actual voltage levels instead of logic states. An

H means the high voltage level (2.0 to 5.0 volts) and the L means a low voltage level (0.0 to 0.8 volts).

The truth table in **Fig. 1-17** exactly specifies how the output of the gate will react to the inputs, regardless of whether we are using positive- or negative-true logic. There are two ways we can interpret this truth table.

We can call this part what the manufacturer calls it, a positive-true NAND gate. All we have to do is say that all the L's in the truth table are to be interpreted as zeroes and all the H's are to be interpreted as ones. This converts the truth table in **Fig. 1-17** into the table in **Fig. 1-6** for a NAND gate.

We could also say that we will interpret the inputs as negative-true and output as positive-true. That means that the inputs are now called A and B instead of A and B. The overscore means that the

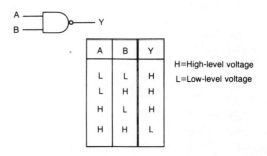

A	B	Y
L	L	H
L	H	H
H	L	H
H	H	L

H=High-level voltage
L=Low-level voltage

Fig. 1-17. A TTL NAND gate with a voltage truth table.

signals are negative-true. With this interpretation, we get the truth table of **Fig. 1-18**. This is the truth table of an OR gate, because the output is a logic 1 (high voltage) if either of the inputs is a logic 1 (low voltage).

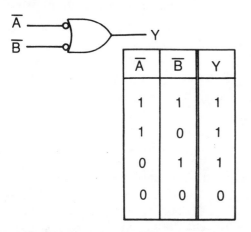

$\overline{A}$	$\overline{B}$	Y
1	1	1
1	0	1
0	1	1
0	0	0

Fig. 1-18. By interpreting the TTL voltage levels with negative-true logic, the TTL NAND gate becomes an inverted-input OR gate with a negative-true output.

By simply reinterpreting the voltage truth table, we now have an OR gate with negative-true inputs and a positive-true output. Note the inversion bubbles on the inputs. These remind us that the inputs are negative-true, that a low-voltage signal represents a logic 1.

Why would we want to make such an interpretation? The reason is that sometimes you have no control over whether signals will be positive- or negative-true. In interfacing, you are provided with a set of signals from an existing circuit. Some will be positive-true and others will be negative-true. It is to our benefit to be able to use logic gates as either positive- or negative-true devices. Otherwise we might have to add a lot of inverters to make every signal positive-true.

Remember, reinterpretation does not change how the part works, it simply makes it easier for you to follow the logic. For example, if you want to produce a signal that is TRUE when the equation A OR B is true, you must use a positive-true OR gate. If the negative-true signals $\overline{A}$ and $\overline{B}$ are avail-

able however, $\overline{A}$ NAND $\overline{B}$ is equivalent, as we have shown in the truth table in **Fig. 1-18**.

The same technique may be used on a positive-true NOR gate. **Figure 1-19** shows a 7402 positive NOR gate with its electrical truth table. Notice that the output is high only when both inputs are low. If we interpret these input and output voltages as positive-true, we do have the two-input NOR gate of **Fig. 1-7**.

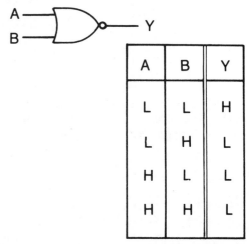

A	B	Y
L	L	H
L	H	L
H	L	L
H	H	L

Fig. 1-19. A TTL NOR gate with a voltage truth table.

We can interpret the inputs as negative-true however, as shown in **Fig. 1-20**. This produces an AND gate with negative-true inputs. If $\overline{A}$ and $\overline{B}$ are both at logic 1, meaning low voltage for negative-true signals, the output will be logic 1, meaning high voltage for positive-true logic.

DEMORGAN'S THEOREMS

There are formal theorems that allow us to make logic transformations. They are DeMorgan's theorems which state:

$$\overline{(AB)} = \overline{A} + \overline{B}$$

and

$$\overline{(A + B)} = \overline{A} \cdot \overline{B}$$

The first equation says that a positive-true NAND gate is equivalent to an OR gate with negative-true inputs. That is what we showed in **Fig.**

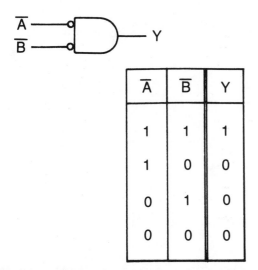

$\overline{A}$	$\overline{B}$	Y
1	1	1
1	0	0
0	1	0
0	0	0

Fig. 1-20. By interpreting the TTL voltage levels with negative-true logic, the TTL NOR gate becomes an inverted-input NAND gate with a negative-true output.

1-18. The second equation says that a positive-true NOR gate is equivalent to an AND gate with negative-true inputs. That was shown in **Fig. 1-20.**

TTL OUTPUT CONFIGURATIONS

So far, we have assumed that all gate outputs will provide the TTL levels we have set; a low level is between 0.0 and 0.8 volts and a high level is between 2.0 and 5.0 volts. The output circuit which can supply these levels is shown in **Fig. 1-21** and is called a Totem-Pole output structure.

There are two transistors in this output structure, one stacked on the other. That's where the name "totem pole" comes from. If the bottom transistor is turned on, current can flow from the output terminal to ground through that transistor. This has the effect of "pulling" the terminal to ground potential. If the top transistor is turned on, current can flow from the 5-volt power supply to the output terminal. This will "pull" the output terminal towards the 5-volt level.

In normal totem-pole-output TTL parts, one of the transistors is always on. There is either a valid high or low voltage-level at the output pin. While the

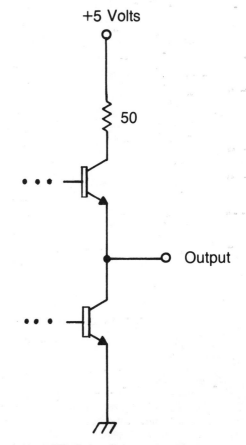

+5 Volts

50

Output

Fig. 1-21. A TTL Totem-Pole output circuit.

output circuit is switching from one level to another, both transistors may be on for a very small amount of time. The 50-ohm resistor in series with the totem pole limits the current through the totem pole during this time, so the circuit will not short out the power supply and burn up.

It is very important to note that if the output terminals from two totem-pole devices are connected, there can be problems—one of the totem-pole outputs may be in the high-voltage state and the other may be at the low-voltage state. A large amount of current will flow through the top transistor of one output and the bottom transistor of the other (see **Fig. 1-22**). The 50-ohm resistor is not intended to limit currents for long periods of time. The output circuits will overheat and may be destroyed. However, it is sometimes necessary to

13

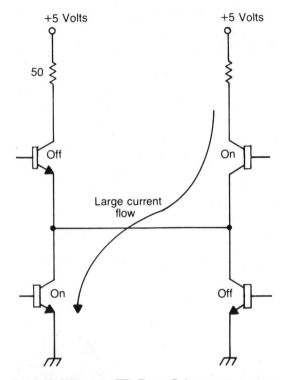

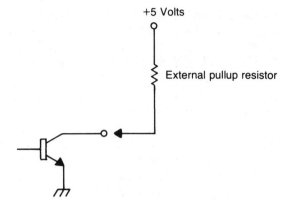

+5 Volts

50

Off

On

Large current flow

On

Off

Fig. 1-22. When two TTL Totem-Pole outputs are connected, the possibility exists that one output will try to drive high while the other is driving low. The result is a high current flowing through the top transistor of one gate output and the bottom transistor of the other gate output. This can result in the destruction of at least one of the gates.

+5 Volts

External pullup resistor

Fig. 1-23. A TTL Open Collector output circuit.

connect more than one output together. Manufacturers have devised alternative output structures for these cases—they are called open-collector and three-state outputs.

An open-collector output circuit is shown in **Fig. 1-23.** Note that the top transistor and 50-ohm resistor from the totem-pole circuit have been removed. Only the bottom transistor remains. This output stage can only supply the low TTL signal. When the transistor is turned off, the output terminal is free to assume whatever voltage it may. Usually, an external resistor is supplied by the circuit designer to "pull" the output into the high-voltage region, thus the name "pullup resistor." The value of the resistor is selected so that the cur-

rent flowing into the output terminal when the transistor is turned on is within the limits specified for the device.

Several open-collector outputs may be connected together with a single pullup resistor used to supply the high-voltage level. There are no top transistors to supply excessive input currents.

Why aren't all TTL outputs open collector? Switching times from the low to the high level are slower for open-collector outputs than for the totem-pole structure, since the pullup resistor has to have a value higher than 50 ohms to keep currents in the safe region. The smaller current supplied by the pullup resistor cannot move the output terminal voltage as fast as the totem-pole output can.

The other alternative output structure is the three-state output. It looks like the totem pole of **Fig. 1-21.** The difference is that a special input to the TTL circuit can instruct both transistors to turn off. Since neither transistor is turned on, current will not flow into or out of the output terminal. The output stage simply becomes disconnected.

Three-state outputs can be connected together, as long as only one output stage is allowed to be active at one time. If two or more outputs are enabled simultaneously, we return to the problem we had with the totem-pole output. If we are careful about enabling the outputs of gates which are connected together, we can have a single signal line driven by one of several outputs. This concept is

14

the foundation of the bus, a structure discussed in Chapters 2 and 3.

NUMBER SYSTEMS

When working with computers, it is impossible to escape numbers. An important part of what computers do is the computation, manipulation, and storage of large quantities of numeric data. One characteristic of computers that makes them more difficult to understand than they might be is that most computers use the binary number system, or a number system closely related to binary.

You are probably familiar with the decimal number system and why we as humans use it. The ten appendages on our hands (fingers and thumbs) are responsible for shaping our arithmetic to a very large degree. Computers do not have hands, or thumbs, or fingers. Computers have transistors. Although we can count from 1 to 10 on our fingers, a computer can only count to 1 on a transistor. A digital circuit can be either on or off, 0 or 1. To count any higher, a computer needs more transistors, meaning more digits.

The Binary Number System

Chances are you are already familiar with binary numbers. In the late 1950s, when the USSR launched Sputnik, there was great concern in the United States that America was falling behind in math and science. School curricula were overhauled to compensate. One of the products of this overhaul was the "new math," and part of this new mathematics was an exposure to the binary number system. Though we weren't told at the time, binary numbers are most useful in the computer sciences.

In order to study binary numbers, we first look at decimal numbers—the number system we are all so familiar with that we take it for granted. Just what does the sequence of numerals "12345" mean? You immediately recognize this number as "twelve thousand three hundred forty-five." Yet what your mind has actually done is something like the following:

1. There are five digits in the number, therefore the leftmost digit is multiplied by ten thousand and saved in a temporary storage area.
2. The second number from the left is multiplied by one thousand, added to the number in temporary storage and the sum is put back into temporary storage.
3. The third number from the left is multiplied by one hundred and added to the number in temporary storage. This new sum is put back into temporary storage.
4. The fourth number is multiplied by ten, added to the number in temporary storage and the new sum is put back into temporary storage.
5. The last number is multiplied by one and added to the number in temporary storage to produce the result.

Our modern number systems use the idea of positional significance. The position of the numeral imparts a weighting to that numeral so that the right hand numeral has a weight of one, the next to the left has a weight of ten and so on.

Not all number systems work like this. A good example of one that does not is the Roman numeral system. The symbol for one, "I," is different from the symbol for ten, "X," which is different from the symbol for one hundred, "C," etc.

The weighting given to a numeral is dependent on both its position and the number system base. For our decimal system, the base is ten. Thus the right-hand position has a weight of one, which is ten raised to the zero power. The next position to the left has a weight of ten, which is ten raised to the first power. The third position has a weight of one hundred, which is ten raised to the second power.

With binary numbers, the base is two. The right-hand position weight is one, just as in the decimal system. In fact, the right-hand position for any base always has a weight of one because any number raised to the zero power is one. The next position to the left has a weight of two, which is two raised to the first power. The next position has a weight of four, then eight, and so on. Each binary digit is called a *bit*, which is a contraction of BInary digiT.

Let's take a binary number and see how to calculate its value. We'll take the number 110010.

1. There are six digits in the number, so the weight of the leftmost digit is two raised to the fifth power, or 32. (Remember, the power starts at zero in the rightmost position. To determine the power of a position, subtract one from the position.) There is a one in this position so one multiplied by 32 is 32. Save thirty-two temporarily.
2. The numeral second from the left is also a 1. Multiply this by two raised to the fourth power, or 16. Add 16 to the saved 32 to get 48 and save this sum.
3. There is a zero in the next position. Multiply this by two raised to the third power, or 8. Since this is zero, we can forget adding it to the temporary sum.
4. There is a zero in the third position from the right. Multiply this by two raised to the second power, or 4. Since this is zero, we don't add anything to the temporary sum.
5. The second from the right position has a 1 in it. Multiply this by two raised to the first power, or 2. Add two to the temporary sum of 48 to get 50. Save the new sum.
6. The right position has a zero in it. Multiply this by one. Since this is zero, and all the positions are now accounted for, the converted number is the saved value of 50.

Sure didn't look like 50, did it? Fortunately, it isn't necessary to deal with binary numbers frequently. There are two other number bases that are easier to use; the *octal* (base 8) and *hexadecimal* (base 16) number systems.

If we take a decimal number three digits at a time, we are working with thousands. If there were a thousand different numerals, we could represent one thousand numbers with a single digit. If we take a binary number three bits at a time, we will be working with eights. This is the octal number system.

Octal numerals are "0" through "7". Note that with three bits we can represent the numbers 0 through 7. Thus octal numbers can be thought of as shorthand notation for binary numbers. The binary number 110010 used in the earlier example can be written as 62 in octal. We could convert this number to decimal by multiplying the 6 by 8 to get 48 and adding the 2 to get 50. Quite a bit simpler than binary manipulation, isn't it?

Since most microprocessors deal with eight-bit quantities, octal notation is not popular. Eight bits is two and two-thirds octal digits. The most common number base used with microprocessors is hexadecimal, base 16. This way, we can deal with an eight-bit byte as two hexadecimal (hex for short) digits.

Now there is a problem. When working with number bases less than our beloved ten, the numerals could be the same as the first few numerals in the decimal numeral set. Base 16 requires sixteen numerals—we are six numerals short.

The extra six numerals are taken from the first six letters of the alphabet. Thus we have the familiar "0" through "9" and the very strange "A" through "F." "A" is worth ten, "B" is eleven and so on until "F," which is worth fifteen.

The binary number 110010 would then convert to 32 hex. To convert this number to decimal, we take the 3 and multiply it by sixteen raised to the first power (16) to get 48. Then we add the 2 to get 50. See **Table 1-3**.

If all of this looks too complex, consider addition, subtraction or worse, multiplication and division in any of these strange number bases. It took you years to memorize the tables and rules for just the decimal numbers.

One way to cope with this deluge of numbers is to always convert the numbers to decimal, perform the arithmetic, and then convert back. A better way is to buy a calculator that can deal with the different number bases. Both Texas Instruments

Table 1-3. Examples of the
Number 50 In Four Number Systems.

Decimal	Binary	Octal	Hexadecimal
50	110010	62	32

(the TI Programmer) and Hewlett-Packard (the HP-16C) make them. A third way is to put a program on your computer which can convert from one number base to another. There is such a program, written in BASIC, in Appendix A of this book.

Although most people associate computers with numbers, the interfacing game is primarily concerned with the transfer of all types of information between devices. Numbers fall in this category, but text is at least as important. Since computers can't deal with anything except binary information, printable characters must be coded into binary format. This takes us into the fascinating world of character codes.

CHARACTER CODES

The problem of coding alphabets has existed long before electricity was harnessed. Semaphore flags, heliographs (solar telegraph) and smoke signals were all used to send information using some sort of code to replace written characters.

When electricity was captured, first in Leyden jars and then in batteries, it was inevitable that the new energy would be harnessed for communications. Samuel Morse finally created a widely used code for the telegraph, the Morse code.

Morse telegraphy involves the transmission of two symbols—dots and dashes (dihs and dahs for purists). Each letter of the English alphabet and the Arabic numerals has a unique string of dots and dashes. Morse code made it possible to send text messages from one telegraph operator to another, as long as they both knew the code. The Morse code was developed between 1832 and 1838.

Even in the 1800s, the cost of human operators was higher than that of machinery, and they were often less reliable. Very early in the history of the telegraph, attempts were made at building mechanical devices for transmitting and receiving Morse code messages. The problem was that Morse had developed a variable-length code. Some characters had two symbols and some had three. Variable-length codes are very hard to mechanize. A constant-length code was needed.

J.M.E. (Emil) Baudot invented the first constant-length teleprinter code in 1874. Following in Morse's footsteps, Baudot's code is called the Baudot code. Each character has five symbols. Since the symbols are binary in nature, either a dot or a dash, we can consider them bits, so Baudot's code is a five-bit code. Baudot code was adopted by the French Telegraph system in 1877. It is also known as the International Telegraph Code Number 1.

Just at the turn of the century, Donald Murray refined the Baudot code. Murray's code also uses five bits per character and is called the International Telegraph Alphabet Number 2 instead of Murray code. Perhaps this is the reason no one remembers Murray. To this day, Murray code is wrongly labeled Baudot. **Table** 1-4 shows the Baudot and Murray codes.

A five-bit code can only represent 32 different characters. This is not sufficient to represent all the letters of the alphabet plus the Arabic numerals. Therefore the Baudot and Murray codes have two special characters called *Letters* and *Figures*. After receipt of a "letters" character, all subsequent characters are to be interpreted as letters of the alphabet. Receipt of a "figures" character causes all following characters to be interpreted as numerals and punctuation marks.

Letters and figures are known as shift codes because they cause interpretation of the received codes to shift between two sets. In this case the two character sets are:

1. the alphabet
2. numerals and punctuation marks

Shift codes create problems. If a shift code is lost or garbled in transmission, all following codes are misinterpreted until another shift code is received. Another disadvantage of the five-bit code is that only capital letters can be represented. There aren't enough bits to specify lowercase letters. A benefit of the short, five-bit code is that no more bits are sent than necessary, since five bits specify a letter of the alphabet.

Clearly, five bits just wasn't enough. Shift codes had reliability problems. As electromechanical devices such as teletypewriters gave way to electronics, the need for a more advanced character code grew.

Table 1-4. Baudot and Murray Character Codes.

DECIMAL	BINARY	HEXADECIMAL	BAUDOT		MURRAY	
			Letters	Figures	Letters	Figures
0	0 0000	00	Note 1	Note 1	No Action	No Action
1	0 0001	01	Letters	Letters	E	3
2	0 0010	02	Figures	Figures	Line Feed	Line Feed
3	0 0011	03	Error	Error	A	-
4	0 0100	04	Y	3	Space	Space
5	0 0101	05	S	•	S	(Apost) '
6	0 0110	06	B	8	I	8
7	0 0111	07	R	-	U	7
8	0 1000	08	E	2	Car. Ret.	Car. Ret.
9	0 1001	09	X	(Comma) ,	D	WRU
10	0 1010	0A	G	7	R	4
11	0 1011	0B	M	)	J	BELL
12	0 1100	0C	I	Note 1	N	(Comma) ,
13	0 1101	0D	W	?	F	Note 1
14	0 1110	0E	F	Note 1	C	:
15	0 1111	0F	N	Note 1	K	(
16	1 0000	10	A	1	T	5
17	1 0001	11	Line Feed	Line Feed	Z	+
18	1 0010	12	J	6	L	)
19	1 0011	13	K	(	W	2
20	1 0100	14	U	4	H	Note 1
21	1 0101	15	T	Note 1	Y	6
22	1 0110	16	C	9	P	0
23	1 0111	17	Q	/	Q	1
24	1 1000	18	Car. Ret.	Car. Ret.	O	9
25	1 1001	19	z	:	B	?
26	1 1010	1A	H	+	G	Note 1
27	1 1011	1B	L	=	Figures	Figures
28	1 1100	1C	O	5	M	•
29	1 1101	1D	V	(Apost) '	X	/
30	1 1110	1E	D	0	V	=
31	1 1111	1F	P	%	Letters	Letters

Note 1: Not assigned
Note 2: Bits are transmitted from least to most significant.
Note 3: In the Baudot code, receipt of a Letters character while in the Letters mode or a Figures
　　　　Character while in the Figures mode causes a space.

There are two ways to fill a technological gap such as that which existed for character codes. First, a group of companies can get together, spend months or years in careful consideration and bring forth a standard. The other way is for one company to create its own solution, quickly implement it and expect all the other companies to follow along.

Both of these paths were taken, producing two competing codes. The group of companies formed under the American National Standards Institute (ANSI) and brought forth the American Standard Code for Information Interchange (ASCII, pro-nounced Askey, rhymes with pass-key). The ASCII code is formally known as ANSI standard X3.4-1977.

ASCII is a seven-bit code which has become the worldwide standard under several standards organizations. It can represent all of the capital and lowercase letters, numerals and popular punctuation marks. In addition, there are codes called control codes such as carriage return and line feed. There are even shift codes, if the standard ASCII character set should prove insufficient. The ASCII code is shown in **Table 1-5.**

Table 1-5. The ASCII Code Table.

BITS 3 2 1 0	HEX	000 / 0	001 / 1	010 / 2	011 / 3	100 / 4	101 / 5	110 / 6	111 / 7
0 0 0 0	0	NUL	DLE	SP	0	@	P	`	p
0 0 0 1	1	SOH	DC1	!	1	A	Q	a	q
0 0 1 0	2	STX	DC2	"	2	B	R	b	r
0 0 1 1	3	ETX	DC3	#	3	C	S	c	s
0 1 0 0	4	EOT	DC4	$	4	D	T	d	t
0 1 0 1	5	ENQ	NAK	%	5	E	U	e	u
0 1 1 0	6	ACK	SYN	&	6	F	V	f	v
0 1 1 1	7	BEL	ETB	'	7	G	W	g	w
1 0 0 0	8	BS	CAN	(	8	H	X	h	x
1 0 0 1	9	HT	EM	)	9	I	Y	i	y
1 0 1 0	A	LF	SUB	*	:	J	Z	j	z
1 0 1 1	B	VT	ESC	+	;	K	[	k	{
1 1 0 0	C	FF	FS	,	<	L	\	l	|
1 1 0 1	D	CR	GS	-	=	M	]	m	}
1 1 1 0	E	SO	RS	.	>	N	^	n	~
1 1 1 1	F	SI	US	/	?	O	—	o	DEL

Then there was IBM, the only company that could reasonably expect to develop a character set without regard for the rest of the industry. IBM's character code is called the Extended Binary Coded Decimal Interchange Code (EBCDIC, pronounced like "eb-sih-dick"). EBCDIC is an eight-bit code introduced with IBM's very successful System/360. The computer did well; the character code did not. IBM has slowly come over to ASCII with the rest of the industry.

Since EBCDIC has one more bit than ASCII, it could theoretically represent twice as many characters. However, not all of the EBCDIC codes are used. Table 1-6 shows the EBCDIC code. You can see that there are many gaps in this table.

ASCII

The ASCII table (Table 1-5) is set up as eight columns of sixteen characters each, for a total of 128 characters. Each column is referred to as a "stick" which is a term brought to us by the creators of ASCII. The sticks are numbered from left to right, starting with stick 0.

When referring to a character, I will refer to it by its position in a specific stick. Thus the upper-case A is the second character in stick 4. A short-hand notation for this character is then 4/1 (the characters are numbered starting with 0 also).

Sticks 4 through 7

These are the printable alphabet. Here we find all the letters (upper- and lowercase) and a few punctuation marks. Some computer and peripheral manufacturers do not strictly conform to all the punctuation mark definitions. For example, character 5/14 is called a circumflex. Some machines replace this character with an up-pointing arrow. That is close, but it isn't standard.

The punctuation marks in sticks 4 through 7 are place holders. Not all languages use 26 character alphabets. For example, Scandinavia's has 29. The punctuation marks [,/, and] in stick 5 and {,|, and } in stick 7 are reserved internationally for nationality-dependent characters. In this book, we will use the characters [,/,{,|,and } as specified in the ASCII definition.

The last ASCII character, 7/15 is not a printable character. It is DEL (delete). DEL was placed at 7/15 because of punched tape. Characters on paper tape are represented as a row of punched holes.

Table 1-6. The EBCDIC Table.

Character	Bit Pattern	Character	Bit Pattern	Character	Bit Pattern	Character	Bit Pattern
NUL	0000 0000	SP	0100 0000		1000 0000	{	1100 0000
SOH	0000 0001		0100 0001	a	1000 0001	A	1100 0001
STX	0000 0010		0100 0010	b	1000 0010	B	1100 0010
ETX	0000 0011		0100 0011	c	1000 0011	C	1100 0011
PF	0000 0100		0100 0100	d	1000 0100	D	1100 0100
HT	0000 0101		0100 0101	e	1000 0101	E	1100 0101
LC	0000 0110		0100 0110	f	1000 0110	F	1100 0110
DEL	0000 0111		0100 0111	g	1000 0111	G	1100 0111
	0000 1000		0100 1000	h	1000 1000	H	1100 1000
RLF	0000 1001		0100 1001	i	1000 1001	I	1100 1001
SMM	0000 1010	¢	0100 1010		1000 1010		1100 1010
VT	0000 1011	.	0100 1011		1000 1011		1100 1011
FF	0000 1100	<	0100 1100		1000 1100	⌐	1100 1100
CR	0000 1101	(	0100 1101		1000 1101		1100 1101
SO	0000 1110	+	0100 1110		1000 1110	⌐	1100 1110
SI	0000 1111	!	0100 1111		1000 1111		1100 1111
DLE	0001 0000	&	0101 0000		1001 0000	}	1101 0000
DC1	0001 0001		0101 0001	j	1001 0001	J	1101 0001
DC2	0001 0010		0101 0010	k	1001 0010	K	1101 0010
DC3	0001 0011		0101 0011	l	1001 0011	L	1101 0011
RES	0001 0100		0101 0100	m	1001 0100	M	1101 0100
NL	0001 0101		0101 0101	n	1001 0101	N	1101 0101
BS	0001 0110		0101 0110	o	1001 0110	O	1101 0110
IDL	0001 0111		0101 0111	p	1001 0111	P	1101 0111
CAN	0001 1000		0101 1000	q	1001 1000	Q	1101 1000
EM	0001 1001		0101 1001	r	1001 1001	R	1101 1001
CC	0001 1010	!	0101 1010		1001 1010		1101 1010
CU1	0001 1011	$	0101 1011		1001 1011		1101 1011
IFS	0001 1100	*	0101 1100		1001 1100		1101 1100
IGS	0001 1101	)	0101 1101		1001 1101		1101 1101
IRS	0001 1110	;	0101 1110		1001 1110		1101 1110
IUS	0001 1111	¬	0101 1111		1001 1111		1101 1111
DS	0010 0000	—	0110 0000		1010 0000	\	1110 0000
SOS	0010 0001	/	0110 0001	~	1010 0001		1110 0001
FS	0010 0010		0110 0010	s	1010 0010	S	1110 0010
	0010 0011		0110 0011	t	1010 0011	T	1110 0011
BYP	0010 0100		0110 0100	u	1010 0100	U	1110 0100
LF	0010 0101		0110 0101	v	1010 0101	V	1110 0101
EOB/ETB	0010 0110		0110 0110	w	1010 0110	W	1110 0110
PRE/ESC	0010 0111		0110 0111	x	1010 0111	X	1110 0111
	0010 1000		0110 1000	y	1010 1000	Y	1110 1000
	0010 1001		0110 1001	z	1010 1001	Z	1110 1001
SM	0010 1010	;	0110 1010		1010 1010		1110 1010
CU2	0010 1011	.	0110 1011		1010 1011		1110 1011
	0010 1100	%	0110 1100		1010 1100		1110 1100
ENQ	0010 1101	—	0110 1101		1010 1101		1110 1101
ACK	0010 1110	>	0110 1110		1010 1110		1110 1110
BEL	0010 1111	?	0110 1111		1010 1111		1110 1111
	0011 0000		0111 0000		1011 0000	0	1111 0000
	0011 0001		0111 0001		1011 0001	1	1111 0001
SYN	0011 0010		0111 0010		1011 0010	2	1111 0010
	0011 0011		0111 0011		1011 0011	3	1111 0011
PN	0011 0100		0111 0100		1011 0100	4	1111 0100
RS	0011 0101		0111 0101		1011 0101	5	1111 0101
UC	0011 0110		0111 0110		1011 0110	6	1111 0110
EOT	0011 0111		0111 0111		1011 0111	7	1111 0111
	0011 1000		0111 1000		1011 1000	8	1111 1000
	0011 1001		0111 1001		1011 1001	9	1111 1001
	0011 1010		0111 1010		1011 1010		1111 1010
CU3	0011 1011	#	0111 1011		1011 1011		1111 1011
DC4	0011 1100	@	0111 1100		1011 1100		1111 1100
NAK	0011 1101	'	0111 1101		1011 1101		1111 1101
	0011 1110	=	0111 1110		1011 1110		1111 1110
SUB	0011 1111	"	0111 1111		1011 1111		1111 1111

The method used to delete a character on punched tape was to punch out all the holes in a row. This created the binary pattern 1111111 which is position 7/15 in the ASCII table.

Sticks 2 and 3

These are the characters used for printing numbers. Included in these two sticks are the digits 0 through 9, most of the punctuation marks, and the space.

The digits were carefully placed in the ASCII table so that the lower four bits of the digit would coincide with the number that digit represents. Thus 0 is in location 3/0 and 9 is in location 3/9. This makes it easy to convert numbers into ASCII equivalents. Simply tack on the high four bits 0011.

There is a wide variation in punctuation marks among countries. For example, the dollar sign is used mainly in North America while other countries have their own monetary denominations. Thus international codes have an international monetary symbol called a scarab in position 2/4.

Sticks 0 and 1

The first two sticks are the control characters. These characters aren't supposed to cause a mark to be placed on the paper or screen. Instead, they are supposed to be used to control the operation of the receiving device. For instance, a Carriage Return (0/13) moves the active printing position to the first column of the current line.

Many manufacturers have redefined the standard definitions of the control characters because there was a function in their device that needed a special code to activate it. This lack of conformance to the ASCII standard can lead to a lot of confusion. It is always best to have the operations manual for a peripheral device whenever you are first interfacing to it. This can help save you from many surprises.

CONTROL CODES

The ASCII control codes are subdivided into five groups: logical communication control, physical communication, device control, field separators and set changers.

Logical Communication Control Characters

These control characters are intended to control the communication channel or are for use in labeling storage media such as magnetic tape. There are ten logical control characters. They are usually used only when communications are block oriented. They are:

SOH (0/1) (Start of Header). This control character signifies that an information header follows. The header will provide information about the message, which follows the header.

STX (0/2) (Start of Text). This control character separates the header from the information block.

ETX (0/3) (End of Text). This is the last character in a text message block.

EOT (0/4) (End of Transmission). This is the last character to be transmitted in the message block.

ENQ (0/5) (Enquiry). This control character requests a return identification message (who are you?) or a return status message (how are you?).

ACK (0/6) (Acknowledge). A character which answers ''yes'' to some inquiry.

DLE (1/0) (Data Link Escape). Allows an extra set of communications control characters to be used by ''escaping'' to an alternate set of character definitions.

NAK (1/5) (No Acknowledge). A character which answers ''no'' to some inquiry.

SYN (1/6) (Synchronous idle). A control character used in synchronous data communications (see Chapter 4) to synchronize receiver to sender. This character is sent whenever there are no messages to send.

ETB (1/7) (End of Transmission Block). This

character is used to separate blocks of information within a message block.

The existence of the Logical Communication Control characters has caused many problems in computer communications. Sometimes, a computer or peripheral manufacturer needs to send raw binary data over the same communications link used for AS-CII characters. This works well until the link between the computer and peripheral is no longer a piece of wire.

Sometimes, a device called a *modem* (contraction of modulator-demodulator) is used to convert the computer signals so they may be transmitted over the telephone lines. The logical communication control characters are designed to control the operation of the modems and the EOT character can cause some modems to hang up the phone! Clearly, if raw binary data is being transmitted, there is a good chance that one of the binary characters will look like an EOT. That is why care is needed when using a communications link for both ASCII and binary transmissions.

Physical Communication Control Characters

These control characters are also used for communicating information about the communications channel or recording medium.

NUL (0/0) (Null). Used as a fill character to hold a channel open or take space in stored data blocks. DEL (7/15) is used for a similar function even though it isn't in the control sticks.

CAN (1/8) (Cancel). This character tells the receiver to ignore everything received before the reception of the CAN character. "Everything" may just mean everything in the current line or word or it may really mean "never mind."

EM (1/19) (End of Medium). This character is strictly used in data storage to inform the device that no characters are to be stored past the point where the EM character is found.

SUB (1/10) (Substitute). This character is substituted for other characters when there is a problem in deciphering just what that other character was. It might have been garbled in transmission and received with an error.

Device Control Characters

The device control characters are the ones that are most familiar to anyone who has used a typewriter. These characters are used to move the active character position to somewhere else. An active character position is the location where the next printable character will be printed or displayed. There are eleven device control characters:

BEL (0/7) (Bell). Used to cause an audible signal to be generated. Teletypewriters actually had bells that rang, but printers and terminals now have all manner of beepers, tone generators, and other noisemakers. Hewlett-Packard manufactured one printer that "beeped" by exciting the metal laminations in the carriage motors.

BS (0/8) (Backspace). Causes the active character position to move back one position. This character can be used for overstriking characters on printers and printing terminals. CRT terminals rarely have overstrike capability, they will replace whatever character was in the position with the character following the backspace.

HT (0/9) (Horizontal Tab). This character causes the active character position to move to the next predetermined position on the current line.

LF (0/10) (Line Feed). This character, interpreted as line feed, causes the active character position to move down one line. It may also be interpreted as new line (NL) which moves the active character position to the first character of the next line.

VT (0/11) (Vertical Tab). This character is used to move the active position to the same column on the next predetermined line. Some terminals move the current active position to the first column of the next predetermined line.

FF (0/12) (Form Feed). Can be used to cause a form to eject so that the active character position is at the beginning of the next form.

CR (0/13) (Carriage Return). Causes the active character position to move to the beginning of the current line. Note that this is different from typewriters which have a carriage return key that effectively performs the new line function.

DC1 through DC4 (1/1-1/4) (Device Controls). The function of the device control characters are not specified by the ASCII standard. One common use of DC1 and DC3 is to start and stop transmissions. This is called the XON/XOFF protocol.

Field Separators

Four control characters were placed in ASCII as hierarchical Field Separators. These are to be used to denote separate fields of data, much like spaces denote separate words and periods separate sentences. The four separators are:

FS (1/12)   (File Separator)

GS (1/13)   (Group Separator)

RS (1/14)   (Record Separator)

US (1/15)   (Unit Separator)

The hierarchy is ordered such that FS is higher than GS which is higher than RS which is higher than US. The Field Separators aren't used much for their intended purpose in microcomputer systems.

Set-Changing Control Characters

There are only three Set Changing Control characters but they are very powerful. These characters are used to alert a peripheral that the AS-CII characters are about to take on different, predefined definitions. The 128 characters of the ASCII set aren't always sufficient. Where are the Greek letters for scientific papers, the math symbols, and the legal characters? For that matter, what do for-eign countries do for their character sets? The set changing control characters allow other character sets to be selected and activated:

ESC (1/11) (Escape). This control character is the most powerful in the ASCII set. It heads a string of characters in an "escape sequence" that can completely alter the way a peripheral will interpret incoming characters. Escape sequences can be used to select foreign language or other special character sets. Other escape sequences may represent extended control functions such as cursor positioning in CRT terminals.

SO (1/14) (Shift Out). Causes the previously selected alternate character set to become active. The escape sequence is intended only to designate an alternate character set while the SO control character activates it.

SI (1/15) (Shift In). Causes the peripheral to return to the standard ASCII character set.

THE MICROPROCESSOR

We have reached a point in this introductory chapter where it is time to discuss the actual hardware of interest. The first sections in this chapter cover the basics of computer technology. The topics in these sections are very general and apply to all types of computers; micro-, mini- and large mainframes. Now we will get a little more specific and start discussing subjects directly related to microcomputers and microcomputer interfacing.

What is a Microprocessor?

High-technology manufacturers have always taken license with language. Superlatives such as "super" and "ultra" abound in the sales literature. When computers started getting smaller, the term minicomputer was invented to represent a computer that was smaller, less expensive and more rugged than the "regular" computers of the day.

When an entire computer central processing unit, or "CPU," was fabricated on a single integrated circuit, it was labeled with the name "microprocessor," a processor built from microcircuitry. A microcomputer then is simply a computer with a microprocessor-based central processing unit (CPU). These microcircuits weren't new to computers. Mini- and large computers used large quantities of less powerful microcircuits as building blocks for their own processors.

What was new with microprocessors is that the computer manufacturer no longer had to design the CPU. It had become a standard, off-the-shelf component. It may not be clear why this was revolutionary. The revolutionary idea was that suddenly a part was available that was a complete computer processor, with a standardized instruction set and standardized signals. The semiconductor manufacturers were making entire computers as standardized as TTL signal levels. In addition, the miniaturization of the central processing unit, coupled with a major reduction in power requirements, meant that microprocessors could take computing power into areas where such power was not even dreamed of.

This new era of standardization had a revolutionary effect on the electronics industry. As designers began to regard computer processors as just another part, the computer revolution was able to relentlessly advance until almost any product that uses electricity had a computer in it. Unlikely products that have been computerized include automobiles, toys, refrigerators, air conditioners, thermostats, door bells, and television sets.

Microprocessor Operation

There are four major components to a microprocessor as shown in Fig. 1-24 which illustrates a generic microprocessor. (Generic means that no particular microprocessor looks exactly like Fig. 1-25, but all microprocessors look something like it.) There is a bank of registers for holding information, an arithmetic logic unit (ALU) for processing the information, and a bus interface responsible for moving information into and out of the microprocessor. The entire operation of the microprocessor is managed by the control sequencer.

In operation, the control sequencer instructs the bus interface to get an instruction. The microprocessor is connected to external memory by the bus. The external memory has instructions stored in it. When instructed to do so, the bus interface will obtain an instruction from the external memory and give it to the control sequencer. This is called an instruction fetch.

What happens next depends on what the instruction says to do. Some instructions require information in one of the registers in the register bank

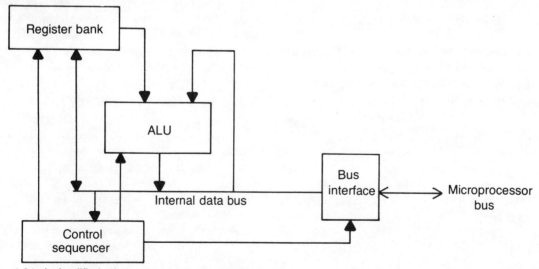

Fig. 1-24. A simplified microprocessor block diagram.

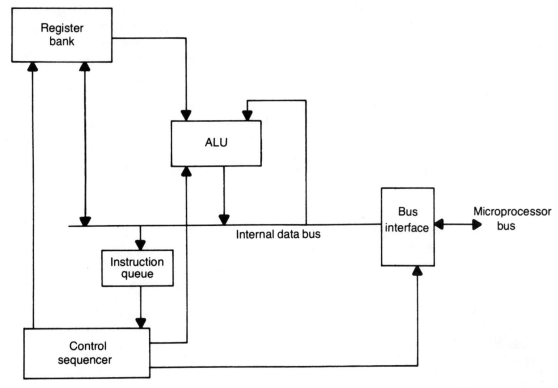

Fig. 1-25. A block diagram of a pipelined microprocessor. An instruction queue has been added to speed up instruction fetches.

to be "fetched," processed by the ALU, and then returned to the register bank. Other instructions cause information to be moved from external memory to a register, from a register to external memory, from one register to another, or from one memory location to another.

Whatever the instruction, the control sequencer issues the proper signals to perform the appropriate operation. This is called instruction execution. After the instruction is executed, the next instruction is fetched.

Pipelining

Most of the early microprocessors had separate fetch and execute cycles. First an instruction is fetched, then the instruction is executed, then another instruction is fetched, and so on. Some instructions do not require the services of the bus interface.

These instructions cause information to move only between the ALU and register bank. While these instructions are being executed, the bus is idle.

Microprocessor designers decided that the fetch/execute cycle could be speeded up if the bus interface could be made to do something useful all the time. This is where the concept of *pipelining* came from.

A pipelined microprocessor is shown in **Fig. 1-25**. What has been added is an instruction queue. This is a piece of hardware that can hold several consecutive instructions. When the bus interface has nothing else to do, it fetches additional instructions from external memory and places them in the queue.

When the control sequencer needs another instruction, it can get it from the instruction queue rather than external memory. If a "branch" instruction has just been executed, however, all the instructions in the queue have to be dumped because they were obtained before the control sequencer knew a branch was about to occur.

Access to the instruction queue is much quicker than to external memory. Overlapping of the fetch and execute cycles can lead to a faster machine, at the expense of not really knowing which instruction the machine is executing at any given time. Pipelined machines lose speed when a lot of branching takes place. Most of the newer microprocessors have pipelined architectures. Their instruction queues range from one to eight instructions in depth.

The Microprocessor Bus

Microprocessor internals are not really important in the study of microcomputer interfacing. We have studied them here to introduce the concept of the microprocessor bus, which is very important in interfacing. The bus moves information into and out of the microprocessor. It is also used to move information to and from the peripheral interface circuitry which is the heart of the interfacing hardware.

Figure 1-26 is a more detailed picture of a generic microprocessor bus. Three components of the bus are shown: the address bus, the data bus, and the control bus. All microprocessors have some form of these three busses.

Information is moved back and forth over the data bus. Eight-bit processors generally have eight-bit data busses. Sixteen-bit processors generally have sixteen-bit busses (though there are exceptions).

The data bus is shown with an arrowhead at each end. This means that data may flow in either direction; either into or out of the processor. However, data flows in only one direction at any given time.

Where the data goes is controlled by the address bus. The microprocessor specifies exactly what external hardware it wishes to communicate with by an address. Each memory location has an address. Each interface port also has an address. These addresses are driven onto the address bus by the microprocessor whenever communications with the external circuitry are desired.

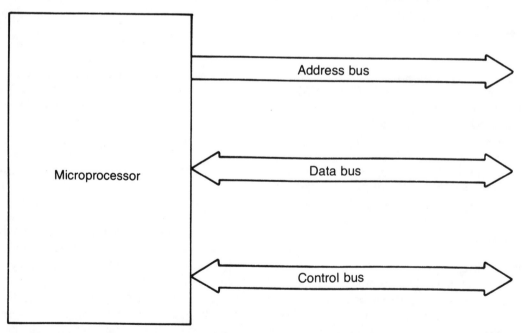

Fig. 1-26. The three major component busses of a microprocessor bus: the address bus, the data bus and the control bus.

Address busses are unidirectional, signified by the single arrowhead on the address bus in **Fig. 1-26**. Eight-bit processors usually have a sixteen-bit address bus which limits the range to 65536 addresses. Sixteen-bit processors have address busses of sixteen to twenty-four bits, which means they can access up to 16,777,216 addresses. This extra addressing capability is one of the main reasons why sixteen-bit microprocessors are more powerful than eight-bit microprocessors.

The control bus is used to sequence the flow of information over the data bus. When the microprocessor wants to output data, it tells the external hardware when information is valid on the data bus. When the microprocessor wants to input information, the control bus allows the external hardware to tell the microprocessor when that data has been made available.

To summarize, the data bus is the "what" bus—it carries information. The address bus is the "where" bus—it determines where the information goes to or comes from. The control bus is the "when" bus—it specifies when the data transfers take place.

Timing Diagrams

The signals that pass over microprocessor busses and to peripherals always have a precise timing relationship. To show these relationships, a timing diagram is generally used. **Figure 1-27** illustrates a simple timing diagram.

The horizontal axis of the timing diagram is labeled "Time." Events shown on the right side of the diagram happen after those shown on the left. The vertical axis shows three sets of signals.

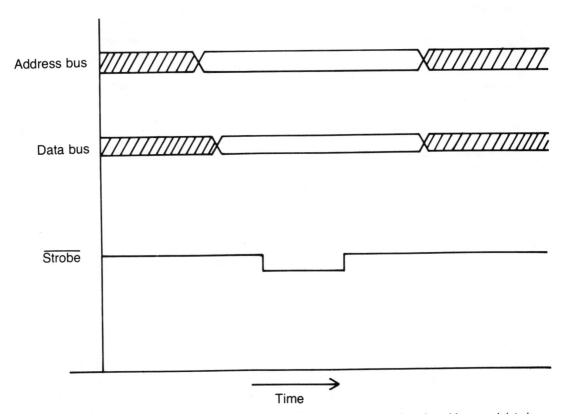

Fig. 1-27. A generic timing diagram. The negative-true Strobe signal indicates when the address and data busses have valid information on them.

The top, labeled "Address Bus," is actually the combination of all the microprocessor address lines. At the left side of the diagram, the address bus signals are shown as a cross-hatched area. The cross-hatching indicates that these signals do not matter at this point in time, they are in a "don't care" state. Towards the center of the diagram, the cross-hatching goes away.

No cross-hatching means the signals must be at valid levels. Since the address bus is really several signals combined, a valid level on the address bus is shown at both high and low levels Some address lines may be high and some may be low. Later in the diagram, the cross-hatching reappears, signifying that the signals are again in a "don't care" region.

Similarly, the data bus is shown with cross-hatching at the beginning and end of the diagram. In the center, the data lines must be at a valid level, either high or low.

Finally, a single signal, called "$\overline{strobe}$" is shown on the diagram. $\overline{Strobe}$ is part of a control bus and is used to indicate when the address and data busses are valid. Remember that the overscore means the signal is asserted or true when it is at a low voltage level.

This diagram then shows the behavior of the address and data busses with respect to the $\overline{strobe}$ line. At some time, the busses take on valid levels. A little later, the $\overline{strobe}$ line indicates that the busses are valid. Whatever device is receiving these signals will then look at the address bus, determine if it is being addressed, and if so, make use of the data.

The $\overline{strobe}$ line is then negated, indicating that the current cycle has ended. Later, after the $\overline{strobe}$ line indicates that the address and data busses are no longer valid, these busses actually become invalid.

MICROPROCESSOR INTERFACES

Microprocessors live on some sort of bus. Usually, this bus carries a collection of signals that the microprocessor manufacturer feels is optimum for that particular processor. Busses cannot be extended for great distances because it takes time for signals to travel over conductors. If the distance is great, the time increases to the point where signal timings on the bus can't be maintained. Most busses are less than two feet in length for this reason.

Most peripheral devices are some distance from the processor. In addition, most peripherals are built by non-microprocessor manufacturers. As a result, the peripherals do not use the same collection of signals to communicate that microprocessors use. on top of all this, we want to be able to use any particular peripheral device with several microprocessors. It would be crazy to have a printer for the 6800, another for the 8080 and yet another for the Z80 microprocessor.

To solve the problems of distance, signal, and timing incompatibility between microprocessors and peripherals, we interpose some specialized circuitry between them. We call this special circuitry an *interface*.

An interface is defined in a dictionary as: "The place at which independent systems meet and act on or communicate with each other; broadly: an area in which diverse things interact."

This is precisely the definition of the circuits we will discuss in this book. Computer-interface circuits allow a diverse group of peripheral devices to interact with microprocessors.

The interface usually takes the form of a circuit board which plugs into the processor bus. The connector which plugs into the bus allows the interface access to the microprocessor signals. At the other end of the board is another connector. A cable is connected between this connector and the peripheral device. Circuitry in the interface will perform four tasks:

1. Transform the processor signals into signals compatible with the peripheral device.
2. Transform the timing on the high-speed processor bus to a speed compatible with the peripheral device.
3. Transform signal levels so that a long cable may be driven, if desired.
4. Transform information from the processor into a format compatible with the peripheral and vice versa.

You can see that the job of an interface is to act as a transformer of many aspects of computer communication. The following chapters will cover these aspects in detail but first I want to introduce the types of interfaces we will be covering.

Interface Types

There are only three major types of electrical interface; parallel, serial, and analog. Within each type however, there are a large number of different species. Chapter 3 covers the parallel species, Chapter 4 covers the serial species, and Chapter 5 covers the analog species.

Parallel interfaces are very similar to microprocessor busses. Data is transferred over a set of wires called data lines, much like the processor data bus. Variation in the parallel interfaces is in the num-

ber of data lines used, and how many signals are used for handshaking. Handshaking is a technique used to control the rate at which information moves from one device to another.

Serial interfaces use a single path to transmit data. Information is transferred one bit at a time. There are two major species of the serial interface; asynchronous and synchronous. Of the two, the asynchronous serial interface is the more common for microcomputers.

Analog interfaces are quite different from serial and parallel interfaces. We have already discussed digital signals, which are either high or low, true or false. Microprocessor busses use digital signals. Serial and parallel interfaces use digital signals to

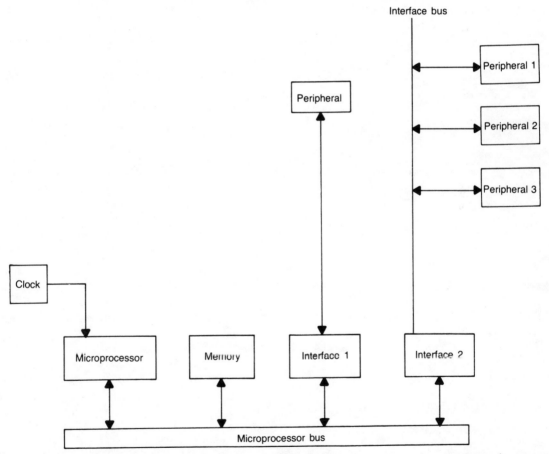

Fig. 1-28. A block diagram of a microcomputer system showing the major components: microprocessor, microprocessor bus, memory, interfaces and peripherals.

29

communicate with peripherals. Analog interfaces convert the digital microprocessor signals into signals that vary continuously.

Examples of values that vary continuously are temperature, pressure, voltage, current, and wind speed. As you can see, these are physical quantities. Analog interfaces are generally used to allow computers to interact with the "real world."

Just how does an interface connect into a computer system? Figure 1-28 illustrates the most common configuration. A microprocessor with its bus is shown, along with memory. There are two interfaces also shown connected to the microprocessor bus. Interface number one is connected to a single peripheral over a cable. Interface number two is connected to three peripherals over a cable which is labeled "interface bus."

Interfaces can also have busses. This allows a single interface to communicate with several peripherals, one at a time. The best known example of an interface bus is the General Purpose Interface Bus (GPIB). The GPIB is a standard, IEEE-488-1979, and is also known as the Hewlett-Packard Interface Bus (HPIB) after the company that developed it.

Chapter 2

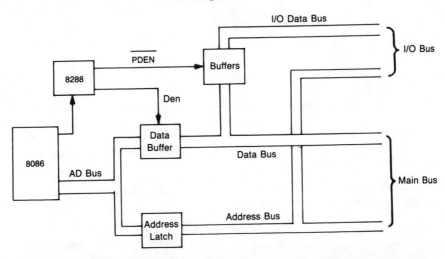

Component-Level Busses

Before we enter into the study of microprocessor interfaces, it is important to first understand just what we are interfacing to. Interfaces are usually connected directly to a microprocessor bus. **Figure 2-1** is a very basic block diagram of a microprocessor-based system. The microprocessor bus is the foundation upon which all other elements are built. A bus is used to carry signals between the three major elements of any microprocessor system: the processor, memory, and the input/output (I/O) devices.

The processor is the computational engine of the microprocessor system. All data processing and calculations are done by the processor. Memory is used to hold both the program and the information that is to be processed. The I/O is used to get information into the system for processing and back out afterwards.

There really isn't anything magic about a microprocessor bus or bus protocol. A bus is simply a carrier of signals which is used by the microprocessor to move data between itself, mem-

ory, and I/O devices. Understanding a microprocessor bus requires that you understand these signals. Once that is accomplished, you can understand how to connect devices to the bus.

The microprocessor busses that we are concerned with in this chapter are component-level busses. Backplane busses are covered in Chapter 3. These classifications were made in 1980 by Paul L. Borril of the University College London.

Component-level busses are created by the microprocessor manufacturers. They originate at the pins of the microprocessor integrated circuit and are routed to other components on the same circuit board. Since most microprocessors have modest signal-drive capability, a component-level bus is rarely routed offboard.

The microprocessor manufacturer completely defines the component level bus because it originates at the microprocessor. Each manufacturer advocates a proprietary blend of signals, claiming this blend to be optimum for a given set of applications. Thus there are almost as many component-level busses

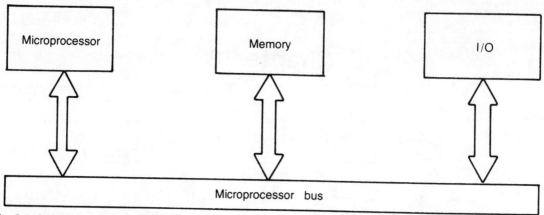

Fig. 2-1. A block diagram of a basic microprocessor system showing the four main components: microprocessor, microprocessor bus, memory, and I/O.

as there are microprocessors. We will study several of the more prominent component-level busses in this chapter.

MICROPROCESSOR BUSSES

Figure 2-2 illustrates a microprocessor with its component-level bus. The bus is further separated into three sub-busses: the data bus, the address bus, and the control bus. Each of these three sub-busses has a particular task which is essential to the proper operation of the microprocessor. Remember, all data entering or leaving the microprocessor does so over this bus.

The Data Bus

The middle sub-bus of Fig. 2-2 is labeled the data bus because it is used to transfer information to be processed into the microprocessor, and processed information out of the microprocessor. You might want to think of the data bus as the "what" bus. Arrowheads at each end of the data bus indicate the bidirectional nature of the data lines which make up the data bus. Data may flow either into or out of the processor, but only in one direction at a time. Which direction the information is flowing in at any given time is controlled by the control bus, to be discussed shortly.

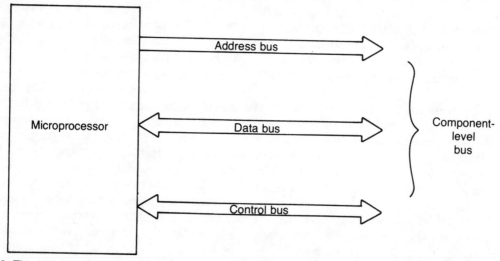

Fig. 2-2. The component-level microprocessor bus compromises the address bus, data bus and control bus.

Microprocessors are frequently characterized by the size of their data busses. Thus if the data bus of a microprocessor is eight bits wide, that microprocessor is considered to be an eight bit-microprocessor. The Intel 8080 and 8085, the Motorola 6800, 6801, and 6802, and the ZILOG Z80 microprocessor are considered to be eight-bit microprocessors. All have eight-bit data busses.

Newer, more powerful microprocessors have sixteen-bit data busses, moving twice the amount of data over the data bus with each transfer. Examples of sixteen-bit microprocessors are the Texas Instruments 9900 and 99000, and Intel 8086, the Motorola 68000, and the Zilog Z8000 microprocessor.

At the top of the processor pyramid are the 32-bit behemoths including Motorola's 68020 and 68030, Intel's 80386, and ZILOG's Z80000. There are also some smaller microprocessors which have four-bit data busses but we will not concern ourselves with them in this book.

The reason the size of the data bus is used to classify the microprocessor is that the data bus frequently indicates the data size the processor is designed to manipulate. An eight-bit data bus implies that the microprocessor internally works with eight bits at a time. Some microprocessors do not conform to this rule. The Motorola 6809 and Intel 8088 have eight-bit data busses but internally can easily work with sixteen-bit data chunks.

Why would the microprocessor manufacturer limit the data bus if the processor can work with larger quantities internally? The reason is one of economics. Eight-bit-wide memory is potentially less expensive than sixteen-bit-wide memory. Also, the I/O devices for eight-bit processors are much less expensive and more available than sixteen-bit versions.

The Address Bus

The top sub-bus in Fig. 2-2 is labeled the address bus. This is the set of lines used by the microprocessor to specify where information will come from or go to on the data bus. Microprocessors divide memory into locations. The address bus is the "where" bus. Each data storage location has a unique address. This address is specified on the address bus whenever the microprocessor needs to communicate with that location.

A single arrowhead on the address bus indicates that the microprocessor always controls the address on the bus. Addresses are never sent to the microprocessor over the address bus by some other device. Most microprocessors can at least be told to release the address bus so that some other device may take over This capability is essential in systems where direct memory access (DMA) is used. DMA is discussed later in this chapter, and Chapter 8 is devoted to a thorough discussion of the technique.

Eight-bit processors generally have sixteen-bit address busses. That means that the address bus is composed of sixteen individual address lines. Sixteen bits give the processor an addressing capability of 65,536 locations. For 8-bit processors, that means a total storage capacity of 65,536 bytes of information. In 1975, when memory was relatively expensive, that was more than most microprocessor systems could use or afford. That much memory is now very inexpensive, costing well under $20. One of the most severe limitations of 8-bit processors is memory-addressing capability.

Sixteen-bit processors are more powerful mainly because of their enhanced addressing range. Some 16-bit processors, such as the Intel 8086, have twenty address lines, giving them an addressing capability of 1,048,576 locations. Others have twenty-four address lines for a capacity of 16,777,216 locations. Though these seemed like unreachable quantities only a few short years ago, PCs with more than 1 megabyte of memory are now fairly common and microprocessor-based workstations commonly have several megabytes of memory.

Thirty-two-bit processors with thirty-two-bit address busses have address spaces in excess of four billion locations, a mind-boggling number. It may help you to remember that one of the reasons why Intel, the first manufacturer of a microprocessor that sold well, built a microprocessor in the first place was to sell memory. Intel was originally founded to make memory circuits, not microprocessors.

The Control Bus

If the data bus is the "what" bus and the address bus is the "where" bus, then the control bus is the "when" bus. The control bus contains timing information used to synchronize other devices with the internal operation of the microprocessor. Memory devices need to know when the address bus contains a valid address and when to place data on the data bus for the processor to read or when the processor has placed information on the data bus to be accepted by the memory. I/O devices have similar needs.

Two arrowheads on the control bus do not necessarily mean that control lines are bidirectional, though some may be. What is represented by the dual arrowheads is that some of the signal lines on the control bus are driven by the microprocessor while other signal lines are driven by other devices in the system. The control bus is not uniformly composed of all data lines as in the data bus or all address lines as in the address bus, but is actually a conglomeration of timing, data-direction, and other system management lines.

You cannot generalize about the control lines as you can with data and address lines. Each microprocessor operates with a completely different set of control lines. Thus the best way to study control lines is to do so in the context of an actual microprocessor, such as the Motorola MC6800 discussed shortly.

Two sets of signal lines in the control bus have special and powerful control over the microprocessor. These are the interrupt and DMA lines. Interrupts allow external devices to get the attention of the processor so that a special task can be initiated. The task may be as simple as the transfer of a single piece of data or as complex as a large routine or program. Interrupts are a complex subject and are treated fully in Chapter 7. DMA, direct memory access, is a technique which allows a specialized piece of hardware to take control of the bus from the processor for a period of time. The special hardware can perform data transfers much faster than the general-purpose processor, so this technique is used for high speed I/O. DMA is covered in Chapter 9.

8-BIT MICROPROCESSORS

Introduced in 1974, the 6800 was the first microprocessor to require only a 5-volt power supply. Earlier microprocessors needed two or three power-supply voltages for operation. Further, the 6800 has a simple bus structure, which makes it ideal as a first example.

Figure 2-3 is a pin diagram of a Motorola MC6800 microprocessor. Note that the processor is supplied in a 40-pin package. Almost all eight-bit processors are built into 40-pin packages. The bi-directional data bus is composed of the pins marked D0 through D7, pin numbers 33 through 26. The address bus is composed of lines A0 through A15 which are on pins 9 through 20 and 22 through 25. There are two pins for power supply ground and signal ground, marked Vss, which are pins 1 and 21. Power is supplied to the 6800 on the Vcc pin which is pin 8. Pins 35 and 38 are marked NC for no connection.

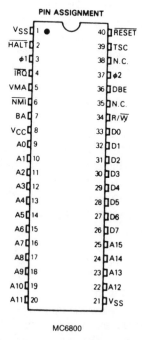

Fig. 2-3. Pin diagram of the Motorola MC6800 microprocessor. Reprinted with permission of Motorola, Inc.

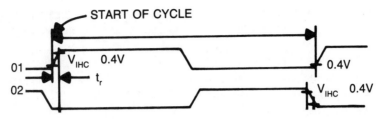

Fig. 2-4. Motorola MC6800 microprocessor clock signals. Reprinted with permission of Motorola, Inc.

The remaining pins are used to control the microprocessor and the rest of the system and thus make up the control bus. There are two clock inputs to the microprocessor marked 01 and 02. These clocks are the main timing signals for the microprocessor system. 01 and 02 are defined as a two-phase, non-overlapping clock. **Figure 2-4** shows the relationship between the two clock signals.

Other signals on the 6800 control bus are: Data Bus Enable (DBE), Bus Available (BA), Read/Write (R/$\overline{W}$), RESET, Interrupt Request (IRQ), Non-Maskable Interrupt (NMI), Three State Control (TSC), Valid Memory Address (VMA) and HALT. Of these, DBE, VMA and R/$\overline{W}$ are used in normal system operation, IRQ and NMI are used for interrupt operation and BA, TSC and HALT are used for DMA. RESET is used to reset the processor which causes the microprocessor to reinitialize and the program to be restarted.

Control Pins

The Data Bus Enable (DBE) pin is an input to the microprocessor and is used to turn on the MC6800 data bus drivers. These drivers are three-state devices and do not always control the signal levels on the data bus. Motorola recommends that the DBE pin normally be connected to the $\phi2$ clock. That allows the 6800 to drive the data bus whenever the $\phi2$ clock is high. It will do so only when a data-write operation is taking place. When the 6800 is performing a read, some other device will be driving the data lines. Internal circuitry disables the 6800 data bus drivers during a read operation.

Data Direction is controlled by the 6800 Read/Write (R/$\overline{W}$) signal line. R/$\overline{W}$ is an output pin on the processor. When the R/$\overline{W}$ line is at a high level, a read operation is taking place. During a processor-write operation, the R/$\overline{W}$ line is low.

The Valid Memory address (VMA) signal is an output from the 6800 which indicates that the address lines are stable and are signaling a valid address. All microprocessor systems have circuitry to decode the address bus. This decoding is used to determine when the processor is addressing the various components of the system. It is very important that this address decoding circuitry not enable any system components until the address bus actually has a valid address on it.

When the processor is executing instructions and not using the processor bus, the address lines may take on random values. The VMA control line is used to qualify the address lines so that system components are only selected when the processor wishes to communicate with them.

There are two or three interrupt inputs to the 6800, depending on how you wish to consider the RESET input pin. Certainly a processor reset is an interrupt to the program, but the old state of the machine is lost, and once a reset has occurred, there is no going back.

The difference between the Interrupt Request (IRQ) and the Non-Maskable Interrupt (NMI) pin is one of processor control. Non-maskable interrupts cannot be ignored. When an interrupt condition is signalled on the NMI pin, program execution will be interrupted.

Interrupts on the IRQ pin can be selectively ignored by the 6800. A bit in an internal register which can be set and cleared by the program determines whether IRQ interrupts will be serviced or not. If the interrupts are not currently being serviced, the 6800 will remember that an $\overline{IRQ}$ was received. When interrupts are later enabled, an $\overline{IRQ}$ will be processed.

The rest of the 6800 control-bus pins are used for DMA. Since we will discuss DMA in detail in Chapter 8, we will only briefly cover the DMA control pins here.

When another device wishes to gain control of the 6800 bus, it asserts the $\overline{HALT}$ pin, which is an input to the processor. After the 6800 completes the current instruction, it will halt and give up control of the address lines, data lines, and the R/$\overline{W}$ line. VMA will be forced low, negating the signal. The 6800 will assert Bus Available (BA) to grant control of the bus to the requesting device.

Notice that the 6800 does not release control of VMA but drives it low. This prevents the VMA line from drifting up to an asserted level and possibly allowing a component to be enabled accidentally. Circuitry external to the 6800 must disconnect the 6800 VMA line from the system VMA line while simultaneously connecting the VMA line from the DMA controller. What usually happens is that both the 6800 VMA signal and the DMA VMA signal drive the system VMA line low for a brief period during the transition.

The Three State Control (TSC) pin may also be used in a DMA operation. TSC is an input to the 6800 and, when asserted, causes the processor to release control of the address and R/$\overline{W}$ pins. The 6800 will also drive VMA and BA low to prevent false selection of system components. External circuitry must also freeze the $\phi1$ and $\phi2$ clocks to halt program execution by the processor.

Use of the TSC control pin with stopped clocks for DMA can only be made for short periods of time. The 6800 is a dynamic device, meaning if it doesn't get clocked within a short period of time, it forgets everything. This time period is specified as 9.5 microseconds maximum.

Memory-Mapped I/O

There are no special pins on the 6800 control bus to indicate that an input or output operation is taking place as opposed to a memory read or write. There are no special I/O instructions in the 6800 instruction set. All bus transactions are performed as though they are to memory. Thus peripheral devices appear to the 6800 as memory locations.

In 6800 systems, a block of memory has to be allocated to I/O devices. This block is usually placed at the bottom of memory because the 6800 uses the highest address locations for reset and interrupt addresses.

The 6800 I/O scheme is called memory-mapped I/O because the I/O is mapped into some memory locations. The advantages of this approach are:

- No special I/O bus signals are needed. Quite often, pins on a microprocessor package are at a premium (though this is not the case with the 6800 since two pins aren't used at all).
- No special I/O instructions are needed. The instruction set is less complex and possibly easier to learn.
- All memory-reference instructions may be used to perform I/O operations. Memory-reference instructions always have more powerful addressing modes than I/O instructions.

A major drawback to memory-mapped I/O is that the full address space is no longer available for program and data storage. Some of the address space has been allocated to I/O devices. Frequently, this can amount to 1024 or more lost address locations. In an eight-bit processor such as 6800, which only can address 65,536 locations, loss of 1024 address locations is appreciable and may cause a problem. On other processors using memory-mapped I/O, such as the Motorola 68000, with an address space of over 16 million locations, loss of even 65,536 locations to I/O functions is not a real problem.

Timing Diagrams

In most 6800 systems, the $\phi1$ signal is used only by the 6800 and is not routed to other system components. System timing is based on the $\phi2$ clock. **Figure 2-5** shows a 6800 read cycle and **Fig. 2-6** shows the write cycle.

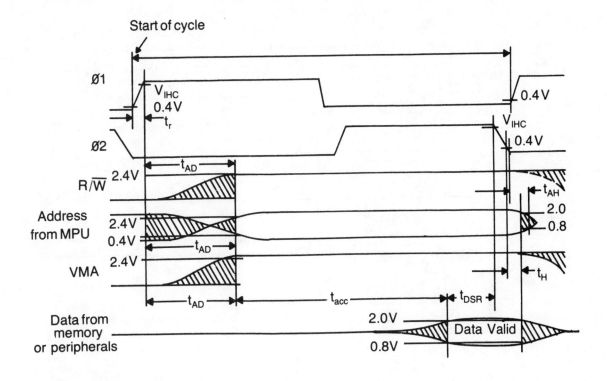

Fig. 2-5. Motorola MC6800 microprocessor read cycle. Reprinted with permission of Motorola, Inc.

Read Cycle

A read cycle starts with the rising edge of the $\phi1$ clock. A period of time after that edge, the 6800 will place an address on the address line, assert the R/$\overline{\text{W}}$ line to signify a read operation, and assert the VMA line. The time between the rising edge of $\phi1$ and valid address on the address lines is labeled t_{AD}, which stands for Address Delay time and is specified at 270 nanoseconds maximum for the standard-speed 6800.

When VMA is asserted, the device being read has only a limited amount of time to get the data to the 6800 input pins. This time is labeled t_{acc} in Fig. 2-5. The term t_{acc} stands for Access Time. On the MC6800, t_{acc} is 530 nanoseconds maximum. This is only if the 6800 is being run at the full 1-MHz clock rate.

The access time is divided up by the various external components. Some time will be required to decode the address. More time will be required to access the requested data in the selected device. Still more time is needed by any buffers on the data lines between the selected system component and the processor. The sum of all these delays must be less than the access time or the processor may get bad data.

Another critical time is marked t_{DSR}. This is the amount of time before the falling edge of the $\phi2$ clock that valid data must be present at the 6800 data inputs for a valid read to take place. The t_{DSR} time is most important in 6800 systems running at speeds less than 1 MHz because the t_{acc} figure is no longer valid. On an MC6800, t_{DSR} is specified to be 100 nanoseconds minimum.

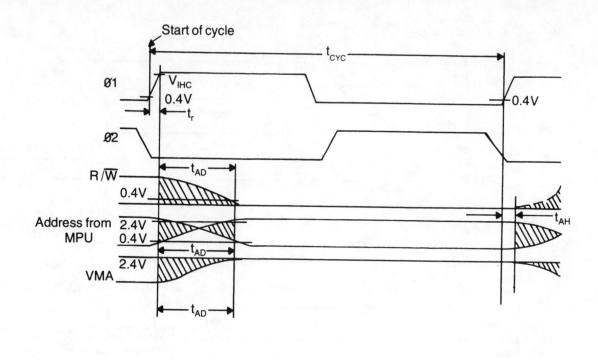

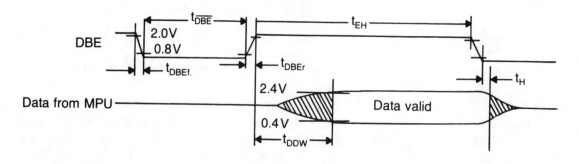

NNNNNN Data not valid

Fig. 2-6. Motorola MC6800 microprocessor write cycle. Reprinted with permission of Motorola, Inc.

Write Cycle

Figure 2-6 shows how a 6800 performs a write operation. Again, the cycle starts with the rising edge of $\phi 1$. After t_{AD} the address lines will be valid, R/$\overline{W}$ will be low signalling a write operation and VMA will be asserted.

Since this is a write operation, the Data Bus Enable (DBE) input to the processor becomes im-

portant. The 6800 will not drive the data lines until DBE is asserted (high). In fact, it will not really place valid data on the data bus until t_{DDW} nanoseconds after DBE is asserted. The term t_{DDW} stands for Data Delay for a Write and is specified at 225 nanoseconds maximum.

If the $\phi 2$ clock is used as the DBE signal, the 6800 will have data on the data bus well before the falling edge of $\phi2$. All Motorola peripheral integrated circuits are designed to accept data on the falling edge of $\phi2$. These peripheral circuits also have data setup times which must be met.

Sychronous Busses

The 6800 component-level bus is an example of a synchronous bus, meaning all bus transactions are synchronized to a common timing signal. In the case of the 6800, the signal is the $\phi2$ clock. 6800 is a second-generation microprocessor. Most second-generation processors have synchronous busses. Any components which are connected to these busses must meet the bus-timing requirements.

There are techniques for allowing slower devices to interact with synchronous busses. For the 6800, the ϕ clocks must be frozen until the slow device has had time to respond. As we have seen, this can only be done for a maximum of 9.5 microseconds before the 6800 forgets everything, a situation which must be avoided at all costs. Some other second-generation microprocessors have special WAIT pins which allow extra wait cycles to be introduced. We will look at these processors shortly.

INTEL 8080

Just before Motorola introduced the 6800, Intel announced the first microprocessor of the second generation, the 8080. First-generation processors had only been manufactured by Intel. They were the 4004, the first commercial microprocessor, and 8008, the first eight-bit microprocessor. The 8080 was designed to be compatible with the 8008 instruction set but was a tremendous improvement over the first-generation microprocessors.

The 8080 was later upgraded and renamed the 8080A. A pinout for the 8080A appears in **Fig. 2-7.** Note that the 8080A is supplied in a 40-pin package. The bidirectional data bus is composed of the pins marked D0 through D7, pin numbers 10 through 3. The address bus is composed of signals A0 through A15 which are on pins 1, 25 through 27 and 29 through 40. There is a ground pin, marked GND,

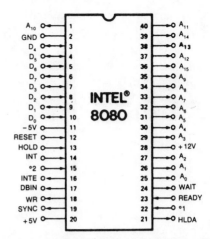

Fig. 2-7. Pin diagram of the Intel 8080 microprocessor. Reprinted by permission of Intel Corporation, Copyright 1983.

which is pin 2. Power is supplied to the 8080A on the +5 volt pin (20), the −5 volt pin (11) and the +12 volt pin (28).

The remaining pins are used to control the microprocessor and the rest of the system and thus make up the control bus. There are two clock inputs to the microprocessor marked $\phi1$ and $\phi2$. These clocks are the main timing signals for the microprocessor system. $\phi1$ and $\phi2$ are defined as a two-phase, non-overlapping clock. **Figure 2-8** shows the relationship between the two clock signals. Also shown is the SYNC output from the 8080A microprocessor. SYNC indicates the start of each new instruction or machine cycle.

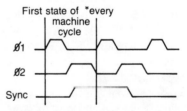

*Sync does not occur in the second and third machine cycles of a dad instruction since these machine cycles are used for an internal register-pair add.

Fig. 2-8. Intel 8080 microprocessor clock signals. Reprinted by permission of Intel Corporation, Copyright 1983.

Other bus signals of the Intel 8080A are: Data Bus In (DBIN), READY, WAIT, Write ($\overline{WR}$), HOLD, Hold Acknowledge (HLDA), Interrupt Enable (INTE), Interrupt (INT) and RESET. Of these DBIN, READY, WAIT and $\overline{WR}$ are used in normal processor operation. INTE and INT are used for interrupts while HOLD and HLDA are used for DMA operations. RESET forces the processor to start executing at location 0.

Control Pins

The 8080A Data Bus In (DBIN) pin is a microprocessor output. It tells the external circuitry that the processor is accepting data at its data-bus input. More important, the DBIN signal indicates when the 8080A is not driving the data bus, which means that some other device may.

Conversely, the 8080A Write ($\overline{WR}$) output indicates when the 8080A is driving the data bus, performing a write or an output operation to an external device. This external device may be either memory or an I/O device. When the $\overline{WR}$ line is low (asserted), the processor has placed valid data on the data bus.

Note that the 8080A DBIN and $\overline{WR}$ outputs serve a similar purpose as the 6800 DBE input, but the technique used is completely different. Which technique is better? Neither—they both serve their purpose admirably.

READY is an input to the 8080A that allows slow devices to stretch out bus operations. The earlier discussion of synchronous busses stated that data transfers were synchronized to a master system clock. That is true for the 8080A bus as well, but with a difference. As long as an external device signals that it is not ready, the 8080A will enter a wait state. In the wait state, the 8080A idles for whole clock cycles until READY is asserted. Then the bus operation is completed on the next clock cycle. The 8080A WAIT output signal tells the external circuitry when the processor has entered a wait state. It serves to acknowledge the "not ready" signal on the READY line.

Interrupts are generated in the 8080A when the Interrupt Request (INT) input is asserted. This interrupt can be masked inside of the 8080A with an "interrupt disable" instruction. Interrupts are allowed after the processor executes an "interrupt enable" instruction. The 8080A Interrupt Enable (INTE) output indicates to external devices whether or not interrupts are currently allowed.

RESET may also be considered an interrupt pin since it alters the execution of the program in the processor. When RESET is asserted, program execution is halted. When RESET is released program execution resumes with the instruction at memory address 0. Interrupts are automatically disabled after a reset but the processor's internal registers are left as they were before the interrupt.

HOLD and Hold Acknowledge (HLDA) are two control lines used for DMA. When another device wishes to gain control of the 8080A bus, it asserts the HOLD input to the processor. The processor acknowledges the bus request by asserting the HLDA output on a rising edge of $\phi 1$ and entering a hold state. Within 120 nanoseconds of the rising edge of the $\phi 2$ clock following the assertion of HLDA, the 8080A will release control of the address and data busses. The DMA control circuitry may then assume control of them.

Extended 8080A Status Information

The designers of the 8080A felt that they needed more status information about the internal state of the processor and devised a way to get eight more status lines out of the package without adding pins. They did this by using the processor data bus as a status-output port during the period when SYNC is asserted.

Take another look at **Fig. 2-8** and remember the SYNC is only asserted at the first machine cycle of each instruction. Unlike the 6800, the 8080A has several clock or machine cycles for every instruction cycle. SYNC is asserted only on the first machine cycle.

Now look at **Fig. 2-9**. It shows an Intel 8212-bit latch used as a status latch for the 8080A. The small timing diagram at the right side of the figure shows that the status byte appears on the 8080A data bus with the falling edge of the $\phi 2$ clock in the

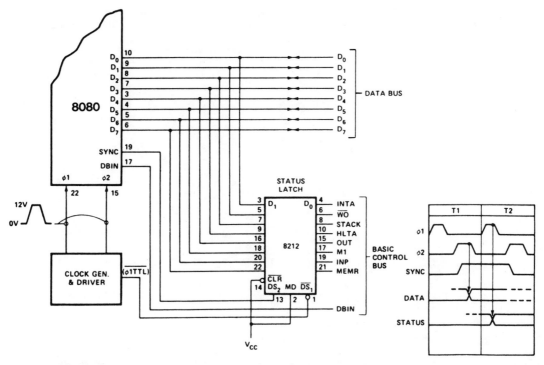

Fig. 2-9. An external status latch for Intel 8080 microprocessor systems. Reprinted by permission of Intel Corporation, Copyright 1983.

T1 machine state. That status byte is latched by the 8212 on the falling edge of the $\phi1$ clock in the second or T2 machine state.

The eight new control lines are: Interrupt Acknowledge (INTA), Write/Output ($\overline{WO}$), Stack address (STACK), Halt Acknowledge (HLTA), Output (OUT), M1, Input (INP) and Memory Read (MEMR). Before we discuss these new control lines, there is something you have to know; the 8080A has special I/O instructions. If you already guessed that from the new OUT and INP control lines, congratulations!

OUT and INP signal to external circuitry that an I/O instruction is executing. The major effect this has on the system is a redefinition of the address bus. During a memory read or write, the address bus is used for sixteen-bit address specifiers. During an I/O input or output, the 8080A drives only the lower eight bits of the address bus, to specify an I/O target address. This creates an I/O address space that is 256 bytes long, which is completely separate from the normal memory-address space. Thus there are 256 input and output "ports".

Actually, the 8080A does drive all sixteen bits of the address bus during I/O transactions. The address on the lower eight bits is reproduced on the upper eight bits. Some systems have taken advantage of this scheme, using the upper eight bits to decode I/O addresses to equalize signal loading on all signal lines. Unfortunately, newer processors, such as the Z80, which emulate the 8080A do not perform this replication. It is always safest to stick with what the manufacturer recommends, unless you really don't care about the consequences.

Let's look at the rest of the extended status lines. Table 2-1 shows what the extended status lines look like for the various types of machine cycles possible with the 8080A. The eight data-bus lines, along with the function they represent as status bits, are shown along the left side of the table.

41

Table 2-1. The Intel 8080 Microprocessor Extended Status Bit Definitions.

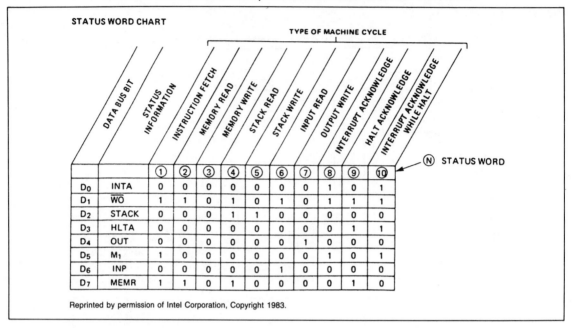

DATA BUS BIT	STATUS INFORMATION	INSTRUCTION FETCH ①	MEMORY READ ②	MEMORY WRITE ③	STACK READ ④	STACK WRITE ⑤	INPUT READ ⑥	OUTPUT WRITE ⑦	INTERRUPT ACKNOWLEDGE ⑧	HALT ACKNOWLEDGE ⑨	INTERRUPT ACKNOWLEDGE WHILE HALT ⑩
D_0	INTA	0	0	0	0	0	0	0	1	0	1
D_1	$\overline{WO}$	1	1	0	1	0	1	0	1	1	1
D_2	STACK	0	0	0	1	1	0	0	0	0	0
D_3	HLTA	0	0	0	0	0	0	0	0	1	1
D_4	OUT	0	0	0	0	0	0	1	0	0	0
D_5	M_1	1	0	0	0	0	0	0	1	0	1
D_6	INP	0	0	0	0	0	1	0	0	0	0
D_7	MEMR	1	1	0	1	0	0	0	0	1	0

STATUS WORD CHART

TYPE OF MACHINE CYCLE

Ⓝ STATUS WORD

Along the top of the table are the possible machine cycles.

INTA is the Interrupt Acknowledge line. When the 8080A wants to acknowledge an interrupt on its INT input, it does a single byte input cycle with INTA asserted. The byte obtained in this manner is executed as an instruction. The 8080A has a set of restart instructions which are eight 1-byte calls to absolute addresses. This mechanism gives the 8080A eight vectored interrupts.

$\overline{WO}$ is the $\overline{Write/Output}$ control line. It is asserted when the 8080A is about to initiate a memory write or an I/O output cycle. Note that this differs from the 8080A $\overline{WR}$ control signal. $\overline{WO}$ is asserted before the data is actually on the data bus to give a warning that a write or output is about to occur, while $\overline{WR}$ is used as a "data bus valid" signal. We will return to these signals shortly, when we explore the timing of the 8080A read, write, input, and output cycles.

STACK indicates that the 8080A is executing a stack instruction and that the address on the address bus is from the stack pointer register inside the 8080A. STACK could be used to create a spe-

cial memory space for the system stack, separate from the I/O and memory spaces. This is rarely done, however.

The M1 control line indicates that the 8080A is fetching the first byte of an instruction. This is useful because it is the best indication of what the processor is doing. Frequently 8080A simulators use M1 to synchronize with the flow of information on the data bus. If the simulator has been set to halt the system when a particular instruction is executed, it helps to be able to separate instructions from data on the bus.

MEMR is the memory-read control signal. It is asserted when the processor is about to initiate a memory-read cycle. This is slightly out of symmetry with the $\overline{WO}$ signal because MEMR is not asserted during an I/O input. That is not a problem because there is an INP signal for that purpose, but the loss of a symmetrical function sometimes confuses the first-time user.

The 8080A has a halt instruction. When executed, this instruction causes the execution of the program to stop and the processor enters a halted state. When this occurs, the Halt Acknowledge

(HLTA) signal is asserted. Only three events can bring the processor out of the halted state:

1. A reset. This will always reset the 8080A and commence program execution at location 0.
2. Assertion of the HOLD input will cause the 8080A to enter the hold state as opposed to the halted state. This allows DMA to take place even when the processor is halted. When HOLD is negated, the halted state is entered once again.
3. An interrupt will cause the 8080A to exit the halted state and begin execution of the interrupt sequence. This will only occur however if interrupts were enabled before the processor entered the halted state. Note that if interrupts are disabled, only a reset can cause the processor to resume execution of the program.

8080A Memory-Cycle Timing

The 8080A bus transactions are slightly more complex than the 6800. Where the entire bus transaction for the 6800 took place in a single clock cycle, the 8080A requires at least three clock cycles per transaction. However, the clock cycles of the 8080A are shorter than those of the 6800. Figure 2-10 illustrates a complete bus cycle for a memory read and write on the 8080A. The read and write do not occur in the same instruction cycle but are shown that way here as a composite timing diagram.

An 8080A instruction cycle is divided up into machine states, labeled across the top of Fig. 2-10 as T_1, T_2, T_W, T_3, T_4, and T_5. Something different occurs during every machine or T state. The standard 8080A runs at 2 MHz so each T state is 500 nanoseconds in duration.

During T_1, SYNC is asserted and the extended status information appears on the data bus. At the same time, the address lines are asserted by the processor, shortly after the rising edge of $\phi 2$.

In the T_2 state, when $\phi 1$ goes high, the extended status lines are also set to the appropriate levels. The 8080A samples the READY, HOLD and HALT inputs. We are concerned here with only the READY input. Since the address and extended status are asserted, we know what part of the system is about to be accessed. If the device is a slow device, READY must remain negated. If the selected device is sufficiently fast, the READY line should be asserted.

The READY line must be at the proper state at least 120 nanoseconds before the falling edge of $\phi 2$ in the T_2 state. If the signal is "ready", the T_3 state will be entered at the next rising edge of $\phi 1$. Otherwise a wait state, T_W will be initiated. During each wait stage, the READY line is again sampled. When READY is finally asserted, the processor will enter the T_3 state on the next rising edge of $\phi 1$. READY must always meet the 120 nanosecond setup time, even during the wait states.

Finally, in the T_3 state, we begin to see a difference between a memory read and memory write cycle. If this is a memory read, DBIN will have been asserted during T_2. If a write is taking place, WR will be asserted at the beginning of the first T_W state or the T_3 state if there are no wait states in this cycle. During a read, the addressed external device will have put data on the data bus in the previous state. If this is a write operation, the processor will have put data on the bus in the previous state.

A read operation ends with the T_3 state. Data on the data bus will be read into the processor's accumulator register on the rising edge of the $\phi 2$ clock. A setup time of 150 nanoseconds must have been met. That is how long before the rising edge of $\phi 2$ the data must be present at the data bus pins of the processor.

Write operations also end in the T_3 state. At the beginning of the state following the T_3 state, WR is negated. The data bus is changed following the next rising edge of $\phi 2$. The state following T_3 in a write may be T_1 of the next bus cycle.

I/O Input Timing

Figure 2-11 is the complete instruction cycle for execution of an 8080A I/O input instruction. Along the top of the figure you will see the labels M_1, M_2 and M_3. These stand for the three bus cycles which take place during the execution of the instruction.

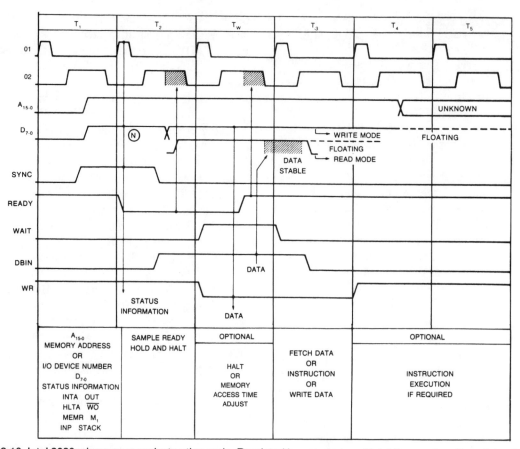

Fig. 2-10. Intel 8080 microprocessor instruction cycle. Reprinted by permission of Intel Corporation, Copyright 1983.

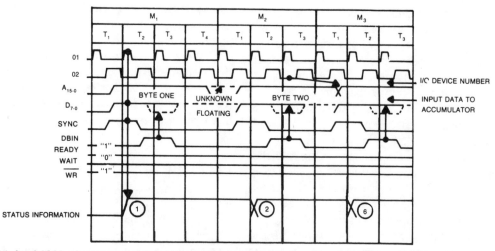

Fig. 2-11. Intel 8080 microprocessor input instruction-execution timing. Reprinted by permission of Intel Corporation, Copyright 1983.

The M_1 cycle is the instruction fetch. The input opcode is fetched from memory where "BYTE ONE" appears. This is a four-T-state instruction cycle. Note that the status information lines are marked with a "1" shown in the T_2 state of the M_1 cycle. This indicates that this is an instruction-fetch cycle. The "1" is keyed to the status-word row of Table 2-1.

The input instruction is a two-byte instruction, so the M_2 cycle is a memory read of the second opcode byte. This byte will specify the I/O port to input from. The second byte appears on the data bus where "BYTE TWO" appears. Again note the status lines. A "2" appears, signifying that this is a memory-read cycle.

Finally, the instruction is executed in cycle M_3. Carefully note the states of all the signals. There is only one difference between the control lines during M_2 and M_3. During M_2, the extended-status information signals a Memory Read (machine cycle 2) while in M_3 an Input Read (machine cycle 6) is shown. Of course, the address on the address bus will be different, and memory supplies the data during M_2 while the input device supplies data during M_3.

Output Timing

A complete 8080A I/O output operation is shown in Fig. 2-12. It is very similar to the I/O input operation during the M_1 and M_2 cycles. This is because the instruction opcode fetch and the memory read are identical to that of the input instruction. The only difference is that the opcode for the output instruction will be fetched during M_1 instead of an input instruction. The difference appears in the M_3 cycle. This cycle appears to be a write operation because $\overline{WR}$ is asserted during the T_3 state. It is identified as an I/O output once again by the extended status information. A "7" appears by the status signal, indicating that this is an Output-Write cycle.

ZILOG Z80

As in most high-technology projects, the designers of the Intel 8080A microprocessor felt that the design could be improved. They left Intel to form Zilog, Inc. Their first product, introduced in 1976, was the ZILOG Z80 microprocessor, which incorporated and extended the instruction set of the Intel 8080A microprocessor. The Z80 processor is considered a 2½ generation device.

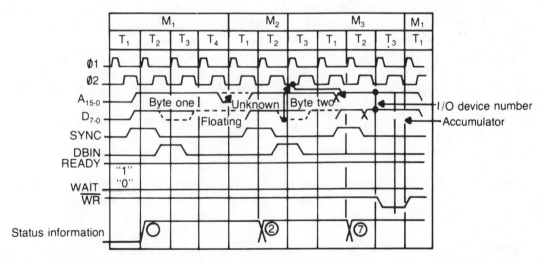

Fig. 2-12. Intel 8080 microprocessor output instruction-execution timing. Reprinted by permission of Intel Corporation, Copyright 1983.

Although the Z80 processor incorporated the 8080A instruction set, the bus was entirely changed. **Figure 2-13** is a pin diagram of the Z80 microprocessor. It is supplied in a 40-pin package.

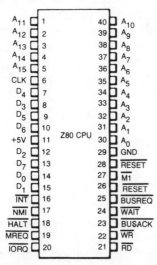

Fig. 2-13. Pin diagram of the Zilog Z80 microprocessor. Reproduced by permission (C) 1979, 1980, 1981 by Zilog, Inc. This material shall not be reproduced without written consent of Zilog, Inc.

Figure 2-14 is a functional pin diagram of the Zilog Z80 microprocessor. There is an eight-bit, bidirectional, data bus, marked D_0 through D_7. The data bus is on pins 7 through 10 and pins 12 through 15. The sixteen-bit address bus, A_0 through A_{15} is on pins 1 through 5 and pins 30 through 40. Ground and power are supplied to the chip on pins 29 and 11 respectively.

The remaining pins make up the Z80 microprocessor control bus. A single phase clock, marked CLK and found on pin 6, drives the microprocessor. Single-phase clocks are easier to build than two-phase clocks. A single-phase clock is one of the distinguishing features of a 2½ generation microprocessor.

Control signals which manage transfer of information over the Z80 data bus are: $\overline{\text{M1}}$, $\overline{\text{MREQ}}$, $\overline{\text{IORQ}}$, $\overline{\text{RD}}$, $\overline{\text{WR}}$ and $\overline{\text{WAIT}}$. Note that these are all negative-true signals. The control signal $\overline{\text{RFSH}}$ is a special signal used to help designers couple the

Z80 microprocessor to dynamic memory. $\overline{\text{INT}}$ and $\overline{\text{NMI}}$ are the two interrupt inputs to the microprocessor. $\overline{\text{BUSREQ}}$ and $\overline{\text{BUSACK}}$ are used for DMA applications. $\overline{\text{HALT}}$ is a signal that indicates that the Z80 processor has executed a halt instruction and is in a halted state. $\overline{\text{RESET}}$ is used to reset the processor.

Z80 Control Pins

Data flow into and out of the Z80 processor is primarily controlled by the $\overline{\text{RD}}$ and $\overline{\text{WR}}$ processor control output pins. $\overline{\text{RD}}$ is asserted when the processor is performing either a memory or I/O read operation. It is asserted only after the address bus has been properly set. $\overline{\text{WR}}$ is asserted during a memory or I/O write operation.

$\overline{\text{MREQ}}$ is used to indicate that the current bus operation is directed at the system memory space. This is to differentiate memory from I/O space, discussed shortly. $\overline{\text{MREQ}}$ is asserted during instruction fetches and data transactions with memory.

During the fetch of the first byte of each instruction, $\overline{\text{M1}}$ is asserted. This serves to synchronize external circuitry with the processor data flow and is especially useful when building emulators. $\overline{\text{RFSH}}$ is asserted during the decoding of an instruction. Normally, a processor bus is idle while a fetched instruction is decoded. The Z80 designers decided to take advantage of this by issuing a dynamic-RAM-refresh command during the idle time. In order for this feature to be useful, the Z80 processor must constantly be fetching instructions. Dynamic memory must be periodically refreshed or the information stored in it will be lost. As we shall see, there are certain conditions where the Z80 instruction fetches can be stopped, which could be a problem for dynamic RAM.

$\overline{\text{IORQ}}$ is asserted during I/O input and output cycles. Since the Z80 processor includes the 8080A processor instruction set, it too has a special I/O space, separate from memory space. Assertion of $\overline{\text{IORQ}}$ indicates that the current operation is targeted at the I/O space, and not the memory space.

There is another use for the $\overline{\text{M1}}$ and $\overline{\text{IORQ}}$ signals. If both are asserted together, the processor is acknowledging an interrupt and is requesting that

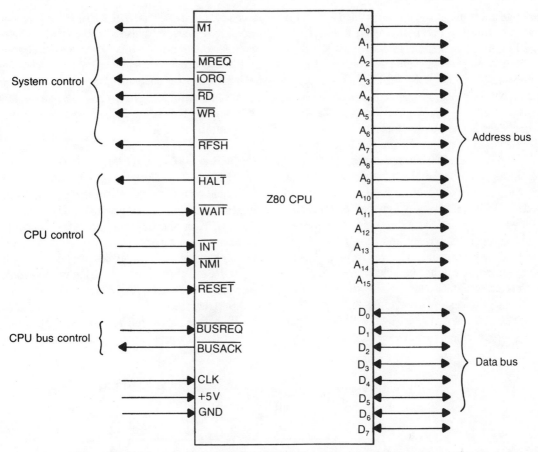

Fig. 2-14. Functional diagram of the Zilog Z80 microprocessor. Reproduced by permission (C) 1979, 1980, 1981 by Zilog, Inc. This material shall not be reproduced without written consent of Zilog, Inc.

an interrupt vector be applied to its data bus. Note the ingenious use of two signals that normally would not be asserted together. Since instructions are never fetched from I/O addresses, $\overline{M1}$ and $\overline{IORQ}$ would ordinarily not be asserted at the same time. This allowed the Z80 designers to multiplex the signal lines, using an unused state (both $\overline{M1}$ and $\overline{IORQ}$ asserted) to represent a third function—interrupt acknowledge. Thus, a special pin to acknowledge interrupts was not needed.

All Z80 bus transactions are synchronized to the processor clock, CLK. The Z80 processor has a synchronous bus. If slow memory or peripheral devices are to be connected to the Z80 bus, some means is needed to make the processor wait for the slower device. That means takes the form of the $\overline{WAIT}$ input. If the $\overline{WAIT}$ signal is asserted during a bus transaction, the processor will enter a wait state at the next clock. It will wait until $\overline{WAIT}$ is negated and then finish the cycle. $\overline{WAIT}$ may be asserted indefinitely, unless the special dynamic RAM refresh features of the processor have been used. Then if the $\overline{WAIT}$ input is asserted for too long a time, the processor will not be able to refresh the RAM and data will be lost.

There are two Z80 interrupt inputs. $\overline{INT}$ is a maskable interrupt, it can be enabled and disabled by executing the proper instructions. This allows the processor to ignore the interrupts at times when operations cannot be interrupted. $\overline{NMI}$ is the nonmaskable interrupt. It cannot be disabled and will always interrupt the processor, even if an INT initiated interrupt is being serviced.

HALT is asserted when the processor has executed a halt instruction. No further instructions are fetched but the processor executes NOPs (no operation) to simulate normal execution so that the RFSH pin continues to operate. Only an interrupt or a reset will release the processor from the halted state.

BUSREQ is a Z80 bus-request input. It is used to kick the processor off the bus so some other device can temporarily control it. This is frequently used for DMA operations. When the Z80 processor acknowledges BUSREQ it releases the data, address, and control busses and then asserts BUSACK. If the processor is deprived from the bus for a long period, it will not be able to refresh RAM, which is a consideration in systems which use DMA and the Z80 refresh feature together.

The processor is reset by the RESET input. During a reset, the Z80 busses are placed in a high-impedance state. Thus, if the RESET signal is asserted long enough, dynamic-RAM refresh will not take place and any dynamic RAM being refreshed by the Z80 processor will lose data. This may not be important, because many systems don't care what was in memory before a reset. Some do, however, and for those, the RESET signal must be of short duration.

Memory-Cycle Timing

Figure 2-15 illustrates a Z80 memory cycle. Both read and write operations are shown, though they cannot occur simultaneously. The processor clock, CLK, is shown at the top of the figure. It is the master timing mechanism for bus transfers. Positive portions of the clock cycles are labeled T_1, T_2, T_W and T_3. These are the T states which make up the read or write cycle. A Z80 processor runs at up to 2.5 MHz, so one T state is at least 200 nanoseconds, with at least 200 nanoseconds between T states. A Z80A processor runs at up to 4 MHz, so

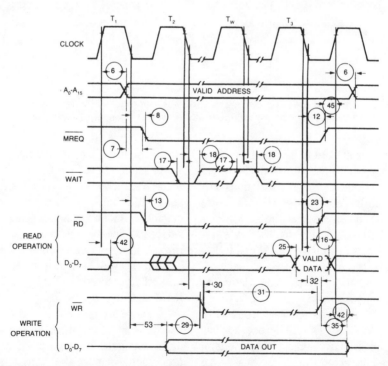

Fig. 2-15. Zilog Z80 microprocessor memory-cycle timing. Copyright 1979, 1980, 1981 by Zilog, Inc. This material shall not be reproduced without written consent of Zilog, Inc.

a T state may be as short as 125 nanoseconds with 125 nanoseconds between T states. A Z80H processor runs at 8 MHz, with a resulting 62.5-nanosecond T state.

Shortly after the start of T_1, the processor places an address on the address bus, specifying the location in memory where the transaction will take place. Shortly after the T_1 cycle, $\overline{MREQ}$ is asserted. If the memory is to be read, $\overline{RD}$ is asserted at about this time also. This indicates to the memory that data should be placed on the data bus. The memory has until just before the end of the T_3 state to place the data on the bus.

If the memory can't supply data in the alotted time, wait states must be generated. $\overline{WAIT}$ must be asserted before the end of the T_2 state to cause the processor to enter a wait state. T_W is shown separated from the rest of the clock cycles because it may or may not be present, depending on the state of the $\overline{WAIT}$ input.

During a write operation, RD is not asserted. The processor places the data to be written on the data bus during T_2. Shortly after the T_2 state, WR is asserted, initiating the memory-write operation. The operation will complete after the next T state, which will be T_3 unless $\overline{WAIT}$ is asserted during T_2. Assertion of $\overline{WAIT}$ will cause the processor to insert T_W states until $\overline{WAIT}$ is no longer asserted. The cycle will then complete with a T_3 state.

I/O-Cycle Timing

The Z80 I/O cycle is very similar to the Z80 memory cycle with a few exceptions. **Figure 2-16** shows both input and output cycles for the Z80 processor. Again, they can't actually happen together but are shown that way to illustrate the similarities.

An input cycle looks like a memory-read cycle with three exceptions. First, $\overline{MREQ}$ has been replaced by $\overline{IORQ}$. That is because $\overline{MREQ}$ is not asserted during I/O cycles, but $\overline{IORQ}$ is. Second, $\overline{RD}$ is asserted shortly after the start of T_2 instead of shortly after the end of the T_1. Third, a special T state marked T_W is shown.

The Z80 processor automatically inserts an extra wait state in I/O operations. This is because the

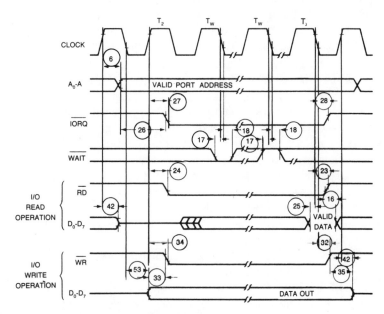

NOTE: T_w^* = One Watt cycle automatically inserted by CPU.

Fig. 2-16. Zilog Z80 microprocessor I/O-Cycle timing. Copyright 1979, 1980, 1981 by Zilog, Inc. This material shall not be reproduced without written consent of Zilog, Inc.

Z80 designers knew that many I/O chips were slower than memory, and were accessed less frequently. Insertion of an automatic wait state during I/O operations allows the Z80 to interface with many I/O circuits without the need for extra wait-state circuitry and without significantly degrading performance.

Refer again to Fig. 2-16. An output operation is similar to a memory-write operation, again with three exceptions. First, $\overline{IORQ}$ is asserted as with the I/O input operation. Second, $\overline{WR}$ is asserted shortly after the start of T_2 instead of shortly after the end of T_2. Third, there is again an automatic insertion of a wait state.

16-BIT MICROPROCESSORS

We are now going to look at 16-bit microprocessors. The first of this generation to become popular was the Intel 8086. National Semiconductor Corporation and Texas Instruments had 16-bit processors on the market before the 8086 was introduced but they never saw wide use.

The Intel 8086, also called the iAPX86/10, has become very popular. It has many advantages over the eight-bit processors including faster, more powerful execution and extended memory and I/O space. Yet it is still supplied in a 40-pin package.

Figure 2-17 shows how this is accomplished, it is a pin diagram for the processor. Gone are the separate address and data busses. Instead we find sixteen pins, marked AD0 through AD15 on pins 2 through 16 and 39, and four other pins marked A16/S3 through A19/S6 on pins 35 through 38.

AD stands for Address and Data. The AD0 through AD15 pins carry address and data, at different times in the processor machine cycle. This is called a multiplexed bus. We have seen multiplexing before. The 8080A multiplexes data and status on the eight data lines. Sixteen address lines allow access to 65,536 memory locations. Address lines A16/S3 through A19/S6 extend the addressing capability of the 8086 to 1,048,576 locations. The extended address lines are also multiplexed. The S stands for status information, present on the extended-address pins at certain times in the machine cycle.

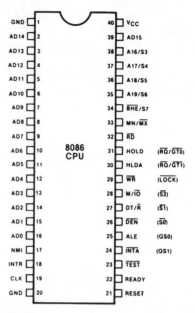

Fig. 2-17. Pin diagram of the Intel 8086 microprocessor. Reprinted by permission of Intel Corporation, Copyright 1983.

Minimum and Maximum Modes

Note that the signals on pins 24 through 31 are doubly labeled. This is because the 8086 has two operating modes: minimum and maximum. The operating mode is determined by the state of the MN/$\overline{MX}$ (Minimum/Maximum) input pin. When this input is high, the processor is in the minimum mode. When the input is pulled low, the processor is in the maximum mode.

Intel made the 8086 a dual mode machine to extend the spectrum of systems which the 8086 could be used in. In the minimum mode, the 8086 generates its own bus signals: HOLD, HLDA, $\overline{WR}$, M/$\overline{IO}$, DT/$\overline{R}$, $\overline{DEN}$, ALE and $\overline{INTA}$. Those are the names shown in parentheses in Fig. 2-17 for pins 24 through 31. An 8086 running in minimum mode is not intended for multi-processor systems.

In the maximum mode, the 8086 generates encoded bus states on the $\overline{S0}$, $\overline{S1}$ and $\overline{S2}$ lines. This encoded information is decoded by an Intel 8288 bus controller. Since only three lines are used for bus control, the remaining pins are available for extended processor functions. These are $\overline{LOCK}$, $\overline{RQ/GT0}$ and

$\overline{RQ}/\overline{GT1}$, used for requesting and granting bus mastership in multiple-processor systems, and QS0 and QS1 which are used to indicate the state of the processor's internal instruction queue. An 8086 running in maximum mode can be coupled with multiple processors on a single bus and can be used with coprocessors for extended capability.

8086 Pins Common to Both Modes

Some of the pins on the 8086 processor operate in the same manner no matter which mode the processor is running in. These are the Address/Data pins AD0 through AD15, the Address/Status pins A16/S3 through A19/S6, $\overline{BHE}$/S7, $\overline{RD}$, READY, INTR, $\overline{TEST}$, NMI, RESET, and CLK.

The low 16 bits of address, and the data bus, are multiplexed over the AD0 through AD15 lines. Early in a machine cycle, these pins are used by the processor to output a target address for the cycle operation.

AD0 is special. Since the 8086 is a 16-bit machine, it normally performs 16-bit transfers onto the data bus. Sometimes execution of an instruction requires a byte-wide transaction. This may involve either the upper or lower byte of the addressed word. A0 serves as a low-byte enable. If A0 is low during the time in the machine cycle when the address is presented on the AD pins, then a low-byte transfer will take place. Bus-High Enable/Status ($\overline{BHE}$/S7) serves a similar purpose for the high byte. Thus either the high byte, the low byte, or both bytes may be transferred in one cycle. The encoding is:

$\overline{BHE}$/S7	AD0	Entity Transferred
0	0	Both high and low bytes
0	1	High Byte only
1	0	Low Byte only
1	1	No bytes transferred

Remember, these pins are only used to specify the address and byte selection early in the machine cycle. Later on, the AD pins are used for the data

bus and the $\overline{BHE}$/S7 pin is used for extended-status information.

$\overline{RD}$ is a read strobe. It is asserted whenever the 8086 is performing a memory or I/O read. READY is the return signal from an addressed device that it is ready to complete the present bus cycle. The 8086 will initiate a bus cycle, be it memory or I/O, read or write, and then wait until READY is asserted.

INTR is the maskable interrupt request pin. The 8086 checks the state of the INTR line just before the end of each machine cycle to determine whether an interrupt should be serviced. NMI is the non-maskable interrupt input to the processor.

$\overline{TEST}$ is a special input which may be tested with a "wait-for-test" instruction. If $\overline{TEST}$ is not asserted when the instruction is executed, the processor enters an "idle" state until $\overline{TEST}$ is asserted. This allows external processes to be synchronized to the execution of a program. RESET simply resets the processor's program counter. Program execution starts over at the reset address FFFF0 hex when RESET is released.

8086 Control Pins - Minimum Mode

When the MN/$\overline{MX}$ pin of the Intel 8086 processor is tied high, minimum-mode operation is selected. This causes pins 24 through 31 to take on the functions labeled in parentheses in Fig. 2-17. The minimum mode is used for smaller 8086-based systems which do not use multiple 8086 processors or coprocessors.

$\overline{WR}$ is the write cycle counterpart of the $\overline{RD}$ signal just discussed. Whenever the 8086 processor performs a memory write or I/O output operation, $\overline{WR}$ is asserted.

ALE, or Address-Latch Enable, is the signal used to indicate when an address is present on the multiplexed address/data and address/status pins. This signal is connected to latches which will hold the address, thus performing a demultiplexing function. ALE is a high-true signal.

Since the 8086 processor has both a memory and an I/O space, some means is required to signal whether the current bus access is directed to memory or I/O. The M/$\overline{\text{IO}}$ pin does this. If the M/$\overline{\text{IO}}$ pin is high during a bus transaction, then a memory access is taking place. If the pin is low, an I/O access is being performed. Usually, the M/$\overline{\text{IO}}$ pin is used in the address decoding circuitry of the system to determine what portion of the system to enable.

The two signals $\overline{\text{DEN}}$ and DT/$\overline{\text{R}}$ are intended to directly control the Intel bus transceivers 8286/8287. The 8286 is a non-inverting buffer while the 8287 inverts. These integrated circuits are used to buffer the 8086 data bus. $\overline{\text{DEN}}$ is a Data-ENable signal. When asserted, data is supposed to be flowing on the address/data bus. The direction the data flows in is determined by the DT/$\overline{\text{R}}$ or Data Transmit/Receive pin. If DT/$\overline{\text{R}}$ is high, data is being transmitted. That means the 8086 processor is driving the data bus. If DT/$\overline{\text{R}}$ is low, the processor is receiving or reading the data bus.

Note that $\overline{\text{DEN}}$ and DT/$\overline{\text{R}}$ could be generated from $\overline{\text{RD}}$ and $\overline{\text{WR}}$. If either $\overline{\text{RD}}$ or $\overline{\text{WR}}$ is asserted, $\overline{\text{DEN}}$ is also asserted. If $\overline{\text{RD}}$ is asserted, DT/$\overline{\text{R}}$ will be low, and if $\overline{\text{WR}}$ is asserted, DT/$\overline{\text{R}}$ will be high. The reason Intel has supplied the DT/$\overline{\text{R}}$ and $\overline{\text{DEN}}$ signals in the minimum mode is to eliminate any external decoding circuitry. $\overline{\text{DEN}}$ and DT/$\overline{\text{R}}$ will directly drive Intel's bus buffers, saving the cost of the decoding logic and the space on the circuit board such logic would require.

$\overline{\text{INTA}}$ is the INterrupT Acknowledge signal. It can be considered a special read signal. When $\overline{\text{INTA}}$ is asserted, the 8086 processor is reading an interrupt vector from an interrupting device. The 8086 processor has only a single interrupt input, INTR. Thus, it cannot tell when more than one device is interrupting and cannot indicate which device it wants the interrupt vector from. This is left to other circuitry in the system. If there is only one device in the system which can interrupt, then the choice becomes obvious. Interrupts are more thoroughly discussed in Chapter 8.

The two remaining signals of the minimum mode requiring explanation are HOLD and HLDA. These are the bus request and acknowledge pins. If another bus master in the system wishes control of the bus, it asserts the HOLD input of the 8086

processor. When the 8086 can relinquish the bus and HOLD is asserted, it releases the bus and asserts HLDA.

HOLD and HLDA are used for direct memory access (DMA) and multiple-processor environments. Although the 8086 minimum mode of operation is not designed to be used in multiple processor systems, a two-processor system can be readily implemented with HOLD and HLDA. DMA operations are discussed in more detail in Chapter 9.

8086 Control Pins - Maximum Mode

Larger 8086 systems may involve multiple processors and/or multiple busses. The 8086 maximum mode is intended to help system designers create such large systems more easily. When the MN/MX pin on the 8086 processor is tied to ground, the processor operates in this maximum mode. This causes the functions QS1, QS0, S0, S1, S2, LOCK, RQ/GT1, and RQ/GT2 to appear on pins 24 through 31.

The status pins $\overline{\text{S0}}$, $\overline{\text{S1}}$, and $\overline{\text{S2}}$ contain encoded information as to the type of bus transaction taking place during a machine cycle. The encoding is:

$\overline{\text{S2}}$	$\overline{\text{S1}}$	$\overline{\text{S0}}$	Transaction
0	0	0	Interrupt Acknowledge
0	0	1	I/O Read
0	1	0	I/O Write
0	1	1	Processor Halt
1	0	0	Code Access
1	0	1	Memory Read
1	1	0	Memory Write
1	1	1	Passive State

There are some interesting aspects to note about the encoded status lines. $\overline{\text{S1}}$ is loosely defined as a read/write specifier. When $\overline{\text{S1}}$ is low, a read is taking place. If $\overline{\text{S1}}$ is high, a write may be taking place.

The Halt and Passive states indicated when $\overline{\text{S1}}$ is high are exceptions to the $\overline{\text{S1}}$ high-write definition. When $\overline{\text{S0}}$ through $\overline{\text{S2}}$ are all high the passive state is signaled. The 8086 processor enters this state to signify that the current bus cycle is ending.

$\overline{RQ}/\overline{GT0}$ and $\overline{RQ}/\overline{GT1}$ are bus request/bus grant pins. They are bidirectional, being both input and output on a single pin. Intel has defined a special bus request/grant protocol using pulses on these pins. The protocol is:

1. A request is indicated when a pulse one clock period wide is received on the $\overline{RQ}/\overline{GT}$ pin.
2. The 8086 processor releases the bus and pulses the $\overline{RQ}/\overline{GT}$ pin to issue a bus grant.
3. When the requesting master has finished with the bus, it issues a third pulse on the same $\overline{RQ}/\overline{GT}$ pin to inform the 8086 processor that it should retake control of the bus.

This protocol is used by Intel's coprocessors, designed to increase the capability of the 8086. An example of a coprocessor is the Intel 8087 math coprocessor which performs floating-point arithmetic.

If there are times when the 8086 does not wish to give up the bus, the $\overline{LOCK}$ signal can be used to indicate that condition. When $\overline{LOCK}$ is asserted, other potential bus masters are not to take control of the bus. $\overline{LOCK}$ will be asserted when a special locking instruction prefix is executed by the 8086. External system circuitry should be designed to ensure this actually happens. Otherwise, some very elusive programming problems will be introduced into the system.

The final two pins of the 8086 in maximum mode are QS0 and QS1. These signals are used to inform external circuits about the 8086 internal instruction queue. These pins are important for in-circuit emulation and debugging of 8086 systems.

The 8086 is a pipelined microprocessor. There is a buffer in the 8086 which can store up to six instruction bytes. Also, there are actually two processing units in the 8086; a Bus Interface Unit (BIU), and an Execution Unit (EU). **Figure 2-18**

shows the internal architecture of the 8086 processor.

The EU actually analyzes and executes the machine instructions. The BIU is responsible for fetching the machine code instructions from memory. In most systems, memory access requires more time than instruction execution. The BIU keeps the six-byte instruction buffer filled so that the EU can get the instruction from the buffer instead of from memory.

Since there is a six-byte buffer in between the processor bus and the Execution Unit, the instruction most recently fetched from memory will probably not be the instruction executed. The instruction being executed could have been fetched up to six bytes previously!

Exceptions to this 6-byte separation occur during branches. The BIU performs simple fetches of sequential addresses. If a conditional branch is executed by the EU, the BIU will not know the outcome of that branch in advance. The instruction buffer may be filled with instructions from the wrong branch in the code. In this case, the buffer has to be emptied, or flushed, and refilled before the EU can continue.

QS0 and QS1 are encoded signals which indicate how the instruction buffer is operating. The signals are encoded as:

QS0	QS1	Buffer Status
0	0	No operation
0	1	First byte of instruction to EU
1	0	Flush instruction buffer
1	1	Subsequent byte of instruction to EU

With the information on the QS0 and QS1 signal lines, an in-circuit emulator can be built which accurately reflects the true internal state of the 8086 processor.

Creating the Maximum-Mode Bus

The 8086 control bus is encoded onto the $\overline{S0}$ through $\overline{S2}$ pins when the processor is in the maxi-

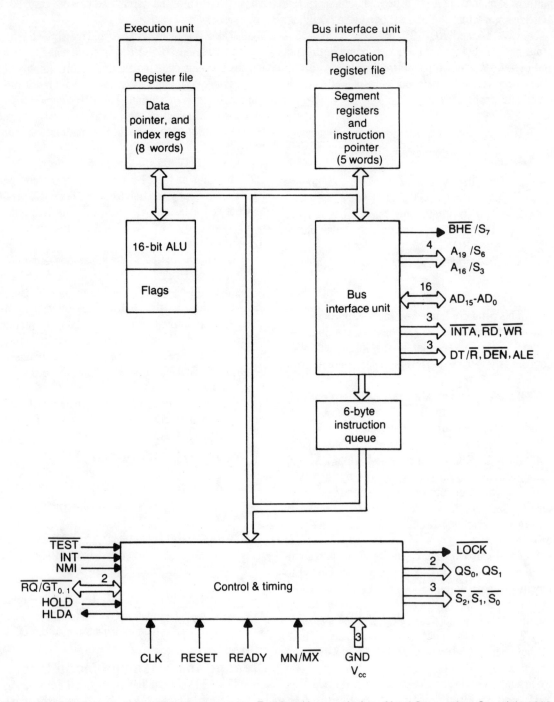

Fig. 2-18. Block diagram of the 8086 microprocessor. Reprinted by permission of Intel Corporation, Copyright 1983.

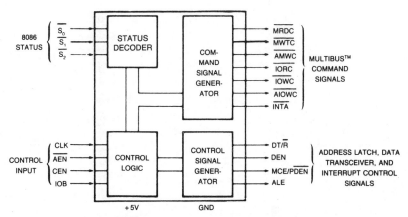

Fig. 2-19. Block Diagram of the Intel 8288 bus controller designed for the Intel 8086 microprocessor. Reprinted by permission of Intel Corporation, Copyright 1983.

mum mode. Circuitry is required to decode these pins and create the bus signals required by the rest of the computer system. Intel has a special integrated circuit to perform this function. It is the 8288 Bus Controller.

Intel has given advanced system designers a very sophisticated part in the bus controller. It can be used to simply run a system bus in a maximum-mode, single-processor 8086 system. It can also be used to drive a system bus shared by several 8086 processors, each with its own 8288 bus controller. Systems with shared system busses and private IO busses can also be accommodated, as can systems with shared I/O busses. The system designer truly has wide latitude in the design of a microprocessor system based on a maximum-mode 8086 processor.

Figure 2-19 is a block diagram of the 8288 Bus Controller and Fig. 2-20 is the pin diagram for the part. The S0, S1 and S2 pins from the 8086 processor are connected to the 8288 status decoder. CLK, the 8086 clock signal, is also fed to the 8288 to synchronize the bus controller with the processor.

This is necessary because the S0, S1 and S2 pins only output status at certain times in the machine cycle. The 8288 must have some means of knowing when these pins have valid information on them. A passive-processor state ($\overline{S0}$ = high, $\overline{S1}$ = high, $\overline{S2}$ = high) alerts the 8288 bus controller when a new machine cycle is about to start. This is the

synchronization mechanism between the processor and the bus controller.

When properly synchronized with an 8086 processor, the 8288 bus controller generates the required bus-control signals to run a large microprocessor system. These signals are produced by the command- and control-signal generators, shown in the block diagram of Fig. 2-19.

Signals from the command-signal generator are labeled Multibus (TM) Command signals. This is because the signals generated by this section of the bus controller are compatible with Intel's system bus, which is called Multibus. The Multibus is discussed in detail later.

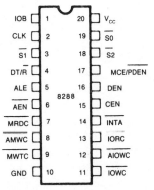

Fig. 2-20. Pin diagram of the Intel bus controller. Reprinted by permission of Intel Corporation, Copyright 1983.

The $\overline{\text{AEN}}$ input to the 8288 bus controller determines whether or not the outputs of the command-signal generator will be actively driven. If $\overline{\text{AEN}}$ is held high, the command outputs will be disabled, and will not drive the bus. When $\overline{\text{AEN}}$ is driven low, the command output signals will be enabled after at least an 85 ns delay.

$\overline{\text{AEN}}$ is most useful in systems where more than one processor may control the bus. Some sort of arbitration logic must be designed in. Then, whenever a processor wishes to drive the system bus, the arbitration logic decides whether that processor can have the bus. If the bus is available, the arbitration logic drives the $\overline{\text{AEN}}$ input of the appropriate 8288 bus controller low, allowing the requesting processor to drive the bus command lines.

$\overline{\text{MRDC}}$ and $\overline{\text{MWTC}}$ are the Memory Read and Write control signals respectively. $\overline{\text{MRDC}}$ is asserted when the processor is performing a read operation from memory (not I/O) space. $\overline{\text{MWTC}}$ is asserted when the processor is performing a memory write operation.

$\overline{\text{AMWC}}$ is an Advanced-Memory-Write control signal. It can be used to give the system memory earlier indication that a write is taking place. $\overline{\text{AMWC}}$ can be used in systems where the write control pulse can occur at the same time that data becomes available on the data bus. For systems that require the data to be valid for some time before the processor write indication is given, $\overline{\text{MWTC}}$ should be used instead of $\overline{\text{AMWC}}$.

$\overline{\text{IORC}}$ and $\overline{\text{IOWC}}$ are the I/O ReaD and Write control signals respectively. $\overline{\text{IORC}}$ is asserted when the processor is performing a read operation from I/O (not memory) space. $\overline{\text{IOWC}}$ is asserted when the processor is performing an I/O write operation. $\overline{\text{AIOWC}}$ is the Advanced I/O Write control signal and serves the same purpose for I/O write operations that $\overline{\text{AMWC}}$ serves for memory write operations.

$\overline{\text{INTA}}$ should look familiar. It is the same interrupt-acknowledge signal generated by the 8086 processor running in minimum mode. The only difference is that the 8288 bus controller generates this signal for the 8086 when running in maximum mode.

Three of the signals from the control-signal generator should also be familiar to you. DT/$\overline{\text{R}}$, DEN, and ALE have already been discussed in the explanation of 8086 minimum mode operation. The two differences are that these signals are generated by the 8288 instead of the 8086, and the DEN signal is high-true when generated by the 8288 while it was low-true ($\overline{\text{DEN}}$) when generated by the 8086.

The last output generated by the control-signal generator serves a dual purpose. That is why it is doubly labeled MCE/$\overline{\text{PDEN}}$. Which function this pin performs is determined by one of the 8288 input pins; IOB.

IOB is used to tell the 8288 whether the system has a separate IO Bus or not. If there are separate data busses for I/O and Memory, then the IOB pin on the 8288 should be tied high. This will enable the $\overline{\text{PDEN}}$ function of the MCE/$\overline{\text{PDEN}}$ pin and will place the 8288 bus controller in the I/O Bus mode. Figure 2-21 shows a possible 8086 system with a separate I/O data bus.

$\overline{\text{PDEN}}$ is the Peripheral-Data-ENable pin. It is used to enable the I/O data bus buffers when an I/O bus transaction is taking place. $\overline{\text{PDEN}}$ serves a similar purpose for the I/O data bus as DEN serves for the processor data bus. Of course, the special I/O data bus must connect to the processor data bus at some point.

When the 8288 is operated in the I/O Bus mode, the I/O command lines $\overline{\text{IORC}}$, $\overline{\text{IOWC}}$, $\overline{\text{AIOWC}}$ and $\overline{\text{INTA}}$ are always enabled. Thus, the I/O bus is committed to a single processor because the I/O command lines will never be disabled.

It is important to think about why a separate I/O data bus might be a desirable feature to have in a system. After all, it requires extra parts to create a separate I/O data bus which costs more and takes up more board space. There must be some advantage to this architecture to justify the extra costs.

The advantage is one of isolation. If the I/O data bus is isolated from the system data bus, transactions on the I/O data bus can take place while unrelated transactions are taking place on the system data bus. This sort of parallel operation can greatly

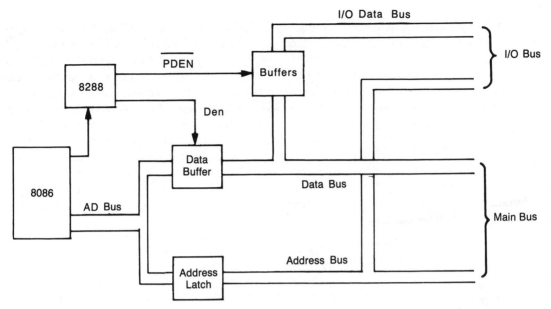

Fig. 2-21. An Intel 8086 microcomputer system with a separate I/O bus.

improve system performance because up to twice the number of bus transactions can occur in a given amount of time.

Unfortunately, the simple system of **Fig. 2-21** cannot take advantage of parallel I/O and system data bus operation. The 8086 processor still can only perform one operation at a time. To make full use of the dual-bus architecture, another processor must be included in the system to control the I/O data bus independent of the 8086. A second 8086 might be used for this, but Intel has a better idea.

A specialized I/O microprocessor, the Intel 8089, can be used for I/O data bus control. The 8089 microprocessor has a special instruction set developed especially for I/O oriented operations. It can move information very quickly with these instructions.

Dual-processor/dual-bus architectures are much more complex topics than I wish to cover in an introduction to I/O such as this book. If such concepts excite you, however, please feel encouraged to go on to more complex texts after you finish reading here. The Intel 8086 data manuals can tell you much more about 8086/8089 architectures, and I urge you to investigate them.

We have almost covered all the signal pins on the 8288 bus controller. The remaining pin is CEN, or the Command-ENable line. This input signal, when driven low, will force the command lines to their inactive state. It does not disable the command outputs from driving the bus, but rather places all command outputs in the negated state. CEN is to be used at the discretion of the system designer for such things as system memory, or other system-resource partitioning where address is not the only qualifying parameter which selects the resource.

Bus-Cycle Timing

Timing for the 8086 bus is shown in **Fig. 2-22**. Remember, this is a multiplexed microprocessor bus, so the address and data lines are combined. At some times, addresses appear on the lines and at other times, data appears. At the top of the figure, the master clock signal, CLK, is shown. All other bus signals generated by the 8086 processor are synchronized to CLK. The CLK period may be as small as 200 ns (5 MHz) in an 8086 system.

An 8086 bus cycle is composed of CLK cycles, called T-states. A bus cycle is four T-states long unless external circuitry causes the processor to en-

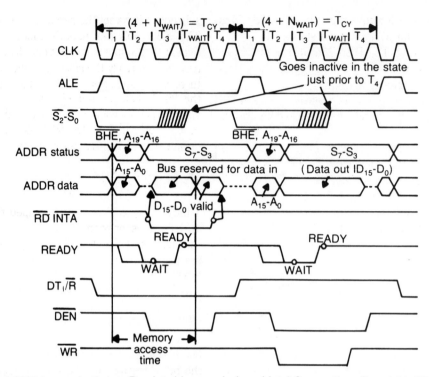

Fig. 2-22. Intel 8086 bus cycle timing. Reprinted by permission of Intel Corporation, Copyright 1983.

ter Wait states, which stretch out the cycle. **Figure 2-22** shows two bus cycles.

An 8086 bus cycle starts at the negative edge of a CLK pulse. In the first T-state, T1, processor status appears on the S0 through S2 lines (maximum mode only), an address appears on the multiplexed address/data lines AD0 through AD15, on the address lines A16 through A19, and BHE is driven to its appropriate level. The read/write line, DT/$\overline{R}$, is also appropriately driven during T1. ALE is asserted and then negated during T1. At the trailing edge of ALE, the address must be latched external to the 8086 so that the address/data lines may be cleared for subsequent data on the bus.

During T2, the multiplexed address/data bus is converted from an address bus to a data bus. The address which was on the AD0 through AD15 lines is removed. The information on A16 through A19 and $\overline{BHE}$ is removed, and A16 through A19 become the extended-status lines S3 and S7. At this time, if a memory read or interrupt acknowledge opera-

tion is taking place, $\overline{RD}$ or $\overline{INTA}$ will be asserted respectively. If this is a maximum-mode system and a memory write or I/O output operation is taking place, $\overline{AMWC}$ or $\overline{AIOWC}$ will be asserted during T2 by the 8288 bus controller. If a write or output is taking place, the data being written, or output, appears on the AD lines during T2.

S3 through S7 provide extra status information about the processor state. S3 and S4 are used to indicate which processor register the address bits A16 through A19 came from. The encoded information is:

S4	S3	Register
0	0	Alternate data register
0	1	Stack register
1	0	Code register or no register used
1	1	Data register

S5 indicates whether interrupts are enabled, S6 is always zero, and S7 is a spare status bit.

Also during T2, DEN (minimum mode) or $\overline{\text{DEN}}$ (maximum mode) will be asserted shortly after the address information has been removed from the AD lines. This prevents conflicts between the 8086 address drivers and any external data drivers in the system.

If the addressed device is going to stretch the bus cycle with the 8086 READY input, indication must be given before the end of T2. If READY is low at the end of the T2 machine state, at least one WAIT T-state will be inserted between T3 and T4. At the end of each succeeding T-state, READY is again sampled to determine whether another WAIT T-state is needed. When READY is finally asserted, the WAIT states will end for this cycle.

During T3, the AD lines are used as the processor data lines. Data being read in will appear on the AD lines during T3 unless WAIT states are requested.

T4 is the last T-state in the bus cycle. If the processor is going to read the data lines, it does so during T4. All asserted control signals are negated during T4 to end the bus cycle.

Intel won big with its 8086 microprocessor architecture. IBM incorporated the 8086's little brother, the 8088, into the original IBM PC, which subsequently swept the personal-computing market. The 8088 duplicates all of the functions of the 8086 except that it sports an 8-bit data bus instead of 16 bits, but internally the chips have the same architecture. Intel estimates that the 8-bit data bus makes the 8088 about 25 percent slower than the 8086 which is quite a good engineering tradeoff. Because of it's 8-bit data bus, the 8088 allows designers to create less expensive 16-bit systems.

INTEL 80286

Programmers quickly found that the 8086's 1-megabyte address space cramped their style. A 16-bit processor seems to need a lot more memory than an 8-bit machine, especially when programmers start to get ambitious. So Intel decided to retool the 8086 architecture and add several enhancements. The result of this architectural refurbishing is the 80286 microprocessor.

Figure 2-23 shows the results of this architectural growth. In addition to the 8086's two internal processing components (the execution unit (EU) and the bus interface unit (BIU)), the 80286 sports an address unit and an instruction unit. Similar to the 8086's BIU, the 80286's bus unit (BU) fetches instructions and operands from memory and performs I/O transfers. The 80286's BU incorporates a 6-byte prefetch queue, just like the 8086's BIU.

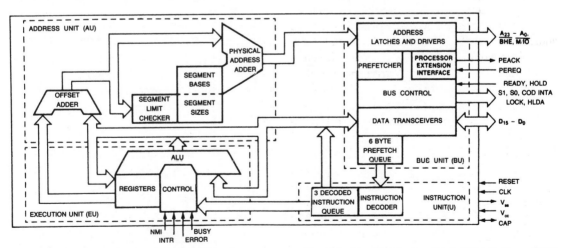

Fig. 2-23. Block diagram of the Intel 80286 microprocessor. Reprinted by permission of Intel Corporation, Copyright 1983.

The 80286's instruction unit (IU) decodes the instructions fetched by the BU and places these decoded instructions in a 3-instruction queue for use by the execution unit. Because the 80286 is a microcoded processor, its machine codes are compacted. Before the 80286 can execute these instructions, the compacted codes must be expanded, a process called decoding, to generate the individual control signals that activate different parts of the microprocessor. Decoding these compacted instructions takes time, so Intel added the IU which decodes instructions in parallel with the EU's instruction execution. This hardware parallelism improves the 80286's overall performance.

Likewise, the 80286's address unit (AU) computes physical addresses from the processor's unique conglomeration of segment registers and addressing modes. The 8086 lacked an AU and thus its execution unit was often diverted from executing program instructions to perform these sorts of calculations. The 80286's AU provides additional parallelism, hence faster processor operation. Finally, the EU executes the fetched and decoded instructions, which of course is the purpose of the whole exercise.

Figure 2-24 illustrates the 80286's memory and I/O maps. Like the 8086, the 80286 has a 64K-byte I/O space. However, Intel's processor designers acknowledged that 16-bit processors need more elbow room for programs by expanding the microprocessor's memory space to 16 megabytes. All of this growth extracts a cost. For the 80286, that cost came in the form of a larger piece of silicon, additional power dissipation, and more pins. The 80286 does not fit in a 40-pin package. Instead, Intel offers the device in a 68-pin leadless chip carrier, shown in **Fig. 2-25**.

Unlike the 8086, the 80286 has separate address (A0 through A23 on pins 7, 8, 10-28, and 32-34) and data (DO through D15 on pins 36 through

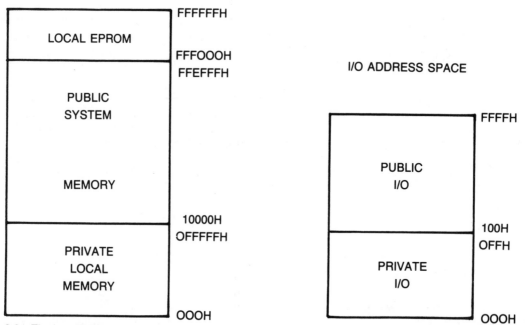

Fig. 2-24. The Intel 80286 microprocessor has separate memory and I/O address spaces. Reprinted by permission of the Intel Corporation, Copyright 1983.

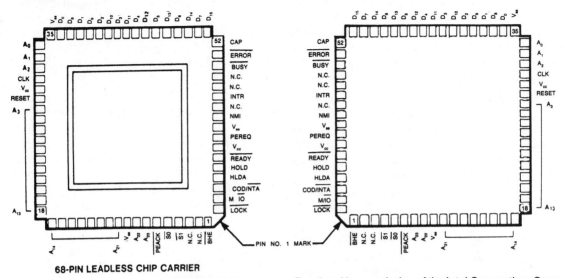

Fig. 2-25. Lead diagram of the Intel 80286 microprocessor. Reprinted by permission of the Intel Corporation, Copyright 1983.

51) busses. That eats up 40 pins right there. Note that the processor has a 24-bit address bus to accommodate its 16-megabyte address space.

By no small coincidence, several of the 80286 signals closely resemble 8086 signals. The HOLD and HLDA (hold acknowledge) signals are used to arbitrate control of the system bus in multiple-processor designs or systems with DMA controllers. Likewise, the LOCK signal allows the 80286 to retain control of the bus. INTR and NMI are the maskable and non-maskable interrupt-request inputs. READY allows an addressed device to stretch a bus cycle. For some reason, Intel decided to change the sense of this pin between the designs of the 8086 and 80286. Thus the 80286's READY is a low-true signal and the 8086's ready input is high-true.

One of the remaining 80286 signals should also look familiar to you. The Bus High Enable signal (pin 1) works in conjunction with the A0 pin to specify which bytes are to be transferred during a bus cycle using a coding scheme quite similar to the 8086's:

BHE	A0	Entity Transferred
0	0	Both high and low bytes
0	1	High byte only
1	0	Low byte only
1	1	No bytes transferred

The 80286 does not directly implement the control signals necessary to control a microprocessor system bus as does an 8086 in minimum mode. Instead, the 80286's $\overline{S0}$ and $\overline{S1}$ bus-cycle status signals (pins 4 and 5), along with the M/$\overline{IO}$ signal (pin 67) and COD/$\overline{INTA}$ signal (pin 66) specify the type of bus cycle the processor is currently executing. You may notice the operational similarity to an 8086 in maximum mode. The complete list of possible cycles is:

COD/INTA	M/IO	S1	S0	BUS CYCLE
0	0	0	0	Interrupt acknowledge
0	0	0	1	Reserved
0	0	1	0	Reserved
0	0	1	1	None
0	1	0	0	Halt if A1 = 1, else shutdown
0	1	0	1	Memory data read
0	1	1	0	Memory data write

COD/ INTA	M/IO	S1	SO	BUS CYCLE
0	1	1	1	None
1	0	0	0	Reserved
1	0	0	1	I/O read
1	0	1	0	I/O write
1	0	1	1	None
1	1	0	0	Reserved
1	1	0	1	Memory instruction read
1	1	1	0	Reserved
1	1	1	1	None

A companion IC, the 82288 bus controller, has the task of generating bus control signals from these four status lines. Pin and block diagrams for the 82288 appear in **Figs. 2-26** and **2-27** respectively and a complete system diagram comprising an 80286 processor, 80288 bus controller, and 82284 clock generator appears in **Fig. 2-28**. The 82288 shares a common clock with the 80286 allowing it to latch the status-line state during the falling edge of the

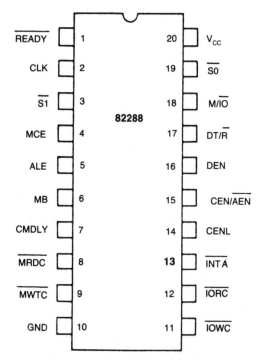

Fig. 2-26. Pin diagram of the Intel 82288 bus controller for the Intel 80286 microprocessor. Reprinted by permission of the Intel Corporation, Copyright 1983.

clock. From these four status lines, plus a few more inputs, the 82288 generates five command signals (INTA, IORC, IOWC, MRDC, and MWTC) and four control signals (DT/R, DEN, ALE, and MCE). All of these outputs except MCE replicate the signals generated by the 8086's bus controller, the 8288, and have thus been covered. MCE is an expansion signal that allows you to expand the 80286's interrupt capabilities with an Intel 8259A programmable interrupt controller.

Now that we have all the signals defined for an 80286 system, we can look at some bus cycles. The interconnection of 80286, 82288, and 82284 forms a synchronous local bus that runs at twice the frequency of the 80286's internal processor clock, called PCLK. Each processor clock cycle or T state thus encompasses two local-bus clock cycles called Phase 1 and Phase 2. The relationship between a T state, PCLK, and clock cycles Phase 1 and Phase 2 appears in **Fig. 2-29**.

The local bus can assume one of four T states: idle (Ti), send-status (Ts), perform-command (Tc), and hold (Th). Each T state lasts one PCLK. If no transfers into or out of the 80286 are required, the processor executes idle T states, signified by both S0 and S1 assuming an 11 state. The 80286 bus-cycle table shows that this condition indicates that no bus-cycle is taking place. Ti states occur when the 80286 is executing an instruction that does not require a bus cycle such as an internal computation or a register-to-register transfer. Of course, the 6-byte prefetch queue must also be full or the BU will be busy bringing in more instructions.

The 80286 enters a Ts state to initiate a bus cycle, indicating the type of cycle on the S0, S1, M/IO, and COD/INTA signal lines. Immediately after a Ts state, the 80286 always enters a Tc state and waits for a READY signal indicating that the bus transfer has completed. The processor will continue to execute Tc states until its READY input is asserted. Then it will start another bus cycle by returning to the Ts state if another cycle is required. Otherwise, the processor will enter the Ti state until more bus cycles are needed. The 80286 enters a Th state when it has relinquished its external bus to another bus master.

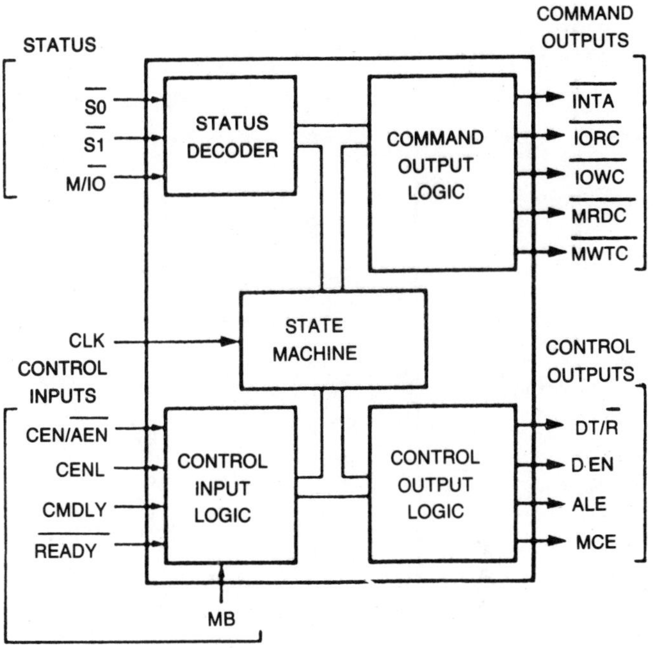

Fig. 2-27. Block diagram of the Intel 82288 bus controller. Reprinted by permission of the Intel Corporation, Copyright 1983.

All of this local-bus activity is fine, but it doesn't get anything done in the real world of the system bus. T states merely send commands from the 80286 microprocessor to the 82288 bus controller. It is the 82288 which drives the bus-control signals that actually move data around the system. So now, let's put Phases and T states together with an 82288 and look at some system bus cycles. Take a look at Figs. 2-30 and 2-31, which show read and write cycles respectively.

A minimum-length read cycle requires two states: a Ts state followed by a Tc state. During Phase 1 of the Ts state, the 80286 places a valid address on the address bus and the 82288 sets the M/$\overline{IO}$, COD/$\overline{INTA}$, $\overline{SO}$, and $\overline{S1}$ signal lines appropriately. During Phase 2 of the Ts state, the 82288 asserts ALE, starting the actual system bus cycle. Then, early in Phase 1 of the Tc cycle, the 82288 sets the DT/$\overline{R}$ data-direction pin low and asserts $\overline{MRDC}$ (for a memory read cycle) or $\overline{IORC}$ (for an I/O read cycle). A little later, the 82288 asserts DEN to enable the system-bus data buffers. If $\overline{READY}$ is asserted before the end of the Tc state, the 80286 will read the data on its data bus and complete the

transaction. Otherwise, the microprocessor will continue to execute Tc states, waiting for the assertion of $\overline{READY}$.

Write cycles operate quite similarly except the 80286 drives the data lines instead of reading them. In addition, during a write cycle the 82288 asserts $\overline{MWTC}$ (for a memory write) or $\overline{IOWC}$ (for an I/O write) and drives DT/$\overline{R}$ high to set the data direction controls on the data-bus buffers.

The 80286 and its companion parts create a fairly complex system. However, you should note that when you take a larger view of a system built from the 80286, 82288, and the 82284, you find the same old signals universally found in all microprocessor systems: read, write, and data direction. Look for familiarity in complex systems to reduce apparent complexity.

ZILOG Z8000

The Z8000 microprocessor is Zilog, Inc.'s entry into the 16-bit processor market. The processor is available in two versions: segmented and nonsegmented. Figure 2-32 shows a pin diagram of the nonsegmented Z8002 processor. Figure 2-33

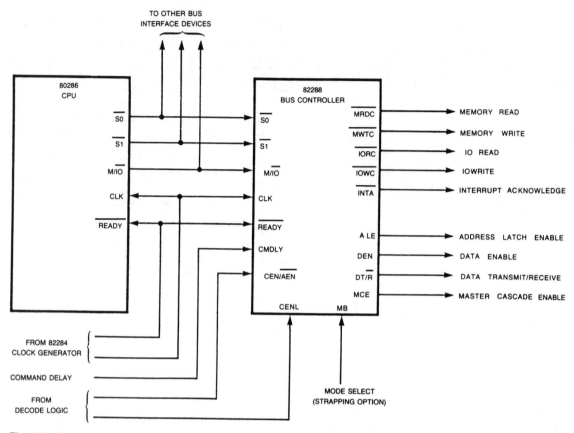

Fig. 2-28. Connections between the Intel 82288 bus controller and 80286 microprocessor. Reprinted by permission of the Intel Corporation, Copyright 1983.

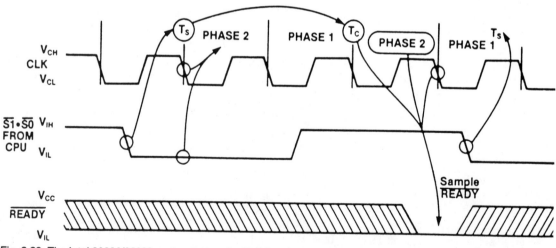

Fig. 2-29. The Intel 80286/82288 system bus cycle. Reprinted by permission of the Intel Corporation, Copyright 1983.

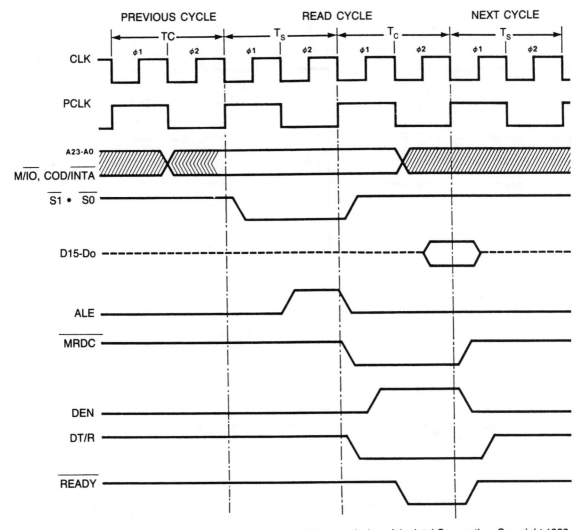

Fig. 2-30. An Intel 80286 microprocessor read cycle. Reprinted by permission of the Intel Corporation, Copyright 1983.

shows the pin diagram of the Z8001 segmented processor. The differences between the two processors are the segment address lines, SNO through SN6 and the Segment-Trap input line, $\overline{SEGT}$. Thus the Z8002 microprocessor is supplied in a 40-pin package while the Z8001 microprocessor is supplied in a 48-pin package.

Figure 2-34 is a functional pin diagram of the Z8000 processor, with the pins grouped according to function. Z8001 segment pins are shown in a dashed box. Note the multiplexed address/data bus

on pins AD_0 through AD_{15}. Also note the grouping of the various bus-control pins into Timing, Status, CPU Control, Bus Control, Interrupt, Multi-Micro Control, and Segment pins.

The address/data pins AD_0 through AD_{15} carry address and data information, at different times in the bus cycle. This is a 16-bit processor so there are sixteen data lines. Their are also 16 address lines. In a nonsegmented Z8002 processor, which has no segment lines, sixteen address lines are all the pins available for address specification. The max-

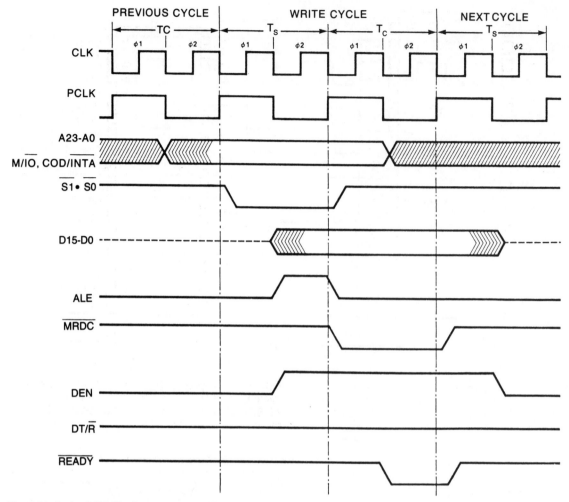

Fig. 2-31. An Intel 80286 microprocessor write cycle. Reprinted by permission of the Intel Corporation, Copyright 1983.

imum address space for this version of the Z8000 processor is therefore 64K bytes.

The segmented Z8001 processor has seven extra segment lines SN_0 through SN_6, which are used as extended-address lines. This makes a total of 23 address lines for a maximum address space of 9,437,184 bytes (loosely called 8M bytes). SEGT, the segment-trap input, is used to alert the processor of a memory-access violation. SEGT is intended to be driven by the Z8010 Memory Management Unit (MMU).

Bus timing is controlled by the $\overline{AS}$, $\overline{DS}$ and $\overline{MREQ}$ processor outputs. Indications of a valid address on the address/data bus is given by the $\overline{AS}$, or Address-Strobe, signal. The rising edge of $\overline{AS}$ indicates a valid address. The Data Strobe, $\overline{DS}$, is used to gate the data onto the multiplexed address/data bus. MREQ is used to indicate whether the address present on the address/data bus is for a memory or nonmemory access.

There are seven status outputs in the status group. Four indicate the type of bus access taking

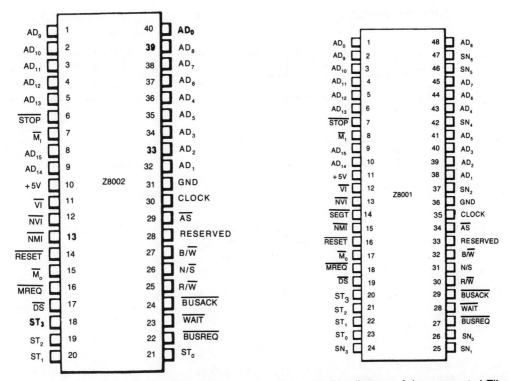

Fig. 2-32. Pin diagram of the non-segmented Zilog Z8000 microprocessor (Z8002). Reproduced by permission (C) 1979, 1980, 1981 by Zilog, Inc. This material shall not be reproduced without written consent of Zilog, Inc.

Fig. 2-33. Pin diagram of the segmented Zilog Z8000 microprocessor (Z8001). Reproduced by permission (C) 1979, 1980, 1981 by Zilog, Inc. This material shall not be reproduced without written consent of Zilog, Inc.

Table 2-2. Status-signal outputs for the Zilog Z800 microprocessor.

ST3	ST2	ST1	ST0	Cycle Definition
0	0	0	0	Internal operation
0	0	0	1	Memory refresh
0	0	1	0	I/O reference
0	0	1	1	Special I/O reference (i.e. MMU)
0	1	0	0	Segment-trap acknowledge
0	1	0	1	Non-Maskable interrupt acknowledge
0	1	1	0	Non-Vectored interrupt acknowledge
0	1	1	1	Vectored interrupt acknowledge
1	0	0	0	Data-memory request
1	0	0	1	Stack-memory request
1	0	1	0	Data-memory request (EPU)
1	0	1	1	Stack-memory request (EPU)
1	1	0	0	Program reference, nth word
1	1	0	1	Instruction fetch, first word
1	1	1	0	Extension-processor transfer
1	1	1	1	Reserved

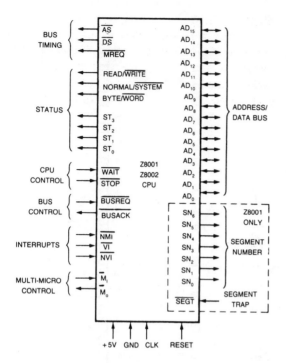

BUS TIMING
- $\overline{\text{AS}}$
- $\overline{\text{DS}}$
- $\overline{\text{MREQ}}$

STATUS
- READ/$\overline{\text{WRITE}}$
- NORMAL/$\overline{\text{SYSTEM}}$
- BYTE/$\overline{\text{WORD}}$
- ST_3
- ST_2
- ST_1
- ST_0

CPU CONTROL
- $\overline{\text{WAIT}}$
- $\overline{\text{STOP}}$

BUS CONTROL
- $\overline{\text{BUSREQ}}$
- $\overline{\text{BUSACK}}$

INTERRUPTS
- $\overline{\text{NMI}}$
- $\overline{\text{VI}}$
- $\overline{\text{NVI}}$

MULTI-MICRO CONTROL
- $\overline{M_I}$
- $\overline{M_O}$

Z8001 Z8002 CPU

ADDRESS/DATA BUS
- AD_{15}
- AD_{14}
- AD_{13}
- AD_{12}
- AD_{11}
- AD_{10}
- AD_9
- AD_8
- AD_7
- AD_6
- AD_5
- AD_4
- AD_3
- AD_2
- AD_1
- AD_0

Z8001 ONLY SEGMENT NUMBER
- SN_6
- SN_5
- SN_4
- SN_3
- SN_2
- SN_1
- SN_0

SEGMENT TRAP
- $\overline{\text{SEGT}}$

+5V   GND   CLK   RESET

Fig. 2-34. Functional diagram of the Zilog Z8000 microprocessor. Reproduced by permission (C) 1979, 1980, 1981 by Zilog, Inc. This material shall not be reproduced without written consent of Zilog, Inc.

place during a bus cycle. These are the ST_0 through ST_3 pins. The encoded status is given in **Table 2-2**.

There are some interesting items of note in the table of processor status codes. Code 1 (0001) shows a memory-refresh operation. Recall that the Zilog Z80 processor has a line called $\overline{\text{RFSH}}$ which served to aid in dynamic-memory-refresh operations. This function is preserved in the Z8000 processor in a status code. Likewise, status code D (1101) indicates when the first word of an instruction is fetched. This corresponds to the $\overline{\text{M1}}$ pin of the Z80 processor.

Extension Processing Units (EPUs) are extra processors which add processing power to the Z8000 processor. These are activated by status codes A (1010), B(1011), and E (1110).

The three other status pins are Read/$\overline{\text{Write}}$, NORMAL/$\overline{\text{SYSTEM}}$, and BYTE/$\overline{\text{WORD}}$. READ/$\overline{\text{WRITE}}$ indicates the direction of data flow on the address/data bus during a bus cycle. NORMAL/SYS-

TEM indicates the operational state of the processor. SYSTEM mode has special privileged instructions which can have a major effect on system operation. This mode is reserved for supervisory or operating-system software. BYTE/$\overline{\text{WORD}}$ indicates whether the current bus cycle requires a full 16-bit word or an 8-bit byte. Byte operations occur only on the lower eight bits of the address/data bus.

Two CPU-control pins, $\overline{\text{WAIT}}$ and $\overline{\text{STOP}}$ can be used to control the speed of operation of the Z8000 processor. $\overline{\text{WAIT}}$ is a signal from a slow device that can stretch the processor bus cycle. $\overline{\text{STOP}}$ can be used to halt the processor entirely and is useful for single-step operation during debugging.

Bus-control pins $\overline{\text{BUSREQ}}$ and $\overline{\text{BUSACK}}$ allow multiple bus controllers in a Z8000 system. A master wishing control of the bus will assert the $\overline{\text{BUSREQ}}$ input to the Z8000 processor. The processor can then relinquish control of the bus and acknowledge the bus request by asserting $\overline{\text{BUSACK}}$. DMA controllers and other processors are examples of devices which may wish to assume control of the system bus.

There are three interrupt inputs to the Z8000 processor; $\overline{\text{NMI}}$, $\overline{\text{NVI}}$ and $\overline{\text{VI}}$. $\overline{\text{NMI}}$ is used to request a Non-Maskable Interrupt. The nonmaskable interrupt has the highest priority of the three interrupts and cannot be disabled (masked) by the processor. A Non-Vectored Interrupt is requested by asserting the $\overline{\text{NVI}}$ input, and a Vectored Interrupt is requested by asserting the $\overline{\text{VI}}$ input.

The processor will do an interrupt poll, reading a word from the interrupting device for all three interrupts. In the case of a nonmaskable or nonvectored interrupt, all sixteen bits read during the poll represent the status of the interrupting device. There can only be one nonmaskable and one nonvectored interrupt routine. For vectored interrupts, the low byte of the polled interrupt word is a jump vector, while the high byte is device status. There can be 256 vectored interrupt routines.

There are two pins on the Z8000 processor for multiple microprocessor systems. These are the $\overline{\text{MI}}$ and $\overline{\text{MO}}$ pins. $\overline{\text{MI}}$ is the Multi-micro In pin, and $\overline{\text{MO}}$ is the Multi-micro Out pin. The two pins form a resource-request daisy-chain with all system processors in the chain.

Finally, there are two utility pins on the Z8000 processor, $\overline{\text{RESET}}$ and CLK. $\overline{\text{RESET}}$ is the processor reset pin. It forces the execution of the processor to stop wherever it is and start up again at the beginning of memory. CLK is the clock input that makes all the internal circuitry in the processor run.

Bus Timing

There are many different bus cycles in the operation of the Z8000 processor. The two that interest us in this book are the Memory-Read/Write cycle and the I/O cycle. A diagram of the Read/Write cycle appears in **Fig. 2-35** and an I/O cycle appears in **Fig. 2-36**.

The clock at the top of **Fig. 2-35** is the mas-

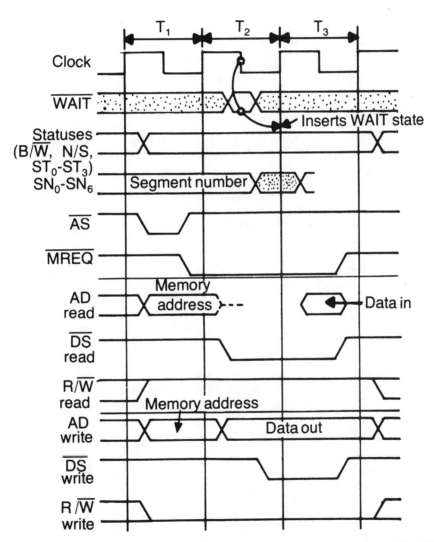

Fig. 2-35. The Zilog Z8000 microprocessor memory-cycle timing. Reproduced by permission (C) 1979, 1980, 1981 by Zilog, Inc. This material shall not be reproduced without written consent of Zilog, Inc.

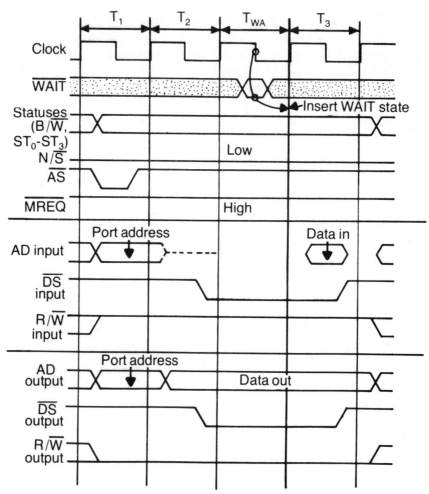

Fig. 2-36. The Zilog Z8000 microprocessor I/O-cycle timing. Reproduced by permission (C) 1979, 1980, 1981 by Zilog, Inc. This material shall not be reproduced without written consent of Zilog, Inc.

ter timing signal for the Z8000 processor and is connected to the CLK input of the device. There are three clock cycles, or T-states, in each cycle. During T_1, status lines B/$\overline{W}$, N/$\overline{S}$, and ST_0 through ST_3 segment lines (segmented version only) and addresses on the address/data lines are asserted. Since the Z8000A processor can have up to a 6-MHz clock, a read/write bus cycle can happen in as little as 500 ns. This makes the Z8000A a very fast processor.

R/$\overline{W}$ is set to the proper level to indicate whether a read or write is taking place. $\overline{AS}$ is generated during T_1 to indicate that the address/data lines

hold an address. This address should be latched on the rising edge of $\overline{AS}$ to clear the address/data lines for the data which is to follow. $\overline{MREQ}$ is asserted late in T_1 to indicate that the current bus cycle is to or from memory.

During T_2, address information is removed from the address/data lines and then DS is asserted to gate data onto the data bus. Note that DS occurs earlier in T_2 for a read than for a write. For a write operation, the processor will place data on the address/data lines early in T_2, before asserting DS. If the addressed device requires a stretched bus cycle, it must assert $\overline{\text{WAIT}}$ by the middle of T_2. Otherwise, no wait T-states will be generated.

In T_3, data is read from the address/data bus if a read is occurring. Then $\overline{\text{DS}}$ is negated, for either a read or a write. Note that the data lines are not disabled in a write operation until after the T_3 cycle has ended.

Once you understand the Read/Write cycle of the Z8000 processor, I/O cycles (shown in **Fig. 2-36**) are easy. There are only two differences. The first is that the segment lines are not valid. Both versions of the processor use only the 16 address lines for I/O addressing. This makes 65,536 (64K) I/O addresses available, more than sufficient for almost any system.

The second difference is that the processor always introduces an extra wait T-state, called T_{WA}. This is because almost all peripheral chips, which would probably be connected as I/O devices, are slower than the Z8000 processor. Automatic wait-state insertion accommodates more peripheral chips, without requiring the system designer to add wait-state circuitry to the system.

MOTOROLA 68000

Motorola was not to be outdone by the other semiconductor manufacturers. The processor designers at Motorola decided that a very bold, advanced-technology processor was required to capture the 16-bit market. Their design, the 68000 microprocessor, is one of the most complex processor designs ever attempted on a single integrated circuit.

The Motorola 68000 processor is actually a 32-bit machine with a 16-bit data bus and a 24-bit address bus. Twenty-four bits of address give the processor a colossal 16,777,215 location address space. Internally, the registers and arithmetic unit are thirty-two bits wide. One of the major reasons the 68000 has a 16-bit data bus at all is a pin limitation on circa 1980 integrated-circuit packaging technology.

Figure 2-37 is a pin diagram of the 68000 processor. You will probably see immediately that there are a lot of pins on this part, sixty-four to be precise. This is the largest number of pins of any

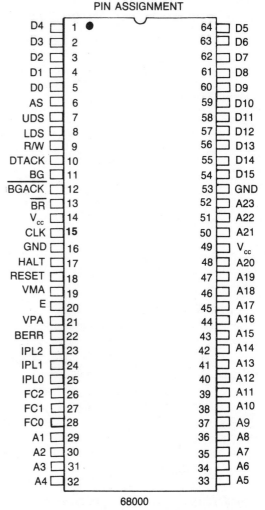

Fig. 2-37. Pin diagram of the Motorola MC68000 microprocessor. Reprinted with permission of Motorola, Inc.

processor we have looked at in this book. **Figure 2-38** is a functional pin diagram of the 68000 processor, with the pins grouped according to function.

68000 Pins

First, look at the address and data pins. There are separate address and data busses. The data bus has sixteen pins labeled D_0 through D_{15}, while the address bus has twenty-three pins labeled A_1 through A_{23}. You may ask, ''You said a 24-bit ad-

71

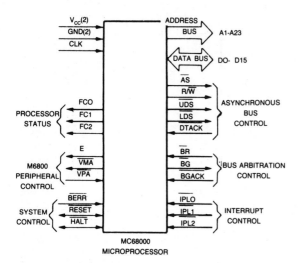

Fig. 2-38. Functional diagram of the Motorola MC68000 microprocessor. Reprinted with permission of Motorola, Inc.

dress bus. What happened to A_0?'' That's an excellent question, which will be answered immediately.

Look at the Bus-Control lines. The two pins LDS and UDS are the Upper and Lower Data Strobes. These pins combined are the missing address bit. The 68000 design allows for full word, upper-byte-only or lower-byte-only bus transfers. This can be quite useful when performing byte I/O, but can cause the system memory to be slightly more complex and costly.

The AS pin is the address strobe. Even though the 68000 doesn't have a multiplexed address/data bus, some indication is still needed as to when the address on the address bus is valid. The read/write, or R/W, line indicates the direction of information flow over the data lines during a bus transaction.

The 68000 processor also has a bus handshaking line called DTACK, for Data Transfer AC-Knowledge. This can be used as a handshake line for each bus transaction. If DTACK is negated, the processor will introduce wait cycles until the signal is asserted. If desired, DTACK can be grounded to allow the processor to run at maximum rates. This requires that all system resources be able to respond to minimum-length bus cycles, something not always possible.

There are three special pins for interfacing to Motorola 6800 peripherals. Recall that 6800 peripheral chips are synchronized to an E clock which is usually between 1 and 2 MHz. Since the 68000 processor can be run at up to 16 MHz, the 68000 clock cannot be used as the peripheral E clock. Note that one of the M6800 Peripheral Interface pins on the 68000 is labeled E. The frequency of the 68000 E pin is one tenth the clock rate of the processor, with a 60/40 low-to-high symmetry. Thus, E is no higher than 1.6 MHz.

When the 68000 processor accesses a 6800 peripheral chip in a system, special circuitry is supposed to assert the VPA input. This tells the 68000 that it has selected a 6800 device and initiates the 6800-device bus cycle built into the 68000. The 68000 responds to assertion of VPA by synchronizing the bus cycle to E and asserting VMA (Valid Memory Address) at the proper point in the E cycle.

There are three interrupt inputs into the 68000 processor. When all three inputs are high, no interrupt is requested. When one or more of the inputs is pulled low, an interrupt request has been made. Up to seven interrupts can be issued in this manner. The priority of the interrupt is determined by the value of the interrupt-input code. All inputs low is interrupt-level 7, the highest level interrupt, which also happens to be non-maskable. Other interrupt levels from 6 to 1 have descending priority. Once in an interrupt-service routine for a certain level, only an interrupt at a higher level will be serviced.

Interrupts are acknowledged by a special interrupt-acknowledge bus cycle. The Function Code lines FC0, FC1, and FC2 indicate the type of bus cycle taking place. The function codes are:

FC2	FC1	FC0	Bus Cycle Type
0	0	0	Undefined, reserved
0	0	1	User data access
0	1	0	User program access
0	1	1	Undefined, reserved
1	0	0	Undefined, reserved
1	0	1	Supervisor data access
1	1	0	Supervisor program access
1	1	1	Interrupt acknowledge

Supervisor and User modes need explaining. There are certain privileged instructions in the 68000 instruction set that can only be executed in supervisor mode. These instructions are useful for operating system programs. It would be potentially dangerous to allow any program to use these instructions, particularly in a multiuser system.

There are three pins on the 68000 processor for managing bus mastership. These are $\overline{BR}$, $\overline{BG}$ and $\overline{BGACK}$. A device may request control of the bus asserting Bus Request ($\overline{BR}$). The 68000 will indicate that it will relinquish the bus at the end of the current bus cycle by asserting Bus Grant ($\overline{BG}$). Assertion of $\overline{BG}$ does not mean that control of the bus may be immediately taken by the requesting device. The bus is not available until $\overline{AS}$, $\overline{DTACK}$, $\overline{BGACK}$ are negated.

A negated $\overline{AS}$ signifies that the 68000 is no longer driving the bus. A negated $\overline{DTACK}$ signifies that no other devices are responding to a 68000 bus cycle. A negated $\overline{BGACK}$ signifies that no other potential bus master controls the bus. $\overline{BGACK}$ is the Bus Grant ACKnowledge, and is asserted by a bus master when it assumes control of the bus.

Three lines remain. $\overline{RESET}$ may appear to be a typical microprocessor reset signal but it isn't. Look carefully and you will notice that it is bidirectional. The pin is not only used to reset the microprocessor but a special reset instruction in the 68000 instruction set will also assert this pin. This feature is useful for programmably resetting the entire system without causing the processor to lose its place in the running program.

$\overline{BERR}$ is a Bus ERRor input. Assertion of $\overline{BERR}$ and $\overline{HALT}$ together can cause the processor to rerun the bus cycle, assuming the problem which caused $\overline{BERR}$ to be asserted can be remedied the second time around. If only $\overline{BERR}$ is asserted, an exception (interrupt) will be generated that will cause the 68000 to branch to a special exception-processing routine.

The Bus ERRor input can be used for several things. First, a special timeout circuit in the system can detect the start of a bus cycle and assert $\overline{BERR}$ if a given amount of time elapses without $\overline{DTACK}$ being asserted. In a system where the bus cycle is

completed by a handshake, it is a good idea to make provision for the time the handshake fails to complete. A bus timeout is one such provision.

A second use for the $\overline{BERR}$ signal is for a memory error. One memory technique involves parity, which adds an extra memory bit to each memory byte or word. The extra bit is used to keep the number of ones stored in that word either even (even parity) or odd (odd parity). The parity bit is generated and stored during a write operation.

If the parity is wrong during a read operation, at least one of the bits stored in that memory location has changed since the location was written to. $\overline{BERR}$ can be asserted by the parity checking circuitry if a parity error is detected. This could cause the processor to branch to an error recovery routine, which is preferable to letting the processor merrily process bad data.

The $\overline{HALT}$ pin has already been mentioned used in conjunction with the $\overline{BERR}$ pin. It can also be used to force the processor to halt at the end of the current bus cycle. Like $\overline{RESET}$ $\overline{HALT}$ is bidirectional. If a double bus fault (BERR and HALT asserted during two bus cycles) occurs, the processor will assert HALT and stop processing instructions. Assertion of RESET is then required to restart the system.

One pin you may find missing in the 68000 set is a memory-I/O indicator. This is because there isn't one. The 68000 has no I/O instructions and no I/O address space. Some portion of the 16M byte address space must be allocated to I/O devices. Usually, the top 32K bytes of address space are so allocated in 68000 systems because there are special short-address processor instructions for manipulating that area of the memory. Even if one million locations are allocated, there are plenty of addresses left for system memory.

Bus Timing

Figure 2-39 shows the timing of three bus cycles on a typical 68000 bus. The processor clock (CLK) is shown at the top of the figure. As with all the other processors we have examined, CLK is the master timing signal for all bus operations.

A 68000 bus cycle consists of at least 8 S-

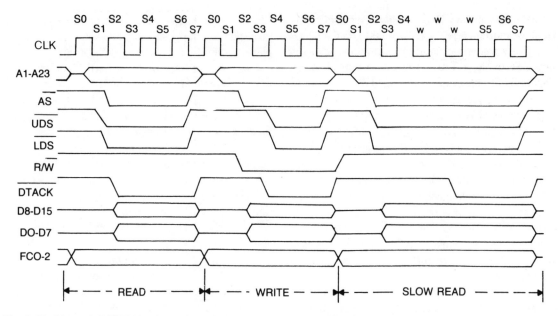

Fig. 2-39. Motorola MC6800 microprocessor bus-timing diagram. Reprinted with permission of Motorola, Inc.

states for a read and 9 S-states for a write. Each S-state is one half of one CLK cycle, a departure from other processors we have studied. The states are labeled S0 through S9. Delayed response on the $\overline{\text{DTACK}}$ bus handshake line can cause additional wait S-states to be inserted after the S4 state, as shown by the third bus cycle in the figure.

S0 is the bus-cycle recovery state. All bus control, address, and data lines are disabled to allow the bus to recover from the previous cycle. In the S1 state, the address for the new cycle is placed on the address lines, and the function-code lines FC0 through FC2 are driven to indicate the type of bus cycle about to take place.

Events which take place during S2 vary depending on whether a read or write is occuring. $\overline{\text{AS}}$ is asserted during S2 regardless of whether a read or write operation is taking place. For a read, $\overline{\text{UDS}}$ and/or $\overline{\text{LDS}}$ will be asserted during S2, determined by which byte(s), upper, lower, or both, are being transferred. During a write operation, neither $\overline{\text{UDS}}$ or $\overline{\text{LDS}}$ will be asserted during S2, but the R/$\overline{\text{W}}$ signal will be driven low to indicate that a write is about to occur.

For a read operation, no signal changes are made during S3 and S4. This is not true for a write, however. If a write is taking place, the processor will drive the data lines during S3 and will assert $\overline{\text{UDS}}$ and $\overline{\text{LDS}}$, as appropriate, during S4.

After the data strobes are asserted, the addressed device has less than one S-state to assert $\overline{\text{DTACK}}$ if wait states are to be avoided. In order to avoid wait states, $\overline{\text{DTACK}}$ must be asserted by S5 for a read and S7 for a write. This is less than 100 ns for a 68000 processor running at 12 MHz. Because of this critical timing, it is very difficult to build a maximum speed 68000 system and use true bus handshaking. Note that the data does not actually have to transfer in this brief period of time, only the handshake has to take place.

At the end of S6 for a read, data on the data bus is read into the processor. Then, during S7, the asserted control lines $\overline{\text{AS}}$, and the data strobes are negated. The address lines and R/$\overline{\text{W}}$ are maintained at their existing levels until the end of S7 so that the situation of $\overline{\text{AS}}$ asserted and address invalid on the bus does not occur. When the data strobes or $\overline{\text{AS}}$ are negated, the device being read must release

74

the data lines and DTACK by S1 of the next cycle to allow another bus cycle to take place.

For a write operation, no signals are changed during S5 or S6. $\overline{\text{DTACK}}$ must be asserted by the start of S7 to avoid wait states. If that happens, $\overline{\text{AS}}$ and the data strobes will be negated during S9, and R/W will be driven high. The address and data busses will be maintained at their previous levels to ensure a proper transfer. The device being written to must release $\overline{\text{DTACK}}$ when $\overline{\text{AS}}$ or the data strobes are negated. This clears the bus for the next cycle. The processor releases the address and data busses at the end of S9.

MOTOROLA 68010

Shortly after introducing its 68000 microprocessor, Motorola debuted an improved version, called the 68010. The key differences between these two parts are internal, as you can see from the 68010 pin diagram in Fig. 2-40. The 68010's pin diagram exactly matches that of the 68000. In fact, the 68010's bus cycles strongly resembles the 68000's bus cycles. The only difference is the operation of the BERR pin.

For the 68000, if $\overline{\text{BERR}}$ is asserted during a bus cycle, the processor aborts the cycle, places some information on the stack, and jumps to an exception-processing program. If the exception processing program decides to attempt the same bus cycle again, the processor restarts the cycle from the beginning.

The 68010 places an additional 22 words of information on the stack during $\overline{\text{BERR}}$ exception processing so that the processor can restart an instruction from the exception point, not from the beginning. This feature is used in virtual memory systems. But the 68010's bus cycles all look like those in the previous discussion of the 68000's operation.

MOTOROLA 68008

Not all 16-bit systems require the performance afforded by a 16-bit data bus. Some cost-sensitive

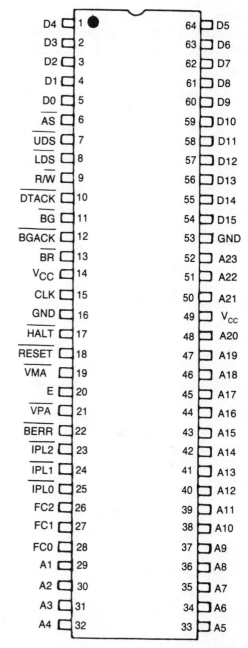

Fig. 2-40. Pin diagram of the Motorola MC68010 microprocessor. Reprinted with permission of Motorola, Inc.

systems merely need 16-bit processing power for computations and can tolerate the somewhat lower performance of an 8-bit data bus. Intel recognized this situation when it decided to produce the 8088, a version of the company's 16-bit 8086 microprocessor with an 8-bit data bus. Motorola also decided to serve this lower-cost market by creating the 68008, a version of the 68000 with an 8-bit data bus.

Figure 2-41 is a functional diagram of the 68008 and shows the microprocessor's strong family resemblance to the 68000. However, there are several differences. Note that the 68008's address bus now includes an A0 pin but lacks A20 through A23 and that the microprocessor has only a single data strobe pin, called $\overline{DS}$. Because the 68008 has an 8-bit wide bus, Motorola had to modify the way in which the A0 address bit was interpreted by the processor. The 68008 bus cycles differ slightly from those of the 68000 and 68010 because the 68008 microprocessor has only a single data strobe. **Figure 2-42 and 2-43** illustrate 68008 read and write cycles respectively. Note that the processor must run two bus cycles for 16-bit (word) data transfers.

Motorola made several other simplifications to the 68008 in addition to reducing its data bus to 8 bits. The processor has only two interrupt inputs:

$\overline{IPL0/2}$ and $\overline{IPL1}$. The 68000 and 68010 support seven interrupt levels with three interrupt inputs. Because Motorola tied $\overline{IPL0}$ and $\overline{IPL2}$ together inside the 68008, the processor supports only three interrupt levels corresponding to the 68000's interrupt levels 2, 5, and 7.

Motorola also eliminated the 68000 VMA signal from the 68008. Recall that the $\overline{VMA}$ output allowed the 68000 to control older peripheral ICs designed for the company's 6800 microprocessor by recreating that older processor's bus. If you wish to design a system that combines the 68000 with 6800-style peripheral chips, you must add external circuitry that generates $\overline{VMA}$ from the 68008's E output and $\overline{VPA}$ input signals.

Looking at the group of bus arbitration control pins, you'll also see that $\overline{BGACK}$ is missing. Motorola again simplified the internal structure of the 68008 by reducing the number of pins that control bus mastership to two. For systems that combine 68000s and 68008s, you must add circuitry to the 68008 to ensure that the 68008 does not request the bus unless $\overline{BGACK}$ on the 68000 side of the system is not asserted.

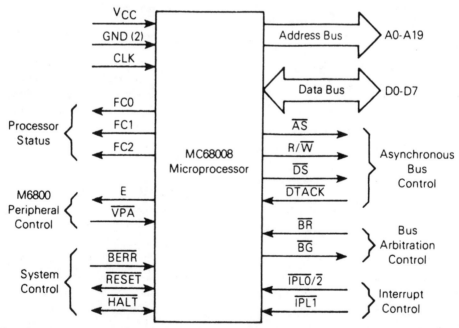

Fig. 2-41. Functional diagram of the Motorola 68008 microprocessor. Reprinted with permission of Motorola, Inc.

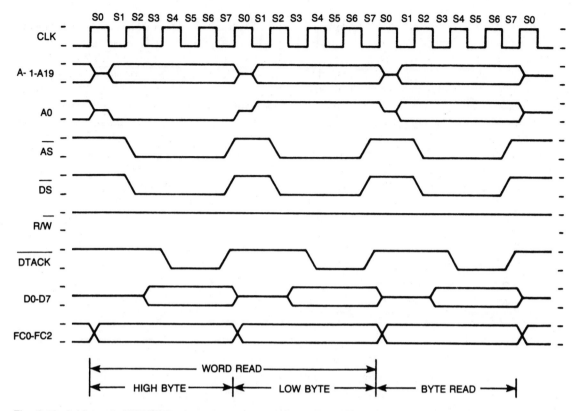

Fig. 2-42. A Motorola MC68008 microprocessor read cycle. Reprinted with permission of Motorola, Inc.

You might well ask why Motorola made all of these functional reductions to produce the 68008. You will find the answer to that question in Fig. 2-44 which shows the pin diagram of the 68008. Because of the reduced number of signal lines, the processor now fits in a 48-pin package which costs less than the 64-pin DIP, often referred to as a "battleship". The 68008 was designed for lower cost systems (remember, that's why it has an 8-bit data bus) and the smaller package costs less and requires less space on a circuit board. Both of these attributes contribute to a lower system cost.

32-BIT MICROPROCESSORS

Progress in electronics grinds on relentlessly and the 16-bit processors no longer hold the top-performance positions. In their efforts to provide parts that are "bigger, better, and faster," semi-conductor vendors now offer 32-bit microprocessors. Many of these processors bear strong family resemblances to their 16-bit forebears and that fact extends to the bus characteristics of these processors as well. However, just as 16-bit processors are more complicated than 8-bit machines, 32-bit microprocessors have attained even higher levels of complexity than the 16-bitters.

MOTOROLA 68020

The 68000 microprocessor family has always been composed of 32-bit machines. The registers of all family members are 32 bits wide and the processors perform 32-bit arithmetic and logical operations. Motorola's foresight in making its 16-bit microprocessors 32-bit machines internally allowed the company to quickly add a full-blown 32-bit processor to its 68000 family, the 68020.

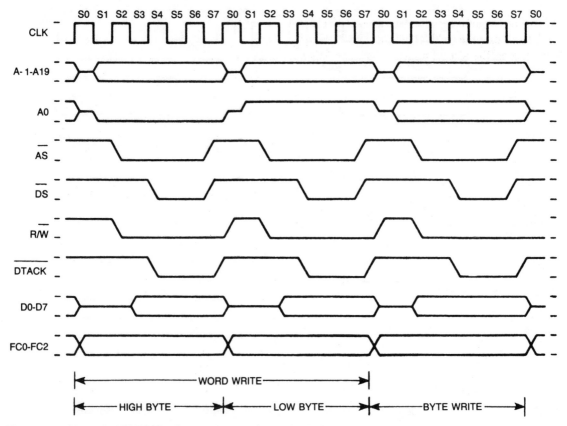

S0 S1 S2 S3 S4 S5 S6 S7 S0 S1 S2 S3 S4 S5 S6 S7 S0 S1 S2 S3 S4 S5 S6 S7 S0

CLK

A-1-A19

A0

AS

DS

R/W

DTACK

D0-D7

FC0-FC2

WORD WRITE

HIGH BYTE | LOW BYTE | BYTE WRITE

Fig. 2-43. A Motorola MC68008 microprocessor write cycle. Reprinted with permission of Motorola, Inc.

With 32 address bits and 32 data bits, the 68020 cannot possibly fit in a 68-pin package. Instead, Motorola put the 68020 in a 114-lead pin-grid-array (PGA) package shown in **Fig. 2-45.** Because the PGA package arranges pins in a 2-dimensional array, Motorola doesn't use pin numbers any more, it uses matrix designators composed of a letter and a number. Most 32-bit processors end up in such packages because conventional DIPs can't support the 32-bit processors' monumental lead requirements.

Figure 2-46 is a functional diagram of the 68020. Before we look at the 68020 signals that differ from those of earlier 68000 family members, let's look at some comforting similarities. The address, data, and function-code busses look pretty familiar, except the data bus has grown from 16 to 32 bits and the address bus has grown from 24 to 32 bits.

Note that the 68020's address bus contains bit A0, just like the 68008, but unlike the 68000 and 68010. More on that in just a moment. The bus-arbitration signals $\overline{BR}$, $\overline{BG}$, and $\overline{BGACK}$ look and work the same as the 68000 signals, as do the interrupt lines $\overline{IPL0}$, $\overline{IPL1}$, and $\overline{IPL2}$. $\overline{AS}$ (address strobe), R/$\overline{W}$ (Read/Write), $\overline{RESET}$, $\overline{HALT}$, and $\overline{BERR}$ should also look familiar. The 68020's $\overline{BERR}$ input works like the 68010's $\overline{BERR}$ line. That about wraps it up for signals that share the 68000's definitions. The rest of the signals, principally the pins that control the 68020's bus operations, constitute a whole new ball game.

Like the 68008, Motorola's 68020 microprocessor has only one data strobe, but the processor performs 8-, 16-, 24-, and 32-bit data transfers. Obviously, one data strobe isn't sufficient to differentiate among these different-sized transfers so Motorola added two transfer-size outputs called SIZ0 and SIZ1 to indicate the width of the transfer. These size pins encode the size of a bus transfer as follows:

SIZ1	SIZ0	Transfer Size
0	1	byte
1	0	word (16 bits)
1	1	3 bytes (24 bits)
0	0	long word (32 bits)

You might well ask why the 68020 would ever perform a 24-bit data transfer. The reason is simple. If a 32-bit quantity is not aligned on a 32-bit, long-word boundary, then the 68020 will have to transfer the quantity in two chunks. Depending on the alignment of that entity in memory, the chunks may both be 16 bits or there may be a 24-bit chunk and an 8-bit chunk. Generally speaking, moving 32-bit operands around in a 32-bit system without making sure that the 32-bit words are aligned on 32-bit boundaries is pretty inefficient and should be avoided. However, Motorola's design accommodates even such sloppy programming habits.

Microprocessors with 32-bit data busses must talk to 8-bit, 16-bit, and 32-bit devices. Motorola's 68020 makes such details invisible to the programmer by allowing hardware to tell the microprocessor how large the data path to a device is during each data transfer, Motorola calls this feature dynamic bus sizing.

The 68020 performs this dynamic bus sizing by replacing the old 68000 DTACK input with two new inputs: DSACK0 and DSACK1. The DSACK pins acknowledge the bus transfer and also indicate how much of the transfer has been accomplished as follows:

DSACK1	DSACK0	Result
HIGH	HIGH	NO ACKNOWLEDGE, INSERT WAIT STATES
HIGH	LOW	8-BIT TRANSFER ACKNOWLEDGE
LOW	HIGH	16-BIT TRANSFER ACKNOWLEDGE
LOW	LOW	32-BIT TRANSFER ACKNOWLEDGE

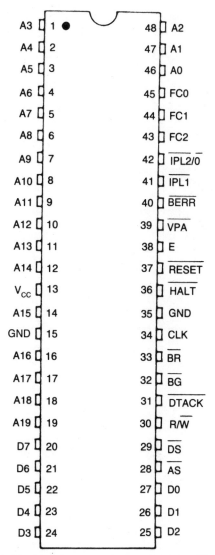

Fig. 2-44. Pin diagram of the Motorola MC68008 microprocessor. Reprinted with permission of Motorola, Inc.

Before we look at a typical 68020 bus cycle, let's look at the remaining 68020 pins. ECS, the external cycle start output, indicates that the 68020 is starting a bus cycle. It appears even before address strobe. OCS, the operand cycle start signal, also indicates the start of a bus cycle, but the 68020 only asserts OCS during the first bus cycle of an operand transfer.

DIM	INCHES		INCHES	
	MIN	MAX	MIN	MAX
A	34.18	34.90	1.345	1.375
B	34.18	34.90	1.345	1.375
C	2.67	3.17	.100	.150
DO	.46	.51	.017	.019
G	2.54 BSC		.100 BSC	
K	4.32	4.82	170	.190
V	1.74	2.28	.065	.095

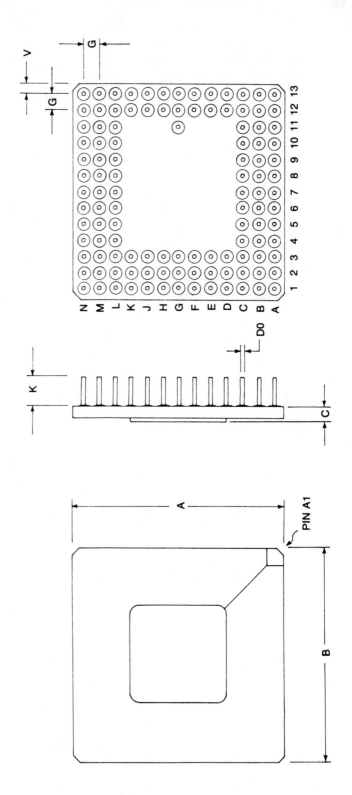

68020 PINS AND SIGNALS GROUPED BY FUNCTION

PIN	SIGNAL	PIN	SIGNAL	PIN	SIGNAL
A3	A31	N1	D31	F2	FC2
B4	A30	L3	D30	F3	FC1
C5	A29	M2	D29	E1	FC0
A4	A28	N2	D28		
B5	A27	L4	D27	F1	SIZ0
A5	A26	M3	D26	G2	SIZ1
C6	A25	N3	D25		
B6	A24	M4	D24	G1	$\overline{ECS}$
A6	A23	L5	D23	E13	$\overline{OCS}$
A7	A22	N4	D22	E2	$\overline{RMC}$
C7	A21	M5	D21	L1	$\overline{AS}$
B7	A20	N5	D20	M1	$\overline{DS}$
A8	A19	L6	D19	L2	$R/\overline{W}$
B8	A18	M6	D18	G3	$\overline{DBEN}$
C8	A17	N6	D17	H3	$\overline{DSACK0}$
C9	A16	M7	D16	J1	$\overline{DSACK1}$
B10	A15	L8	D15	H1	$\overline{CDIS}$
A11	A14	N9	D14	H12	$\overline{IPL2}$
B11	A13	M9	D13	J13	$\overline{ILP1}$
C10	A12	N10	D12	J12	$\overline{IPL0}$
A12	A11	L9	D11	F13	$\overline{IPEND}$
B12	A10	M10	D10	H2	$\overline{AVEC}$
C11	A9	N11	D9	B3	$\overline{BR}$
A13	A8	N12	D8	B2	$\overline{BG}$
C12	A7	L10	D7	A1	$\overline{BGACK}$
B13	A6	M11	D6	C1	$\overline{RESET}$
C1	A5	M12	D5	K2	$\overline{HALT}$
D12	A4	M13	D4	J2	$\overline{BERR}$
D13	A3	L12	D3		
E12	A2	L13	D2	C2	CLK
A2	A1	K12	D1		
C4	A0	K13	D0		
A9	VCC	A10	GND	B1	NC
D1	VCC	B9	GND	C	NC
D2	VCC	G12	GND	D3	NC
E3	VCC	H2	GND	F12	NC
G11	VCC	J3	GND	K3	NC
G13	VCC	K1	GND	L11	NC
M8	VCC	L7	GND	N13	NC
N8	VCC	N7	GND		

NOTE: NC = NOT CONNECTED

Fig. 2-45. Pin diagram of the Motorola MC68020 microprocessor. Reprinted with permission of Motorola, Inc.

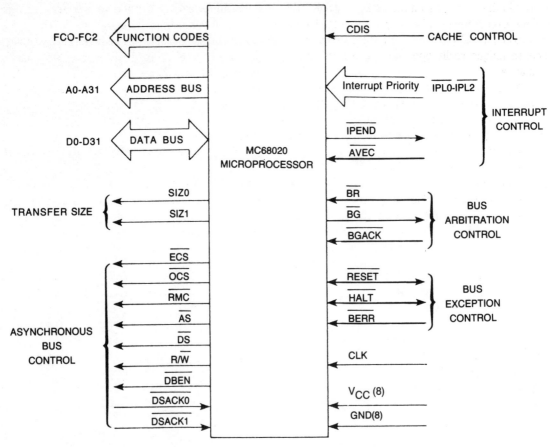

Fig. 2-46. Functional diagram of the Motorola MC68020 microprocessor. Reprinted with permission of Motorola, Inc.

The 68020 can perform a read-modify-write data transfer as an indivisible operation. However, in multiprocessor systems, another processor could acquire the bus and access the same location in between the read and the write by the first microprocessor. To prevent this problem the 68020 has a read-modify-write cycle (RMC) pin that can be used to prevent the loss of the bus by the processor while it completes the instruction. The 68020 also has a data bus enable (DBEN) pin that controls external data-bus buffers. You can use this pin to prevent bus contention during transitions of the R/W pin, but not all 68020 systems need to make use of this pin.

IPEND (Interrupt pending) acknowledges an interrupt. The 68020 asserts this pin when it

receives an interrupt at a level higher than the current interrupt level or when it receives a nonmaskable interrupt request. The AVEC (autovector) input allows external circuitry to request that the 68020 generate an interrupt vector internally. Recall that on the 68000, this function was performed by the VPA input. Because the 68020 does not support 6800 bus cycles, the E, VPA, and VMA signals have disappeared from this processor.

The last pin, CDIS, disable's the 68020's internal, 256-byte instruction memory cache. Instructions fetched by the 68020 are not just executed, they're also stored in this instruction cache. If the processor enters a small loop of instructions, after the first execution of the loop, the entire set of instructions comprising this software loop will be stored in the cache. From that point on, the 68020 will not execute external bus cycles to fetch loop instructions; it will get them from the on-chip cache. This technique really boosts the processor's performance.

With all of those 144 pins described, the 68020's bus cycles look pretty simple. Figures 2-47 and 2-48 show 68020 read and write cycles respectively. Each cycle requires a minimum of three clock cycles, barring wait states. For a read cycle, the 68020 sets the R/$\overline{\text{W}}$, FC0-3, A0-31, and SIZ0-1 output pins to appropriate values. It then asserts $\overline{\text{ECS}}$ and $\overline{\text{OCS}}$ (for the first cycle of an operand transfer) for one-half clock cycle. Then the processor asserts $\overline{\text{AS}}$, $\overline{\text{DS}}$, and $\overline{\text{DBEN}}$. That sequence completes the first portion of the cycle. The cycle completes when the 68020 receives acknowledgement of the bus transfer on its $\overline{\text{DSACK0}}$ and $\overline{\text{DSACK1}}$ inputs. All in all, a very simple transfer protocol when taken at the simplest level.

MOTOROLA 68030

Not content to have a single 32-bit microprocessor in its stable, Motorola now offers the 68030, an enhanced version of its 68020. The key difference between the two microprocessors is that the 68030 has a data cache in addition to the 68020's instruction cache, as shown in Fig. 2-49. The 68030 performs bus cycles in the same manner as the 68020.

INTEL 80386

Intel has not had the same ease in making a 32-bit microprocessor out of its existing 16-bit products. Both the 8086 and 80286 are really 16-bit machines with 16-bit registers. Thus the 32-bit 80386 includes the 8086 and 80286 instructions as subsets of its own, much larger, 32-bit instruction repertoire.

The block diagram of the 80386, shown in Fig. 2-50, illustrates the complexity of this microprocessor. It contains several independent units that operate in parallel to provide additional performance. In addition, this microprocessor contains a paging unit that provides memory management. Systems that run multiple tasks or serve several users simultaneously use this feature to provide each task or program its own working environment.

Like the 68020 and 68030, the 80386 has so many signal lines that it will not fit into a DIP. Intel places this microprocessor in a 132-lead PGA package, shown in Fig. 2-51. The 80386 has separate address and data lines that consume 32 leads. The 80386 has only 30 address lines. It does not output A0 and A1. Instead, the microprocessor decodes A0 and A1 into the four byte enable lines BE0# through BE3#. In order to address bytes individually, the 80386 uses the lower two address bits as byte specifiers. This arrangement allows the 80386 to address any combination of bytes within its 32-bit data word.

The 80386 devotes 41 pins to ground and power and 8 leads on the package are not connected, leaving 21 leads to perform the bus-control functions. Unlike its 80286 microprocessor, Intel's 80386 does not require a separate bus controller to generate bus control signals, making its bus cycles fairly easy to describe and to understand.

However, the 80386 does need a clock generator, which Intel calls the 82384. The 82384 generates both a reset signal and a clock signal, called CLK2, for the 80386, as shown in Fig. 2-52. CLK2 runs at double the rated microprocessor speed. For example, if a designer wants to run an 80386 at 16 MHz, CLK2 will be 32 MHz. The 80386 divides CLK2 by 2 to generate an internal clock and the 82384 also generates a CLK signal at the lower frequency for any peripheral devices you may connect to the 80386. Figure 2-53 illustrates the relationship between CLK2 and the 80386's internally-generated clock.

The rest of the 80386 signals are going to look pretty familiar. Figure 2-54 gives you a good picture of the signal groupings. Four signal lines define the type of bus cycle taking place. These are W/R#, D/C#, M/IO#, and LOCK#. Note that Intel uses the # symbol as a suffix to denote a low-true signal. W/R# differentiates between read and write cycles, D/C# differentiates between data and control cycles, M/IO# indicates whether a bus cycle is directed at memory or I/O space, and LOCK# allows the 80386 to retain control of the bus during

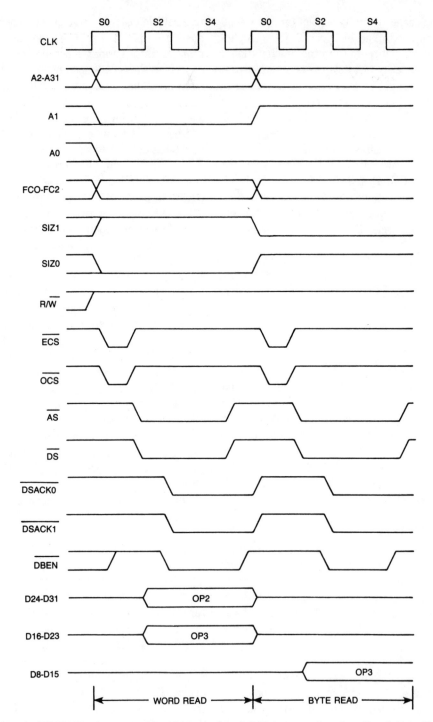

Fig. 2-47. Motorola MC68020 microprocessor 16-bit word and 8-bit byte read cycles. Reprinted with permission of Motorola, Inc.

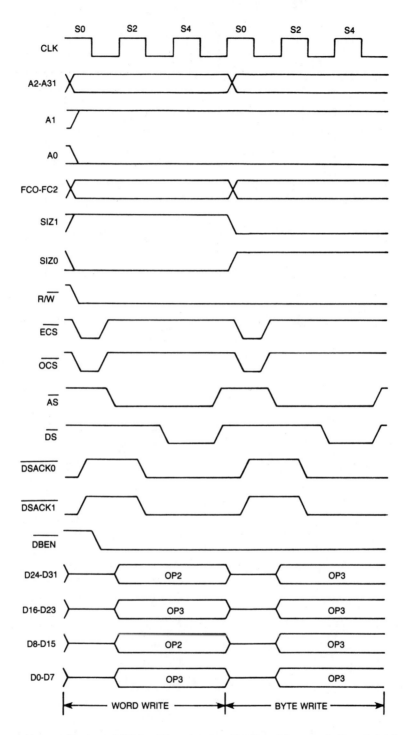

Fig. 2-50. Block diagram of the Intel 80386 microprocessor: Reprinted by permission of the Intel Corporation Copyright 1986.

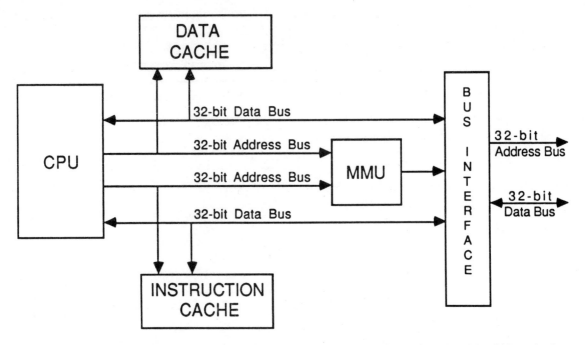

Fig. 2-49. Block diagram of the Motorola MC68030 microprocessor. Reprinted with permission of Motorola, Inc.

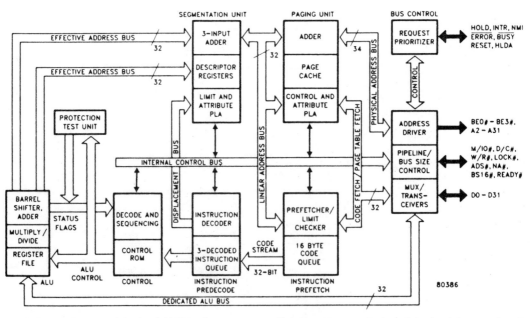

Fig. 2-50. Block diagram of the Intel 80386 microprocessor. Reprinted by permission of the Intel Corporation, Copyright 1986.

pipelined address cycles. (More on address pipelining in just a bit.) The states of the M/IO#, D/C#, and W/R# signals for the various 80386 bus cycles is as follows:

M/IO#	D/C#	W/R#	Bus Cycle Type
LOW	LOW	LOW	INTERRUPT ACKNOWLEDGE
LOW	LOW	HIGH	IDLE, NO CYCLE
LOW	HIGH	LOW	I/O DATA READ
LOW	HIGH	HIGH	I/O DATA WRITE
HIGH	LOW	LOW	MEMORY CODE READ
HIGH	LOW	HIGH	HALT OR SHUTDOWN
HIGH	HIGH	LOW	MEMORY DATA READ
HIGH	HIGH	HIGH	MEMORY DATA WRITE

We have now seen the types of bus cycles the 80386 can perform, but not the actual bus-cycle mechanism. To do that, we must introduce the four bus-control signals: ADS#, NA#, BS16#, and READY#. You might guess that ADS# stands for Address Strobe. Good guess, but not quite correct. ADS# is the Address Status line. When the 80386 asserts ADS# at the beginning of a bus cycle, it signifies that the address, byte-enable, and bus-definition lines are valid. Please refer to **Fig. 2-55** for the following bus-cycle discussion.

To start a bus cycle, the 80386 places the address, byte-enable, and cycle-definition signals at the appropriate signal levels and then asserts ADS#. Eventually, whatever the 80386 is addressing will assert the READY# signal, acknowledging the cycle. The 80386 terminates the cycle after receiving READY#. In order to speed up consecutive cycles, Intel's designers incorporated the NA# (Next Address) signal that allows a peripheral device to accept and acknowledge an address before it acknowledges the cycle. When NA# is asserted, the 80386 can place the next cycle's address on the address bus to help speed up address decoding by the rest of the system. However, the 80386 cannot actually start the next cycle until READY# acknowledges the current cycle.

The last bus-control signal, BS16 (Bus Size 16), allows a 16-bit peripheral device to signal its inability to accommodate 32-bit bus cycles. The 80386 will adapt to this situation by splitting 32-bit transfers into two 16-bit transfers. This is Intel's version of dynamic bus sizing.

Besides RESET, an interrupt of considerable importance to any microprocessor, the 80386 has two more interrupt inputs: a maskable interrupt request (INTR) and a non-maskable interrupt request (NMI). The 80386 services only one non-maskable interrupt request at a time, but it will acknowledge a maskable request by reading an 8-bit interrupt vector with an interrupt-acknowledge bus cycle. The 8-bit vector directs the 80386 to any one of 256 possible interrupt service routines.

Like most microprocessors, the 80386 can operate in a multiprocessor environment. Intel's standard HOLD and HLDA signals allow the 80386 to share a common bus with other microprocessors. In addition, Intel added three signals that allow the 80386 to communicate with a coprocessor. PEREQ (coprocessor request) allows a coprocessor to request that the 80386 transfer an operand between the coprocessor and memory. The coprocessor uses BUSY# to tell the 80386 that it is busy executing an instruction and cannot accept another command just yet. ERROR# allows the coprocessor to signal an error condition to the 80386. Currently, Intel offers numeric coprocessors that conform to this protocol and add floating-point calculation capabilities to the 80386.

THE MOTEL CIRCUIT

Before we leave the world of microprocessor busses, we will briefly consider the problem of adapting from one bus to another. Two of the most popular bus designs derive from the Motorola and Intel 8-bit microprocessors.

The Motorola design has a data-direction line, R/$\overline{\text{W}}$, an address strobe, AS, and a data strobe, DS. Intel chose instead to have a read line $\overline{\text{RD}}$, a write line $\overline{\text{WR}}$, and an address strobe, ALE. Note that there are three lines in either case.

Engineers at Motorola developed a simple circuit which would automatically determine which type of bus, Motorola or Intel, was being used and adapt to it. This circuit is called MOTEL, a strange con-

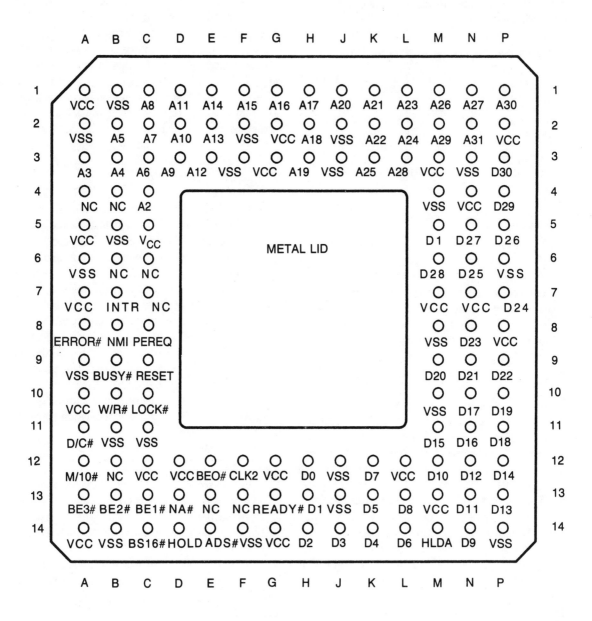

Fig. 2-51. Pin diagram of the Intel 80386 microprocessor. Reprinted by permission of the Intel Corporation, Copyright 1986.

80386 PINS AND SIGNALS GROUPED BY FUNCTION

PIN	SIGNAL	PIN	SIGNAL	PIN	SIGNAL	PIN	SIGNAL
N2	A31	M5	D31	A1	VCC	A2	VSS
P1	A30	P3	D30	A5	VCC	A6	VSS
M2	A29	P4	D29	A7	VCC	A9	VSS
L3	A28	M6	D28	A10	VCC	B1	VSS
N1	A27	N5	D27	A14	VCC	B5	VSS
M1	A26	P5	D26	C5	VCC	B11	VSS
K3	A25	N6	D25	C12	VCC	B14	VSS
L2	A24	P7	D24	D12	VCC	C11	VSS
L1	A23	N8	D23	G2	VCC	F2	VSS
K2	A22	P9	D22	G3	VCC	F3	VSS
K1	A21	N9	D21	G12	VCC	F14	VSS
J1	A20	M9	D20	G14	VCC	J2	VSS
H3	A19	P10	D19	L12	VCC	J3	VSS
H2	A18	P11	D18	M3	VCC	J12	VSS
H1	A17	N10	D17	M7	VCC	J13	VSS
G1	A16	N11	D16	M13	VCC	M4	VSS
F1	A15	M11	D15	N4	VCC	M8	VSS
E1	A14	P12	D14	N7	VCC	M10	VSS
E2	A13	P13	D13	P2	VCC	N3	VSS
E3	A12	N12	D12	P8	VCC	P6	VSS
D1	A11	N13	D11			P14	VSS
D2	A10	M12	D10				
D3	A9	N14	D9	F12	CLK2	A4	NC
C1	A8	L13	D8			B4	NC
C2	A7	K12	D7	E14	ADS#	B6	NC
C3	A6	L14	D6			B12	NC
B2	A5	K13	D5	B10	W/R#	C6	NC
B3	A4	K14	D4	A11	D/C#	C7	NC
A3	A3	J14	D3	A12	M/IO#	E13	NC
C4	A2	H14	D2	C10	LOCK#	F13	NC
A13	BE3#	H13	D1				
B13	BE1#	H12	D0	D13	NA#	C8	PEREQ
C13	BE1#			C14	BS16#	B9	BUSY#
E12	BEO#			G13	READY#	A8	ERROR#
		D14	HOLD				
C9	DRESET	M14	HLDA	B7	INTR	B8	NMI

NOTE: NC = NOT CONNECTED

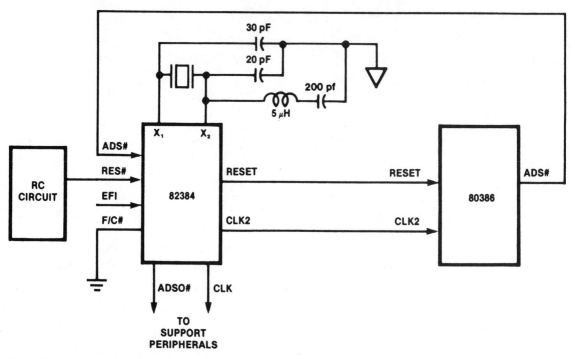

Fig. 2-52. Connection between the Intel 82384 clock generator and the Intel 80386 microprocessor. Reprinted by permission of the Intel Corporation, Copyright 1986.

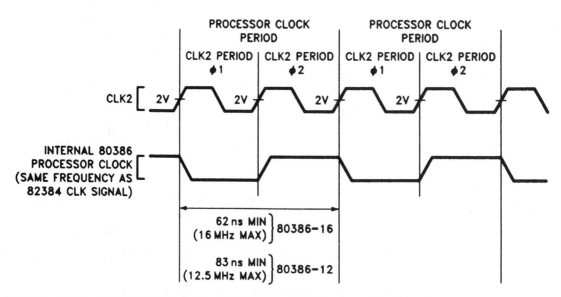

Fig. 2-53. Phase relationship between the Intel 82384's CLK2 signal and the internal clock of the Intel 80386 microprocessor. Reprinted by permission of the Intel Corporation, Copyright 1986.

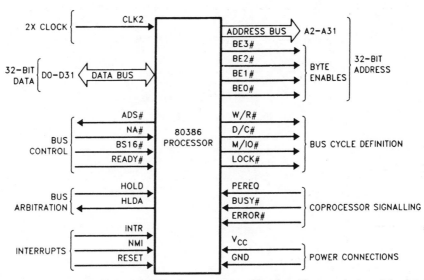

Fig. 2-54. Functional diagram of the Intel 80386 microprocessor. Reprinted by permission of the Intel Corporation, Copyright 1986.

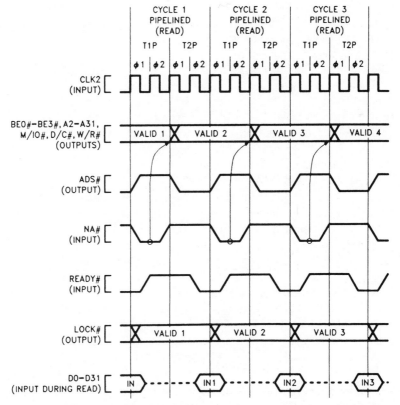

Fig. 2-55. Intel 80386 pipelined read cycles. Reprinted by permission of the Intel Corporation, Copyright 1986.

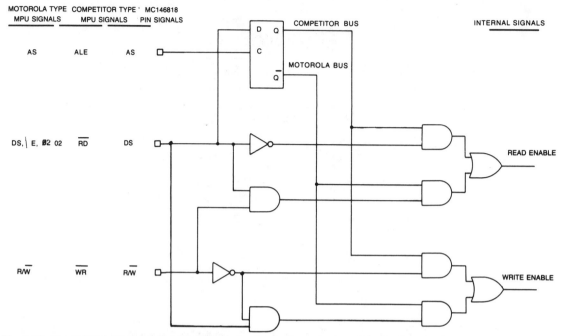

MOTOROLA TYPE MPU SIGNALS	COMPETITOR TYPE MPU SIGNALS	MC146818 PIN SIGNALS		COMPETITOR BUS	INTERNAL SIGNALS

AS   ALE   AS

COMPETITOR BUS

MOTOROLA BUS

DS,\ E, Ø2 02 $\overline{RD}$ DS

READ ENABLE

R/W $\overline{WR}$ $\overline{R/W}$

WRITE ENABLE

Fig. 2-56. The MOTEL (Motorola/Intel) interface circuit translates the bus signals of either Motorola's or Intel's 8-bit microprocessor into read-and write-enable signals.

traction of Motorola and Intel. The MOTEL circuit is shown in Fig. 2-56. Motorola now builds MOTEL circuits into their interface chips so they are compatible with more microprocessors.

Operation of the MOTEL circuit is quite simple. It takes advantage of the fact that, on either bus, address strobe and data strobes are never asserted together. On a Motorola bus, AS and DS are never at a high level together because they are both positive-true signals. On an Intel bus, when ALE is high, $\overline{RD}$ will also be high because ALE is positive true and $\overline{RD}$ is negative true.

On the falling edge of the AS input to the MOTEL circuit, if the DS pin is low, the flip flop will be cleared, asserting the Motorola-bus signal. If DS is high when AS falls, the Intel bus signal is asserted. After the type of bus has been determined, a few gates decode the DS and R/$\overline{W}$ inputs to the MOTEL circuit to generate a read-enable and write-enable signal. For Intel busses, the read enable is simply the inverse of $\overline{RD}$, and the write enable is the inverse of $\overline{WR}$.

Read enable for a Motorola bus is a little more complex and is generated by ANDing DS and R/$\overline{W}$. Write enable is generated by ANDing DS and the inverse of R/$\overline{W}$. The MOTEL circuit is a good example of an ingenious solution to an interfacing problem.

MICROPROCESSORS TO COME

Many more microprocessors are on their way from the semiconductor vendors. A raft of 32-bit RISC (Reduced Instruction Set Computer) microprocessors emerged in 1988 though none show signs of becoming a dominant factor, yet. You can be sure that 64-bit microprocessors are just around the corner. However, the basic analysis tools you can extract from this chapter will help you understand the bus of any microprocessor that may come down the pike for the foreseeable future. Microprocessors get bigger and faster, but when you examine their bus structures, they all look pretty much the same.

Chapter 3

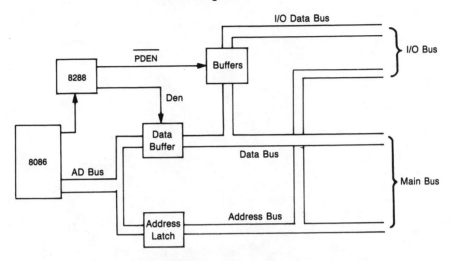

Backplane Busses

When a microprocessor system cannot fit on a single board, an interconnection scheme is needed to connect the multiple boards in a system. A backplane approach is the most commonly used technology for this purpose. The backplane is a circuit board with several connectors on it. Boards which have processors, memory and I/O circuits plug into the backplane. The backplane supplies communications paths between circuit boards and power to them. **Figure 3-1** shows a typical backplane with circuit boards plugged into it.

There are four important factors in a backplane design. The first is the set of signals that will make up the backplane bus. This set is usually heavily influenced by the processor which will be used in the system. Signals which appear on the bus will frequently resemble the component-level bus of the processor used.

The second factor in a backplane design is the power supply voltage or voltages that will be supplied to the boards in the system by the backplane. Most every backplane has a source of 5 volts because most digital integrated circuit technologies require this voltage for power. An exception to this is the S100 bus, which has an unregulated 8-volt supply. Each S100 system card is responsible for regulating this voltage and generating the 5-volt supply on the card.

Other power-supply voltages found on backplanes are +/− 12 volts and +/− 15 volts. The 12-volt supplies are generally used for RS-232 serial-communication circuits and older memory designs. The 15-volt supplies are used mostly for analog-to-digital and digital-to-analog circuits. Some backplanes also have a special battery-supply line which can be used to maintain information in memory after the power fails.

The third factor in backplane design is the connector or connectors used to attach the circuit boards to the backplane. These connectors are usually edge-type connectors, where the circuit board has metallic fingers on its surface which insert into an edge connector on the backplane. Edge connectors are low in cost, but some reliability prob-

Fig. 3-1. The inside of a bus-based computer system. This computer was the author's first computer, a NorthStar Horizon (nicknamed Liberator) based on the S100 microcomputer bus.

lems have been discovered. This led to the use of two-piece connectors where both the circuit board and backplane have metal and plastic connectors which mate together.

Finally, most backplane specifications define the size and shape of the circuit boards which may be plugged in. Backplanes are usually installed in a card cage which mechanically supports the circuit cards and the backplane. The size of the cage is determined by the size of the boards which will be used. Board size has a very powerful effect on the complexity of a microprocessor system, and the number of boards required to build a system. At one time, small boards were coming into favor for microprocessor systems. This kept the complexity, and thus the cost, of each board low. A low cost-per-board encouraged the repair philosophy of board replacement and discard of nonfunctioning boards.

As the 16-bit processors have been introduced, however, more and more functions are being designed into microprocessor systems. This would

tend to drive the number of boards up if the small size was retained. That is why you see larger circuit boards defined in newer backplane designs. The more boards you have in a system, the more connectors you have. Connectors are relatively expensive, compared to integrated circuits, and connectors can also generate reliability problems. Thus, for more complex systems, fewer, larger boards are favored.

In this chapter, we will look at several backplane schemes. Each scheme has a colorful name to differentiate it from the ''lesser'' busses. These busses represent widely varying design philosophies. Yet you should still see great similarities in each of the examples, just as the microprocessor component-level busses are similar.

THE STD BUS

The STD (pronounced Ess-Tee-Dee) bus was originally developed by Pro-Log, a manufacturer of microprocessor-based systems. It was quickly adopted by Mostek, a defunct manufacturer of microprocessors and other integrated circuits. Today, the STD bus is supported by many different board manufacturers.

Table 3-1 is a list of the 56 pins that make up the STD bus. I have conformed to the STD custom of representing negative-, or low-true, signal lines with a "/" prefix instead of the overscore which is used in most of the rest of this book. The reason for this is twofold. First, it isn't my bus, and I don't care to use my own signal names. Second, nonstandard terminology is part of the interfacing game, and it's better if you become accustomed to its use.

STD Bus Pins

The first thing to notice about the pin layout of the STD bus is the location of the power pins. Note that 5-volt power is supplied on pins 1 and 2.

These pins are on opposite sides of the circuit board so a hole through the board can be drilled and filled with solder to link the two pins together. Since the 5-volt supply is used by most all logic circuits on the board, the backplane designers wanted to use two pins for extra current capacity.

There are two pins for ground, 3 and 4, for the same reason since ground is the current return path for the 5-volt supply, as well as the other supplies. Pins 5 and 6 carry a negative 5-volt supply. This negative voltage was frequently needed by dynamic RAM chips until the late 1970s. Newer dynamic RAMs require a single positive 5-volt supply.

Finally, +/- 12 volts is supplied at the other end of the bus, on pins 55 and 56 respectively. Since the need for these supplies is much less than the 5-volt supply, a single backplane pin suffices for positive 12 volts and another serves for the negative 12-volt supply. It is important that there not be a

Table 3-1. STD Bus Signals and Pin Numbering.

PIN	FUNCTION	PIN	FUNCTION
1	+5 volts	2	+5 volts
3	GND	4	GND
5	−5 volts	6	−5 volts
7	D3	8	D7
9	D2	10	D6
11	D1	12	D5
13	D0	14	D4
15	A7	16	A15
17	A6	18	A14
19	A5	20	A13
21	A4	22	A12
23	A3	24	A11
25	A2	26	A10
27	A1	28	A9
29	A0	30	A8
31	/WR	32	/RD
33	/IORQ	34	/MEMRQ
35	/IOEXP	36	/MEMEX
37	/REFRESH	38	/MCSYNC
39	/STATUS 1	40	/STATUS 0
41	/BUSAK	42	/BUSRQ
43	/INTAK	44	/INTRQ
45	/WAITRQ	46	/NMIRQ
47	/SYSRESET	48	/PBRESET
49	/CLOCK	50	/CENTRL
51	PCO	52	PCI
53	AUX GND	54	AUX GND
55	+12 VOLTS	56	−12 VOLTS

hole drilled between pins 55 and 56 on the STD bus since that would short the +12 and −12 supplies together. There is also an auxiliary ground on pins 53 and 54 of the bus. These may or may not be grounded in a particular system.

The orientation of the power supply pins represents a power-distribution design philosophy popular in the middle 1970s. Power is brought to the circuit cards on the outermost conductors. This is because all power conductors are low impedance; they are designed to carry a significant amount of current. Power conductors tend to make good radio-frequency grounds, no matter what dc voltage they happen to be carrying. The rf-grounding effect is used to shield the signal conductors on the bus from stray electromagnetic interference. This philosophy is effective for busses with a few pins, such as the STD bus. However, as the number of pins on the bus increase, the edges of the connector get farther apart and the shielding effects of the power conductors lessen on the more-central signal lines.

Data is transferred on pins 7 through 14, data lines D0 through D7. The address bus is on pins 15 through 30, address lines A0 through A15. There isn't anything remarkable about the address or data pins. Both are driven with three-state drivers. The data bus must be three-state because it is bidirectional. The address must be three-state so the processor can relinquish the bus to other bus masters. Eight data bits and sixteen address bits mean the STD bus is strictly for 8-bit processors.

Pin 31 is the write strobe, /WR. It is asserted when the processor is performing a write operation. Prior to the assertion of /WR, the processor must drive the address and data lines to valid levels. Similarly /RD, pin 32, is the read strobe. Prior to asserting /RD, the processor must place a valid address on the address bus. (Again, the ''/'' before the term denotes negative-true.)

There are two address qualifiers on the STD bus, /IORQ and /MEMRQ. These are found on pins 33 and 34. /IORQ is asserted when the processor is performing an I/O transaction. /RD and /WR are still used to indicate when the data is to be transferred. In a similar manner, assertion of /MEMRQ indicates a memory transaction on the bus.

In addition to the address qualifiers, there are two address expansion pins. These are /IOEXP and /MEMEX on pins 35 and 36 respectively. The address expansion pins are intended to allow for greater address spaces on the STD bus by redefining other bus pins as additional address pins, when the expansion pins are asserted.

A special refresh pin, /REFRESH on pin 37 is used to allow a RAM refresh address to be placed on the lower byte of the address bus. This pin is important mainly in Z80 systems where the processor directly supports RAM refresh. /MCSYNC on pin 38 is a synchronization pin. It is asserted when /RD, /WR or /INTAK is asserted. This pin indicates when a bus transaction is taking place. Some STD processor cards use /MCSYNC for the second phase of a two-phase processor clock. Another use for the pin is the Address Latch Enable (ALE) generated by many microprocessors.

Two general purpose status lines, /STATUS 0 and /STATUS 1 can be found on pins 39 and 40. In Z80 systems using the STD bus, /STATUS 1 is assigned the function /M1, which is a low-true version of the processor M1 signal. Recall that M1 is used to indicate the reading of the first byte of an instruction. /M1 also occurs with /IORQ to signal an interrupt-acknowledge cycle. Other uses for /STATUS 1 are Valid Memory Address (VMA) found in 6800 systems and DT/$\overline{R}$, the 8080 processor's data-direction status line.

Pins 41 and 42 are used for DMA. /BUSRQ, the bus request is asserted when a bus master wishes to assume control of the bus. /BUSAK is asserted by the processor card when it has disabled its data, address and control line drivers.

/INTAK is a single-line interrupt acknowledge. It is found on pin 43. In a Z80 system, it is equivalent to simultaneous assertion of /IORQ and /M1. Pin 44 carries the interrupt request signal, /INTRQ. The /INTRQ signal is a maskable interrupt,.

Pin 45 is the wait request signal, /WAITRQ. Wait request is used to stretch bus cycles for slow memory or I/O devices. The nonmaskable-interrupt signal /NMIRQ is found on pin 46. It has a higher priority than /INTRQ and cannot be ignored by the processor.

There are two reset lines on the STD bus. Pin 47 is /SYSRESET. When this pin is asserted, either power has just been applied to the system, causing a power-on reset, or some device on the bus is resetting the system. The other reset line, /PBRESET is for a debounced reset pushbutton. Either of these lines can reset the processor when asserted.

Pin 49 is the clock line, appropriately labeled /CLOCK. Usually clock lines are not thought of as either positive or negative true but the STD has a negative-true clock line anyway. Pin 50 is a control line, /CNTRL, used for ''auxiliary timing''.

A priority-interrupt daisy chain is formed by pins 51 and 52. Priority-Chain In (PCI) is the input to the link of the daisy chain on each STD card. Priority is assigned by proximity to the processor or interrupt controller card. Cards which are closer have higher priority. If a card finds its PCI input high,

it may respond to an interrupt-acknowledge poll. Otherwise, it can't.

PCO on pin 51 is the Priority-Chain Output. If a card does not wish to respond to an interrupt poll, usually because it didn't request an interrupt, it passes to PCO whatever level it finds on PCI. Thus, if a high is found on PCI, the card will drive PCO high also.

If the card did issue an interrupt request, and the PCI pin is high, the card will reserve the next interrupt poll for itself by driving PCO low. This will tell all lower priority cards to not respond to the next interrupt poll.

STD Board Configuration

Figure 3-2 shows an STD board. Note the size of the board and the 56-pin edge connector for comparison with the other boards and busses we will dis-

Fig. 3-2. The Octagon 9500, an STD card. Though small in size, this card incorporates a NEC V25 microprocessor, two serial ports, an alphanumeric display port, a keypad port, a floppy-disk port, a 24-bit parallel port, 384K bytes of RAM or ROM, a battery-backed clock/calendar, and the BASIC programming language in ROM. Courtesy of Octagon Systems Corporation.

cuss. A standard-size STD board is 6.5 inches long and 4.5 inches wide. Excluding the edge-connector blade, the board is 6.1 inches long. This is considered a small board. STD board manufacturers do sometimes stretch the length of their boards to accommodate more complex designs.

STD Bus Status

The Institute of Electrical and Electronic Engineers (IEEE) promoted the STD bus specification to the status of a standard in late 1987. The standard is called the IEEE std 961-1987 and is available (as are all the IEEE standards mentioned in this chapter) from:

> IEEE, Inc.
> 345 E 47th St
> New York, NY 10017

In addition, several makers of STD cards joined to form the STD Manufacturers Group (STDMG) to promote the STD bus and to further its development. You can contact the group at:

> STDMG
> 3414 N Kennicott Ave
> Suite B
> Arlington Heights, IL 60004

THE S100 BUS

The roots of the S100 bus reach back to the January, 1975 issue of *Popular Electronics*. That issue had an article about a new computer kit offered by MITS (formerly Micro Instrumentation and Telemetry Systems, a company now defunct). The kit used the then new 8080 microprocessor. It had a backplane that was based on 100-pin connectors. This was the first S100 bus computer and was called the MITS Altair 8800. Back in 1975, the S100 bus was called the Altair bus.

The reason for the 100-pin connector had nothing to do with careful engineering or design considerations. MITS simply found a large number of 100-pin connectors for very little money. This was the beginning of one of the major microcomputer busses.

One of the reasons that the S100 bus caught on so quickly was the inability of MITS to deliver much hardware. The company barely had the manufacturing ability to keep up with orders for minimal Altair systems. Many people saw a market opportunity and dozens of companies sprang up overnight with hastily designed add-on boards for the Altair and its competitor, the IMSAI 8080. Some of these add-on boards even worked!

Problems in the S100 bus started to appear as soon as the number of S100 board manufacturers started to mushroom. All 100 pins on the bus had not been defined by MITS in the original Altair design, and whenever there are undefined pins, there are designers who will define them. Systems built with boards from three or four different manufacturers tended to not work the first time.

In addition, MITS had simply designed a bus to go with the Intel 8080 processor. Minimum and maximum bus timings were not specified, or even known. Also, in the flush of having so many pins, MITS placed redundant control signals on the bus. This meant that other manufacturers felt free to use whatever signals on the bus best met their needs while ignoring the rest. Even worse, other processors soon started appearing with Altair-like bus signals, though maybe not all of them. It became fairly easy to get lost in trying to determine if the control signals generated by processor board A would be able to control I/O board B or memory board C. Chaos reigned on the S100 bus.

Then the IEEE (Institute of Electrical and Electronic Engineers) stepped in. A project was initiated under the Microprocessor Standards Committee to standardize the S100 bus. The working PAR (project authorization request) number was P696. A proposed standard was published by the P696 subcommittee in 1979. It was finally approved in early 1983.

Manufacturers can't always wait for standards, however. Soon, "IEEE-696" compatible S100 boards started to appear. Even though the proposed standard had not been approved, the S100 board manufacturers saw a chance to rid themselves of the chaos and they adopted the proposed standard. This has greatly helped purchasers of new S100-based systems. In this book, even though the IEEE-696 is an approved standard, I will refer to the bus, as the S100-bus which is historically more comfortable.

S100 Bus Pins

Table 3-2 is a list of the pins in the 1979 proposal for the IEEE-696 bus. There are still 100 pins, but you won't find many of them undefined anymore. Following the name of each bus pin is an "M," "S," or "B" in parentheses. These indicate what type of bus card drives the line: a Master, Slave, or general Bus resource.

Masters are bus controllers such as processor cards and DMA-controller cards. There are two types of master: permanent and temporary. There is a single permanent master per system and it is usually a processor card. A system may have several temporary masters which may be other processor cards or DMA controller cards. Slaves are controlled by masters and may be memory or I/O cards.

There are up to 24 address lines on the S100 bus. The original Altair bus had only 16. The proposed standard allows bus masters to either drive 16 address lines, A0 through A15, or extended addressing using all 24 bus address lines, A0 through A23 for memory locations. For standard I/O addressing, only the lower eight address lines are used while the lower 16 address lines are used for extended I/O addressing. The address bus may be disabled on the bus master by asserting $\overline{\text{ADSB}}$. This line is used by a temporary master when assuming control of the bus in a DMA operation for example.

The S100 data bus is a good study in luck. Originally, the Altair bus had two eight-bit data busses, one for output and one for input. The reason for this was the RAM chips used by MITS in the Altair 8800, which had separate input and output pins. MITS extended this split input and output structure to the bus. For years, many grumbled about having 16 bus lines devoted to a data bus which only required 8 lines. These people just didn't have foresight.

The 16-bit processors came along, and sixteen S100 data bus lines suddenly looked ideal. These lines could be used as a single 16-bit bidirectional data bus instead of two unidirectional 8-bit data busses. That is how the data lines appear in the proposed standard.

In the 8-bit mode, the output-data bus, lines DO0 through DO7 are driven by the processor during a memory write or I/O output. The input data bus, DI0 through DI7, is read by the processor during a memory read or I/O input. In the 16-bit input mode, DO0 through DO7 become DATA0 through DATA7, and DI0 through DI7 become DATA8 through DATA15. This creates a 16-bit bidirectional data bus.

Data bus configuration is controlled by a status line called $\overline{\text{sXTRQ}}$ and an acknowledge line $\overline{\text{SIXTN}}$. When the bus master wishes to perform a 16-bit transfer, it asserts $\overline{\text{sXTRQ}}$ to indicate to the slave that such a transfer is about to occur. If the slave can perform 16-bit transfers, it asserts $\overline{\text{SIXTN}}$ to acknowledge the request. When both $\overline{\text{sXTRQ}}$ and $\overline{\text{SIXTN}}$ are asserted, the data bus is to be configured as a 16-bit bus. The data bus may be disabled by asserting $\overline{\text{DODSB}}$. This is used when a temporary master needs to take control of the bus. An example of this might be a DMA operation.

Since we have already covered one status line, we may as well discuss the rest. All status lines have a lowercase "s" as a prefix to make them easy to recognize. The remaining seven status lines are: sMEMR, sM1, sINP, sOUT, sWO, sINTA and sHLTA. These names should look very familiar. They come directly from status-bit names of the Intel 8080 processor. Remember, the Altair bus was designed specifically for that processor.

Since MITS brought these status bits directly out onto the bus, a strange lack of symmetry can be seen. The sMEMR signal indicates a memory read is taking place. There is no status line indicating a memory-write operation. This can, however, be created by combining sOUT, the I/O output indicator, with $\overline{\text{sWO}}$ which indicates that a memory write or an I/O output is taking place. The equation is:

$$\text{s Memory Write} = (\overline{\text{sOUT}}) \text{ AND sWO}$$

There is a signal on the S100 bus which indicates when a memory write is taking place. It is MWRT, which was generated by the front panel cir-

Table 3-2. S100 Bus Signals and Pin Numbering.

Pin	Function		Pin	Function	
1	+8 volts	(B)	51	+8 volts	(B)
2	+16 volts	(B)	52	−16 volts	(B)
3	XRDY	(S)	53	GND	(B)
4	$\overline{VI0}$	(S)	54	SLAVE $\overline{CLR}$	(B)
5	$\overline{VI1}$	(S)	55	DMA0	(M)
6	$\overline{VI2}$	(S)	56	DMA1	(M)
7	$\overline{VI3}$	(S)	57	$\overline{DMA2}$	(M)
8	$\overline{VI4}$	(S)	58	sXTRQ	(M)
9	$\overline{VI5}$	(S)	59	A19	(M)
10	$\overline{VI6}$	(S)	60	SIXTN	(S)
11	$\overline{VI7}$	(S)	61	A20	(M)
12	$\overline{NMI}$	(S)	62	A21	(M)
13	$\overline{PWRFAIL}$	(B)	63	A22	(M)
14	$\overline{DMA3}$	(M)	64	A23	(M)
15	A18	(M)	65	NDEF	
16	A16	(M)	66	NDEF	
17	A17	(M)	67	$\overline{PHANTOM}$	(M/S)
18	$\overline{SDSB}$	(M)	68	MWRT	(B)
19	$\overline{CDSB}$	(M)	69	RFU	
20	GND	(B)	70	GND	(B)
21	NDEF		71	RFU	
22	$\overline{ADSB}$	(M)	72	RDY	(S)
23	$\overline{DODSB}$	(M)	73	$\overline{INT}$	(S)
24	0	(M)	74	$\overline{HOLD}$	(M)
25	pSTVAL	(M)	75	$\overline{RESET}$	(B)
26	pHLDA	(M)	76	pSYNC	(M)
27	RFU		77	$\overline{pWR}$	(M)
28	RFU		78	pDBIN	(M)
29	A5	(M)	79	A0	(M)
30	A4	(M)	80	A1	(M)
31	A3	(M)	81	A2	(M)
32	A15	(M)	82	A6	(M)
33	A12	(M)	83	A7	(M)
34	A9	(M)	84	A8	(M)
35	DO1 (M)/DATA1	(M/S)	85	A13	(M)
36	DO0 (M)/DATA0	(M/S)	86	A14	(M)
37	A10	(M)	87	A11	(M)
38	DO4 (M)/DATA4	(M/S)	88	DO2 (M)/DATA2	(M/S)
39	DO5 (M)/DATA5	(M/S)	89	DO3 (M)/DATA3	(M/S)
40	DO6 (M)/DATA6	(M/S)	90	DO7 (M)/DATA 7	(M/S)
41	DI2 (S)/DATA10	(M/S)	91	DI4 (S)/DATA12	(M/S)
42	DI3 (S)/DATA11	(M/S)	92	DI5 (S)/DATA13	(M/S)
43	DI7 (S)/DATA15	(M/S)	93	DI6 (S)/DATA14	(M/S)
44	sM1	(M)	94	DI1 (S)/DATA 9	(M/S)
45	sOUT	(M)	95	DIO (S)/DATA8	(M/S)
46	sINP	(M)	96	$\overline{sINTA}$	(M)
47	sMEMR	(M)	97	sWO	(M)
48	sHLTA	(M)	98	$\overline{ERROR}$	(S)
49	CLOCK	(B)	99	$\overline{POC}$	(B)
50	GND	(B)	100	GNB	(B)

cuitry in early S100 systems. Current systems generate this signal on the system's processor board.

The first fetch of an instruction is indicated by asserting sM1. This has become a problem when adding new processors to the S100 bus because many processors don't indicate when they are fetching the first byte or word of an instruction.

I/O operations are indicated by sOUT and sINP. When one of these two status signals is asserted, the address on the address lines is an I/O address, not a memory address. Data direction is indicated by the sWO status line. When asserted, the bus master is writing, or outputting, to the bus. When negated, a read, or input, is taking place.

An interrupt acknowledge cycle is indicated by sINTA. Interrupt acknowledges are a weak part of the S100 design. Every processor responds to an interrupt in a different manner (A Z80 processor has three different interrupt-acknowledge sequences). The IEEE-696 proposal does not specify how an interrupt acknowledge is to take place.

The final status line is sHLTA, the 8080 halt acknowledge. It is to be asserted when the processor has halted. Again, many processors don't halt, and others cannot indicate a halted condition. These should simply leave sHLTA negated.

All the status lines may be disabled with the SDSB line, in the same manner as ADSB disables the address bus and DODSB disables the data bus. Again, this might be done for a DMA operation.

Timing and sequencing of data flow on the S100 bus are controlled by the Control-Output bus. All control output lines start with a lowercase "p." This is because the signals originally were driven by the Altair processor. The five control-output bus lines are: pSYNC, pSTVAL, pDBIN, pWR and pHLDA. All control-output lines may be disabled by asserting the CDSB (Control DiSaBle) line.

Since these are the "when" bus lines, indicating when transfers occur, we had best discuss the master bus clock, Φ first. The frequency of Φ is whatever the processor card cares to make it. This is another possible source of incompatibility between S100 cards. Some are not fast enough to be run by certain processor cards.

Whatever frequency Φ is, the control-output signals are synchronized with that clock. The pSYNC line indicates the start of every bus cycle, whether it be first instruction fetch, memory read, memory write, I/O operation or interrupt acknowledge. It starts during the first cycle of Φ and lasts for one cycle. In conjunction with pSYNC, pSTVAL signals that the status bus is valid. When both pSYNC and pSTVAL are asserted, the slaves may read the status bus to determine the type of bus cycle in progress.

Read and write for both memory and I/O operations are controlled by pDBIN (Data Byte IN) and pWR (WRite) respectively. Ignore the word "byte" in pDBIN, it is the read signal for 16-bit transfers also. The pDBIN signal is also used during interrupt acknowledge bus transactions to read in vector information.

The final control-output signal is pHLDA, or HoLD Acknowledge. This pin is asserted in response to a hold request by a bus master attempting to gain control of the bus. Hold requests are issued by assertion of HOLD, a signal of the control-input bus.

Just as there is a control-output bus, there is also a control-input bus, with six lines which are to be driven by slave boards. The six control-input lines are: RDY, XRDY, INT, NMI, HOLD and SIXTN. We have already covered the last two, HOLD and SIXTN.

Most of the processors discussed in Chapter 2 had a signal that could initiate the insertion of wait states in the bus cycle. RDY and XRDY are the two S100 signals which serve this function. Both RDY and XRDY must be asserted for the S100 bus cycle to complete. These lines may also be thought of as wait-request lines, driven low by a slave when bus cycle stretching is required. A slave may use either RDY or XRDY to control the length of the bus cycle.

INT and NMI are two general purpose interrupt lines. INT is the maskable interrupt and NMI is nonmaskable. There are also eight vectored-interrupt lines VI0 through VI7. In many S100 systems, the vectored-interrupt lines are monitored by a priority-interrupt circuit which then uses the INT line to interrupt the processor. This does not have to be the case, however. The vectored-interrupt lines may be received directly by the processor board.

DMA management on the S100 bus is performed by eight lines. I have already mentioned four of them: ADSB, SDSB, DODSB and CDSB. These are the bus-disable control signals which a temporary bus master asserts to disable the address, status, data, and control drivers of the permanent master.

The other four DMA control lines are the four request lines DMA0 through DMA3. These lines are used by temporary masters to request access to the address, data, status and control lines of the bus. Arbitration among several requesting temporary masters is performed using these lines.

Bus lines remaining to be discussed are the nine system-utility lines. There are three supply voltages on the S100 bus. The main logic supply is +8 volts and it is supplied to each card on two bus pins. The 8-volt supply is specified to be greater than 7 volts with an average voltage of less than 11 volts. Pulses of up to 25 volts are allowed. This type of power supply will not run most digital logic. Each S100 card is responsible for regulating the 8-volt supply to 5 volts, or whatever else the card happens to need.

Positive and negative 16-volt supplies are also available on the S100 bus. These are specified as being greater than 14.5 volts, with an average voltage less than 21.5 volts. Pulses of up to 35 volts are allowed. These supplies are used to power RS-232 communications circuits, which usually run on positive and negative 12-volts supplies. Again, the cards must have on-board regulators to obtain the 12-volt supplies. The 16-volt bus lines may also be used to power analog circuitry. However, many commercially available analog integrated circuits require positive and negative 15-volt supplies, which cannot be guaranteed from the specification.

The system clock, Φ, also falls into the utility category, and has already been discussed. Another clock signal, CLOCK, is a constant 2-MHz clock with a 0.5 percent tolerance. It is to be used for any purpose and cannot be relied upon to be synchronized with any bus transactions.

There are three reset lines on the S100 bus: RESET, SLAVE CLR and POC. RESET is supposed to reset all bus masters, permanent and temporary, when asserted. SLAVE CLR resets all slaves. POC is the power-on clear line. When POC is asserted, RESET and SLAVE CLR are to be asserted also, for a complete system reset.

MWRT is a most peculiar bus line. It is a memory-write strobe generated by ANDing the inverted versions of pWR and sOUT. This should logically be a control-output line, with the lowercase "p" prefix. It is not because MWRT is not necessarily generated by the permanent master, or any master for that matter. In older S100 systems, MWRT was generated by the front panel! That is why it is considered a bus-utility pin.

PHANTOM is another interesting bus line. It is present mainly for the case of what happens to microcomputer systems when power is turned on. Most systems have a special program, called a "boot," stored in ROM somewhere in the processor memory space. When the system starts up, the boot is used to initialize all the hardware, and usually to bring an operating system in from disk. After the power-on sequence, that boot ROM is no longer needed.

When PHANTOM is asserted, special slave boards called phantom slaves are enabled. Also, normal slaves are disabled. Thus PHANTOM is a good way of waking the system up with one memory space and changing over to another space for normal operation. PHANTOM may also be program-driven, to allow the processor access to larger amounts of memory than it might normally be able to access.

ERROR is a general error-condition indicator. A slave is supposed to assert ERROR when some problem arises during a bus transaction. Examples of such problems are memory parity errors during a read operation, or a 16-bit transfer request to a slave which cannot support such transfers.

PWRFAIL is an indicator, usually from the power supply, that power to the bus is about to fall out of specification. A good PWRFAIL signal generator will give the system sufficient time to prepare for the power outage. A poor $\overline{\text{PWRFAIL}}$ generator will alert the system just as the supplies are going out of specifications.

Finally, there are two groups of lines on the S100 bus which have no specific definitions. Three of these lines are marked NDEF, for not-to-be-defined. This means the IEEE-696 subcommittee has no intention of defining these lines now or in the future. They are for system manufacturers to use as desired. There are four stipulations, however: the lines are to be used only for optional functions; they are for 5-volt logic signals only; any use of the line must be fully documented; and jumper wires should be supplied on the board so these lines may be disconnected from the bus in case of conflict with another board in the system.

The last three lines are marked RFU, reserved for future use. They have been reserved by the IEEE-696 subcommittee for future definition by the subcommittee. They should not be used at this time.

S100 Bus Timing

Timing on the S100 bus is easy to understand because the read and write strobe signals, pDBIN

and $\overline{\text{pWR}}$, are generalized. This means that the same tunings apply to both memory and I/O accesses. Thus, a read operation can perform either a memory read or an I/O input, and a write operation is either for a memory write or I/O output. Figure 3-3 shows timing for a bus read, and Fig. 3-4 shows timing for a bus write.

A read-bus cycle is made up of at least three "bus states;" BS1, BS2 and BS3. Wait states may be generated by negating RDY or XRDY, but the basic read cycle is three states. Each bus state is a complete cycle of Φ, starting with a rising edge.

At the beginning of BS1, address and status lines are driven to set the bus up for the transaction. The pSYNC line is asserted during BS1 to mark the start of the bus cycle. During the last half of BS1, pSTVAL is asserted, indicating that the address and status busses have been driven long enough to be stable and valid. The data-input bus is not to be driven during BS1.

During BS2, pDBIN is asserted to indicate that the bus slave selected by the address and status information on those busses should place the requested data on the data input bus.

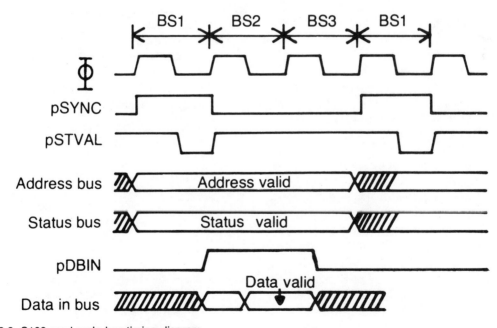

Fig. 3-3. S100 read-cycle bus-timing diagram.

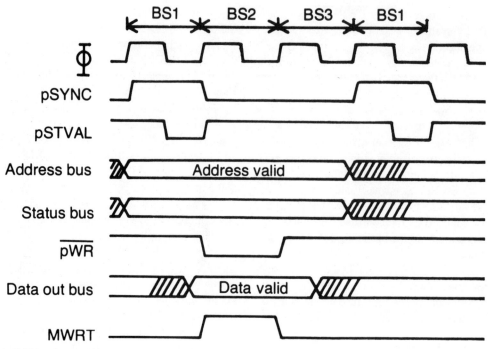

Fig. 3-4. S100 write-cycle bus-timing diagram.

The data on the data-input bus is read by the master at the start of BS3, and then pDBIN is negated and the address and status information is removed. That terminates a read cycle. If RDY or XRDY is negated by the start of BS2, wait states will be inserted between BS2 and BS3, extending the time allowed for the slave to drive the data input bus in response to a pDBIN request. Wait states are inserted until both RDY and XRDY are asserted.

Write-bus cycles are quite similar to read cycles. The pSYNC and pSTVAL signals are driven as they were during a read, as are the address and status busses. Since this is a write operation, the master must drive the data output bus. This occurs early in BS2. After the data has had time to settle on the data output bus, the master asserts pWR. MWRT will also be asserted, if this is a write to memory.

Finally, in BS3, pWR is negated, signifying that the slave had better have the data by this time. The master then stops driving the address and status busses. A delay between the negation of pWR and

loss of drive on the address and data busses is essential because many slaves use the rising edge of pWR to clock the data into their internal latches. The IEEE-696 specification calls for a delay of two-tenths of a bus state for the delay. Writes may also be stretched by negation of RDY and XRDY.

S100 Physical Description

Figure 3-5 illustrates a typical S-100 bus card. A standard card is 9.925 inches wide, usually rounded to 10 inches, and 5.125 inches tall, excluding the edge connector. Cards are available which are both shorter and taller, creating a problem in a standard-size card cage. The proposed IEEE-696 standard has defined an optional-height card which is taller than the standard card.

S100 Bus Status

In 1983, the S100 bus became IEEE std 696-1983. Since then, the bus has declined in popularity, mainly giving way to systems based on

Fig. 3-5. An S100 RAM card with a 24K-byte capacity. Like most S100 boards, this RAM card is now a relic of a bygone era in computing.

the IBM PC bus variations. However, a few manufacturers continue to support the S100 bus and it remains the patriarch of the microcomputer-bus family.

THE MULTIBUS

Shortly after the S-100 bus took off, Intel Corporation developed what became the major industrial microprocessor bus of the middle-to-late 1970s. This is the Multibus. Originally designed specifically for Intel 8-bit microprocessors, the Multibus has evolved and has been adapted to most of the other 8-bit microprocessors. With the addition of some newly defined address and data lines, many 16-bit processors have been placed on the Multibus as well.

Currently, the Multibus is defined with 20 address lines, 16 bidirectional data lines, 8 interrupt lines, and the usual assortment of control, status, and power supply lines. These lines appear on the 86-pin P1 connector of the Multibus. An auxiliary

P2 connector with 60 pins remains officially undefined, although many manufacturers have found uses for this connector. As with the other popular busses, the Multibus is standardized by IEEE-796.

Multibus Lines

Table 3-3 lists the defined Multibus signals of the P1 connector. Power connections are at the edge of the connector, with the signal lines nicely collected into groups.

1. Power supply
2. Bus control
3. Bus controls and extended address
4. Interrupt
5. Address
6. Data
7. Power Supply

Power supplies on the Multibus are regulated. There are four supply voltages available to each

Table 3-3. Multibus Signals and Pin Numbering.

PIN GROUP	COMPONENT SIDE		CIRCUIT SIDE	
	PIN	DESCRIPTION	PIN	DESCRIPTION
Power Supplies	1	GND	2	GND
	3	+5V	4	+5V
	5	+5V	6	+5V
	7	+12V	8	+12V
	9	−5V	10	−5V
	11	GND	12	GND
Bus Controls	13	BCLK/	14	INIT/
	15	BPRN/	16	BPRO/
	17	BUSY/	18	BREQ/
	19	MRDC/	20	MWTC/
	21	IORC/	22	IOWC/
	23	XACK/	24	INH1/
Bus Controls and Extended Address	25	RESERVED	26	INH2
	27	BHEN/	28	AD10/
	29	CBRQ/	30	AD11/
	31	CCLK/	32	AD12/
	33	INTA/	34	AD13/
Interrupts	35	INT6/	36	INT7/
	37	INT4/	38	INT5/
	39	INT2/	40	INT3/
	41	INT0/	42	INT1/
Address	43	ADRE/	44	ADRF/
	45	ADRC/	46	ADRD/
	47	ADRA/	48	ADRB/
	49	ADR8/	50	ADR9/
	51	ADR6/	52	ADR7/
	53	ADR4/	54	ADR5/
	55	ADR2/	56	ADR3/
	57	ADR0/	58	ADR1/
Data	59	DATE/	60	DATF/
	61	DATC/	62	DATD/
	63	DATA/	64	DATB/
	65	DAT8/	66	DAT9/
	67	DAT6/	68	DAT7/
	69	DAT4/	70	DAT5/
	71	DAT2/	72	DAT3/
	73	DAT0/	74	DAT1/
Power Supplies	75	GND	76	GND
	77	RESERVED	78	RESERVED
	79	−12V	80	−12V
	81	+5V	82	+5V
	83	+5V	84	+5V
	85	GND	86	GND

card; positive and negative 5 volts and positive and negative 12 volts. A total of eight bus pins are used for the positive 5-volt supply and the ground return, with two bus pins devoted to each of the other three power supply voltages. This allows Multibus cards to draw substantial power from the bus.

The 12-volt supplies are convenient for older NMOS parts and RS-232 signal voltages, but limited for analog conversion designs. This limitation can be eliminated with on-board dc-to-dc supplies which create positive and negative 15 volts from the 12-volt supplies.

There are 20 address lines, ADR0/ through ADR13/. Again note the use of a ''/'' suffix to denote low-true signals. Also note the use of hexadecimal notation instead of decimal in the numbering of all Multibus lines. Thus, the first 16 address lines and ADR0/ through ADRF/ and the last four address lines are ADR10/ through ADR13/. It's just another notation, no better or worse than the others.

Originally, only 16 address lines were defined. They were nicely grouped in pins 43 through 58 of the P1 connector. Later, Intel introduced the 8086 and 8088 microprocessors which required 20 address lines. ADR10/ through ADR13/ were placed on the even pins 28 through 34. Since some newer microprocessors require even more address lines, the P2 connector has become a likely candidate for expansion.

Data lines on the Multibus have been bidirectional since the original 8-bit definition. There are 16 data lines, DAT0/ through DATF/. For 8-bit systems, only DAT0/ through DAT7/ are used. A special Byte High ENable (BHEN/) control signal is asserted by a bus master when 16-bit transfers are to take place. The least significant address bit, ADR0/, is driven high for 16-bit transfers, making it always zero in 16-bit systems.

Some systems may have both 8- and 16-bit masters. The Multibus has a method, called ''byte swapping,'' which allows 8-bit masters to communicate with 16-bit slaves. BHEN/ is never asserted by 8-bit masters. When an 8-bit master drives ADR0/ low during access to a 16-bit slave, a special byte-swapping buffer on the slave is enabled. This allows the high byte of the 16-bit slave to cross to the low-byte-bus data lines. Essentially, the slave appears 8-bits wide for 8-bit accesses.

Data transfers on the Multibus are not synchronized to a bus clock. The transactions are initiated by one of four control lines; MRDC/, MWTC/, IORC/, and IOWC/. Memory transfers are controlled by MRDC/ and MWTC/, the read and write strobes respectively. I/O transactions are controlled by the input strobe IORC/, and the output strobe IOWC/.

No matter which of the four control-strobe lines is being used to initiate the transfer, the addressed slave device responds to the transfer request by asserting XACK/. Handshaking is fully interlocked. First, one of the strobes is asserted by the bus master. Then the slave performs the requested operation and asserts XACK/ to signify completion. In the case of a memory write or I/O output, completion is the acceptance of the information being transferred. For a memory read or I/O input, completion is the placing of the requested information onto the bus.

When the master observes XACK/ asserted, it completes its part of the transfer by negating the asserted control strobe line. For reads or inputs, the information on the bus is accepted before negating MRDC/ or IORC/. Then the slave completes the handshake by negating XACK/, clearing the bus for the next transaction.

There are two inhibit lines on the Multibus; INH1/ and INH2/. Inhibit 1 (INH1/) is a RAM inhibit line. This can be used to allow ROM in the system to override RAM at certain times. Uses for this feature include the hiding of ROM code for system initialization and for debugging purposes. A good example of the use of this line would be for a system that ran completely out of RAM. The INH1/ line could be used to switch in the boot ROM long enough to load the main code from a disk. In a similar manner, INH2/ is used to inhibit some ROM devices from responding to bus transactions to allow boot ROMs to overlay normal system ROMs.

There are eight interrupt-request lines on the Multibus, INT0/ through INT7/. These are prioritized, with INT0/ having the highest priority. An interrupt-acknowledge cycle, initiated by a request, is signaled by the assertion of INTA/.

Multiple-bus masters are accommodated by six lines. All bus arbitration is synchronized to the bus clock, BCLK/, which may have a frequency of up to 10 MHz. A master requests the bus by asserting its BREQ/ pin. The BREQ/ pins on the Multibus are not bussed together. They are individually supplied to a parallel-bus arbitrator. This implies that a parallel arbitrator cannot exist on a Multibus card, since there is a single BREQ/ pin to each card.

A second bus-arbitration scheme on the Multibus uses a serial technique. The CBRQ/, or Common Bus ReQuest, pin is connected to all boards on the bus. A master requests the bus by asserting this line with an open-collector driver. The bus arbitrator signals the availability of the bus by asserting its Bus PRiorty Output (BPRO/) signal, thus granting the bus request. Each BPRO/ line is connected to the Bus PRiority iNput (BPRN/) pin of the next adjacent board. This forms a daisy chain which prioritizes the boards according to their proximity to the bus arbitrator.

If a card's BPRN/ input is asserted and the card is not requesting the bus, it asserts its BPRO/ output, causing the BPRN/ input of the next card to be asserted. If, however, the card is requesting the bus, it takes control and does not pass the bus grant on. When a board takes control of the bus,

in either the parallel or serial priority case, it asserts BUSY/ to signify that it has taken over the bus.

All bus arbitration must take place within one clock cycle of BCLK/. That places some restrictions on the speed of a parallel-bus arbitrator, and on the number of boards that can be daisy-chained in a serial priority system. With a 10 MHz clock, there is only 100 ns for arbitration of requests.

Finally, there are two utility lines on the Multibus, INIT/ used for system reset, and CCLK/. The INIT/ line may be driven by a bus master or a reset switch. A constant clock supplied on the CCLK/ (Constant CLocK) line may be used by any card on the bus. The frequency of CCLK/ is not specified but has an upper limit of 10 MHz.

Multibus Timing

Figure 3-6 illustrates a read or input cycle on the Multibus. The master first places the target address for the transaction on the bus. After a minimum of 50 ns, the read strobe, MRDC/, or the input strobe, IORC/, is asserted. The slave responds to the request by placing the requested information on the bus-data lines. At the same time, or later, the slave asserts XACK/ to signal the presence of the information on the data lines. The master then acknowledges the assertion of XACK/ by negating the asserted strobe and removing the address from the address lines within 50 ns of the negation of the

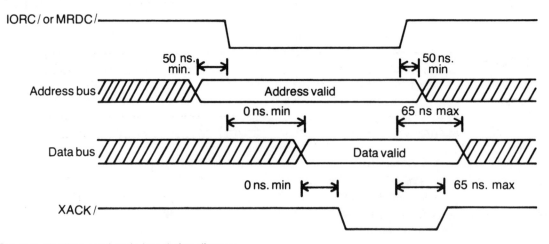

Fig. 3-6. Multibus read-cycle bus-timing diagram.

strobe. After the strobe is negated, the slave must release XACK/ and the data bus within 65 ns.

Note the lack of critical timing specifications for this bus-transfer protocol. Except for setup and hold requirements, the bus is fully asynchronous. A single transfer could take an hour or a week without violating the timing specification. The only consequence would be a very slow system. This approach allows boards of different speed to be mixed in a system without having to run them all at the rate of the slowest card.

A write, or output, cycle is shown in Fig. 3-7. As in the read or input cycle, the master places the target address on the address bus and waits at least 50 ns before asserting a strobe. Since this is a write or output cycle, the data bus is also driven, with similar setup requirements. The slave responds to the transfer request by accepting the information on the data bus and then asserting XACK/. This causes the master to negate the strobe and release the address and data busses within 50 ns of that negation. The slave then has 65 ns to release XACK/, clearing the bus for the next cycle.

Multibus Physical Description

Figure 3-8 illustrates a typical Multibus card. A standard card is 12 inches wide and 6.75 inches tall including the edge connector. Looking at the component side of the board, the P1 connector (86 pins on 0.156 inch centers) is on the left, and the P2 connector (60 pins on 0.1 inch centers) is on the right. Excluding the edge connectors, the Multibus card is 6.5 inches tall.

Multibus Status

Since introduced by Intel in the middle of the 1970s, Multibus systems have become very popular in industrial applications. Many manufacturers now offer Multibus-compatible boards, and several smaller companies have been founded to do nothing more than build boards for Multibus systems.

The Multibus specification is now standardized as IEEE std 796-1983. Intel has renamed the Multibus, calling it Multibus I. The company has developed a 32-bit bus, which it calls Multibus II. The Multibus II specification does not resemble the origi-

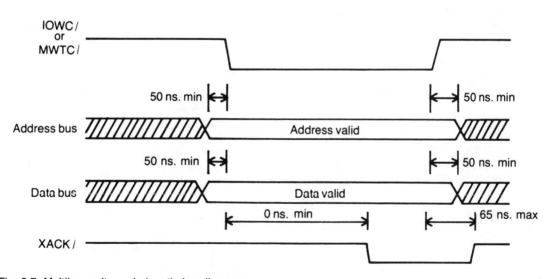

Fig. 3-7. Multibus write-cycle bus-timing diagram.

Fig. 3-8. A Multibus single-board computer card containing an 8-bit microprocessor, ROM, RAM, and I/O circuitry.

nal Multibus in any way. Only the name has remained the same, to confuse you.

In addition, several companies that build Multibus I boards have banded together and formed a trade association with data book containing information about the Multibus and its member's products. You can contact the group at:

Multibus Manufacturers Group
PO Box 6208
Aloha, OR 97007
(503) 629-8497

THE IBM PC BUS

The earth shook in the microcomputer industry on August 12, 1981. That was the day IBM introduced their PC, or Personal Computer. A microcomputer from IBM is a lot like a moped from Caterpillar Tractor. IBM had not been in the microcomputer market but rather controlled the minicomputer, medium-sized, and large-mainframe markets. In one product introduction, IBM validated personal microcomputers and carved out a large share of the market.

There are many interesting aspects of the IBM PC. IBM violated many of the "traditional" IBM rules. A non-IBM processor (an Intel 8088) is at the heart of the computer. The operating-system software is from another vendor, Microsoft. Most important for us, in our study of busses, IBM published the complete specifications of their special PC bus, which is like no other bus on the market.

There is an 8-bit, bidirectional data bus, 20 address lines, 6 interrupt lines, 3 sets of Direct-Memory-Access control lines, and the usual assortment of data-transfer control and status lines. There are also four power-supply voltages on the bus. An unusual signal on the IBM PC bus is an error line.

This is asserted if a slave card detects a problem during a bus transaction. An example of such an error might be a parity error on a memory card with parity. Assertion of the error line causes a nonmaskable interrupt to the processor.

IBM PC Bus Pins

Table 3-4 is a list of the 62 pins which make up the IBM PC bus. The IBM PC is a single board computer; the processor and some of the computer I/O circuitry and memory reside on a large board. Also on this board are five edge connectors forming the IBM PC bus.

Data is transferred on the IBM PC bus over the data line D0 through D7. Target addresses for all bus transfers are specified on the 20 address lines A0 through A19. Note that IBM selected the 8-bit version of the Intel 8086 16-bit processor. This sim-

Table. 3-4. IBM PC Bus Signals and Pin Numbering.

PIN	SIGNAL NAME	PIN	SIGNAL NAME
B1	GND	A1	I/O CH CK
B2	RESET DRV	A2	D7
B3	+5V	A3	D6
B4	IRQ2	A4	D5
B5	−5V	A5	D4
B6	DRQ2	A6	D3
B7	−12V	A7	D2
B8	RESERVED	A8	D1
B9	+12V	A9	D0
B10	GND	A10	I/O CH RDY
B11	MEMW	A11	AEN
B12	MEMR	A12	A19
B13	IOW	A13	A18
B14	IOR	A14	A17
B15	DACK3	A15	A16
B16	DRQ3	A16	A15
B17	DACK1	A17	A14
B18	DRQ1	A18	A13
B19	DACK0	A19	A12
B20	CLK	A20	A11
B21	IRQ7	A21	A10
B22	IRQ6	A22	A9
B23	IRQ5	A23	A8
B24	IRQ4	A24	A7
B25	IRQ3	A25	A6
B26	DACK2	A26	A5
B27	T/C	A27	A4
B28	ALE	A28	A3
B29	+5V	A29	A2
B30	OSC	A30	A1
B31	GND	A31	A0

plified the bus by reducing the number of data lines required. IBM also avoided the nagging problem of byte transfers in 16-bit systems.

The IBM PC uses the 8088 processor in maximum mode, which means that an Intel 8288 bus controller is present in the system. IBM simply brought out the 8288 control signals to the bus, so we find the familiar signals ALE (Address Latch Enable) and AEN (Address ENable) on the bus. Assertion of ALE signals that a valid address is on the bus address lines. AEN signals whether the processor or the DMA controller is driving the bus. Assertion of AEN signals that a DMA transaction is taking place.

Four other 8288 signals, with new names, can also be found on the bus. These are I/O Read ($\overline{\text{IOR}}$), I/O Write ($\overline{\text{IOW}}$), MEMory Read ($\overline{\text{MEMR}}$) and MEMory Write ($\overline{\text{MEMW}}$). These signals are the same as the 8288 signals $\overline{\text{IORC}}$, $\overline{\text{IOWC}}$, $\overline{\text{MRDC}}$ and $\overline{\text{MWTC}}$ respectively.

A bus handshake line, I/O CH RDY, can be used to ask the processor to stretch the current bus cycle. IBM states that this line may only be asserted for a maximum of 2.1 microseconds. This is to assure that the dynamic memory in the computer is properly refreshed. RAM refresh in the IBM PC is handled by one channel of the system DMA controller, which requires the bus to perform its job. I/O CH $\overline{\text{CHK}}$ is the error line mentioned earlier. When asserted, a nonmaskable interrupt is generated in the processor.

There are six interrupt lines, IRQ2 through IRQ7. These are connected to an interrupt controller on the processor board which automatically generates vectors for the interrupt service routine. As a result, there is no explicit interrupt-acknowledge signal on the IBM PC bus. Interrupts are acknowledged by data transactions with the processor.

Also, there are three pairs of DMA handshake lines. DRQ1 through DRQ3 are the DMA request lines and $\overline{\text{DACK1}}$ through $\overline{\text{DACK3}}$ are the acknowledge lines. $\overline{\text{DACK0}}$ is a special line used to refresh dynamic RAM boards which may be plugged into the bus. Another signal, T/C, is pulsed when the proper number of DMA bus cycles have occurred during a DMA transfer.

Utility-signal lines include OSC, a 14 .31818-MHz clock, and CLK, the 4.77-MHz clock which runs the processor. The RESET DRV line is a reset signal for all cards on the bus. Power supplies available to bus cards includes +5 volts, −5 volts, and positive and negative 12 volts. Three ground pins complete the bus.

IBM PC Bus Timing

IBM did not publish timing diagrams for their PC bus in the technical manual for the computer. Bus cycles take four clock cycles, or 840 ns, while DMA cycles take five clock cycles, or 1.05 microseconds. It isn't hard to determine what an IBM PC bus cycle looks like, however, since the cycles are controlled by an 8288 bus controller running at 4.77 MHz. Please refer to the section on the 8086 processor for a discussion of how the 8088 bus works.

IBM PC Physical Description

There is no standard size IBM PC bus card. Figure 3-9 shows a typical card. One of the unusual aspects of the IBM design is that each bus card has a metal plate attached to one end. This plate is designed as both a card guide for the back of the card and a support for any I/O connectors which may be attached to the card. This approach eliminates cabling inside the computer.

IBM PC Bus Status

Although it has never reached the position of a recognized industry standard, the IBM PC bus has become the most popular microprocessor backplane bus ever to be introduced. That just shows you that the presence of a market representing several million computers outweighs the best efforts of determined engineers to create balanced, well-considered standards. Currently, you can find the IBM PC bus used in desktop computers, portable computers, and industrial computer systems.

The IBM PC bus achieved its popularity despite being poorly specified by the IBM and in defiance of the abuse it was subjected to by early board

Fig. 3-9. An IBM PC RAM card with a 512K-byte capacity. Though 512K bytes was quite large when the IBM PC was first introduced, it no longer represents very much storage for a personal computer.

designers. Literally thousands of boards from hundreds of companies have been designed to plug into the IBM PC bus and the market momentum generated by these products ensures that the IBM PC bus remains popular well into the 1990s.

THE IBM PC/AT BUS

Only two years after introducing its PC, IBM debuted a full 16-bit version, the PC/AT, which incorporated Intel's 80286 microprocessor. Because the 80286 has a full-blown 16-bit data bus, IBM created a new expansion bus for the PC/AT with a wider data path, more interrupt lines, and more DMA signals. Like the earlier PC bus, IBM's PC/AT bus strongly resembles the Intel microprocessor on which the computer is based.

To maintain compatibility with expansion boards designed for the PC, IBM kept the original 62-pin connector and pin definitions from the original PC bus and added a second connector with 36 pins to carry the additional signals. The second connector is just in front of the 62-pin connector, so some boards designed for the IBM PC physically interfere with the new PC/AT expansion connector. Remember, IBM didn't establish a standard board size and shape for the PC expansion boards and some manufacturers decided to make use of all available space by dropping the bottom edge of the board just in front of the PC's edge connector. Figure 3-10 is a photograph of a typical board for the PC/AT bus.

IBM PC/AT Bus Pins

Table 3-5 lists the assignments for signals on the PC/AT's 62-pin connector and Table 3-6 lists the assignments for the 36-pin connector. Although most of the signals on the PC/AT's 62-pin connector retain the same names they had on the PC's bus, a few signals have new names, but similar functions. For example, $\overline{\text{DACK0}}$ on the PC became $\overline{\text{RE-FRESH}}$ on the PC/AT and IRQ2 on the PC became IRQ9 on the PC/AT. In addition, B8 on the 62-pin connector, a reserved pin on the PC bus, became 0WS (zero wait state), a signal that allows an ex-

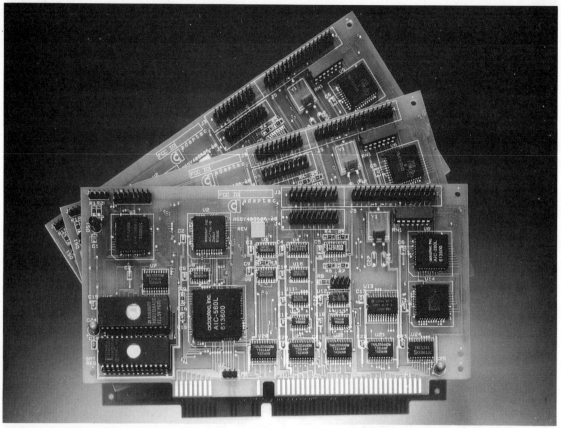

Fig. 3-10. The Adaptec ACB-2300 Series family of hard-disk controller cards for the IBM PC/AT bus. Note the second edge connector to the left of the original IBM PC bus connector. Courtesy of Adaptec, Inc.

pansion board to signal it does not require the motherboard to insert wait states into the bus cycle.

Most of the signals on the 62-pin connector didn't change in the transition between the IBM PC and PC/AT so you can refer back to the discussion of the PC's bus for definitions of the signals the two busses share. The new signals on the PC/AT bus give the computer a 16-bit data bus (with the addition of D8 through D15), a 24-bit address bus (resulting in a 16M-byte address space), more interrupt lines, and more DMA channels.

Note that the address lines LA17 through LA23 on the 36-pin connector partially replicate the addresses on the 62-pin connector and in addition, are labeled slightly different. Unline the PC's original address lines, the PC/AT's LA address lines are not latched on the computer's motherboard. Expansion boards that use these lines must latch the address values on the falling edge of ALE.

The MEM CS16 and I/O CS16 signals allow an expansion board to indicate, on a cycle-by-cycle basis, that it will accept a 16-bit, 1-wait-state transfer. The bus effects transfers in the lowest 1M-byte of address space using the SMEMR (memory read) and SMEMW (memory write) signals. Transfers to addresses above 1M byte use the MEMW and MEMR signals, which are also active for transfers to addresses below 1M-byte.

Because the 80286 can perform both byte and 16-bit-word transfers, IBM added the BHE (byte

Table 3-5. IBM PC/AT Bus Signals and Pin Numbering, 62-pin Connector.

PIN	SIGNAL NAME	PIN	SIGNAL NAME
B1	GND	A1	I/O CH CHK
B2	RESET DRV	A2	D7
B3	+5V	A3	D6
B4	IRQ9	A4	D5
B5	−5V	A5	D4
B6	DRQ2	A6	D3
B7	−12V	A7	D2
B8	OWS	A8	D1
B9	+12V	A9	D0
B10	GND	A10	I/O CH RDY
B11	SMEMW	A11	AEN
B12	SMEMR	A12	A19
B13	IOW	A13	A18
B14	IOR	A14	A17
B15	DACK3	A15	A16
B16	DRQ3	A16	A15
B17	DACK1	A17	A14
B18	DRQ1	A18	A13
B19	REFRESH	A19	A12
B20	CLK	A20	A11
B21	IRQ7	A21	A10
B22	IRQ6	A22	A9
B23	IRQ5	A23	A8
B24	IRQ4	A24	A7
B25	IRQ3	A25	A6
B26	DACK2	A26	A5
B27	T/C	A27	A4
B28	ALE	A28	A3
B29	+5V	A29	A2
B30	OSC	A30	A1
B31	GND	A31	A0

high enable) signal to the PC/AT's bus. BHE is really just an additional address bit that allows the bus to address individual bytes. Refer back to Chapter 2's explanation of the 80286 bus signals for more detailed information about BHE.

The original PC's 8088 microprocessor ran at 4.77 MHz and the first PC/AT's 80286 ran at 6 MHz. Thus, for the PC/AT bus, IBM increased the

clock frequency on the CLK pin from 4.77 to 6 MHz. However, the 14.31818 MHz signal on the OSC pin remained the same.

You'll find three more DMA request and acknowledge signals (DRQ5-7 and DACK5-7) on the PC/AT's bus, reflecting the additional DMA channels the PC/AT supports. Where did DRQ4 and DACK4 go? DMA Channel 4 is reserved for the

Table 3-6. IBM PC/AT Bus Signals and Pin Numbering, 36-pin Connector.

PIN	SIGNAL	PIN	SIGNAL
D1	MEM CS16	C1	BHE
D2	IO CS16	C2	LA23
D3	IRQ10	C3	LA22
D4	IRQ11	C4	LA21
D5	IRQ12	C5	LA20
D6	IRQ15	C6	LA19
D7	IRQ14	C7	LA18
D8	DACK0	C8	LA17
D9	DRQ0	C9	MEMR
D10	DACK5	C10	MEMW
D11	DRQ5	C11	D8
D12	DACK6	C12	D9
D13	DRQ6	C13	D10
D14	DACK7	C14	D11
D15	DRQ7	C15	D12
D16	+5V	C16	D13
D17	MASTER	C17	D14
D18	GND	C18	GND

IBM PC/AT Bus Timing

Just as with its PC bus, IBM did not specify the timing of the PC/AT bus in the computer's technical manual. Manufacturers of expansion cards for the IBM PC/AT bus must either use the basic 80286 and 80288 timing specifications or hang a logic analyzer on the bus and reverse engineer the timing. Since IBM introduced its original PC/AT, the clock speeds of compatible computers have climbed to 8, 10, 12, 16, and finally 20 MHz as Intel and other microprocessor vendors have improved their manufacturing processes.

Physical Description

Again, like the IBM PC, IBM did not specify a standard expansion card size for the PC/AT. A representative card appears in **Fig. 3-10**. Note the additional edge connector on the back edge of the card.

IBM PC/AT Bus Status

Many manufacturers of compatible computers adopted IBM's PC/AT bus for their 80286-based machines. Chip manufacturers such as Chips and Technologies Inc. (San Jose, CA) and Western Digital (Irvine, CA) developed ICs that shrank IBM's entire PC/AT motherboard into a few chips and replicated the PC/AT's expansion bus. These chips ensured the popularity of the PC/AT bus by making it easy for many, many computer designers to create machines that incorporate the bus.

In addition to machines based on the 80286 microprocessor, several 80386-based machines also employ the PC/AT bus, adding extensions for 32-bit memory boards. Unfortunately, every vendor of an 80386-based computer has developed a different technique for extending the PC/AT bus to 32 bits so memory boards for these computers are not mutually compatible.

Some computer vendors have even developed extensions to the PC/AT bus. For example, AST Research Inc. of Irvine, CA developed a PC/AT-bus extension called Smartslot by adding an additional 8 pins to the bus. These pins allow multiple proces-

motherboard and does not appear on the PC/AT's bus. So IBM's PC/AT actually supports four more DMA channels than the IBM PC.

Finally, the MASTER signal allows a microprocessor or possibly a DMA controller, installed on an expansion card, to take over the PC/AT's bus. To do this, the expansion card's circuitry must first assert one of the DMA request lines (DRQ) and wait for a data acknowledge (DACK). Upon receiving the acknowledge, the card can then assert MASTER. After waiting one clock cycle (on CLK) for components on the motherboard to relinquish the PC/AT's expansion bus, the card can assume control and drive the address, data, and control lines on the bus.

While an expansion card owns the bus, no memory refresh cycles are occurring, so a card can only retain the bus for 15 microseconds at a time. It can give up the bus and then rerequest ownership to allow refresh cycles to sneak in.

sors on several expansion cards to share the bus through an arbitration scheme. A central arbiter for all Smartslot cards grants the bus to one of the requesting cards. AST offers to license the Smartslot technology on a royalty-free basis to interested parties.

The IEEE created the P996 PC Bus committee to study the feasibility of standardizing IBM's PC/AT bus, but before the committee could produce a standard, IBM introduced its PS/2 line of personal computers that use a completely new, and totally incompatible, bus. IBM's PS/2s took the wind out of the committee's sails.

THE IBM
PS/2 MICRO CHANNEL BUS

Many aspects of computer architecture take on the airs of religious issues and computer busses are no exception. In April, 1987, when IBM introduced the PS/2 computers and the all-new Micro Channel bus, it said that the bus represented a vast technological improvement over the PC and PC/AT busses. IBM's competitors said IBM changed its personal computer bus to thwart them, and that the Micro Channel did not represent a leap forward in technology. Indeed, IBM patented several aspects of the PS/2's bus so competitors must pay IBM for a license to copy the Micro Channel. By mid-1988, only Tandy Corp. (Ft Worth, TX) and Dell Computer Corp. (Austin, TX) had announced computers with PS/2 busses, and neither company had put these machines on the market.

Micro Channel Bus Pins

Whether or not the Micro Channel represents a great leap forward, we can find many interesting similarities and differences between IBM's old and new personal-computer busses. IBM's Micro Channel currently supports three types of cards: 16-bit, 16-bit with a video extension, and 32-bit. The pin assignments for the 16-bit slot appears in Table 3-7, the pin assignments for the video extension to the 16-bit slot appears in Table 3-8, and the pin assignments for the full 32-bit slot appear in Table 3-9.

Note that a minus sign in front of the signal name means that the signal is low-true.

IBM designed the Micro Channel bus to support multiple bus masters. Normally, the processor or DMA controller on the PS/2 motherboard controls the bus. However, the Micro Channel contains a set of signals that allow expansion cards to also become bus masters. In fact, the Micro Channel allows as many as 15 masters to share the bus with the motherboard.

The first thing to note about the Micro Channel pin assignments is the power and ground scheme. Compare the number of ground (GND) and power ($+5V$ and $+12V$) pins on the Micro Channel assignments with the configuration of the earlier PC and PC/AT busses. You'll find a lot more power pins on the PS/2 bus. This increase provides two benefits.

The most obvious benefit of these additional power and ground pins is that expansion cards can draw more power from the computer because the extra ground and power pins provide a lower-impedance path to the computer's power supply. The ground and power pins also serve as low-impedance paths for radio-frequency interference (RFI) to drain off the expansion card. IBM designed this bus to help it cut down on computer interference emissions and to improve data integrity by reducing noise on the bus.

One pair of unusual pins on the Micro Channel bus are the AUDIO and AUDIO GND signals. Someone at IBM decided that expansion cards might make use of the PS/2's audio amplifier and speaker. These two pins give every card the ability to inject sound signals into a mixing amplifier. Expect a regular cacophony of sound from these machines as designers start to exploit this feature. In a similar manner, the video expansion connector allows an expansion card to override the video circuitry on the PS/2 motherboard.

A lot of the signals on the Micro Channel busses should look pretty familiar, unless you just started to read this book at this section. The data bus comprises signals D0 through D15 on the 16-bit Micro Channel slot and D0 through D31 on the

Table 3-7. IBM Micro Channel Architecture (MCA) PS/2 Bus Signals and Pin Numbering, 16-bit Version.

PIN	SIGNAL	PIN	SIGNAL
B1	AUDIO GND	A1	– CD SETUP
B2	AUDIO	A2	MADE 24
B3	GND	A3	GND
B4	OSC	A4	A11
B5	GND	A5	A10
B6	A23	A6	A9
B7	A22	A7	+ 5V
B8	A21	A8	A8
B9	GND	A9	A7
B10	A20	A10	A6
B11	A19	A11	+ 5V
B12	A18	A12	A5
B13	GND	A13	A4
B14	A17	A14	A3
B15	A16	A15	+ 5V
B16	A15	A16	A2
B17	GND	A17	A1
B18	A14	A18	A0
B19	A13	A19	+ 12V
B20	A12	A20	– ADL
B21	GND	A21	PREEMPT
B22	– IRQ2	A22	BURST
B23	– IRQ3	A23	+ 12V
B24	– IRQ4	A24	ARB0
B25	GND	A25	ARB1
B26	– IRQ5	A26	ARB2
B27	– IRQ6	A27	+ 12V
B28	– IRQ7	A28	ARB3
B29	GND	A29	ARB/ – GNT
B30	RESERVED	A30	TC
B31	RESERVED	A31	+ 5V
B32	– CHCK	A32	– S0
B33	GND	A33	– S1
B34	– CMD	A34	M/ – IO
B35	CHRDYRTN	A35	+ 12V
B36	– CD SFDBK	A36	CD CHRDY
B37	GND	A37	D0
B38	D1	A38	D2
B39	D3	A39	+ 5V
B40	D4	A40	D5
B41	GND	A41	D6
B42	CHRESET	A42	D7

B43	RESERVED	A43	GND
B44	RESERVED	A44	– DS 16 RTN
B45	GND	A45	REFRESH
— — — — — —	— KEY —	— — — —	— —
B48	D8	A48	+ 5V
B49	D9	A49	D10
B50	GND	A50	D11
B51	D12	A51	D13
B52	D14	A52	+ 12V
B53	D15	A53	RESERVED
B54	GND	A54	– SBHE
B55	– IRQ10	A55	CD DB 18
B56	– IRQ11	A56	+ 5V
B57	– IRQ12	A57	– IRQ14
B58	GND	A58	– IRQ15

NOTE: THE – USED AS A PREFIX MEANS THE SIGNAL IS LOW-TRUE

32-channel version. A0 through A23 form the address bus for the 16-bit bus and the 32-bit bus adds A24 through A31.

Several of the remaining signals on the Micro Channel bus have been carried over all the way from

Table 3-8. IBM Micro Channel Architecture (MCA) PS/2 Bus Signals and Pin Numbering, Video Extension.

PIN	SIGNAL	PIN	SIGNAL
BV10	ESYNC	AV10	VSYNC
BV9	GND	AV9	HSYNC
BV8	P5	AV8	BLANK
BV7	P4	AV7	GND
BV6	P3	AV6	P6
BV5	GND	AV5	EDCLK
BV4	P2	AV4	DCLK
BV3	P1	AV3	GND
BV2	P0	AV2	P7
BV1	GND	AV1	EVIDEO
— — — — KEY —	— — —		
16-BIT MICRO CHANNEL SLOT STARTS HERE			

the original PC bus. These signals include -REFRESH, OSC (14.31818 MHz), the byte high enable (-SBHE) signal that identifies the 80286 derivation of the 16-bit bus, CD CHRDY (channel ready), CD DS 16 (card data-size 16 bits) a combination of the PC/AT's MEM CS16 and IO CS16 identification signals, CHRESET (channel reset), and TC which indicates the last bus cycle of a DMA transfer.

That still leaves a lot of signals to tackle so let's start with the 16-bit bus. One of the first differences you might note about the Micro Channel when comparing it to the PC/AT bus is that the memory and I/O read and write control lines are gone. Instead, you'll see three lines (M/– IO, – SO, and – S1) that look like they are straight from the 82288 bus controller. According to IBM, these lines denote the following types of bus transfers:

M/– IO	– SO	– S1	Bus transfer type
0	0	0	not defined (IBM reserved)
0	0	1	I/O Read
0	1	0	I/O Write

0	1	1	not defined (IBM reserved)
1	0	0	not defined (IBM reserved)
1	0	1	memory read
1	1	0	memory write
1	1	1	not defines (IBM reserved)

That list certainly looks a lot like the 82288 signals, with a few deletions of bus cycle types IBM doesn't think expansion cards should deal with.

In addition, the MADE 24 and TR32 signals also modify the meaning of the address lines. MADE 24, when asserted, indicates that the address bus carries a 24 bit address. TR32 (Translate 32 bits) indicates the occurrence of a 32-bit wide memory data transfer (M/–I0 = 1) and the use of the -BE0 through -BE3 byte-enable signals. You should recognize the byte-enable signals, they're generated by the 80386 microprocessor that IBM just happens to use in 32-bit Micro Channel machines.

To start a bus cycle, the computer asserts -ADL (address decode latch). The expansion card that recognizes the address on the bus then asserts either -CD DS 16 or -CD DS 32 to indicate whether it is a 16- or 32-bit card, and -CD SFDBK to acknowledge the cycle. The PS/2 motherboard generates -DS 16 RTN or -DS 32 RTN to acknowledge the width of the transfer.

Once a card has acknowledged the address, the bus master can initiate data transfer. If this is a write cycle, the master places data on the bus and asserts -CMD (command). If the cycle is a read, the master asserts -CMD, indicating that the addressed card should place data on the bus. At the same time, the master negates -ADL. The bus cycle completes when the master negates -CMD.

An addressed expansion card can negate CD CHRDY to stretch the bus cycle until it has completed the bus transaction. PS/2 motherboards generate a signal in response to the assertion of CD CHRDY called CHRDYRTN (channel ready return) that it broadcasts to all the Micro Channel expansion slots.

The Micro Channel bus also supports a faster, 32-bit bus transfer called a matched memory cycle. A 32-bit memory card that can perform such cycles asserts -MMCR (matched memory cycle request) when addressed. The bus master responds to this request by asserting -MMC (matched memory cycle) and using -MMC and CMD (matched memory cycle command) to initiate the data transfer instead of -CMD. The matched-memory signals appear on a special extension of the 32-bit version of the Micro Channel at the top of the connector (pins AM1-4 and BM1-4).

At any time, an expansion card can assert -CHCK (channel check) to indicate that some error has occurred. Such errors include parity errors and time outs. The -CHCK signal causes an interrupt. In addition to the -CHCK interrupt, the Micro Channel supports 11 conventional interrupts numbered -IRQ3, 4, 5, 6, 7, 9, 10, 11, 12, 14, and 15.

Micro Channel Bus Arbitration

To support multiple bus masters, IBM designed an arbitration scheme that uses seven signals on the bus. ARB0-3 form a 4-bit arbitration address bus that indicates the current bus master. IBM reserved eight of these 16 addresses for the DMA controller on the motherboard. The ARB/-GNT signal line indicates when bus masters may contend for control of the bus.

A potential bus master requests an arbitration cycle by asserting -PREEMPT. That event initiates re-arbitration of the bus. When no bus transfers are taking place, the bus arbiter, a circuit on the motherboard IBM calls the "central arbitration control point" (CACP), drives ARB/-GNT high to allow potential bus master to contend for the bus.

When ARB/-GNT is high, potential bus masters compete for control of the bus by driving their address onto the ARB0-3 lines. Contending cards must not only drive the ARB0-3 lines, they must also monitor the state of these lines. If a higher-priority address (one with a lower numeric value) appears on the arbitration address bus, the lower-priority cards must stop driving the ARB0-3 lines. Eventually, the bus arbiter on the motherboard drives ARB/-GNT low and the address that remains on the ARB0-3 lines at that time indicates the address of the master that has successfully acquired control of the bus.

Table 3-9. IBM Micro Channel Architecture (MCA) PS/2 Bus Signals and Pin Numbering, 32-bit Version.

PIN	SIGNAL	PIN	SIGNAL
BM4	GND	AM4	RESERVED
BM3	RESERVED	AM3	– MMC CMD
BM2	– MMCR	AM2	GND
BM1	RESERVED	AM1	– MMC
B1	AUDIO GND	A1	– CD SETUP
B2	AUDIO	A2	MADE 24
B3	GND	A3	GND
B4	OSC	A4	A11
B5	GND	A5	A10
B6	A23	A6	A9
B7	A22	A7	+ 5V
B8	A21	A8	A8
B9	GND	A9	A7
B10	A20	A10	A6
B11	A19	A11	+ 5V
B12	A18	A12	A5
B13	GND	A13	A4
B14	A17	A14	A3
B15	A16	A15	+ 5V
B16	A15	A16	A2
B17	GND	A17	A1
B18	A14	A18	A0
B19	A13	A19	+ 12V
B20	A12	A20	– ADL
B21	GND	A21	PREEMPT
B22	– IRQ2	A22	BURST
B23	– IRQ3	A23	+ 12V
B24	– IRQ4	A24	ARB0
B25	GND	A25	ARB1
B26	– IRQ5	A26	ARB2
B27	– IRQ6	A27	+ 12V
B28	– IRQ7	A28	ARB3
B29	GND	A29	ARB/ – GNT
B30	RESERVED	A30	TC
B31	RESERVED	A31	+ 5V
B32	– CHCK	A32	– S0
B33	GND	A33	– S1
B34	– CMD	A34	M/ – IO
B35	CHRDYRTN	A35	+ 12V
B36	– CD SFDBK	A36	CD CHRDY
B37	GND	A37	D0
B38	D1	A38	D2
B39	D3	A39	+ 5V
B40	D4	A40	D5
B41	GND	A41	D6
B42	CHRESET	A42	D7

B43	RESERVED	A43	GND
B44	RESERVED	A44	– DS 16 RTN
B45	GND	A45	REFRESH

— — — — — — KEY — — — — — — —

B48	D8	A48	+ 5V
B49	D9	A49	D10
B50	GND	A50	D11
B51	D12	A51	D13
B52	D14	A52	+ 12V
B53	D15	A53	RESERVED
B54	GND	A54	– SBHE
B55	– IRQ10	A55	CD DB 18
B56	– IRQ11	A56	+ 5V
B57	– IRQ12	A57	– IRQ14
B58	GND	A58	– IRQ15
B59	RESERVED	A59	RESERVED
B60	RESERVED	A60	RESERVED
B61	RESERVED	A61	GND
B62	RESERVED	A62	RESERVED
B63	GND	A63	RESERVED
B64	D16	A64	RESERVED
B65	D17	A65	+ 12V
366	D18	A66	D19
B67	GND	A67	D20
B68	D22	A68	D21
B69	D23	A69	+ 5V
B70	RESERVED	A70	D24
B71	GND	A71	D25
B72	D27	A72	D26
B73	D28	A73	+ 5V
B74	D29	A74	D30
B75	GND	A75	D31
B76	– BE0	A76	RESERVED
B77	– BE1	A77	+ 12V
B78	– BE2	A78	– BE3
B79	GND	A79	– DS 32 RTN
B80	TR 32	A80	– CD DS 32
B81	A24	A81	+ 12V
B82	A25	A82	A26
B83	GND	A83	A27
B84	A29	A84	A28
B85	A30	A85	+ 5V
B86	A31	A86	RESERVED
B87	GND	A87	RESERVED
B88	RESERVED	A88	RESERVED
B89	RESERVED	A89	GND

NOTE: THE – USED AS A PREFIX MEANS THE SIGNAL IS LOW-TRUE

Micro Channel Bus Setup

IBM's Micro Channel design allows designers to eliminate addressing and option-configuration switches from expansion cards. The scheme that allows this, which IBM calls the Programmable Option Select (POS), is a technique originally developed and patented by Computer Automation (Irvine, CA). Upon power up, the PS/2 motherboard individually addresses each expansion card by asserting its -CD SETUP line. This line is not bussed across the PS/2 backplane. Instead, each slot has its own -CD SETUP signal.

When a card observes the assertion of its -CD SETUP line, it responds to I/O addresses 100-107. This standard address range allows the motherboard processor to read a 16-bit identification (ID) code (issued by IBM) from the expansion card. IBM has divided the available ID codes up as follows:

ID Code (Hexadecimal)	Definition
0000	Device not ready
0001-0FFF	Bus Master
5000-5FFF	DMA Devices
6000-6FFF	Direct program control and Memory-Mapped I/O
7000-7FFF	Memory Storage
8000-8FFF	Video Adapters
9000-FFFE	Reserved for IBM
FFFF	No device present

The processor on the motherboard matches the ID with configuration data stored in the computer's non-volatile memory and downloads that data into the expansion card. Configuration data includes the card's bus-master arbitration level, the address range of the card's on-board I/O ROM (if any), and the I/O address range assignment for the card. Every different card from every different manufacturer is supposed to have a unique POS ID code. Because IBM issues these codes, the Micro Channel architecture allows IBM some degrees of control over vendors that want to make PS/2-compatible products.

Micro Channel Bus Timing

Normally, a bus transfer on the Micro Channel requires 250 nanoseconds, representing four clock cycles for a 16-MHz microprocessor. Matched memory cycles occur in three clock cycles and therefore last 187.5 nanoseconds. As the processor speeds increase in newer models of the PS/2 family, you can expect to see faster bus transfer times.

Micro Channel Physical Description

IBM defined the board dimensions for a Micro Channel expansion card in the PS/2 Technical Reference Manual. This policy markedly differs from the company's previous efforts on behalf of the PC and PC/AT busses. A Micro Channel card is 11.5 inches long and 3.475 inches high, including the edge connector. Additional dimensions are provided in the IBM PS/2 Technical Reference Manual to precisely locate the edge connector on the board. **Figure 3-11** shows a Micro Channel card.

One reason for this policy change may be because of the change in the type of edge connector used by the Micro Channel. The PC and PC/AT busses use edge connectors with fingers placed on a 0.100-inch pitch. The Micro Channel places fingers on a 0.050-inch pitch, so precise fit is essential to prevent shorted fingers. Plastic positioning keys, occupying two finger positions on each side of the printed-circuit board, residing in the Micro Channel slots mate with notches in the expansion-card edge connectors to further ensure a precise fit.

A full-size Micro Channel expansion card is about 40 percent smaller than a full-size PC/AT card. The reduced card size will force board designers to use more highly-integrated ICs and surface-mount components which require less room on a printed-circuit board than conventional IC packages. Thus, the cost of entering the PS/2 expansion board market for a manufacturer can be higher than it was for the PC and PC/AT markets.

Micro Channel Bus Status

Several board manufacturers offer boards compatible with IBM's Micro Channel. As mentioned

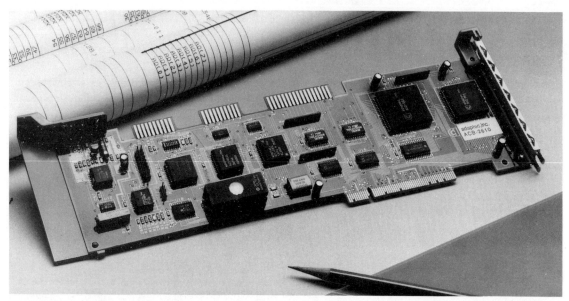

Fig. 3-11. The Adaptec ACB-2610 hard disk controller board for IBM's PS/2 (Micro Channel Architecture) bus. Contrast the 0.05-inch edge-connector fingers for the PS/2 bus (along the bottom of the card) with the more conventional 0.100-inch fingers for the disk-drive cables (along the top of the card). Courtesy of Adaptec, Inc.

previously, as of mid-1988, at least two computer vendors have announced plans to market PS/2 machines. In addition, chip makers including Chips and Technology, Inc. and G2 Inc. (Milpitas, CA) have announced chip sets that make building a Micro Channel motherboard much easier. Even with these chip sets, the Micro Channel may be adopted by only a limited number of companies. IBM wants royalty fees of as much as 5 percent of a products's selling price for the privilege of using its patented technology.

THE NUBUS

Designers need not make 32-bit backplane busses as complex as IBM's Micro Channel to achieve high-performance features. A case in point is the NuBus (A name trademarked by Texas Instruments Inc., Dallas, TX). The NuBus started as a concept at the Massachusetts Institute of Technology and appeared in a paper written by Professor Steve Ward and Chris Terman. In 1983, Texas Instruments adopted the NuBus for its Explorer line of artificial intelligence (AI) workstations.

However, the big break for the NuBus came in 1987 when Apple Computer, Inc. (Cupertino, CA) introduced the Macintosh II with a NuBus architecture. **Figure 3-12** shows a series of boards for the Macintosh II version of the NuBus. Previous versions of the Apple Macintosh had no expansion bus at all. Texas Instruments sells unrestricted licenses for incorporation of the NuBus into other manufacturer's equipment.

NuBus Pins

Unlike all of the busses we have previously studied in this book, the NuBus does not use printed-circuit board edge connectors and edge-card sockets. Instead, the NuBus uses a 96-pin 2-piece connector used internationally. One piece of the connector solders to the motherboard and the other piece solders to the expansion card. This type of connector has several advantages over edge connectors including tighter dimensional tolerances, much less susceptibility to fret corrosion, and fewer abrasion problems. The 96 pins are arranged as three rows with 32 pins per row.

Fig. 3-12. The National Instrument's NB series of data-acquisition cards for the Apple Macintosh II's NuBus. Courtesy of National Instruments Corp.

The P1196 draft specification defines three connectors to be used on the NuBus: a P1 connector that carries the bus signals (shown in **Table 3-10**) and P2 and P3 connectors that carry I/O signals from the expansion board to other devices (shown in **Table 3-11**). At the minimum, a NuBus board must have P1 connector to communicate with the bus.

The NuBus differs from the other busses discussed in this chapter so far in many other ways as well. The NuBus is a synchronous bus: every bus transfer occurs in lock step with a 10-MHz clock. The clock, which appears on P1 pin C32, has a 75/25 duty cycle, as shown in **Fig. 3-13**.

In addition, the NuBus uses a multiplexed address/data bus (the AD signals) instead of separate address and data busses. A multiplexed bus cuts 32 signal lines from the NuBus, allowing it to fit on a 96-pin connector and still allocate a substantial number of pins to power and ground.

The SP* (system parity) signal is an optional bus-parity line that allows NuBus systems to be used in high-reliability applications. If used, SP* carries a bit of even parity generated over the 32 AD bits. SP* can carry parity for both address and data bus cycles. SP* can be used on a cycle-by-cycle basis, meaning that in one system, some transfers may use SP* and others may not. When asserted during a cycle, SPV* (System Parity Valid) indicates that the SP* bit is valid.

Two signals affect the transfer of data over the NuBus. The bus master asserts START* for one clock cycle to initiate a transfer and the target of the transfer (called the slave) asserts ACK* (acknowledge) for one clock cycle when the transfer is done. Thus, the minimum time for a single bus transfer on the NuBus requires two clock cycles or 200 nanoseconds.

NuBus transfers can be 32-bits wide (a word), 16-bits wide (a half-word), or 8-bits wide (a byte).

Table 3-10. NuBus Signals and Pin Numbering, Connector P1.

SIGNALS

ROW PIN	A	B	C
1	– 12V	– 12V	RESET*
2	RESERVED	GND	RESERVED
3	SPV*	GND	+5V
4	SP*	+5V	+5V
5	TM1*	+5V	TMO*
6	AD1*	+5V	ADO*
7	AD3*	+5V	AD2*
8	AD5*	– 5.2V	AD4
9	AD7*	– 5.2V	AD6*
10	AD9*	– 5.2V	AD8*
11	AD11*	– 5.2V	AD10*
12	AD13*	GND	AD12*
13	AD15*	GND	AD14*
14	AD17*	GND	AD16*
15	AD19*	GND	AD18*
16	AD21*	GND	AD20*
17	AD23*	GND	AD22*
18	AD25*	GND	AD24*
19	AD27*	GND	AD26*
20	AD29*	GND	AD28*
21	AD31*	GND	AD30*
22	GND	GND	GND
23	GND	GND	PFW*
24	ARB1*	– 5.2V	ARB0*
25	ARB3*	– 5.2V	ARB2*
26	ID1*	– 5.2V	ID0*
27	ID3*	– 5.2V	ID2*
28	ACK*	+5V	START*
29	+5V	+5V	+5V
30	RQST*	GND	+5V
31	NMRQ*	GND	GND
32	+12V	+12V	CLK*

NOTE: THE * USED AS A SUFFIX MEANS THE SIGNAL IS LOW-TRUE

Table 3-11. NuBus Signals and Pin
Numbering, Connectors P2 and P3.

		SIGNALS	
Row	A	B	C
PIN			
1	-	-	-
2	-	GND	-
3	-	GND	-
4	-	-	-
5	-	+5V	-
6	-	+5V	-
7	-	+5V	-
8	-	-	-
9	-	-	-
10	-	−5.2ENAB	-
11	-	−5.2OUT	-
12	-	GND	-
13	-	-	-
14	-	+12ENAB	-
15	-	+12OUT	-
16	-	GND	-
17	-	-	-
18	-	-	-
19	-	GND	-
20	-	−12OUT	-
21	-	−12ENAB	-
22	-	-	-
23	-	GND	-
24	-	-	-
25	-	-	-
26	-	-	-
27	-	-	-
28	-	+5V	-
29	-	-	-
30	-	GND	-
31	-	GND	-
32	-	-	-

NOTE: - = NOT ASSIGNED, AVAILABLE
FOR USE

Figure 3-14 shows the relationship and numbering between NuBus words, half-words, and bytes. During the START* pulse, transfer mode signals TM0* and TM1*, used in conjunction with address bits AD0* and AD1*, indicate the transfer direction (read or write), the data transfer size, and the portion of the AD bus to use for the transfer (see Table 3-12).

Note that two of the transfer modes in Table 3-12 perform block reads and writes. A slave need not support this capability, but the block-transfer technique allows the NuBus to achieve very high transfer rates, approaching 40M bytes/second. The NuBus specification only allows the block transfer of 32-bit words.

To initiate a block transfer, the bus master asserts START* for one clock cycle just as with a single bus transfer, however it encodes the TM1*, TM0*, AD1*, and AD0* lines to signal a block-mode read or write and encodes AD5*, AD4*, AD3*, and AD2* to indicate the number of words to be transferred. Following that block-transfer START* pulse, the slave acknowledges intermediate transfers by asserting TM0* and the final transfer in the block by asserting ACK*.

The TM0* and TM1* transfer-mode lines also allow the slave to send back a coded transaction response to the master when it asserts ACK*. Slave transaction responses appear in Table 3-14. These responses apply only to single-transfer bus cycles, however, a slave can use the Transfer Complete response to indicate that it does not support block transfers by generating an ACK* acknowledgment to a block-mode transfer request with the Transfer Complete message encoded on the transfer-mode signal lines. This response does not indicate an error condition and the bus master is supposed to handle the situation gracefully.

Three other possible transaction responses give the bus master quite a bit of information about its bus transactions. The error response means that data supplied during a read may not be valid or that a write may not have completed. A slave memory board might generate this response as the result of a parity error on the memory card.

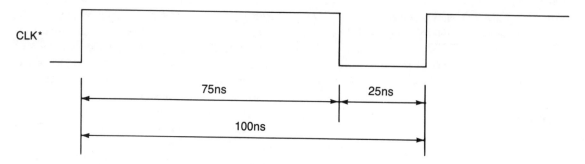

CLK*

75ns

25ns

100ns

Fig. 3-13. The NuBus uses an asymmetrical, 10-MHz clock as a timing signal for all bus transactions.

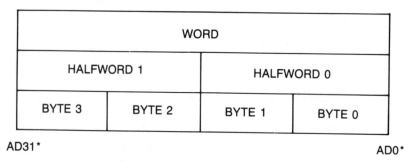

WORD			
HALFWORD 1		HALFWORD 0	
BYTE 3	BYTE 2	BYTE 1	BYTE 0

AD31*   AD0*

Fig. 3-14. Relationship between bytes, halfwords, and words on the NuBus.

The Bus Timeout Error response is not generated by the addressed slave but by timeout circuitry somewhere in the NuBus system. A slave must respond to a START* request within 255 clock cycles following the request. If the slave fails to respond, that is a bus-timeout error. To prevent the NuBus from locking up, the timeout circuitry generates a Bus Timeout Error response, freeing the bus so that the system can get on about its business.

Slaves that cannot respond within the 255-clock window can avoid generating bus-timeout errors by responding with the Try Again Later message. The bus specification states that "There is a strong indication that the transfer can be accomplished by some future request."

The NuBus supplies the NMRQ* (Non Master ReQuest) signal to allow a slave to generate an interrupt without becoming a bus master first. The only other interrupts on the bus are the PFW* (Power Failure Warning) and the RESET* signals. RESET* has an obvious function. The PFW* function is closely interwoven with the NuBus reset.

When circuitry monitoring the ac power line detects a loss of power, it must assert PFW* at least two milliseconds before RESET*. Typically, RESET* will become asserted when the dc power-supply voltages drop below tolerances. Similarly, when power is supplied to the NuBus, the PFW* signal must be negated at least one millisecond before RESET* is negated.

NuBus Arbitration

NuBus allows multiple bus masters to share the bus, although only one master can control the bus at a time. Bus masters competing for bus mastership must compete for control of the bus through an arbitration mechanism. The NuBus arbitration sequence occurs concurrently with data transfers so it allows very efficient bus sharing.

Bus arbitration uses five NuBus lines, plus information supplied by four, dual-use signals. The five arbitration lines are RQST* (ReQueST) and the four arbitrate lines ARB0*, ARB1*, ARB2*, and ARB3*. Each NuBus card has an arbitration priority,

Table 3-12. NuBus Transfer-mode Encoding.

TM1*	TMO*	AD1*	AD0*	TYPE OF CYCLE
L	L	L	L	WRITE BYTE 3
L	L	L	H	WRITE BYTE 2
L	L	H	L	WRITE BYTE 1
L	L	H	H	WRITE BYTE 0
L	H	L	L	WRITE HALF-WORD 1
L	H	L	H	BLOCK WRITE
L	H	H	L	WRITE HALF-WORD 0
L	H	H	H	WRITE WORD
H	L	L	L	READ BYTE 3
H	L	L	H	READ BYTE 2
H	L	H	L	READ BYTE 1
H	L	H	H	READ BYTE 0
H	H	L	L	READ HALF-WORD 1
H	H	L	H	BLOCK READ
H	H	H	L	READ HALF-WORD 0
H	H	H	H	READ WORD

NOTE: H = HIGH, L = LOW

Table 3-13. NuBus Block Transfer Sizes.

AD5*	AD4*	AD3*	AD2*	BLOCK SIZE (WORDS)	BLOCK STARTING ADDRESS
X	X	X	H	2	(A31-A3)000
X	X	H	L	4	(A31-A4)0000
X	H	L	L	8	(A31-A5)00000
H	L	L	L	16	(A31-A6)000000

NOTE: H = HIGH, L = LOW, X = DON'T CARE

Table 3-14. NuBus Transaction-response Encoding.

TM1*	TMO*	RESPONSE
L	L	TRANSFER COMPLETE
L	H	ERROR
H	L	BUS TIMEOUT ERROR
H	H	TRY AGAIN LATER

NOTE: H = HIGH, L = LOW

set by the four ID lines, discussed in the next section.

Arbitration starts when one or more cards asserts RQST* on the rising edge of a clock pulse. No module may assert RQST* unless that signal was negated during the previous clock cycle. Thus, several cards may wait for a clock edge and then assert RQST*, but latecomers cannot jump into the arbitration after the clock edge has passed.

Once the request is issued, each requesting card places its 4-bit ID, assigned by the ID lines, onto the ARB lines and the contest begins. At the same time that a card places its ID on the ARB lines, it starts monitoring the ARB lines as well. If the card senses that a higher-priority (higher ID number) is being asserted on the ARB lines, it stops driving the lines.

Eventually, within two clock cycles, only the card with the highest priority continues to drive the ARB lines. The winning card has become the bus owner and can initiate bus transfers after the current transfer completes. When the winning bus master asserts START*, it stops asserting RQST*.

However, the losing cards do not stop asserting the RQST* line, preventing latecomers from participating in the next arbitration cycle. When the current bus owner decides to relinquish the bus, it stops driving the ARB lines, signaling the start of the next arbitration cycle. Cards requesting the bus by asserting RQST* again put their IDs on the ARB lines and again they allow the highest-priority ID to assume ownership. This sequence repeats until all of the original requesters get a turn to own the bus.

When the last requester negates RQST*, the next group of requesters can jump in. NuBus designers call this arbitration scheme "fair." No card can monopolize the bus and every bus master that wants to use the bus gets a turn, eventually.

NuBus Setup

Like IBM's Micro Channel cards, NuBus cards do not need on board switches to set addresses. However, the NuBus accomplishes this feat in a completely different manner. The four ID signals (ID0* through ID3*) are prewired on the motherboard. Each NuBus card slot has a different ID number, so a NuBus backplane can hold as many as 16 cards. A card plugged into a NuBus card slot takes the 4-bit ID code and incorporates it into its slot address.

Slot addresses occupy the top 256 megabytes of the 4 gigabyte address space supported by the NuBus. Thus, each of the 16 slots gets its own 16-megabyte space. The remainder of the 4 gigabyte space is considered general purpose. The slot ID code becomes the second most significant nibble of the slot-space address. Thus slot 0's slot address starts at F0000000 and runs up to F0FFFFFF, slot 1's address starts at F1000000 and runs up to F1FFFFFF, and so on. The NuBus address map appears in Fig. 3-15.

When the system starts up, it can interrogate the highest-order word in each slot space (address FXFFFFFC) to find out if the slot is occupied by a card (or module). Modules that are present respond with either a Transfer Complete or Error response to signal their presence. In addition, each module is supposed to have a configuration ROM located at the top of the slot's address space to assist the system in configuring the module. The 16-megabyte slot space allows for a lot of configuration information.

NuBus Timing

You have already seen the NuBus system clock in Figure 3-13. NuBus cards must assert bus signals on the rising edge of CLK* and sample the state of these signals on the falling edge. The asymmetry of the clock thus gives the signals about 75 nanoseconds to settle on the bus before they are sampled.

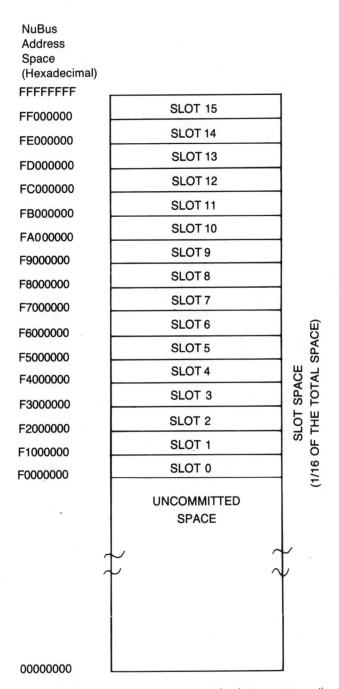

NuBus
Address
Space
(Hexadecimal)

Address	Slot
FFFFFFFF	
	SLOT 15
FF000000	
	SLOT 14
FE000000	
	SLOT 13
FD000000	
	SLOT 12
FC000000	
	SLOT 11
FB000000	
	SLOT 10
FA000000	
	SLOT 9
F9000000	
	SLOT 8
F8000000	
	SLOT 7
F7000000	
	SLOT 6
F6000000	
	SLOT 5
F5000000	
	SLOT 4
F4000000	
	SLOT 3
F3000000	
	SLOT 2
F2000000	
	SLOT 1
F1000000	
	SLOT 0
F0000000	
	UNCOMMITTED SPACE
00000000	

SLOT SPACE
(1/16 OF THE TOTAL SPACE)

Fig. 3-15. The 4G-byte NuBus address space is divided into uncommitted space, representing $^{15}/_{16}$ of the total available addresses, and 16 individual address spaces, each assigned to individual card slots on the NuBus. Each slot space measures 16M-bytes in size.

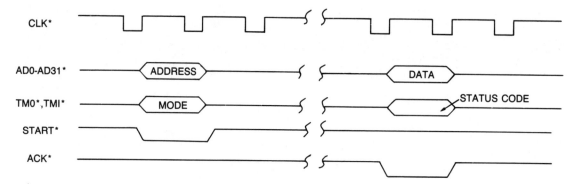

Fig. 3-16. A NuBus read-cycle bus-timing diagram.

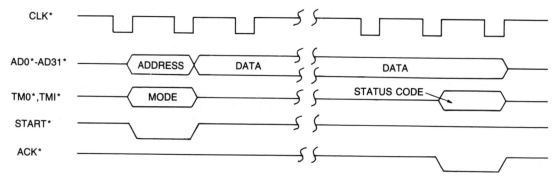

Fig. 3-17. A NuBus write-cycle bus-timing diagram.

Figure 3-16 illustrates a single read cycle on the NuBus and Figure 3-17 illustrates a single write cycle. Because the transfer-mode signals encode the read/write status of the cycle, you'll have to look closely to see the difference between the transfer cycles.

During a read, the bus master drives the AD lines with a target address, encodes the proper transfer mode on the TM lines, and asserts START* for one clock cycle, starting on the rising edge of the clock. At the next falling edge of the clock, the slave samples the status of these lines, recognizes the read request, and takes the necessary actions. At the next rising edge of the clock, the bus master stops driving the AD, TM and START* lines.

At that same rising clock edge, or at some subsequent rising clock edge, the slave places the requested data on the AD lines, an appropriate transaction response on the TM lines, and asserts

ACK*. Even if the slave is only supplying requested data on part of the AD bus, it must drive all of the AD lines to ensure that the lines assume valid logic levels during the data transfer. The bus master samples the states of these lines at the next falling edge of the system clock. On the next rising clock edge, the slave stops driving the AD, TM and START* lines, completing the transfer cycle. Thus, a single data transfer over the NuBus requires at least two CLK* cycles.

NuBus writes work in much the same way as reads. The bus master drives the target address on the AD lines, encodes the proper transfer mode on the TM lines, and asserts START* for one CLK* cycle. At the rising edge on the end of that cycle, the master replaces the target address on the AD lines with the data being written. Just as with the read cycle, the bus master must drive all of the AD lines, not just the ones carrying valid data bits.

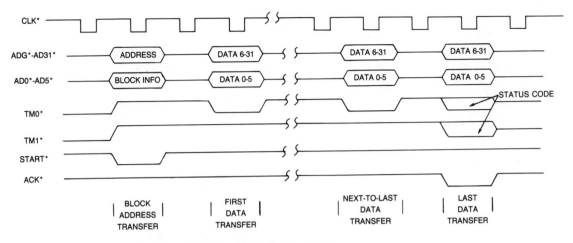

Fig. 3-18. A NuBus block-mode, read-cycle, bus-timing diagram.

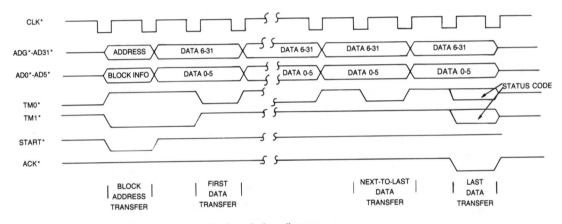

Fig. 3-19. A NuBus block-mode, write-cycle, bus-timing diagram.

At that same rising clock edge, or at some subsequent rising clock edge, the slave accepts the data, places an appropriate transaction response on the TM lines, and asserts ACK* for one clock cycle. This completes the write cycle.

You can see from Fig. 3-18 and 3-19 that NuBus block reads and writes work in much the same manner. In fact, the initiating and terminating cycles exactly match the operation of single-cycle reads and writes. Only the intermediate block-mode transfer cycles differ. During a block-mode reads and writes, the slave asserts TM0* instead of ACK* for each data transfer. That's the only change made to the block-mode transfer cycles.

NuBus Physical Description

The P1196 specification allows two different sizes of NuBus board: a triple-height card and a PC style card. The triple-height card conforms to the international IEC 297 SC 48D standard and is 280 millimeters (11.024 inches) high and 366.7 millimeters (14.437 inches) wide. The triple-height card holds all three connectors defined by the P1196 specification (P1, P2, and P3).

The triple-height card is great for rackmounted, industrial systems but it's a bit large to fit into a desktop computer. The PC-style card is a much better size for small computers at 4 inches high by 12.875 inches long. Figure 3-12 is a picture of a PC-style NuBus card designed to fit in the Apple Macintosh II.

NuBus Status

As of mid 1988, the IEEE P1196 committee was working to finalize the NuBus standard. When finished, the NuBus will become IEEE std 1196. In addition, several companies have banded together to form a NuBus manufacturers and users group called the NuGroup. You can contact the NuGroup by writing to:

NuGroup
c/o CMC (Attn: Ann Weber)
222 Fashion Lane
Suite 201
Tustin, CA 92680
Phone: (714) 669-1201

THE VMEBUS

When Motorola developed the 68000 microprocessor, it decided that the new 16-bit processor required a new bus. Previously, Motorola built systems for its 8-bit 6800 microprocessor based on the company's proprietary EXORbus. Motorola had big plans for the 68000 family and wanted to place a bus before the public that was worthy of the 68000's capabilities and could support the capabilities of planned successors to the 68000.

Motorola developed the VERSAbus as its candidate for the 16-bit backplane bus of choice. The company's first VERSAbus specification appeared in November, 1979. The VERSAbus comprises two connectors: a 140-pin connector that supports a 16-bit data bus and a 24-bit address bus, and a 120-pin connector that carries the data- and address-bus extensions that allow the VERSAbus to accommodate 32 bits of address and data. The VERSAbus card is huge, measuring 14 inches by 9.25 inches. Motorola builds a number of VERSA Modules based on the VERSAbus specification and the IEEE is working on a VERSAbus standard.

However, the VERSAbus did not meet some needs of the European engineering community. In particular, the VERSAbus employed a non-standard form factor for the card size and it used edge connectors for the bus. Motorola's European Microsystems Group in Munich, West Germany therefore created a new bus, based on the VERSAbus, but with a standard European card size and using 2-piece, 96-pin, European DIN connectors instead of the VERSAbus edge connectors. The German engineers dubbed this derived bus VERSA Module Europe, or VME. Revision A of the VMEbus specification appeared in 1981. Since then, the VMEbus has completely overshadowed its parent bus.

VMEbus Signal Lines

The VMEbus is composed of four sub busses: the data transfer bus (DTB), the priority interrupt bus, the DTB arbitration bus, and a utility bus. The DTB further divides into addressing lines, data lines, and control lines. Tables 3-15 and 3-16 give the signal names and pin numbering for the two VMEbus connectors: P1 and P2. P1 implements the 16-bit VMEbus and P2 provides the additional lines needed to flesh out the bus to a full 32 bits.

VMEbus address lines consist of the traditional address signals A01 through A31, plus address-modifier signals AM0 through AM5, data strobes DS0* and DS1*, and LWORD*. Address lines A02 through A31 select the address of a 32-bit word and A01, DS1*, DS0*, and LWORD* specify the byte or bytes within that 32-bit word to be transferred. The allowable combinations of the four byte-specifier signals appears in Table 3-17.

The six address-modifier lines create a myriad of address spaces on the VMEbus. Many of these spaces are reserved , meaning they should not be used. Table 3-18 lists the meanings of the various address-modifier codes. A few of the spaces specify block transfers, which we'll look at in a bit. The primary use of the VMEbus address spaces is to divide memory into supervisor space and non-supervisor (or nonprivileged) space. The concepts of supervisor and non-supervisor space directly reflect the 68000 lineage of the VMEbus.

In addition to the differentiation between supervisory and nonprivileged space, certain address-

Table 3-15. VMEbus Signals and Pin Numbering, Connector P1.

PIN	ROW A	SIGNALS B	C
1	D00	BBSY*	D08
2	D01	BCLR*	D09
3	D02	ACFAIL*	D10
4	D03	BG0IN*	D11
5	D04	BG0OUT*	D12
6	D05	BG1IN*	D13
7	D06	BG1OUT*	D14
8	D07	BG2IN*	D15
9	GND	BG2OUT*	GND
10	SYSCLK	BG3IN*	SYSFAIL*
11	GND	BG3OUT	BERR*
12	DS1*	BR0*	SYSRESET*
13	DS0*	BR1*	LWORD*
14	WRITE*	BR2*	AM5
15	GND	BR3*	A23
16	DTACK*	AM0	A22
17	GND	AM1	A21
18	AS*	AM2	A20
19	GND	AM3	A19
20	IACK*	GND	A18
21	IACKIN*	SERCLK	A17
22	IACKOUT*	SERDAT*	A16
23	AM4	GND	A15
24	A07	IRQ7*	A14
25	A06	IRQ6*	A13
26	A05	IRQ5*	A12
27	A04	IRQ4*	A11
28	A03	IRQ3*	A10
29	A02	IRQ2*	A09
30	A01	IRQ1*	A08
31	−12V	+5V STANDBY	+12V
32	+5V	+5V	+5V

modifier codes signal the use of short (16-bit), standard (24-bit), and extended (32-bit) addressing. The standard addressing is 24-bits because the 68000 and many other 16-bit microprocessors support 24-bit address spaces. A small address space, using short (16-bit) addressing, creates a nice-sized space for designers who just can't live without a separate address space for memory and I/O. Extended addresses support the large addressing needs of 32-bit microprocessors.

The VMEbus supports both 16- and 32-bit data busses. When a VMEbus-based system implements

Table 3-16. VMEbus Signals and Pin Numbering, Connector P2.

ROW	A	B	C
PIN			
1	USER-DEFINED	+5V	USER-DEFINED
2	USER-DEFINED	GND	USER-DEFINED
3	USER-DEFINED	RESERVED	USER-DEFINED
4	USER-DEFINED	A24	USER-DEFINED
5	USER-DEFINED	A25	USER-DEFINED
6	USER-DEFINED	A26	USER-DEFINED
7	USER-DEFINED	A27	USER-DEFINED
8	USER-DEFINED	A28	USER-DEFINED
9	USER-DEFINED	A29	USER-DEFINED
10	USER-DEFINED	A30	USER-DEFINED
11	USER-DEFINED	A31	USER-DEFINED
12	USER-DEFINED	GND	USER-DEFINED
13	USER-DEFINED	+5V	USER-DEFINED
14	USER-DEFINED	D16	USER-DEFINED
15	USER-DEFINED	D17	USER-DEFINED
16	USER-DEFINED	D18	USER-DEFINED
17	USER-DEFINED	D19	USER-DEFINED
18	USER-DEFINED	D20	USER-DEFINED
19	USER-DEFINED	D21	USER-DEFINED
20	USER-DEFINED	D22	USER-DEFINED
21	USER-DEFINED	D23	USER-DEFINED
22	USER-DEFINED	GND	USER-DEFINED
23	USER-DEFINED	D24	USER-DEFINED
24	USER-DEFINED	D25	USER-DEFINED
25	USER-DEFINED	D26	USER-DEFINED
26	USER-DEFINED	D27	USER-DEFINED
27	USER-DEFINED	D28	USER-DEFINED
28	USER-DEFINED	D29	USER-DEFINED
29	USER-DEFINED	D30	USER-DEFINED
30	USER-DEFINED	D31	USER-DEFINED
31	USER-DEFINED	GND	USER-DEFINED
32	USER-DEFINED	+5V	USER-DEFINED

only 16 of the data lines, Byte(0) and Byte(2) appear on the D08-D15 lines and Byte(1) and Byte(3) appear on the D00-D07 lines. Naturally a system cannot perform 3-and 4-byte data transfers across a 16-bit data bus so the high bytes are folded into the lower 16 bits of the data bus. In VMEbus systems that implement the full 32-bit data bus, Byte(0) appears on the D24-D31 lines, Byte(1) appears on the D16-D23 lines, Byte(2) appears on the D08-D15 lines, and Byte(3) appears on the D00-D07 lines.

Table 3-17. VMEbus Byte-specifier Signal Combinations.

BYTE LOCATIONS SELECTED	DS1*	DS0*	A01	LWORD*
SINGLE-BYTE ACCESS				
BYTE(0)	LOW	HIGH	LOW	HIGH
BYTE(1)	HIGH	LOW	LOW	HIGH
BYTE(2)	LOW	HIGH	HIGH	HIGH
BYTE(3)	HIGH	LOW	HIGH	HIGH
DOUBLE-BYTE ACCESS				
BYTE(0,1)	LOW	LOW	LOW	HIGH
BYTE(1,2)	LOW	LOW	HIGH	LOW
BYTE(2,3)	LOW	LOW	HIGH	HIGH
TRIPLE-BYTE ACCESS				
BYTE(0,1,2)	LOW	HIGH	LOW	LOW
BYTE(1,2,3)	HIGH	LOW	LOW	LOW
QUAD-BYTE ACCESS				
BYTE(0,1,2,3)	LOW	LOW	LOW	LOW

Six signals effect data transfer over the VMEbus: AS*, WRITE*, DS0*, DS1*, DTACK*, and BERR*. When asserted by a bus master, the leading (falling) edge of AS*, the address strobe, indicates that the address lines are stable and contain a valid address. Assertion of AS* initiates a VMEbus data-transfer cycle. WRITE* indicates the direction of the data transfer. When WRITE* is asserted, the bus master is writing data to the bus slave.

Data strobes DS0* and DS1* not only designate the selected byte locations to be transferred, as discussed above, they also indicate the timing of these data transfers. During a write cycle (when WRITE* is asserted), the falling edge of a data strobe indicates that the data bus is stable and contain valid data. During a read cycle, the rising edge of a data strobe signals the end of read cycle which means that the bus slave should stop driving the data bus.

The VMEbus is an asynchronous bus. The bus master initiates a transfer cycle by putting an ap-propriate address on the bus, asserting WRITE* if necessary, and then asserting AS* and one or both data strobes. The slave then asserts DTACK* (data transfer acknowledge) when it has successfully received the data (during a write cycle) or when it has put the requested data onto the bus (during a read). If something goes wrong with the transfer cycle, the slave can assert BERR* (bus error) to signal the problem. An example of such a problem might be a parity error on a memory board. When a bus master receives BERR* instead of DTACK*, it should take some appropriate action.

For block transfers, the bus master does not negate AS* after the first data transfer. Instead, it leaves AS* asserted but toggles one or both data strobes for each succeeding transfer. The continuously-asserted AS* allows the bus master to lock the bus, but removes the master's ability to signal the presence of a new address. Therefore, slaves that support block transfers must latch the initial address presented by the master at the start of the

Table 3-18. VMEbus Address-modifier Codes.

HEX CODE	AM5	AM4	AM3	AM2	AM1	AM0	FUNCTION
3F	H	H	H	H	H	H	STANDARD SUPERVISORY BLOCK TRANSFER
3E	H	H	H	H	H	L	STANDARD SUPERVISORY PROGRAM ACCESS
3D	H	H	H	H	L	H	STANDARD SUPERVISORY DATA ACCESS
3C	H	H	H	H	L	L	RESERVED
3B	H	H	H	L	H	H	STANDARD NONPRIVILEGED BLOCK TRANSFER
3A	H	H	H	L	H	L	STANDARD NONPRIVILEGED PROGRAM ACCESS
39	H	H	H	L	L	H	STANDARD NONPRIVILEGED DATA ACCESS
38	H	H	H	L	L	L	RESERVED
37	H	H	L	H	H	H	RESERVED
36	H	H	L	H	H	L	RESERVED
35	H	H	L	H	L	H	RESERVED
34	H	H	L	H	L	L	RESERVED
33	H	H	L	L	H	H	RESERVED
32	H	H	L	L	H	L	RESERVED
31	H	H	L	L	L	H	RESERVED
30	H	H	L	L	L	L	RESERVED
2F	H	L	H	H	H	H	RESERVED
2E	H	L	H	H	H	L	RESERVED
2D	H	L	H	H	L	H	SHORT SUPERVISORY ACCESS
2C	H	L	H	H	L	L	RESERVED
2B	H	L	H	L	H	H	RESERVED
2A	H	L	H	L	H	L	RESERVED
29	H	L	H	L	H	L	SHORT NONPRIVILEGED ACCESS
28	H	L	H	L	L	L	RESERVED
27	H	L	L	H	H	H	RESERVED
26	H	L	L	H	H	L	RESERVED
25	H	L	L	H	L	H	RESERVED
24	H	L	L	H	L	L	RESERVED
23	H	L	L	L	H	H	RESERVED
22	H	L	L	L	H	L	RESERVED
21	H	L	L	L	L	H	RESERVED
20	H	L	L	L	L	L	RESERVED
1F	L	H	H	H	H	H	USER-DEFINED
1E	L	H	H	H	H	L	RESERVED USER-DEFINED
1D	L	H	H	H	L	H	USER-DEFINED
1C	L	H	H	H	L	L	USER-DEFINED

1B	L	H	H	L	H	H	USER-DEFINED
1A	L	H	H	L	H	L	USER-DEFINED
19	L	H	H	L	L	H	USER-DEFINED
18	L	H	H	L	L	L	USER-DEFINED
17	L	H	L	H	H	H	USER-DEFINED
16	L	H	L	H	H	L	USER-DEFINED
15	L	H	L	H	L	H	USER-DEFINED
14	L	H	L	H	L	L	USER-DEFINED
13	L	H	L	L	H	H	USER-DEFINED
12	L	H	L	L	H	L	USER-DEFINED
11	L	H	L	L	L	H	USER-DEFINED
10	L	H	L	L	L	L	USER-DEFINED
0F	L	L	H	H	H	H	ENTENDED SUPERVISORY BLOCK TRANSFER
0E	L	L	H	H	H	L	EXTENDED SUPERVISORY PROGRAM ACCESS
0D	L	L	H	H	L	H	EXTENDED SUPERVISORY DATA ACCESS
0C	L	L	H	H	L	L	RESERVED
0B	L	L	H	L	H	H	EXTENDED NONPRIVILEGED BLOCK TRANSFER
0A	L	L	H	L	H	L	EXTENDED NONPRIVILEGED PROGRAM ACCESS
09	L	L	H	L	L	H	EXTENDED NONPRIVILEGED DATA ACCESS
08	L	L	H	L	L	L	RESERVED
07	L	L	L	H	H	H	RESERVED
06	L	L	L	H	H	L	RESERVED
05	L	L	L	H	L	H	RESERVED
04	L	L	L	H	L	L	RESERVED
03	L	L	L	L	H	H	RESERVED
02	L	L	L	L	H	L	RESERVED
01	L	L	L	L	L	H	RESERVED
00	L	L	L	L	L	L	RESERVED

L = LOW SIGNAL LEVEL

H = HIGH SIGNAL LEVEL

block transfer and then increment that address at the end of each transfer cycle.

This same bus-locking feature permits a master to perform a read-modify-write cycle which is very important in multiprocessor systems because memory locations can contain information regarding the availability of system resources. This information, often called a semaphore, indicates whether or not a resource is in use. A bus master can read the memory location, determine whether the resource is in use, and then write to the location to signal that it has taken possession of the resource.

Without bus locking, one master could read the semaphore location and while it was making a determination of the resource's status, another bus master could (theoretically) get control of the bus and also read the semaphore. Thus, both bus masters could decide that the resource was available and then both bus masters would take possession of the resource. Pandemonium would result when both bus masters issued conflicting instructions to the luckless resource.

To prevent this situation, a read-modify-write cycle allows a bus master to get the semaphore value and change it in one, uninterruptable bus cycle. The VMEbus supports this indivisible transfer cycle by allowing a bus master to keep AS* asserted between the read and write portions of the read-modify-write cycle. A 68000's test-and-set instruction makes good use of this type of cycle.

The VMEbus supports multiple bus masters through its DTB arbitration sub-bus. Three types of signal lines comprise the DTB arbitration sub-bus: bus requests (BR1*-BR3*), bus-grant inputs (BG1IN*-BG3IN*), and bus-grant outputs (BG1OUT*-BG3OUT*). A bus master requests control of the bus by asserting a bus request. This request is received by a bus arbiter. The arbiter grants control of the bus by asserting the proper bus-grant input of slot 1 (the first card slot) in the VMEbus card cage.

Bus-grant lines are daisy-chained among VMEbus boards. That means that a bus-grant signal enters a board through its BGXIN* pin and exits the board through its BGXOUT* pin. A board's BGXOUT* pin is connected to the BGXIN* pin of the next board in the card cage. Thus, a board that is not requesting the bus on a particular bus-request level passes bus grants that it receives on down the line. Therefore, you can prioritize VMEbus masters by assigning bus-request levels to them and by arranging the boards physically in the card cage. The farther away a bus master is from the bus arbiter, the less priority it has.

When a bus master gets control of the bus, it asserts BBSY* (bus busy) to prevent any other master from taking control of the bus. To prevent bus hogging, the bus arbiter can assert BCLR* (bus clear) when it receives a bus request. BCLR* is designed to kick a bus master off the bus to allow another master to take control.

The VMEbus interrupt structure also employs this daisy-chain concept. Requesters generate interrupts by asserting one of seven interrupt-request lines (IRQ1*-IRQ7*). When a VMEbus interrupt handler receives an interrupt request, it generates an interrupt acknowledge cycle by driving the low three address-bus lines (A01-A03) with the interrupt level being acknowledged and by asserting IACK* (interrupt acknowledge).

A VMEbus interrupt handler can reside on any card in a VMEbus system. In fact, multiple handlers can reside on multiple cards, as long as each handler manages a different group of interrupt request lines. The IACK* signal line runs the length of the VMEbus so it can be driven by any card. In addition, the IACK* line is connected to the IACKIN* pin of slot 1. The card in slot 1 passes this signal through to slot 2 through its IACKOUT* pin, and so on.

When an interrupt-acknowledge cycle occurs, the appropriate interrupt handler acknowledges the interrupt and obtains an interrupt status/ID byte by conducting an interrupt-acknowledge cycle. IACK* is asserted at the beginning of the cycle and ripples through the card cage, starting at slot 1, until the requesting card intercepts the acknowledge and places its response on the data bus. Thus, like the DTB bus arbitration, interrupters are prioritized by the interrupt-request level they generate and by their proximity to slot 1.

The utility sub-bus, comprising six lines, supplies the VMEbus with several essential or potentially-useful signals. SYSRESET* (system reset) puts all of the cards on the bus into a known, stable state. Any card and more than one card on the VMEbus can drive SYSRESET*. A power-monitor module incorporated into every VMEbus system can also drive SYSRESET* when the ac or dc power falls out of tolerance. The power-monitor module also asserts ACFAIL* when the 60-Hz power line disappears.

SYSFAIL* (system failure) works in conjuction with a system's power-on self test. All boards in a system are supposed to assert SYSFAIL* with an open-collector driver until they verify their own operation or until a bus master checks them out and tells them they're OK. A board can also drive SYSFAIL* low if it detects a failure in its operation or feels ill for any other reason.

SYSCLK (system clock) is a fixed-frequency, 16-MHz clock with a 50% duty cycle. It has no fixed phase relationship with any of the other signals on the VMEbus. It's there in case a VMEbus card should happen to need a 16-MHz signal. Of course, a card can also divide the 16-MHz SYSCLK down to a lower frequency.

That leaves two signal lines on the VMEbus for us to explore: SERCLK (serial clock) and SERDAT* (serial data). These lines allow an entirely separate, serial bus to operate in tandem with the VMEbus. Motorola and the IEEE are working on such a bus, called the VMSbus, but the signal definitions and timings are not part of the VMEbus specification.

VMEbus Bus Timing

Figure 3-20 illustrates the timing for a VMEbus transfer cycle. To start the cycle, the bus master places the address, the address-modifier, and the LWORD* signal lines at appropriate signal levels. At least 35 ns after those lines have stabilized, the bus master can assert AS*. The bus master can also assert the appropriate data strobe or strobes 10 ns after the address has stabilized. The data strobes must both be asserted within 10 ns of each other but either one can be asserted first.

After AS* and at least one data strobe are asserted, the addressed slave can respond to the cycle. It does this by asserting DTACK* to successfully complete the transfer cycle or BERR* to abort the cycle. The bus master can terminate the cycle by negating AS* and the data strobes immediately upon receiving the asserted DTACK*.

The only difference in the control-line states between VMEbus read and write cycles is the state of the WRITE* line. The bus master must assert WRITE* at least 35 ns before it asserts a data strobe if it wishes to perform a write cycle. During a write data transfer, the bus master must also place data onto the data bus at least 35 ns before asserting a data strobe. During a read cycle, the bus slave must place the requested data on the data bus before asserting DTACK*.

VMEbus Physical Description

The VMEbus specification describes two sizes for VMEbus boards: a single-height board and a double-height board. The single-height board incorporates only the P1 VMEbus connector and measures 3.937 inches by 6.299 inches (100 mm by 160mm). The double-height board may incorporate both the P1 and P2 connectors, but it may only have a P1 connector. The double-height board measures 9.187 inches by 6.299 inches (233.35 mm by 160

Fig. 3-20. A VMEbus data-transfer (read or write) bus-timing diagram.

Fig. 3-21. The Force CPU-32 single-board computer for the VMEbus incorporates a Motorola 68030 microprocessor running as fast as 30 MHz, 1M bytes of static RAM, 4 sockets that hold as much as 512K bytes of EPROM storage, a real-time executive and operating-system software kernal called VMEPROM, two multiprotocol RS-232C serial ports, the VMEbus interface, and a private bus interface based on the VSB extension to the VMEbus. Courtesy of Force Computers, Inc.

mm). VMEbus card cages can be designed to accommodate single-height boards, double-height boards, or a combination of both board sizes.

Some companies have designed single-height VMEbus cards with an additional connector along the side. This extra connector allows you to plug a second board onto the first, adding functions and turning the board into a double-height card.

VMEbus Status

In 1987, the VMEbus became an IEEE and ANSI standard 1014-1987. In addition, many manufacturers make a wide variety of boards for the VMEbus. Also, the bus has its own trade association that supports VMEbus activities around the world, publishes a magazine called VMEbus Systems, and produces a product catalog containing information about member-company products. The VMEbus International Trade Association can be reached at:

VITA
10229 N Scottsdale Rd
Suite E
Scottsdale, AZ 85253
(602) 951-8866

Chapter Summary

We've looked at quite a few busses in this chapter, from simple 8-bit to the high-performance, 32-bit architectures. Every bus represents an engineer's or group of engineers' solution for supporting multi-board microprocessor systems. Every bus excels in certain applications and does not fit very well into others. The large and more complex the bus, the more it costs. The smaller and less expensive busses have somewhat reduced performance. Therefore, the more bus architectures you study, the better you will be able to select the appropriate bus for any given application.

Chapter 4

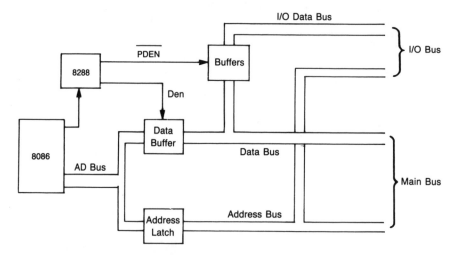

Parallel Interfacing

Microcomputer-to-peripheral interfaces are designed to link microprocessor busses with peripheral devices. As such, they usually take the form of a board plugged into the microprocessor bus. A cable links the interface board with the peripheral. The major concern is with the signals which are passed across this cable, and the circuitry on the interface board required to generate these signals.

This study starts with the parallel type of interface because they are the least complex. Some parallel interfaces can be built with a single TTL integrated circuit. Conversely, some parallel interfacing techniques, such as HPIB, are quite intricate and require much more complex circuitry. The full spectrum of parallel interfaces will be discussed in this chapter.

CLASSIFICATIONS

Parallel interfaces can be classified by two features. The first is the number of bits transferred in parallel by the interface (the data path), and the second is the type of handshake used to move these bits between the computer and the peripheral.

Data-paths range from a single bit to 16-bit, 32-bit and even wider. The most common size for 8-bit microprocessors is the 8-bit data path. This allows the microprocessor to transfer a full data word over the interface during each transfer. What is most interesting about the 8-bit parallel interface is that it is also the most popular size for 16-bit microprocessors. There are two reasons for this. The first is because of the number of 8-bit peripherals available which were originally designed for 8-bit microcomputers, such as printers. The second reason is that ASCII, the most popular character code (see Chapter 1) requires at least a 7-bit interface. Usually, that is rounded up to 8 bits.

The second factor used to classify parallel interfaces is the type of handshake used to move information over the data lines. There are zero-wire handshakes, one-wire handshakes, two-wire handshakes and three-wire handshakes. Within these four classifications there is variation as to how the wires are actually used for the handshake. There are pulsed and interlocked handshake methods. All will be discussed.

Classification by handshaking method is more useful for this discussion than the width of the data path. This is because the same handshake wires can be used for any number of data lines. Therefore, this chapter has been written using handshaking as the classification. Please remember that the methods discussed apply to any data-path width.

THE ZERO-WIRE HANDSHAKE

If ever there was a simple interface, the parallel output, zero-wire handshake is it. Figure 4-1 illustrates how the interface may be constructed. An eight-bit latch is used to store the state of the processor's data bus when an output occurs to the address the circuit has been designed to respond to.

The NAND gate at the bottom of the figure has two inputs. One is asserted when the address of the circuit appears on the microprocessor address bus. Generation of "my address" may require the comparison of the states of address and control lines from the microprocessor. This comparison is frequently done with exclusive-OR gates.

A write pulse may be directly generated by the microprocessor or may have to be decoded from microprocessor address- and control-line states.

When "write pulse" is asserted at the same time "address valid" is asserted, the output of the NAND gate is driven low. When the write pulse is negated, the output of the NAND gate is driven high, the resting state.

We are concerned with that point in time where the write pulse has ended and the NAND gate output is driven high. On the rising edge of that signal, the latch takes the states of the processor data bus lines and freezes them inside the latch. The states are reproduced on the output lines of the latch.

The circuit in Fig. 4-1 is capable of remembering the state of the microprocessor data bus at a specified point in time. This time corresponds to when the microprocessor is outputting information to the parallel interface. Thus we can output an 8-bit value to this circuit and that value will remain on the output lines of the latch until we output another value to the parallel interface or turn off the computer.

We can build a 16-bit interface by adding a second 8-bit latch. By connecting the data inputs of this second latch to the upper 8-bits of a 16-bit data bus, and the clock input to the NAND-gate output, we have a 16-bit parallel output interface.

A zero-wire handshake, parallel-output interface can be used to drive simple peripherals such as lights or relays. Devices such as these do not have handshaking requirements. Each of the output lines

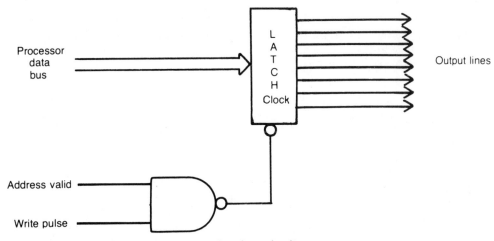

Fig. 4-1. A parallel, zero-wire handshake, output-interface circuit.

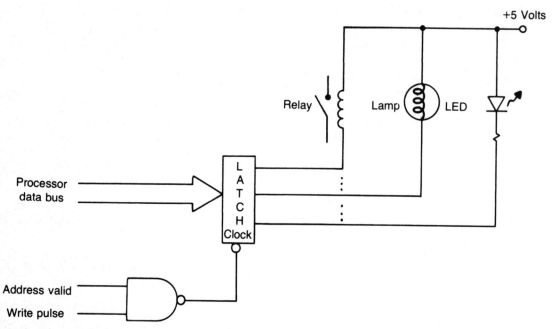

Fig. 4-2. A parallel, zero-wire handshake, output interface used to drive a relay, a lamp, and a light-emitting diode (LED).

from the interface can be used to drive a light or relay. Such configurations are shown in **Fig. 4-2** with relays, incandescent lamps and light-emitting diodes (LEDs) connected to the interface outputs.

Note that the lights and relays are connected between the latch outputs and the +5 volt power supply. This design will light the lamp or activate the relay when the associated bit in the latch is a zero. Most designs using TTL circuits use this approach because TTL outputs are much better at sinking current than they are at sourcing current. The more current drawn through the lamp, the brighter the light.

Also note the resistor in series with the LED. This is called a current-limiting resistor. It prevents excessive current from flowing through the LED when it is turned on. An LED operates with a voltage drop of approximately 2 volts, so the current-limiting resistor drops the remaining voltage. Typical resistor values for 5-volt LED drivers are 220 to 330 ohms.

Figure 4-3 shows a zero-wire handshake, parallel-input interface. It too is 8-bits wide. There

is a great similarity between the zero-wire handshake input and output interfaces. The NAND gate is present once again and one of its inputs is tied to "my address." The other input, however, is connected to a processor "read pulse." When the processor reads a value from the address assigned to this parallel input interface, the buffer is enabled and the information present on the buffer inputs is placed on the processor data bus. All of this must occur within the read-cycle time of the processor.

A very good use for the zero-wire handshake, parallel interface is to read the status of a bank of switches. A simple circuit is shown in **Fig. 4-4**. Each of the buffer inputs is connected to a switch and a resistor. The resistors are called "pullups." They "pull" the buffer inputs up to near +5 volts when the associated switch is open. When the switch is closed, the input is grounded.

A read to the proper address performed by the microprocessor will cause the states of the input lines of the interface buffer to be placed on the processor data bus so that the processor may read them. The input lines are controlled by the states

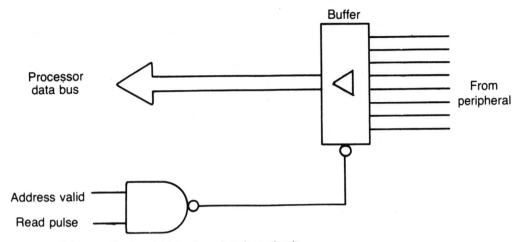

Fig. 4-3. A parallel, zero-wire handshake, input-interface circuit.

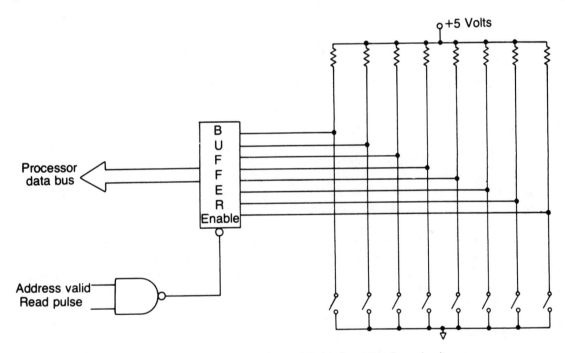

Fig. 4-4. Reading switches using a parallel, zero-wire handshake, input-interface circuit.

of the attached switches, as discussed in the previous paragraph. This 8-bit parallel input interface is limited to reading only eight switches.

A more complex switch interface can be built with one 8-bit output interface and one 8-bit input interface. Such a circuit is shown in **Fig.** 4-5, it is called a switch matrix, or keyboard scanner. A grid of wires is used to connect to the switches. A switch is wired between row and column wires at each grid intersection. Other than the switch connections, the rows and columns are not connected together. A pullup resistor on each row wire pulls the wire up

147

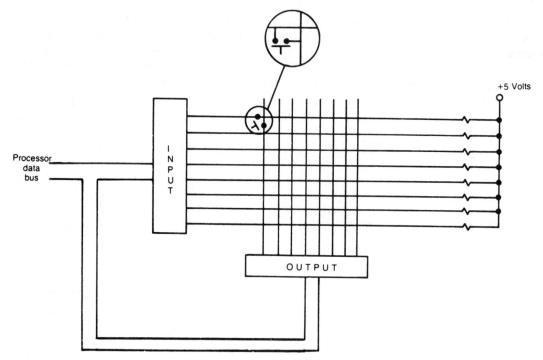

Fig. 4-5. Using a zero-wire handshake input and output interface to read a matrix of switches.

to +5 volts if all switches connected to that row are open.

Operation of this scanner is simple. The microprocessor initializes the circuit by placing an FF_{hex} in the latch of the output interface. This causes all the column wires to be driven high. If a switch in the matrix is closed, it will try to drive its attached row wire high also. Since the row wires are already high from the pullup resistors, no change is observed at the input to the parallel input interface.

The microprocessor then outputs a $7F_{hex}$ to the output interface, causing one column wire to be driven low. This is because the most significant bit of the byte written to the output interface is a zero, forcing the associated latch output to be driven low. If any of the switches attached to that column are closed, the row or rows attached to the closed switch or switches will also be driven low. The microprocessor can now read the input interface to discover the closed switches by looking for zeroes in the byte obtained from the interface.

Switches are uniquely identified by a row and column address. Each switch will force only one row low, and only when the appropriate column is driven low. The microprocessor scans the columns by outputting 7F, BF, DF, EF, F7, FB, FD, and FE (hex) in sequence. These numbers represent the eight, 8-bit values which have a single zero bit. Try writing down the values in binary to observe the "walking zero." The single zero bit corresponds to the column to be driven.

In between each output, the microprocessor reads the input interface. If the value FF_{hex} is read back, no switches attached to the low column wire are closed. If some other value than FF_{hex} is read back, at least one switch for the energized column is closed and the processor looks at the individual bits to determine which switch or switches are closed.

Parallel input interfaces may be used to read any signal which is normally in one state or another. A zero-wire parallel input interface is not especially useful for looking at signals which frequently change state. This is because there is no time information supplied by the interface—there is no way of knowing when a signal changed state, only that it was in one state last time the interface was read and in the opposite state this time.

Parallel interfaces with no handshake wires are always unidirectional. There are no wires to indicate direction on the data path. If the data direction over the interface must be controlled, then the timing of the data transfer over the data lines must be controlled. Handshake lines are the answer.

THE ONE-WIRE HANDSHAKE

Peripheral devices which are more complex than lights and switches generally require more complex interfaces. The next level of complexity is achieved by adding a single handshake wire to indicate when information is valid on the data lines.

We really have already looked at one-wire handshakes. The output latch and input buffer of the zero-wire-handshake parallel interface were connected to the microprocessor through an 8-bit data bus and a single wire which informed the latch or buffer when the microprocessor was accessing the interface. The clock input on the latch and the enable input on the buffer are the essence of the single-wire output and input handshakes.

A one-wire parallel-output interface is shown in **Fig. 4-6**. Note that it has been built from a zero-wire parallel-output interface. Three D-type flip-flops and an inverter have been added to generate the peripheral-write-pulse handshake signal. A timing diagram for this circuit is shown in **Fig. 4-7**.

The sequence starts when the microprocessor write pulse (WP) ends, on the negative edge. This edge is converted to a positive edge by the inverter, and used to toggle the first D flip-flop. The

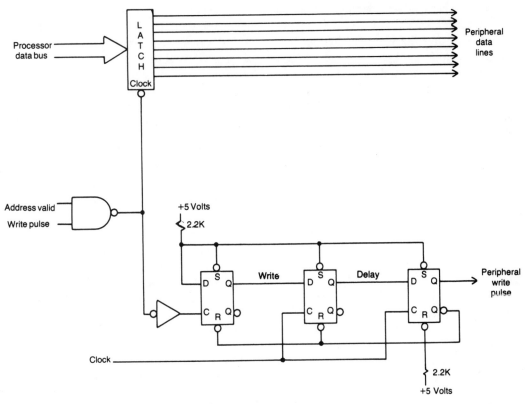

Fig. 4-6. A parallel, one-wire handshake, output-interface circuit.

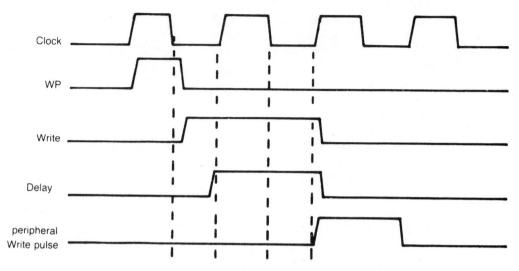

Fig. 4-7. Timing diagram for a parallel, one-wire handshake, output-interface circuit.

D input to this flip-flop is tied high, so the flip-flop is always set when a positive edge appears at its clock input. The set flip-flop indicates that an output operation has been started.

Some time after the write flip-flop has been set, the second flip-flop will receive a positive edge from the clock signal. This will cause the flip-flop to set also, because its D input is high. This is a delay flip-flop. Its purpose is to create a delay between the time the microprocessor places information in the latch and the time the interface signals an output operation to the peripheral device.

A delay is necessary to give the data lines to the peripheral device time to settle after being changed. Settling time required is determined by the length of the cable between the microprocessor and the peripheral device and by how well the latch can drive the cable and the peripheral.

The delay will range from slightly more than one cycle of clock, to almost two cycles. The range of delay is caused by the uncertainty of when a processor write pulse will occur with respect to clock's positive edge. This uncertainty can be eliminated by using the microprocessor clock as the clock to the interface's delay flip-flop. Then the write pulse will always have a well defined relationship to the clock, since microprocessor control signals are all synchronized to the microprocessor's clock input.

Delay can be adjusted by varying the frequency of clock.

On the next positive edge of clock, the peripheral-write-pulse flip-flop will be set. This flip-flop performs two tasks. The first is the generation of the peripheral write pulse while the second is to reset the write and delay flip-flops with the Q output. The peripheral write pulse lasts exactly one cycle of clock. Then, on the next positive edge of clock, the peripheral-write-pulse flip-flop will be cleared because its D input is a zero. Remember that the delay flip-flop was cleared at the start of the peripheral write pulse. This brings the circuit back to a stable state. Nothing more will happen until the processor writes another byte to the latch.

An important feature of the one-wire parallel-output interface is the ability to stretch the write pulse from the microprocessor. There are two reasons to do this. The first is cable settling time, discussed previously. The second is that the device being interfaced may be too slow to respond to the microprocessor write pulse. Some circuits built of CMOS must have write pulses of a microsecond or more while write cycles on many processors last for only about 0.5 microsecond.

A one-wire-handshake parallel-input interface is shown in Fig. 4-8. Again, the interface has been built from a zero-wire handshake interface, of the

150

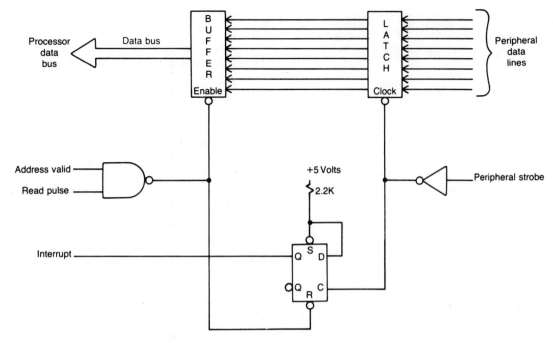

Fig. 4-8. A parallel, one-wire handshake, input-interface circuit.

input type this time. In this example, the peripheral device wishes to send the microprocessor some information at a particular time. It places the information on the peripheral data lines and then pulses the peripheral strobe. This causes the latch to capture the information on the peripheral data lines and sets the interrupt flip-flop, both on the trailing edge of the peripheral-strobe pulse. **Figure 4-9** illustrates the timing for this interface.

Interrupts are a means of getting the microprocessor's attention at any time. The interrupt will cause the microprocessor to enter an interrupt service routine, written so that the processor reads the input interface when an interrupt occurs.

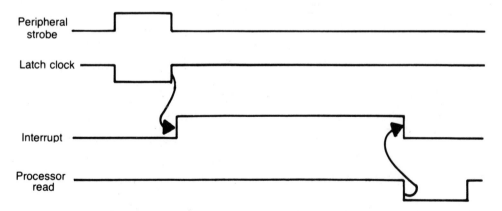

Fig. 4-9. Timing diagram for a parallel, one-wire handshake, input-interface circuit.

151

The read of the input buffer will place the contents of the latch on the processor data bus for the processor to read and will automatically reset the interrupt flip-flop.

Note that the peripheral strobe is connected to the clock input of the interrupt flip-flop. The inverted peripheral-strobe line which drives the clock input to the latch could have been connected to the set input to the flip-flop. This would have produced an interrupt at the appropriate time also.

There are two reasons why that would be a poor design. The interrupt would occur at the start of the peripheral-strobe pulse instead of at the end since the flip-flop set input has an immediate effect. It is possible that the microprocessor would be interrupted and respond to that interrupt before the peripheral strobe was negated. In that case, the interrupt would remain because the set input to the flip-flop would still be asserted. A second interrupt would occur, although the peripheral only transferred one piece of data.

Also, the interrupt would occur before the latch had actually accepted the data, since it does so at the trailing edge of the peripheral-strobe pulse. That means the processor could possibly get bad data if it serviced the interrupt too quickly. Using the clock input to the flip-flop to generate the interrupt avoids both of these problems.

Though we have now brought interface timing under control with a single handshake wire, there is still no data-direction control line. A bidirectional interface can be built with a single line for handshaking and another to control data direction. The

direction-control line may control only the data direction or it may also control which device, computer or peripheral, controls the handshake line also. You might want to try combining the one-wire handshake input and output example circuits to create a bidirectional interface as an exercise.

THE TWO-WIRE HANDSHAKE

A major problem with interfaces having a single handshake wire is that there is no way to tell if the receiving device is ready for a data transfer. The lone handshake line is used to present an endless series of "here it is" messages. There is no way for the receiving device to say, "Hold up a while, I'm not ready yet." By adding a second handshake line, this problem is solved.

From this point on, the circuits become too complex to show with simple designs using latches, buffers, flip-flops, and gates. Therefore, we will study the handshaking signals here and postpone the study of the circuits and software to implement the handshakes until later in this chapter, when we discuss the integrated circuits specially designed for parallel interfaces.

Figure 4-10 illustrates one type of two-wire handshake for parallel output ports, the pulsed handshake. The interface circuitry places the data to be output on the data lines and then the strobes are pulsed. So far, this is exactly how the one-wire handshake for parallel output interfaces operates. The difference is that the peripheral has an acknowledge line which it controls.

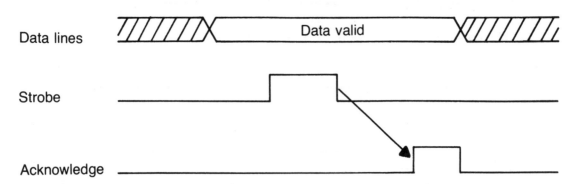

Fig. 4-10. Timing diagram for a pulsed, two-wire handshake, output interface.

The acknowledge line is used to inform the parallel-interface circuitry when the peripheral has taken the information. It is also used to signal the readiness of the peripheral for another data transfer. Both of these messages are conveyed by the trailing edge of the acknowledge pulse.

The disadvantage of pulsed handshakes is that the state of the interface cannot be determined at all times. For example, the resting state of both the strobe and acknowledge lines is low. However, this same state is encountered in the middle of a transfer, when strobe has just been negated but acknowledge has not yet been asserted. Edge-detection circuitry must be used to determine where in the cycle we are. The rising edge of strobe starts the data transfer and the falling edge of acknowledge ends it.

A better use of two handshake lines is the fully interlocked handshake technique, shown in Fig. 4-11. The same two handshake wires, strobe and acknowledge, are used but with different timings. Data is placed on the data bus and strobe is then asserted, starting the transfer. Strobe is maintained in the asserted state until acknowledge is asserted. Then strobe is negated and acknowledge follows, ending the cycle.

The fully interlocked handshake allows us to determine the state of the transfer at any time. If neither strobe nor acknowledge is asserted, no transfer is currently taking place. If strobe is asserted and acknowledge is not, the transfer has just started. If both strobe and acknowledge are asserted, the transfer is about to complete. There is no possibility of losing or missing pulses because each signal is held asserted until acknowledged by the other signal.

There are four signal transitions in the fully interlocked handshake technique: assertion of strobe, assertion of acknowledge, negation of strobe, and negation of acknowledge. Each transition adds a delay to the handshake, since the last three are results of preceding transitions. For very high speed data transfers, the number of transitions in the handshake can be reduced by a technique called *Non-Return-to-Zero*, or NRZ.

An interlocked, NRZ handshake is shown in Fig. 4-12. Two data transfers are shown. There is only a single transition of strobe and acknowledge per transfer. When both strobe and acknowledge are at the same logic level, no transfer is in progress. A transfer starts when data is placed on the data bus and strobe changes state. Later, the peripheral responds by changing the state of acknowledge. This results in both strobe and acknowledge being at the same state again, completing the transfer.

Note that there are two resting states and two "transfer in progress" states. The two resting states are:

1) Strobe = 0, Acknowledge = 0

2) Strobe = 1, Acknowledge = 1

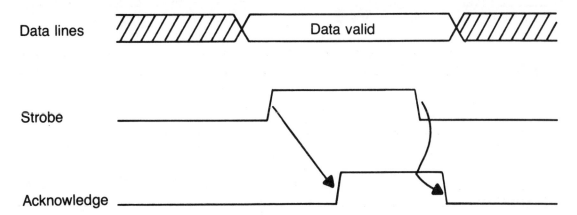

Fig. 4-11. Timing diagram for an interlocked, two-wire handshake, output interface.

153

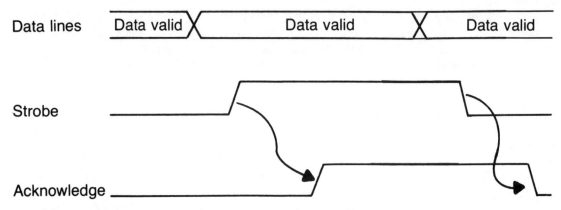

Fig. 4-12. Timing diagram for an interlocked, non-return-to-zero (NRZ) two-wire handshake, output interface.

The two active, transfer-in-progress states are:

1) Strobe = 1, Acknowledge = 0

2) Strobe = 0, Acknowledge = 1

An exclusive-OR gate connected to strobe and acknowledge can be used to detect the resting/busy status of the interface. If both inputs are zero or both inputs are 1, the output of the exclusive-OR gate will be 0, signaling a resting state. If the inputs don't match, the output of the exclusive-OR gate will be 1, signaling a busy interface, with a transfer in progress.

Two-wire-handshake, parallel-input interfaces work in a manner very similar to their output counterparts. Figure 4-13 shows a pulsed two-wire parallel input handshake. The interface requests information from the peripheral by pulsing strobe.

The peripheral obtains the requested information, places it on the data lines and pulses acknowledge. The interface must have a data latch similar to the one used in the one-wire-handshake parallel input interface to capture the data during the acknowledge pulse.

Figure 4-14 illustrates a fully interlocked, two-wire input handshake. Again the interface requests information from the peripheral by asserting strobe. This time, however, strobe remains asserted. The peripheral obtains the requested information, places it on the data lines and asserts acknowledge. At this point, the data lines are to remain valid until strobe is negated. This gives the processor ample time to read the data lines, no latch is needed. When the data has been accepted by the processor, strobe is negated. The processor may then negate acknowledge, completing the transfer.

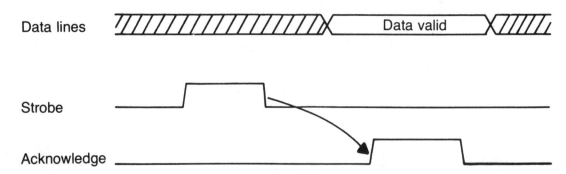

Fig. 4-13. Timing diagram for a pulsed, two-wire handshake, input interface.

154

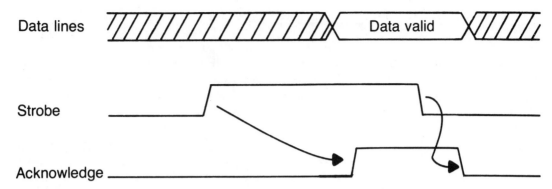

Fig. 4-14. Timing diagram for an interlocked, two-wire handshake, input interface.

Once again, the interlocked handshake has proven its superior operation. No data latch is needed in the interface because the data remains valid as long as strobe and acknowledge are asserted. Timing problems are much easier to handle in fully interlocked interface designs.

An NRZ, fully-interlocked, input handshake is shown in **Fig. 4-15**. The resting state for the interface is when both strobe and acknowledge are at the same logic levels. When strobe is toggled, the transfer is initiated. The peripheral obtains the requested information and places it on the data bus. Then the peripheral toggles acknowledge to complete the cycle. As long as strobe is not toggled again, the information is on the data lines to be read, maintaining the advantage of the interlocked signals.

Note that with two handshake lines, the computer initiates the data transfer with a strobe line and the peripheral completes it with the acknowledge line. By adding a data-direction line to the interface

design, bidirectionality can be achieved. This may require bidirectional hardware on the data lines also.

THE THREE-WIRE HANDSHAKE

Even though a two-wire handshake protocol is entirely adequate for interfacing a single peripheral to a computer, three-wire handshakes have been developed. Some of these designs seem to not really need the third wire: it is there to confound and confuse. Others use the third wire to create a protocol which allows several peripherals to use a single interface. We will study two 3-wire handshake protocols; the Centronics Parallel interface and the IEEE-488-1978 interface bus.

The Centronics Parallel Interface

One of the earliest parallel interfaces to gather a large amount of industry support is a protocol developed by Centronics, a printer manufacturer. The

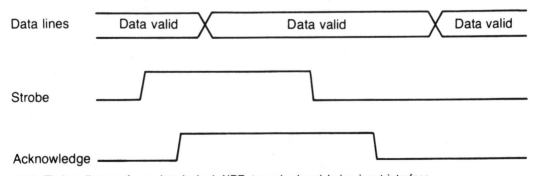

Fig. 4-15. Timing diagram for an interlocked, NRZ, two-wire handshake, input interface.

155

interface has eight data lines and three signal lines for handshaking: DATA STROBE, ACKNOWLEDGE and BUSY.

DATA STROBE is a signal line from the computer which indicates to the peripheral that the data lines have valid information on them. The data lines must have valid data on them at least one microsecond before the negative-true DATA STROBE is asserted. Data must be held valid at least one microsecond after DATA STROBE is negated. The length of time DATA STROBE is asserted may range from 1 to 500 microseconds.

The trailing edge of DATA STROBE causes the peripheral to assert ACKNOWLEDGE. In Centronics printers, the delay between the negation of DATA STROBE and the assertion of ACKNOWLEDGE is on the order of 2.5 to 10 microseconds. ACKNOWLEDGE is asserted anywhere from 2.5 to 5 microseconds.

These times assume that "normal" data transfer are occurring. Figure 4-16 illustrates the timing for the interface. Centronics calls the above sequence "Normal-Data-Input Timing." For Centronics printers, normal transfers take place when the printer is filling an internal line buffer and isn't

printing or performing some other special operation. If one of these operations is being performed, a "busy" condition exists.

A busy condition occurs when the printer is given a command to print the line in the print buffer (carriage return), or when a vertical tab, form feed, line feed, delete, bell, select, or deselect character is sent. Receipt of one of these special characters causes the printer to perform some mechanical operation that takes considerably more time than a few microseconds. In these cases, the handshake changes to "Busy Condition Timing."

The handshake mechanism during a busy condition brings the BUSY handshake line into action. After DATA STROBE is negated, BUSY is asserted instead of ACKNOWLEDGE. This indicates that the peripheral is busy and will not complete the handshake for some time. Centronics printers are busy for durations of 2 to over 300 milliseconds.

Some time after negating BUSY, the peripheral asserts the negative-true ACKNOWLEDGE line. The delay is only a few microseconds and ACKNOWLEDGE is asserted for a few microseconds. Note that busy-condition timing ends with the negation of ACKNOWLEDGE, as does normal-data-

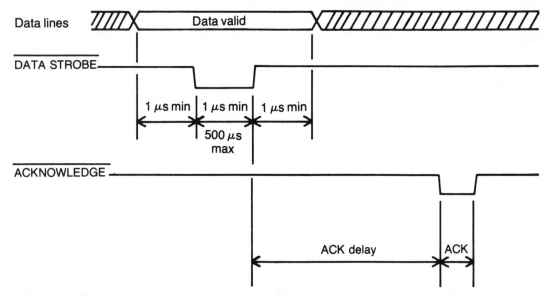

Fig. 4-16. Timing diagram for the Centronics parallel interface—normal data-input timing. Input refers to the printer receiving information from the computer, which is really an output operation from the computer's perspective.

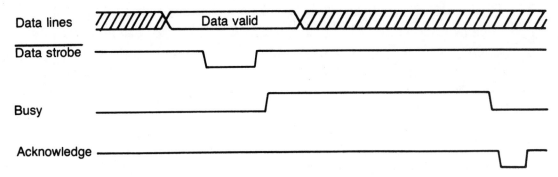

Fig. 4-17. Timing diagram for the Centronics parallel interface—BUSY—condition timing.

input timing. **Figure 4-17** illustrates the busy-condition timing for the Centronics parallel interface.

Though this is a simple handshake protocol, it has caused problems. Many manufacturers simply cannot decide what to do with the third handshake line. Why have BUSY at all, since both normal and busy handshake protocols end with the $\overline{AC}$ $\overline{KNOWLEDGE}$ pulse? To complicate matters, other manufacturers of printers which use the Centronics handshake don't always bother to implement both $\overline{ACKNOWLEDGE}$ and BUSY. They pick one or the other or include a switch that allows the end user to decide which handshake signal the printer will drive. After all, you really need only $\overline{AC}$ $\overline{KNOWLEDGE}$.

A timing example of a non-Centronics printer which uses the Centronics interface is shown in **Fig. 4-18**. This diagram is derived from an illustration in the back of the printer manual. First look at the relationship between the data lines and $\overline{DATA}$ $\overline{STROBE}$. This printer requires the data to be valid only 0.5 microsecond before $\overline{DATA\ STROBE}$ is asserted and to be held valid only 0.5 microsecond after $\overline{DATA\ STROBE}$ is negated. In addition, $\overline{DATA}$ $\overline{STROBE}$ need only be asserted for 0.5 microsecond. These times are all half of the original Centronics specification. Any computer interface designed for a Centronics printer can also drive this printer, with wide margins.

Now look at the BUSY and $\overline{ACK}$ signals of **Fig. 4-18**. These signals have a behavior different from the corresponding signals on the Centronics printer. BUSY is activated on the falling edge of $\overline{DATA}$ $\overline{STROBE}$ instead of the rising edge, and is negated after $\overline{ACK}$ is negated. Recall that the Centronics specification requires that $\overline{ACK}$ not even be asserted until BUSY is negated, if a busy condition exists.

Some computer interfaces designed for Centronics printers assume that the rising edge of $\overline{ACK}$ is the end of the transfer. That will not be quite right, since negation of BUSY will follow negation of $\overline{ACK}$ by another 5 microseconds or so. Most microcomputers can't respond to the completion of one transfer cycle with another for well over 5 microseconds, so this printer interface will work like the Centronics printers, even though the signal timings are different.

Along with a standard handshake mechanism, the Centronics interface offers a standardized connector and pin designation. The connector, a 36-pin Amphenol "Blue Ribbon" connector, is shown in **Fig. 4-19** while **Table 4-1** lists the connector input as defined by Centronics' early printers. Not all of the signals have been retained in newer printers. The key part of the standard Centronics interface are the data and handshake lines.

Other peripherals are available with Centronics-type parallel interfaces. Among these are plotters and digitizers. Many microcomputers now are manufactured with built-in Centronics parallel interfaces. It is a powerful and useful interface, despite its minor drawbacks.

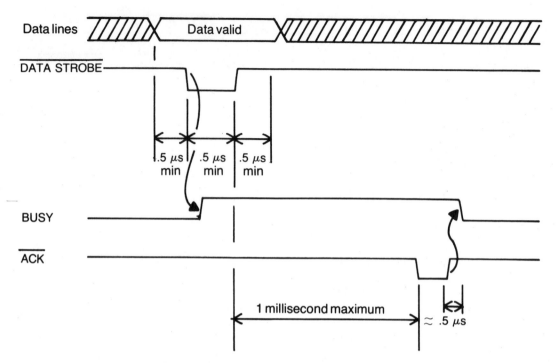

Fig. 4-18. Timing diagram for the Centronics parallel interface taken from the user's manual of a non-Centronics printer.

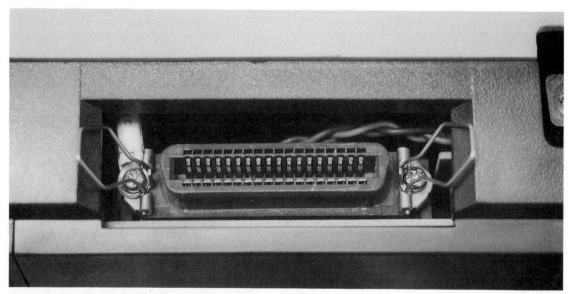

Fig. 4-19. The 36-pin, Centronics parallel-interface connector.

Table 4-1. Pinout for the Centronics Parallel Interface.

SIGNAL NAME	POSITIVE- OR NEGATIVE-TRUE	SIGNAL PIN NUMBER	ASSOCIATED GROUND WIRE PIN NUMBER
DATA STROBE	Negative	1	19
DATA 1	Positive	2	20
DATA 2	Positive	3	21
DATA 3	Positive	4	22
DATA 4	Positive	5	23
DATA 5	Positive	6	24
DATA 6	Positive	7	25
DATA 7	Positive	8	26
DATA 8	Positive	9	27
ACKNOWLEDGE	Negative	10	28
BUSY	Positive	11	29
PAPER OUT	Positive	12	None
SELECT PRINTER	Positive	13	None
Signal Ground	-	14	None
OSCXT (OSC Out)	-	15	None
Signal Ground	-	16	None
Chassis Ground	-	17	None
+5 volt supply	-	18	None
INPUT PRIME (Printer reset)	Negative	31	30
FAULT	Negative	32	None
Line Count		34	35

The IEEE-488-1978 Interface

You may have noticed the increasing complexity of the parallel interfaces as the number of handshake lines increases. Zero-wire-handshake interface protocols were quite simple and could communicate with simple devices only. One- and two-wire handshake protocols, though more complex, are useful in communicating with peripherals of moderate complexity and little intelligence. Even the Centronics parallel interface with its three handshake lines does little more than a two-wire handshake interface.

In addition, simple interfaces are designed to connect to only one peripheral. To attach a second device to your computer, you must replicate the interface circuits. This is necessary because no device-selection protocol is built into the simpler interfaces.

Computer-peripheral designers have been free for years to custom design parallel interfaces for each new peripheral; there was no standard. As a result, we have 0-, 1-, 2-, and 3-wire handshake protocols and widely varying data-path widths. This situation is similar to that which the American Railroads found

themselves in during the early 1800s. Dozens of track gauges existed and cars of one railroad could not travel on the tracks of another. Just as the railroads found it advantageous to standardize on track width, peripheral manufacturers have found it to their advantage to create standard interfaces.

As the microprocessor began to find its way into more products, a need arose for an interface which could link intelligent devices to a computer. The interface had to support high data rates and advanced interface concepts such as interrupts. In addition, there was a need for an interface protocol that could connect a computer to several peripherals with a single set of interface circuitry, to reduce the cost of interfacing.

Hewlett-Packard, a manufacturer of both computers and instruments, felt these needs strongly. In the early 1970s, engineers at Hewlett-Packard developed a very complex interface protocol which they called the Hewlett-Packard Interface Bus or HPIB. In 1975, the Institute of Electrical and Electronic Engineers (IEEE) adopted the HPIB protocol as a standard computer interface, the IEEE-488-1975. In 1978, the standard was revised and became IEEE-488-1978, the "IEEE Standard Digital Interface for Programmable Instrumentation."

A very wide assortment of peripherals can be obtained with IEEE-488 interfaces. Printers, plotters, disk drives, digitizers, voltmeters, power supplies and signal generators are a few examples. The combination of a standard interface and wide availability of devices for that interface has resulted in a new flexibility in system configuration. A computer and a few peripheral devices can be purchased and quickly connected together to create complex configurations such as circuit board testers and radiofrequency analysis systems.

Connector and pin usage are precisely specified in IEEE-STD-488-1978, as are signal levels (both voltage and current) and signal timings. Thus, building a system can be as simple as a "remove-from-the-box-and-plug-together" operation. The hardware of interconnection is defined so that two interconnected instruments can communicate. Understanding the communications, however, is not guaranteed by the standard.

Using the IEEE-488 is like the international telephone system. You can call anywhere on the Earth because a compatible communications network called the telephone system exists. Sounds that you make can reach the other end, and you will be able to hear the sounds made by the person at the other end of the connection. The hardware for communications is all in place but there is no guarantee that you will understand what the other person is saying.

Unlike the other parallel interfaces, which connect a single device with the computer, the IEEE-488 interface makes it possible to connect as many as 15 devices, including the computer. IEEE-488 is a bus, similar in concept to a microcomputer's bus.

Controllers, Talkers, and Listeners

Three types of devices exist on the IEEE-488 bus: controllers, talkers, and listeners. These entities are actually attributes, and may exist alone or in combination within any given peripheral. For ex-

ample, the IEEE-488 interface allows a computer to be a talker, listener, and controller. A voltmeter might only be a talker, able to supply the system with information, while a printer might only be a listener, accepting data from the system. Additionally, these attributes may be active or not at any given time.

Figure 4-20 illustrates how an IEEE-488 system might be configured. The lines on the right of the figure represent the signal lines of the interface. There are a total of sixteen signal lines divided into

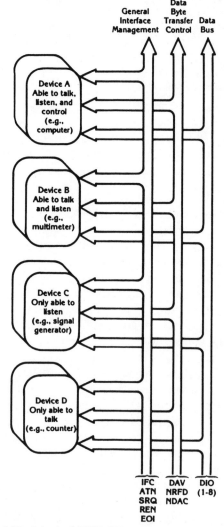

Fig. 4-20. A typical IEEE-488 system.

three groups. The first group is composed of eight data lines, forming the data bus. These signal lines are bidirectional and carry information and messages between devices on the bus.

The data-byte-transfer control group is composed of three lines called DAV (data valid), NRFD (not ready for data) and NDAC (not data accepted). As these names imply, this group is used to sequence the flow of information over the data lines. These lines form the three-wire handshake. The five remaining lines form the general interface-management group. These lines are used for control and status information pertaining to the devices connected to the bus.

Four devices are shown attached to the bus. Device A has the talker, listener, and controller attributes. As a controller, it may assign the role of active talker to any device on the bus capable of being a talker, including itself. As a talker, it can supply information to other devices on the bus. As a listener, it can accept information from the other talkers on the bus. A computer is typical of a device that would have all three attributes.

Although device A is the only controller shown in Fig. 4-20, more than one controller is allowed in an IEEE-488 system. Only one controller is allowed to be active at a time, however, to prevent conflicts. Control may be passed from one controller to another using sequences defined in the standard. One controller, designated the "system controller," becomes the active controller when the system is turned on. All other controllers must remain passive until control is passed to them.

Device B is both a talker and a listener. It can be addressed by the controller and made an active talker or listener. An active talker controls the DAV signal line in the data-byte-transfer control group. An active listener controls the NRFD and NDAC signal lines. Device C can only be a listener. Device D is only a talker. Either of these devices may be made active by the controller.

A data transaction is controlled by both the active talker and the active listener. The talker drives the bus with data. The listener accepts the information transmitted by the talker. To avoid conflict, only one talker may be active at a time. However, several simultaneous active listeners are allowed.

Transferring Information

The potential existence of several active listeners receiving data simultaneously presents a problem. The active listeners may not all accept data at the same rate. The speed of data transfer must therefore be paced by the slowest active listener, or data may be lost by some of the listeners.

Data transfer rate on the IEEE-488 bus is controlled by an electronics voting system called *open collector*. This voting system requires unanimous agreement before the data transaction is completed. Transfer of information takes place as follows:

1. All active listeners indicate on the NRFD line their state of readiness to accept a new piece of information. This signal line is usually connected to five volts through a resistor. If an active listener is not ready, it pulls the NRFD line down to zero volts by turning on a transistor connected to the signal line. The activated transistor acts as a short to ground, pulling the voltage on the NRFD line to ground potential, or zero volts. When the listener is ready to accept data, it turns off this transistor. When all active listeners turn off their transistors, the resistor connected to five volts pulls the NRFD signal line up to approximately five volts. The active talker observes the state of the NRFD line and will not start the data transfer until the signal line reaches a high voltage level.

2. The active talker observes that the NRFD line has gone high. It places a data byte on the data lines and waits two microseconds. It then asserts DAV by pulling it low to zero volts. This two microsecond wait allows the data to reach valid logic levels on the data lines. This is called *settling time*. The assertion of DAV is a signal to the active listener(s) to read the information on the data bus. The listeners acknowledge the assertion of DAV by pulling back down on NRFD immediately.

3. Previous to this point, the active listeners have held NDAC low. When DAV is asserted and all of the active listeners accept the data on the data lines, they will release NDAC. As the slowest active listener releases NDAC, the pullup resistor will cause the signal line to go high.

4. The active talker observes the NDAC line in a high state. It acknowledges the acceptance of the data by the listeners by releasing DAV. The release of DAV signals the listeners that the data transfer is complete and they again pull NDAC low in preparation for the next transfer.

A timing diagram of the complete handshake is shown in **Fig. 4-21**. Note that control of the data transfer is effected by the *active* talkers and listener(s). Once the controller has configured the bus, it takes no part in subsequent transactions until reconfiguration is desired.

Now that we have examined data transfer on the IEEE-488 bus, let's consider how the bus gets configured. One of the general interface management lines is called ATN (attention). This line is controlled by the active controller. It signifies whether the data transfers on the bus are data or control information. Data transactions are controlled by the active talker, as explained above but control transfers are controlled by the active controller.

When the controller wishes to configure the bus, it asserts the ATN line. This causes any active talker to relinquish control of the DAV line. Transmission of control information occurs in the same

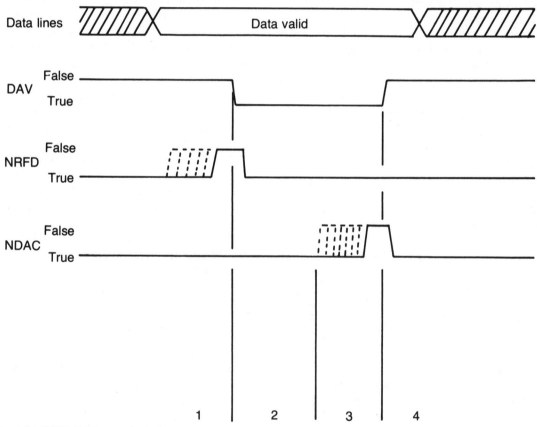

Fig. 4-21. IEEE-488 bus-cycle timing.

manner as transfer of data as explained above. The difference is that when ATN is asserted, the active controller takes the place of the active talker and both talkers and listeners accept the information. All devices, whether active or not, accept information transmitted by the controller when ATN is asserted.

The active talker and active listeners may be designated during the transmission of control information. Information is transmitted over the data lines. Table 4-2 shows what the control information means.

Note that bit 7 is not used. Bits 6 and 5 are used to classify the control information as to command type. A control transfer with bits 6 and 5 set to zero is a bus command and is used to directly control devices on the bus. Examples of bus commands are triggering of a function or the passing of control from the active listener to a passive one.

Transmission of a control byte with bit 6 set to zero and bit 5 set to 1 is used to activate a listener. A listener that observes its address in the lower 5 bits of a Listen Address control byte becomes active. When ATN is negated, it will assume control of NDAC and NRFD. Listeners that do not observe their listen addresses in a control transfer do not change state. They will be as they were before the controller asserted ATN.

There is a way to deactivate all active listeners with a single command. The five bits of the Listen Address allow 32 listen addresses. These addresses are from zero to 31. Address 31 is the "unlisten" address. Active listeners observing the unlisten address in the address field of a listen command will go inactive.

Definition of the talk addresses is similar to that for listen addresses with one exception: Any active talker that observes a talk command for another device will go inactive. Thus activating one talker guarantees deactivation of any other active talkers. This prevents conflicts on the bus. Talk address 31 is the "untalk" address. When the controller issues an untalk command, no active talkers are left on the bus.

Secondary addresses are used to address subunits within a device. Some HPIB instruments are actually clusters of devices. Secondary addressing allows addressing of a device in a cluster.

The remaining four lines in the general interface management group are used to control the interface sections of the HPIB devices. IFC (interface clear) may be used by the active controller to override all bus activity and place the bus in a known state. Such an action is abortive to any data transfers in progress and is typically used when something has gone wrong.

REN (remote enable) is a signal that allows the HPIB to control a device. The active controller indicates to an active listener whether it will use the information sent to it by a talker by the state of the REN line.

EOI (end of identify) may be used in two ways. The active talker may assert it to designate a data byte as the last in a message. EOI is also used in a serial poll, discussed later.

SRQ (service request) is a signal from a device to the active controller used to get the controller's attention. This signal is a request, not a demand. The controller may ignore SRQ as long as it wishes.

When the controller finally does acknowledge SRQ, it has to determine which device is requesting service. Since SRQ is shared by all devices on

Table 4-2. Control Information on the IEEE-488 Bus.

Bit # Information Type	7	6	5	4	3	2	1	0
Bus command	X	0	0	C	C	C	C	C
Listen Address	X	0	1	L	L	L	L	L
Talk Address	X	1	0	T	T	T	T	T
Secondary Address	X	1	1	S	S	S	S	S

the bus, the requester is not immediately known.

There are two methods a controller may use to determine the address of the device requesting service. Both methods are called *polls*. A poll is a request made by the controller for status information. The controller may request the status of each device individually, by addressing the device as a talker and sending it a serial-poll-enable command. This is one of the bus commands a controller may send when it asserts ATN. Using the serial poll, the controller can obtain eight bits of status information from the addressed device. A serial-poll-disable command is sent to the device to return it to data mode.

The advantage of serial polling is that eight bits of poll information are obtained from each device polled. One bit may be used for indicating whether the device is requesting service. The other seven bits are available for other purposes. A disadvantage of the serial poll is speed. Each device on the bus must be polled in turn since more than one device may be requesting service. A faster method of polling is called parallel poll.

A parallel poll is performed when the active controller asserts both ATN and EOI. Up to eight devices may respond, each using a different data line. The only information obtained in a parallel poll is whether a device is requesting service. This is because the device has only one bit to respond with.

One of the best features of the IEEE standard is that a system user does not have to know anything about the bus or its protocol. The standard, if followed by all the manufacturers of devices attached to the bus, guarantees that devices may talk to each other. This assumes the system builder didn't violate the standard by placing two devices at the same address or connect two system controllers to the bus.

In the early days of IEEE-488 instruments, the interfaces were quite difficult to build, due to the complexity of the bus protocol. Fortunately, the chip manufacturers saw an opportunity and designed integrated circuits which implement the IEEE-488 interface. We will look at one of these ICs later in this chapter.

The Small Computer System Interface (SCSI)

One of the most complex parallel interfaces to be developed is the Small Computer System Interface (SCSI, pronounced "scuzzy"). SCSI is based on a disk-drive interface developed by Shugart Associates. The original Shugart interface, called the SASI bus (for Shugart Associates System Interface and pronounced "sassy"), reflects the Shugart designers' preoccupation with the disk-drive side of the interface. In most SASI and SCSI systems composed of a disk controller and a computer, the disk controller board (sometimes called a bridge controller) sequences data transfers over the SASI (and SCSI) bus, not the computer. However, no matter which end controls the bus, data seems to make it from one end of the SCSI bus to the other without any problems.

The SCSI bus uses a 50-pin connector even though it's an 8-bit interface. Two different definitions for SCSI allow for single-ended (ground-referenced) and differential transmissions. **Table 4-3** lists the pin assignments for the single-ended SCSI cable and **Table 4-4** lists the differential pin assignments. A single-ended SCSI cable can be as long as 6 meters and a differential SCSI cable can stretch 25 meters.

Like the IEEE-488 standard, SCSI is a bus interface and supports as many as eight devices, numbered 0 through 7. Thus, one SCSI bus can connect several computers and peripherals together. In SCSI terminology, the device that initiates a data transfer is called the initiator (makes sense, doesn't it?) and the responding device is called the target. Each data transfer requires the presence of an initiator and a target device.

The SCSI bus supports multiple initiators, however only one initiator can control the bus at any given time. To effect a data transfer, an initiator must first obtain control of the SCSI bus through arbitration. Before arbitration can start, an initiator must wait for the SCSI bus to become inactive (the bus-free phase), signaled by the negation of both the BSY (busy) and SEL (select) control lines. After the

Table 4-3. Single-ended SCSI Signals and Pin Assignments.

PIN	SIGNAL NAME	PIN	SIGNAL NAME
1	GND	2	– DB(0)
3	GND	4	– DB(1)
5	GND	6	– DB(2)
7	GND	8	– DB(3)
9	GND	10	– DB(4)
11	GND	12	– DB(5)
13	GND	14	– DB(6)
15	GND	16	– DB(7)
17	GND	18	– DB(PARITY)
19	GND	20	GND
21	GND	22	GND
23	GND	24	GND
25	NOT CONNECTED	26	TERMINATION POWER
27	GND	28	GND
29	GND	30	GND
31	GND	32	– ATN
33	GND	34	GND
35	GND	36	– BSY
37	GND	38	– ACK
39	GND	40	– RST
41	GND	42	– MSG
43	GND	44	– SEL
45	GND	46	– C/D
47	GND	48	– REQ
49	GND	50	– I/O

NOTE: A - PREFIX SIGNIFIES A LOW-TRUE SIGNAL

bus has been in the bus-free phase for at least 800 nanoseconds, an initiator can start the arbitration phase by asserting BSY and by asserting the SCSI data bit (DB(0) through DB(7)) that corresponds to its own ID code.

More than one initiator can vie for the SCSI bus during the arbitration phase. Imagine several initiators all waiting for a turn on the bus. The last data transaction of an earlier transfer completes and the bus enters the bus-free phase. When the SCSI bus has been in the bus-free phase for 800 nanoseconds, all the initiators that want a turn assert BSY and place their ID codes on the bus data lines.

After 2.2 microseconds, the initiators examine the data lines and determine which of the competing initiators has won control of the bus. The initiator with the highest priority (highest-numbered ID code) wins control of the bus and indicates its

Table 4-4. Differential SCSI Signals and Pin Assignments.

PIN	SIGNAL NAME	PIN	SIGNAL NAME
1	SHIELD GND	2	GND
3	+ DB(0)	4	-DB(0)
5	+ DB(1)	6	-DB(1)
7	+ DB(2)	8	-DB(2)
9	+ DB(3)	10	-DB(3)
11	+ DB(4)	12	-DB(4)
13	+ DB(5)	14	-DB(5)
15	+ DB(6)	16	-DB(6)
17	+ DB(7)	18	-DB(7)
19	+ DB(PARITY)	20	-DB (PARITY)
21	DIFFSENS	22	GND
23	GND	24	GND
25	TERMINATION POWER	26	TERMINATION POWER
27	GND	28	GND
29	+ ATN	30	-ATN
31	GND	32	GND
33	+ BSY	34	-BSY
35	+ ACK	36	-ACK
37	+ RST	38	-RST
39	+ MSG	40	-MSG
41	+ SEL	42	-SEL
43	+ C/D	44	-C/D
45	+ REQ	46	-REQ
47	+ I/O	48	-I/O
49	GND	50	GND

NOTE: A - PREFIX SIGNIFIES A LOW-TRUE SIGNAL
A + PREFIX SIGNIFIES A HIGH- TRUE SIGNAL

assumption of bus mastership by asserting SEL. This event terminates the bus arbitration phase. The losing initiators stop driving the bus and wait to compete in the next arbitration cycle that will start when the bus again enters a bus-free phase.

The successful initiator must execute a selection sequence to ready a target device for the data transfer. This sequence is called the SCSI selection phase. While continuing to assert BSY, SEL, and its own ID bit, the initiator asserts the ID bit for the target. Then the initiator negates BSY. The rising edge of BSY alerts potential targets that a target ID is on the data bus. The targets examine the ID codes and the selected target recognizes its ID and asserts BSY in response. When the initiator senses the assertion of BSY by a target, it releases SEL and the data bus, completing the selection phase that creates a logical connection between target and initiator. The transfer of data can now begin.

The transfer of data over the SCSI bus employs a 2-wire handshake using the REQ (request) and ACK (acknowledge) lines. The target must de-

Table 4-5. SCSI Group 0 and 1 Commands.

GROUP 0

COMMAND CODE	COMMAND
00	TEST UNIT READY
01	REZERO UNIT
03	REQUEST SENSE
04	FORMAT UNIT
05	READ BLOCK LIMITS
07	REASSIGN BLOCKS
08	READ
0A	WRITE OR PRINT
0B	SEEK
0F	READ REVERSE
10	WRITE FILE MARK (FLUSH BUFFER)
11	SPACE
12	INQUIRY
13	VERIFY
14	RECOVER BUFFERED DATA
15	MODE SELECT
16	RESERVE UNIT
17	RELEASE UNIT
18	COPY
19	ERASE
1A	MODE SENSE
1B	START/STOP (LOAD/UNLOAD)
1C	RECEIVE DIAGNOSTIC
1D	SEND DIAGNOSTIC
1E	PREVENT/ALLOW MEDIA REMOVAL

GROUP 1

COMMAND CODE	COMMAND
25	READ CAPACITY
28	EXTENDED ADDRESS READ
2A	EXTENDED ADDRESS WRITE
2E	WRITE AND VERITY
2F	VERIFY
30	SEARCH DATA HIGH
31	SEARCH DATA EQUAL
32	SEARCH DATA LOW
33	SET LIMITS
39	COMPARE
3A	COPY AND VERIFY

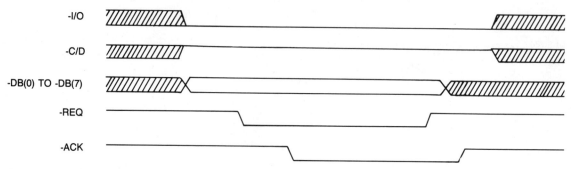

Fig. 4-22. SCSI target-to-initiator transfer timing.

termine the type of transfer the initiator desires by obtaining a command. SCSI commands are multi-byte messages transferred from the initiator to the target specifying the type of data transfer desired.

The SCSI specification defines eight command groups, 0 through 7. Groups 0, 1, and 5 form a core group of common commands every SCSI device should support. Group 0 contains 6-byte commands and groups 1 and 5 contain extended 10- and 12-byte commands respectively. Groups 2, 3, and 4 are reserved. Groups 6 and 7 are defined as vendor-specific commands meaning a company building a SCSI product may define them as necessary. The individual command definitions for command groups 0 and 1 are shown in **Table 4-5.**

The target requests the first command byte by setting the -I/O (input/output) control line high, signaling that it wants the initiator to output a byte, and the -C/D (command/data) control line low, signaling that it wants a command byte. Then the target asserts REQ, requesting the first command byte. The initiator places the requested byte on the data lines and asserts ACK, indicating that the tar-

get can now accept the byte. The target reads the byte and negates REQ. The byte transfer completes when the initiator negates ACK.

This REQ/ACK sequence must transpire several times to effect the transfer of the entire command. The target knows exactly the number of bytes to request for each command because each command within a command group comprises a predetermined number of bytes. When the initiator has transferred all of the command bytes to the target, the target can then interpret and act upon the command.

Data transfers occur in much the same way as command transfers. The target, acting on a command from the initiator, sets the proper levels on the -I/O line to set the data direction, on -C/D to differentiate command and status bytes from data bytes, and then asserts REQ to get things moving. The initiator responds by asserting ACK to complete the handshake. **Figures 4-22** and **4-23** illustrate SCSI target-to-initiator and initiator-to-target transfers respectively.

Though we have now covered basic SCSI-bus

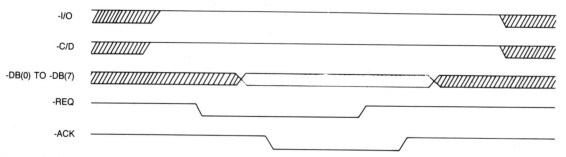

Fig. 4-23. SCSI initiator-to-target transfer timing.

transfers, a few more SCSI details remain undiscussed. The transfer of commands and data over the SCSI bus fall into a group of transfer cycles collectively called the information-transfer phase. Two other types of transfers can occur during an information-transfer phase: status and message.

A status transfer is the opposite of the command transfer; The target transfers some number of status bytes. During a status transfer the target drives -C/D is low, signaling a command (actually status) transfer, and -I/O low, signaling data movement from the target to the initiator. Many SCSI commands request that the target send status information back to the initiator. Thus the target may send back status bytes to the initiator in response to a command instead of sending or receiving other data.

Messages serve as a SCSI interrupt mechanism. An initiator can indicate to the target that an unusual condition has occurred and that the initiator wants to send the target a message by asserting the ATN (attention) control line. The initiator in control of the SCSI bus can assert ATN during the command, data-transfer, status-transfer, and selection phases but not during the bus-free and arbitration phases. The initiator must assert ATN during a REQ/ACK transfer cycle, before asserting ACK, to ensure that the target recognizes the attention condition in a predictable manner.

The target responds to the ATN request by creating a message-out bus state: setting -MSG and -C/D low and -I/O high. Then the target asserts REQ, requesting the first message byte. The initiator supplies this byte and asserts ACK. If the message is several bytes long, the initiator continues to assert ATN until the target receives the entire message.

The SCSI bus supports a reselection phase that allows a target to temporarily disconnect itself from the initiator and free up the SCSI bus. Typically, a system might use this feature to allow other bus traffic to take place while a target device was busy executing a command.

A target disconnects from an initiator simply by releasing BSY and creating a bus-free phase on the SCSI bus. At some later time, when the target

wishes to reconnect to the initiator, it waits for a bus-free phase to appear on the bus, and then arbitrates for the bus as though it were an initiator. When the target wins the bus during an arbitration phase, it selects the initiator using the same mechanism that the initiator originally used to select the target, and thus re-establishes the target-initiator connection.

The last line in the SCSI bus is the RST (reset) line. Any device, target or initiator, can assert RST. When a device asserts RST, all devices attached to the SCSI bus must immediately release control of all bus signals (except RST). The reset condition will also have some effect on the state of the SCSI devices. The extent of this effect depends on the way the device interprets reset.

A device that implements a hard SCSI reset will clear all uncompleted commands and return to its power-up default state in response to the assertion of RST. A device that implements a soft SCSI reset will attempt to complete any commands it is currently executing and will preserve its current configuration in response to a reset condition. The soft reset condition allows an initiator to clear the SCSI bus without disturbing the execution of commands issued by other initiators on the bus.

Clearly, the SCSI protocols are somewhat complex. Designers created early SASI and SCSI interfaces using simple parallel I/O ICs and a lot of software. Because of its popularity, especially in the small hard-disk market, several IC manufacturers now make one-chip solutions for SCSI. We will study one of these later in the chapter.

PARALLEL I/O INTEGRATED CIRCUITS

We have already looked at some of the least-complex integrated circuits used to build parallel interfaces. These are the latches and buffers discussed in the early part of this chapter. Now we turn our attention to the more-complex chips, specially designed for parallel interfacing. They have various names: Parallel I/O (PIO), Parallel Interface Adapter (PIA), Versatile Interface Adapter (VIA), ad nauseum. All are the chip manufacturers' idea of what a microprocessor needs to speak to parallel interfaces.

In this chapter we will look at three of the general-purpose parallel integrated circuits. These are Intel's 8255A Programmable Peripheral Controller (PPC), the Motorola 6821 Peripheral Interface Adapter (PIA), and Motorola's 68230 Parallel Interface and Timer (PIT). We will also look at the Texas Instruments 9914A, an integrated circuit which implements the IEEE-488 talker, listener, and controller functions, and the NCR 5380, which implements the SCSI protocol.

Peripheral chips must be built so that microprocessors can control them. Otherwise, they are of little use in building microprocessor-based systems. Each chip contains a number of registers which are simply storage areas for bits. Some registers can be both read and written to, and are called read/write registers. Others may only be read and are therefore called read-only, while still others are write-only.

You may be initially amused at the idea of read- or write-only registers. How could they be of any possible use? These registers inside the peripheral chips are the links into the microprocessor address spaces. The integrated circuits are wired so that internal registers correspond to address locations. Then, when the microprocessor reads or writes to those locations, it is transacting with the I/O chip's on-board registers. By placing bit patterns into these registers, the microprocessor controls the operation of the I/O chip.

How does one wire a peripheral chip to make it appear in a microprocessor's address space? Most I/O integrated circuits follow a similar pattern. One input to the chip is called Chip Select. When this pin is asserted the chip is activated. Some circuits have two or three chip selects. These can be used to make address decoding easier.

Chip Select is wired to an address decoder which determines when the address being output on the microprocessor address lines corresponds to the portion of address space occupied by the I/O chip. When an address match occurs, the decoding circuitry asserts Chip Select, activating the I/O chip and allowing a data transaction to take place. In microprocessor systems where there are separate I/O and memory spaces, the address decoder must also determine whether the proper address space is being accessed.

Figure 4-24 illustrates how an address decoder is wired between a microprocessor address bus and an I/O chip. Note that not all of the address bits are connected to the decoder; some are connected directly to the I/O chip. These low-order address bits are used as register select bits. They

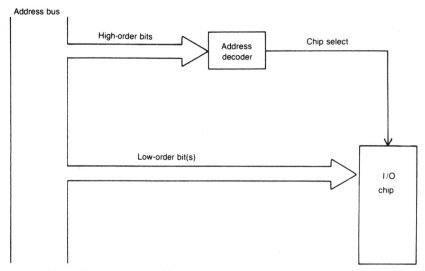

Fig. 4-24. Connection of an I/O chip to a microprocessor bus with an address decoder.

specify which registers in the chip are being accessed.

The number of low-order bits used as register selects varies depending on the number of registers in the integrated circuit. Some have only one or two while others have 32 registers. Also be aware that many system designers only partially decode addresses. Though a circuit may only have two registers, a block of sixteen or more may be decoded. The I/O chip will be activated whenever any of the decoded addresses is accessed.

In this example, the lower four bits of the address bus are not connected to the address decoder but only the lowest bit is used for register selection. This leaves three bits unconnected. The result of this approach is that the two registers of the I/O chip appear eight times in the 16-address block because three address bits are unused. Thus, register 0 also appears as register 2, 4, 6, 8, 10, 12, and 14 while register 1 appears as registers 3, 5, 7, 9, 11, 13, and 15.

Why partially decode addresses? The most common reason is cost. Each address bit in the decoder requires circuitry for decoding that bit. If fewer bits are decoded, less circuitry is required, thus the cost is less. In many systems, wasted I/O address space is not of great concern but system costs always are.

Address decoders can be built from several types of devices. Exclusive-OR and Exclusive-NOR gates are good because they indicate when both of their inputs match. Comparators, which are built from Exclusive-OR and Exclusive-NOR gates, are also popular and provide for decoding more address lines in one package.

Figure 4-25 fills out the picture started in **Fig. 4-24**. The data and control busses have also been connected to the chip. Remember, the address bus is the "where" bus, the data bus is the "what" bus, and the control bus is the "when" bus. The data bus is used for the actual transfer of information between the microprocessor and the I/O chip, and the control bus allows the transfers to take place with appropriate timing.

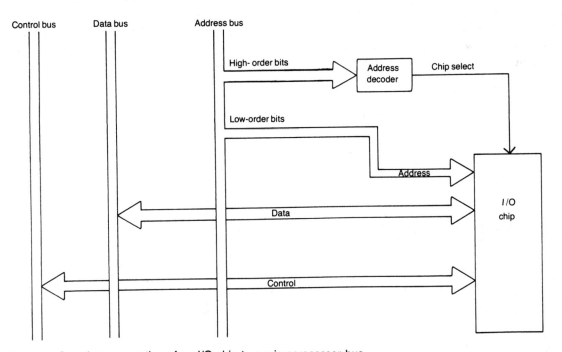

Fig. 4-25. Complete connection of an I/O chip to a microprocessor bus.

THE INTEL 8255A PROGRAMMABLE PERIPHERAL INTERFACE

Our first parallel I/O chip is also the simplest. Intel's 8255A has but four registers and only a few peculiarities to confuse and befuddle you. **Figure 4-26** is a block diagram of the part and **Fig. 4-27** is a pin diagram. Don't be put off by any apparent complexity. It is really easy to understand.

On the left side of the block diagram is the in-interface to the microprocessor. It is composed of a chip select pin called CS (as promised), two address pins (A0 and A1), the three control pins $\overline{\text{READ}}$ (RD), $\overline{\text{WRITE}}$ (WR), and RESET, and eight bidirectional data pins (D0 through D7).

From these few pins we can immediately deduce several facts about the chip. First, it has at most four registers, since it has two address inputs. Next, it is designed for Intel-type control busses because it has separate $\overline{\text{READ}}$ and $\overline{\text{WRITE}}$ pins. Finally, we deduce that this is an eight-bit part because of the eight data pins.

The preceding paragraph is intended to illustrate to you how I set about understanding a new I/O chip. Start with the block diagram and work your way from the microprocessor interface through the chip until you reach the I/O side.

On the right side of **Fig. 4-26** we see what appears to be four groups of I/O pins: Port A, Port C Upper, Port C Lower, and Port B. Ports A and B are eight bits wide, while ports C Upper and C

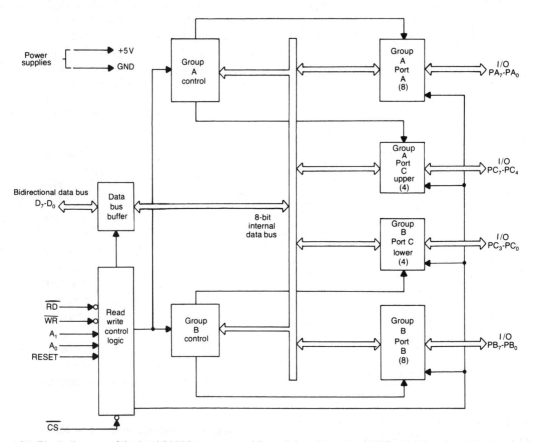

Fig. 4-26. Block diagram of the Intel 8255A programmable peripheral interface (PPI) chip. Reprinted by permission of Intel Corporation, Copyright 1983.

172

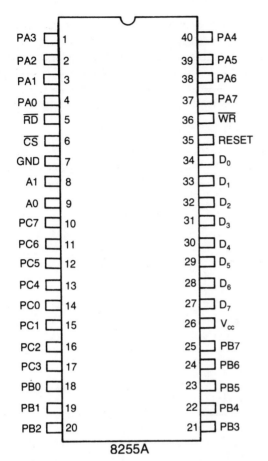

PA3 □ 1   40 □ PA4
PA2 □ 2   39 □ PA5
PA1 □ 3   38 □ PA6
PA0 □ 4   37 □ PA7
$\overline{RD}$ □ 5   36 □ $\overline{WR}$
$\overline{CS}$ □ 6   35 □ RESET
GND □ 7   34 □ D_0
A1 □ 8   33 □ D_1
A0 □ 9   32 □ D_2
PC7 □ 10   31 □ D_3
PC6 □ 11   30 □ D_4
PC5 □ 12   29 □ D_5
PC4 □ 13   28 □ D_6
PC0 □ 14   27 □ D_7
PC1 □ 15   26 □ V_{cc}
PC2 □ 16   25 □ PB7
PC3 □ 17   24 □ PB6
PB0 □ 18   23 □ PB5
PB1 □ 19   22 □ PB4
PB2 □ 20   21 □ PB3

8255A

Fig. 4-27. Pin diagram of the Intel 8255A PPI. Reprinted by permission of Intel Corporation, Copyright 1983.

Lower are four bits each. Note that Port C Upper is controlled by the Group A control and port C Lower is controlled by the Group B control. We have a total of 24 I/O pins.

Operation of the 8255A is quite simple. Certain combinations of levels on the microprocessor-interface pins of the 8255A give the microprocessor read and write access to the 8255A internal registers. Table 4-6 provides a summary of how those registers are accessed.

What each of the above register transactions do is determined by the bit pattern placed in the 8255A control register. The 8255A has three modes of operation. These are:

Mode 0: Basic input and output, also called bit I/O.
Mode 1: Strobed input/output.
Mode 2: Bidirectional bus.

Port A and Port B may be set to different modes. Port C Upper is configured according to how Port A is set and Port C Lower is configured according to how Port B is set. Figure 4-28 illustrates the port configurations in the various modes. To fully understand 8255 modes, we must study the control register.

Figure 4-29 illustrates the bit assignments of the 8255A control register. Note first that bit 7 must always be written as a 1. We will see why shortly. Bits 5 and 6 set the Port A mode. Bit 4 is the Port A data-direction bit which determines whether the Port A pins are input or outputs. It is important to remember that input and output are from the perspective of the 8255A. Bit 3 determines the direction of the Port C Upper pins. Bit 2 of the 8255A control register is the mode-select bit for Port B. Note that port B may not be configured to mode 2,

Table 4-6. Register Access Codes for the Intel 8255A.

PIN	A0	A1	$\overline{RD}$	$\overline{WR}$	CS	OPERATION
	0	0	0	1	0	Read Port A pins
	0	1	0	1	0	Read Port B pins
	1	0	0	1	0	Read Port C pins
	0	0	1	0	0	Write to Port A
	0	1	1	0	0	Write to Port B
	1	0	1	0	0	Write to Port C
	1	1	1	0	0	Write to control register
	X	X	X	X	1	No transaction
	1	1	0	1	0	Illegal
	X	X	1	1	0	No transaction

(Note: X indicates that the pin may assume either level - it is called a "don't care")

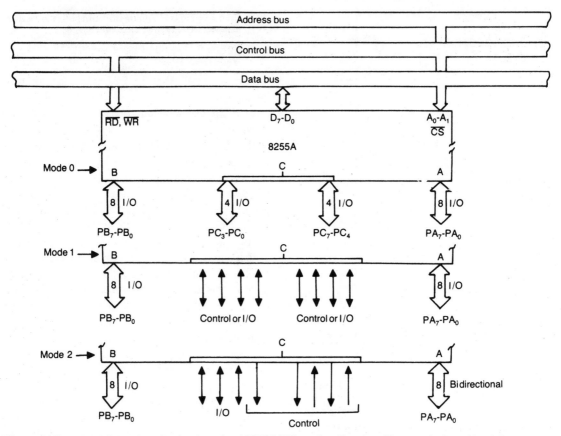

Fig. 4-28. Output configurations for the three Intel 8255A PPI modes. Reprinted by permission of Intel Corporation, Copyright 1983.

the bidirectional-bus mode. Bit 1 determines the direction of the Port B pins and Bit 0 determines the direction of the Port C Lower pins.

In addition to this definition, the 8255A control register may also be defined as shown in **Fig. 4-30**. In this configuration, Port C pins are directly set or reset according to the definitions shown in the figure. Bit 7 must be 0 to differentiate this format from the control register format in **Fig. 4-27**. Bits 4, 5 and 6 are "don't cares." Bits 1 through 3 specify which Port C bit is to be manipulated and bit 0 specifies the state which the bit is to assume.

Mode 0

In mode 0, the 8255A operates in the "basic I/O" or bit I/O configuration. That means that pins defined as outputs will stay at the level set by an output to the 8255A by the microprocessor until changed by the microprocessor with another output instruction. Instantaneous input-pin levels are read by the microprocessor by an input to the microprocessor. The outputs in mode 0 are latched and are said to be single buffered. The inputs are not latched.

An 8255A can be configured in sixteen different ways when set to mode 0. This covers all combinations of setting ports A, B, C Upper, and C Lower to inputs or outputs. All bits of port A are set to be either inputs or outputs. Likewise the pins of port B, C Upper, and C Lower can be defined as inputs or outputs.

Note that the data direction must be the same for all signal lines in a given port. That means that port A cannot be defined as six inputs and two out-

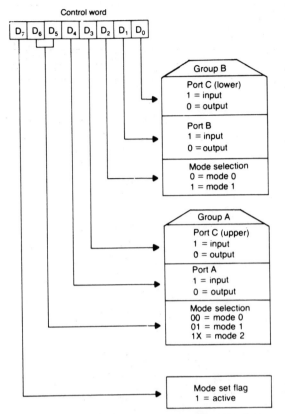

Control word

D_7 D_6 D_5 D_4 D_3 D_2 D_1 D_0

Group B

Port C (lower)
1 = input
0 = output

Port B
1 = input
0 = output

Mode selection
0 = mode 0
1 = mode 1

Group A

Port C (upper)
1 = input
0 = output

Port A
1 = input
0 = output

Mode selection
00 = mode 0
01 = mode 1
1X = mode 2

Mode set flag
1 = active

Fig. 4-29. Bit definitions for the Intel 8255A PPI control register. Reprinted by permission of Intel Corporation, Copyright 1983.

puts. Port C is split and can therefore be defined as eight outputs, eight inputs, or four inputs and four outputs. Table 4-7 lists the bit patterns in the 8255A control register to produce the sixteen configurations of mode 0.

Operation in mode 0 is classified as a zero-wire handshake. No timing information is passed between computer and peripheral. A one-, two- or three-wire handshake could be implemented using mode 0 operation of the 8255A. This would require software running in the microprocessor to manage the handshake control signal levels and monitor incoming status lines.

Mode 1

Mode 1 is the strobed-I/O mode for the 8255A. The data ports are A and B, and the C ports serve as control and status lines for the strobed handshake. Signals in Port C take on slightly different meanings for input and output. Port A uses Port C bits 3, 4, and 5 for handshaking while Port B uses Port C bits 0, 1, and 2. That leaves Port C, bits 6 and 7 available for bit I/O.

For the input configuration, the three handshake lines are called strobe ($\overline{STB}$), Input Buffer Full (IBF), and Interrupt Request (INTR). An external device may place a byte of data into the input latch of the data port by pulsing $\overline{STB}$ low. This causes the data on the data lines to be latched, and IBF is asserted by the 8255A. For Port A, $\overline{STB}$, IBF, and INTR correspond to Port C bits 4, 5, and 3 while for Port B they correspond to Port C bits 2, 1, and 0.

$\overline{STB}$ is low true while IBF is high true. When $\overline{STB}$ is subsequently negated by raising it to a high logic level, the 8255A asserts the INTR signal, raising it to a high logic level to signal the acquisition of a data byte. INTR is negated at the start of a read cycle by the microprocessor to the port input latch. IBF is negated by the 8255A at the end of this read cycle. Figure 4-31 illustrates a typical transfer into the 8255A input buffer.

This handshake mechanism can be used to implement a fully interlocked handshake with a peripheral. The peripheral must wait for IBF to be in a false state. Then it can place data on the data lines and assert $\overline{STB}$. When the 8255A accepts the data and asserts IBF, the peripheral can negate $\overline{STB}$ and then wait for IBF to be negated, signaling readiness for the next transfer.

Output-handshake pin definitions differ only slightly from the input-handshake pin definitions. In this mode, the microprocessor places a data byte in the port output latch and that bit pattern appears on the output-data pins. This causes a signal called Output Buffer Full ($\overline{OBF}$) to be asserted. The peripheral has a handshake pin called Acknowledge ($\overline{ACK}$) to assert when the data has been accepted. An Interrupt-Request (INTR) pin is supplied to indicate when the peripheral has accepted the data from the output lines by pulsing $\overline{ACK}$.

Figure 4-32 shows the timing for a typical 8255A mode 1 output handshake. The sequence is started by an output of a data byte by the

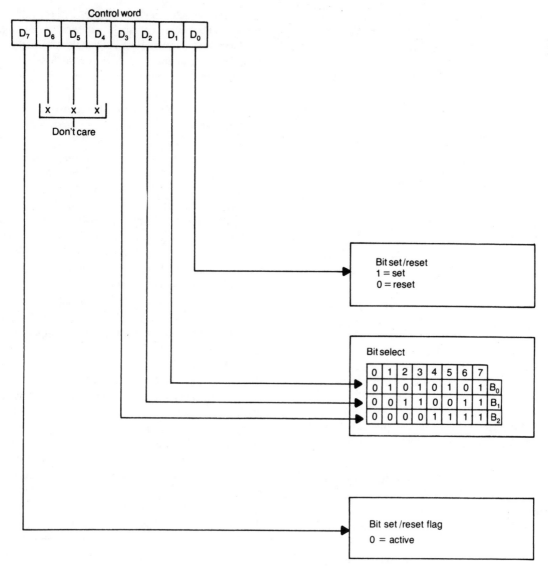

Fig. 4-30. Bit definitions for the Intel 8255A PPI control register, port C bit set/reset mode. Reprinted by permission of Intel Corporation, Copyright 1983.

microprocessor into the output-data latch in the 8255A. This is shown as an assertion of the $\overline{WR}$ (write) control signal. The start of the write cycle causes the 8255A to negate INTR. The completion of the write cycle causes the 8255A to assert $\overline{OBF}$, signaling the peripheral that a byte of data is ready to be accepted. When the peripheral accepts the data by asserting $\overline{ACK}$, the 8255A negates $\overline{OBF}$. When the peripheral returns $\overline{ACK}$ to the false level, the 8255A asserts INTR, requesting another data byte from the microprocessor.

INTR in both the input and output operations does not have to be used as an interrupt request. The two INTR lines may be buffered so that the microprocessor can read the state of the lines. The 8255A can then be operated as a polled device. The

176

Table 4-7. Intel 8255A Mode 0 Configurations.

BITS D4	A D3	B D1	D0	GROUP A PORT A	PORT C (UPPER)	GROUP B PORT B	PORT C (LOWER)
0	0	0	0	Output	Output	Output	Output
0	0	0	1	Output	Output	Output	Input
0	0	1	0	Output	Output	Input	Output
0	0	1	1	Output	Output	Input	Input
0	1	0	0	Output	Input	Output	Output
0	1	0	1	Output	Input	Output	Input
0	1	1	0	Output	Input	Input	Output
0	1	1	1	Output	Input	Input	Input
1	0	0	0	Input	Output	Output	Output
1	0	0	1	Input	Output	Output	Input
1	0	1	0	Input	Output	Input	Output
1	0	1	1	Input	Output	Input	Input
1	1	0	0	Input	Input	Output	Output
1	1	0	1	Input	Input	Output	Input
1	1	1	0	Input	Input	Input	Output
1	1	1	1	Input	Input	Input	Input

Note: Bits D4, D3, D1 and D0 are bits in the 8255A control register.

microprocessor must periodically read the status of the INTR lines and determine whether either of the data ports is requesting service.

Two flip-flops inside the 8255A can be used to enable the Port A and Port B interrupt request pins. Interrupt-enable A (INTE A) is set and reset with Port C bit 6, and interrupt enable B (INTE B) is set and reset with Port C bit 2. When the interrupt enable bits are set, the corresponding INTR signal line is allowed to be asserted at the proper time. When

the INTE bits are reset, the corresponding INTR line is disabled.

Mode 1 operation can be used for either a one- or two-wire handshake. A two-wire input handshake follows naturally from the design of the 8255A. The peripheral places data on the data lines and strobes the information into the 8255A input latch with the $\overline{STB}$ signal while the 8255A signals readiness for another transfer with the IBF line. For a one-wire handshake, the peripheral may ignore the IBF signal. To

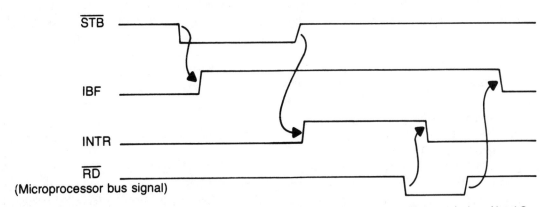

Fig. 4-31. Timing diagram for the Intel 8255A PPI Mode 1 input handshake. Reprinted by permission of Intel Corporation, Copyright 1983.

177

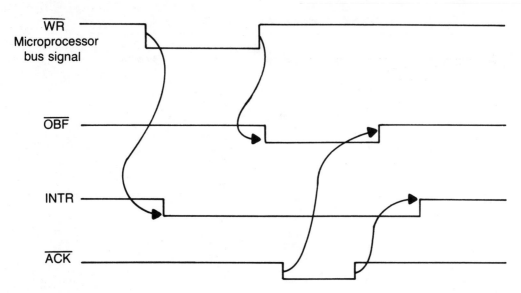

Fig. 4-32. Timing diagram for the Intel 8255A PPI Mode 1 output handshake. Reprinted by permission of Intel Corporation, Copyright 1983.

do this however, the system designer must be sure that the peripheral will not try to transfer information faster than the computer will accept it. This is an implicit return handshake.

Mode 1 may also be used for one- or two-wire output handshakes. The two-wire version is again in keeping with the design of the 8255A. A one-wire handshake becomes more of a problem, however, since there is no signal returned from the peripheral to acknowledge the transfer. One solution is to let the 8255A handshake with itself. By connecting $\overline{OBF}$ with $\overline{ACK}$, the 8255A will receive $\overline{ACK}$ as soon as it asserts $\overline{OBF}$ and the output cycle will complete.

Mode 2

Mode 2 is the most complex 8255A operating mode. Only Port A may be operated in mode 2. Port A is used as a bidirectional data port while five bits of Port C are used as handshake lines. Port B may be operated in either mode 0 or mode 1 while Port A is operating in mode 2. The remaining Port-C bits are available either for bit I/O or as handshake lines for Port B.

One mode-2 handshake line, Interrupt Request (INTR) is common to both input and output opera-

tions in mode 2. It is asserted when the data port requires service. For output operations, two additional handshake lines are used; Output Buffer Full ($\overline{OBF}$) and Acknowledge ($\overline{ACK}$). Input handshake lines are Strobe ($\overline{STB}$), and Input Buffer Full (IBF). INTR corresponds to Port C, bit 3. $\overline{OBF}$ and $\overline{ACK}$ correspond to Port C, bits 7 and 6 while $\overline{STB}$ and IBF correspond to Port C, bits 4 and 5.

The handshake timings for mode 2 look similar to those of the mode 1 transfers. An important difference is that data is now flowing in both directions on the data pins of Port A. In order to control data direction, the output handshake is modified. The 8255A will not place data in the output latch onto the Port-A data lines until the peripheral asserts $\overline{ACK}$. This signifies that the peripheral is ready to accept data even though the data lines are not yet valid.

When the 8255A receives an asserted $\overline{ACK}$, it will place the contents of the output latch onto the Port-A data lines within 300 nanoseconds. The peripheral must therefore wait at least that long before actually latching in the data or it will get bad information. **Figure 4-33** illustrates overlapped input and output operations for an 8255A operating in mode 2.

178

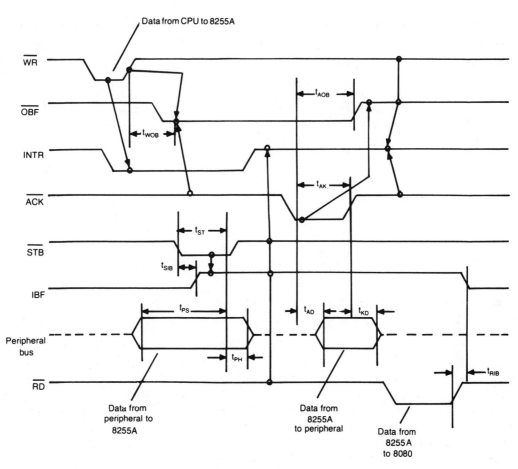

Fig. 4-33. Timing diagram for the Intel 8255A PPI Mode 2 handshake. Reprinted by permission of Intel Corporation, Copyright 1983.

The interrupt-request line may be enabled for input transfers, output transfers, or both. INTE 1, corresponding to Port C bit 6, enables the INTR line for output transfers, and INTE 2, which corresponds to Port C bit 4, enables the INTR line for input transfers. The INTE bits enable when set.

If both INTE 1 and INTE 2 are set, the INTR line will be asserted when the 8255A requires service for either the input or output latch. Then the microprocessor must determine the cause of the request. The input latch may be full, the output latch may be empty, or both conditions may be true. The type of request is determined by reading Port C to determine the status of the IBF and $\overline{OBF}$ lines.

If IBF (Port C, bit 1) is high there is data in the input register. If $\overline{OBF}$ (Port C, bit 7) is high, signifying that the output data latch is empty, another byte is being requested from the microprocessor. Software must determine what is required.

Since the mode-2 handshakes work similarly to the mode-1 handshakes, they have the same potential uses for one- and two-wire protocols.

THE MOTOROLA 6821 PARALLEL INTERFACE ADAPTER

Next on our list of parallel I/O chips is the Motorola 6821 Peripheral Interface Adapter (PIA).

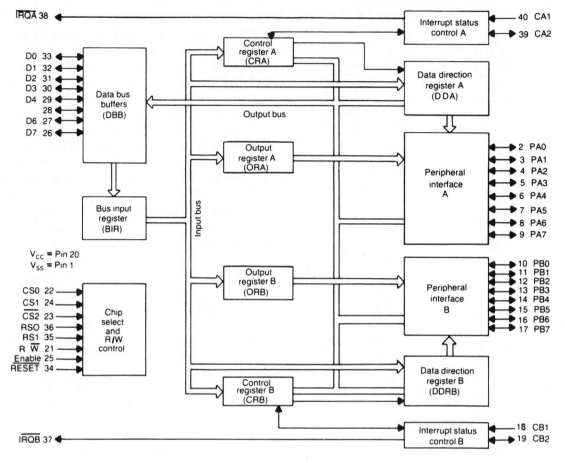

Fig. 4-34. Block diagram for the Motorola MC6821 Peripheral Interface Adapter (PIA). Reprinted with permission of Motorola, Inc.

The PIA has a Motorola-style bus interface, two eight-bit I/O ports with two handshake lines each, and two interrupt-request lines. Figure 4-34 is a block diagram of the 6821, and Fig. 4-35 is a pin diagram of the chip.

Looking at the bus interface portion of the PIA, we see eight bidirectional data pins (D0 through D7), three chip selects (CS0, CS1, and CS2), two register selects (RS0 and RS1), a read/write line, an enable-clock input, and a reset line. From these, we can conclude that the chip is an eight-bit part. It has at most four internal registers since there are two register-select lines.

Three chip-select inputs help the system designer in the task of address decoding. If the register selects are connected directly to the two lowest address lines, two of the chip selects can be connected to the next two address lines. This leaves one chip select for the rest of the address lines. The net effect is to reduce the address decoding circuit complexity, which may be important if the system is being designed for lowest cost.

We have already discussed how the Motorola 6800 bus works in Chapter 2. To briefly review, all bus transactions are synchronized with the enable clock, which is the main system timing signal. The rising edge of the enable clock signifies that a valid address is present on the address lines. By the time the falling edge of enable occurs, the PIA must have either accepted or produced the data for the cur-

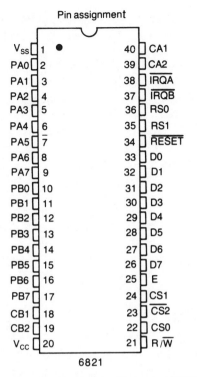

Pin assignment

```
              ___
        Vss [ 1 •        40 ] CA1
        PA0 [ 2          39 ] CA2
        PA1 [ 3          38 ] IRQA
        PA2 [ 4          37 ] IRQB
        PA3 [ 5          36 ] RS0
        PA4 [ 6          35 ] RS1
        PA5 [ 7          34 ] RESET
        PA6 [ 8          33 ] D0
        PA7 [ 9          32 ] D1
        PB0 [ 10         31 ] D2
        PB1 [ 11         30 ] D3
        PB2 [ 12         29 ] D4
        PB3 [ 13         28 ] D5
        PB4 [ 14         27 ] D6
        PB5 [ 15         26 ] D7
        PB6 [ 16         25 ] E
        PB7 [ 17         24 ] CS1
        CB1 [ 18         23 ] CS2
        CB2 [ 19         22 ] CS0
        Vcc [ 20         21 ] R/W
```

6821

Fig. 4-35. Pin diagram for the Motorola MC6821 PIA. Reprinted with permission of Motorola, Inc.

rent bus transaction, based on whether a read or write is taking place.

Although the presence of two register-select lines led us to believe that there were at most four registers in the PIA, there are actually six. This bit of magic is accomplished through a technique called register pointers, or indirect addressing. For some addresses, the register select lines are not sufficient to completely specify an internal register. Pointer bits in a pointer register must also be taken into consideration.

If this seems confusing, hang on. The concept really isn't that difficult to understand. More impor-

tant, many of the more complex I/O chips use pointer registers, so it is vital that you conquer this bit of technology now.

Without telling you how to access it, I present the PIA control register in **Fig. 4-36**. For the moment, ignore all the bit positions except bit 2, the DDRA Access bit. The 6821 has two control registers like the one shown in **Fig. 4-36**. One has a DDRA access bit, and the other a DDRB access bit in position 2. One control register is for Port A and the other is for Port B, the two eight-bit data ports of the PIA.

DDR stands for data-direction register. The state of the DDRA access bit determines which of two registers is accessed when a certain register address is presented on the PIA register select lines. When the DDRA bit in control register A (CRA) is "0," the data direction register for Port A is available. When the bit is a "1," peripheral register A, the Port-A data register is available. DDRB in control register B (CRB) has the same control over access to the Port B data-direction and port-data registers.

With that explanation out of the way, look at Fig 4-37, which shows register locations within the PIA. There are six registers. Also, the data-direction and peripheral registers have the same address; register address 0 for Port A and register address 2 for Port B. The term that differentiates the two registers is the state of the associated control-register bit. Note that control-register A is at register address 1, and control-register B is at address 3.

Data direction for each bit in Ports A and B can be individually configured. This is done by placing appropriate values in the data direction register for the associated port. A "0" in a bit location of a data-direction register causes the associated port bit to be defined as an input. A "1" causes the port

Control register	b7	b6	b5	b4	b3	b2	b1	b0
	IRQA(B)1 Flag	IRQA(B)2 Flag	CA2 (CB2) Control			DDR Access	CA1 (CB1) Control	

Fig. 4-36. Motorola MC6821 PIA control-register bit definitions. Reprinted with permission of Motorola, Inc.

181

Internal addressing				
		Control register bit		
RS1	RS0	CRA-2	CRB-2	Location selected
0	0	1	X	Peripheral register A
0	0	0	X	Data direction register A
0	1	X	X	Control register A
1	0	X	1	Peripheral register B
1	0	X	0	Data direction register B
1	1	X	X	Control register B

X = Don t care

Fig. 4-37. Motorola MC6821 PIA register map. Reprinted with permission of Motorola, Inc.

bit to become an output. The port data lines can be read simply by reading the peripheral register. Output-pin levels are set by writing to the peripheral register.

Figure 4-38 again illustrates the bit definitions of the control registers. We have already discussed bit 2, the data-direction-register access bit. Bits 0 and 1 are called CA1 and CB1, control for Ports A and B respectively. Bits 3, 4, and 5 control CA2 and CB2 for Ports A and B. The CA and CB lines are the two handshake lines associated with each port. CA1 and CB1 are inputs to the PIA and CA2 and CB2 are outputs. Control register bits 6 and 7 cannot be written to, they are read-only. These two bits represent the states of the handshake lines and we shall see what they are used for in a moment.

Figure 4-39 shows how control-register bits 0 and 1 are used to control the CA1 and CB1 inputs. From here on, we will refer to both the CA1 and CB1 input lines as the C1 line and both CA2 and CB2 as the C2 line. Keep in mind that both Port A and Port B work in the same manner.

If control-register bits 1 and 0 are "0," then the C1 line is asserted by the negative edge of the incoming signal. In addition, this negative edge will cause bit 7 of the control register to be asserted. The setting of bit 7 in the control register informs

the microprocessor that the C1 line was asserted. The bit will be cleared when the microprocessor reads the associated peripheral register. With control register bits 0 and 1 set to "0," the associated port interrupt-request line is disabled.

A similar situation exists when control register bits 1 and 0 are set to "0" and "1" respectively. A negative edge on the C1 line asserts it, causing bit 7 of the control register to be set to a 1. The difference is that the interrupt-request line for the associated port is activated and will be asserted when CR1 is asserted.

States "10" and "11" for control register bits 1 and 0 work nearly the same as states "00" and "01." The difference here is that the CR1 input line is asserted by a positive edge. Operation of control register bit 7 and the interrupt request line follow the rules listed in the figure.

Control signals CA2 and CB2 can be configured as either inputs or outputs. From this point on, both CA2 and CB2 will be referred to as simply C2 since the discussion applies equally well to Port A and Port B. Configuration of the signal pin is done with bits 3, 4, and 5 of the related control register. Figures 4-40, 4-41, and 4-42 list the bit patterns for these three bits and their effect on 6821 operation.

First, note that bit 5 determines whether the C2 signal pin is an input or an output. If bit 5 is a "0," C2 is an input, and if bit 5 is a "1," C2 is an output. This leaves two remaining bits to determine the operation of C2 as an input or an output pin. Thus there are four input configurations and four output configurations for C2.

As an input, C2 works similarly to C1. Control register bits 4 and 3 create the same input relationships for C2, control register bit 6, and the interrupt request line as does control register bits 1 and 0 for C1. Note that C2 is associated with control register bit 6 instead of bit 7 as C1 is, but both

		b7	b6	b5	b4	b3	b2	b1	b0
Control register		IRQA(B)1 Flag	IRQA(B)2 Flag		CA2(CB2) Control		DDR Access		CA1(CB1) Control

Fig. 4-38. Motorola MC6821 PIA control register. Reprinted with permission of Motorola, Inc.

182

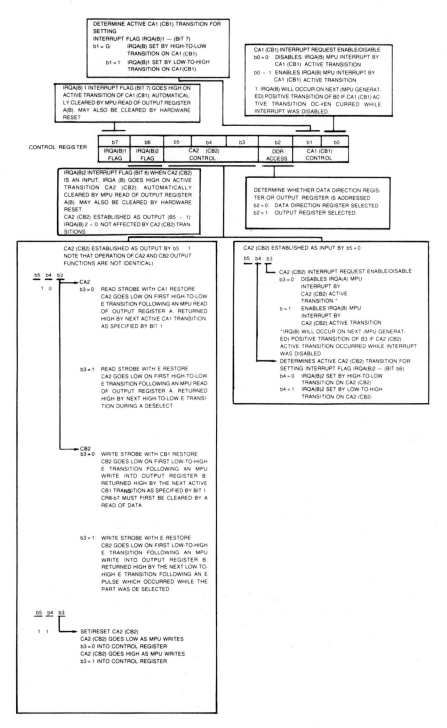

Fig. 4-39. Configuration of CA1 and CB1 bits in the Motorola MC6821 PIA control register. Reprinted with permission of Motorola, Inc.

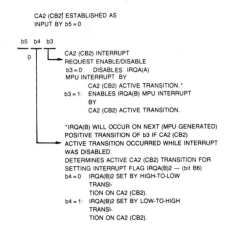

CA2 (CB2) ESTABLISHED AS
INPUT BY b5 = 0

b5 b4 b3
0

CA2 (CB2) INTERRUPT
REQUEST ENABLE/DISABLE
b3 = 0: DISABLES IRQA(A)
MPU INTERRUPT BY
CA2 (CB2) ACTIVE TRANSITION.*
b3 = 1: ENABLES IRQA(B) MPU INTERRUPT
BY
CA2 (CB2) ACTIVE TRANSITION.

*IRQA(B) WILL OCCUR ON NEXT (MPU GENERATED)
POSITIVE TRANSITION OF b3 IF CA2 (CB2)
ACTIVE TRANSITION OCCURRED WHILE INTERRUPT
WAS DISABLED.
DETERMINES ACTIVE CA2 (CB2) TRANSITION FOR
SETTING INTERRUPT FLAG IRQA(B)2 — (bit B6)
b4 = 0   IRQA(B)2 SET BY HIGH-TO-LOW
TRANSI-
TION ON CA2 (CB2).
b4 = 1: IRQA(B)2 SET BY LOW-TO-HIGH
TRANSI-
TION ON CA2 (CB2).

Fig. 4-40. Configuration of CA2 and CB2 bits in the Motorola MC6821 PIA control register. Reprinted with permission of Motorola, Inc.

C1 and C2 share the same interrupt-request line.

As an output, C2 can be defined as a handshake pin in either an interlocked or pulsed mode. As outputs, CA2 and CB2 differ in operation. CA2 can either be defined as a general-purpose output pin, following the sense of control-register A bit 3, or as an input-handshake pin in either an interlocked or pulsed handshake mode. Similarly, CB2 can be configured as a general-purpose output pin following the sense of control register-B bit 3, or as an output-handshake pin in either an interlocked or pulsed handshake mode. Pulsed-mode operation is useful for implementing one-wire handshakes, and the interlocked mode is useful for two- and three-wire handshakes.

Figure 4-41 lists the operating characteristics for CA2 as an output. With control-register A bit 4 set to "0," the pin acts as an input-handshake pin. If control-register A bit 3 is also a "0," the handshake works in an interlocked manner. That is, the handshake output is asserted by a read from peripheral register A. This should send a read request to the attached peripheral. When the data is made available by the peripheral and placed on the Port A data lines, the CA1 input pin should be asserted by the peripheral to signal the completion of the requested operation, which will negate CA2.

If control-register A bit 4 is "0" and control register bit 3 is "1," pulsed operation of CA2 results. When the microprocessor reads the peripheral register A, CA2 is asserted for one E cycle and then negated. When control-register A bit 4 is a "1," the CA2 output will follow the state of control-register bit 3.

CB2 operates in a similar manner but as an output-handshake pin. With both control-register B bits 4 and 3 set to "0," CB2 acts as an interlocked output-handshake signal. It is asserted when the microprocessor writes to peripheral register B to signal the availability of data at the Port-B data-output pins. When the attached peripheral accepts the data it should assert CB1, which will negate CB2 completing the output operation.

In pulsed operation (control-register bits 4 and 3 set to "01"), CB2 is pulsed for one E cycle when the microprocessor writes to peripheral-register B.

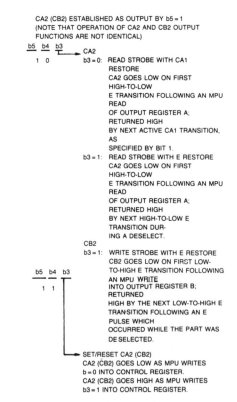

CA2 (CB2) ESTABLISHED AS OUTPUT BY b5 = 1
(NOTE THAT OPERATION OF CA2 AND CB2 OUTPUT
FUNCTIONS ARE NOT IDENTICAL)

b5 b4 b3
1 0

CA2
b3 = 0: READ STROBE WITH CA1
RESTORE
CA2 GOES LOW ON FIRST
HIGH-TO-LOW
E TRANSITION FOLLOWING AN MPU
READ
OF OUTPUT REGISTER A;
RETURNED HIGH
BY NEXT ACTIVE CA1 TRANSITION,
AS
SPECIFIED BY BIT 1.
b3 = 1: READ STROBE WITH E RESTORE
CA2 GOES LOW ON FIRST
HIGH-TO-LOW
E TRANSITION FOLLOWING AN MPU
READ
OF OUTPUT REGISTER A;
RETURNED HIGH
BY NEXT HIGH-TO-LOW E
TRANSITION DUR-
ING A DESELECT.

CB2
b3 = 1: WRITE STROBE WITH E RESTORE
CB2 GOES LOW ON FIRST LOW-
TO-HIGH E TRANSITION FOLLOWING
AN MPU WRITE
INTO OUTPUT REGISTER B;
RETURNED
HIGH BY THE NEXT LOW-TO-HIGH E
TRANSITION FOLLOWING AN E
PULSE WHICH
OCCURRED WHILE THE PART WAS
DESELECTED.

b5 b4 b3
1 1

SET/RESET CA2 (CB2)
CA2 (CB2) GOES LOW AS MPU WRITES
b = 0 INTO CONTROL REGISTER.
CA2 (CB2) GOES HIGH AS MPU WRITES
b3 = 1 INTO CONTROL REGISTER.

Fig. 4-41. CA2 configured as an output pin. Reprinted with permission of Motorola, Inc.

184

This should have the effect of strobing the data into the attached peripheral device. Finally, if control-register B bit 4 is a "1," then CB2 will follow the state of control-register B bit 3.

MOTOROLA 68230 PARALLEL INTERFACE AND TIMER

Up to this point, the parallel-interface chips we have studied have been designed to work primarily with eight-bit microprocessors. They may be adapted to work with sixteen-bit processors but do not offer quite the power that such a more complex system can use. Motorola has developed a newer parallel I/O chip, called the 68230 Parallel Interface/Timer (PIT), which offers more complex parallel I/O capability than the older chips. You also get a timer/counter thrown in for good measure.

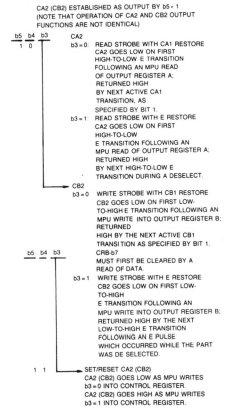

Fig. 4-42. CB2 configured as an output pin. Reprinted with permission of Motorola, Inc.

Figure 4-43 is a block diagram of the 68230 PIT. At this level, the chip appears quite simple. At the top of the diagram are the pins used to interface the PIT to the microprocessor. There are eight bi-directional data pins (D0 through D7), a read/write line, a Data-Transfer Acknowledge ($\overline{\text{DTACK}}$) line for handshaking with the microprocessor, a chip select ($\overline{\text{CS}}$), a clock input, and a reset pin. Also, at the bottom-right side of the diagram are five register-select inputs, RS1 through RS5.

First, we note that this chip has an eight-bit data bus to the microprocessor. Though this device is designed especially for the Motorola 68000 16-bit processor, it has an 8-bit-wide interface. However, since the PIT is designed for the 68000, its register select inputs start at RS1 instead of RS0, because the 68000 has no "0" address line.

The next items to look for in a parallel I/O chip are the number and type of I/O ports available. The PIT has three 8-bit ports: A, B, and C. Ports A and B are simple data ports which may be used in either a unidirectional or bidirectional mode.

Port C can be used in a similar manner but with other capabilities possible on the various Port C pins. For example, Port C bit 5 can be used as an interrupt request pin to the microprocessor for the parallel-port data transfers of Ports A and B. We will look in more detail at these added functions a little later.

Another look at the block diagram reveals four pins used for handshaking. These are signals H1 through H4. H1 and H3 are inputs while H2 and H4 may be used as either inputs or outputs. The PIT has extensive flexibility for handshaking and we will be studying the handshake lines more thoroughly. Figure 4-44 is a pin diagram of the 68230. You should immediately see one big difference between the PIT and the other parallel I/O chips reviewed in this chapter. The PIT comes in a 48-pin package while the other chips are in 40-pin packages. The extra functions available from the PIT do not come for free; there is a price to pay and it is in the package.

With five register-select lines, we expect the PIT to have at most 32 registers. Actually, it is nine

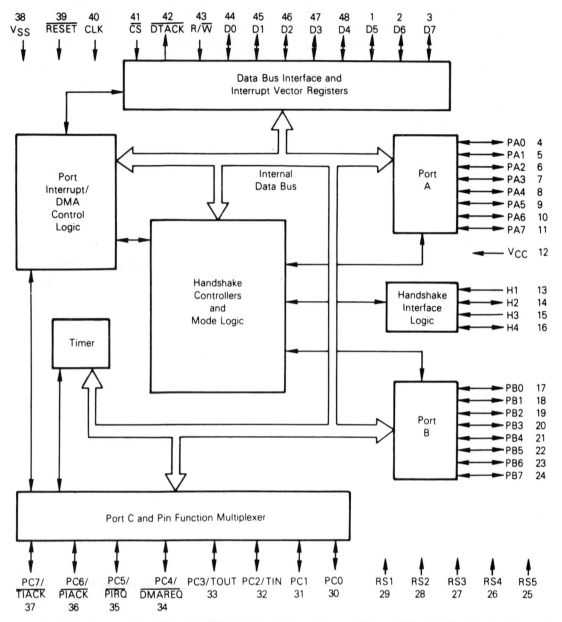

Fig. 4-43. Block diagram of the Motorola MC68230 Parallel Interface and Timer (PIT) chip. Reprinted with permission of Motorola, Inc.

short of that number—23 registers. The nine unused registers can be read but will only read as "0." **Figure 4-45** lists all of the registers inside the PIT. We aren't going to look at each register in detail. The PIT is complex enough to have its own chapter. Instead, we are more interested in what the PIT can be programmed to do.

There are four major operating modes for Ports A and B: modes 0, 1, 2, and 3. Mode 0 has three submodes, mode 1 has 2 submodes, and

PIN ASSIGNMENT

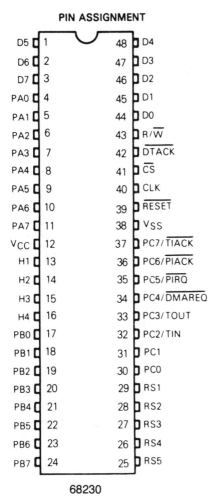

68230

Fig. 4-44. Pin diagram of the Motorola MC68230 PIT. Reprinted with permission of Motorola, Inc.

modes 2 and 3 have no submodes. The various modes and submodes are illustrated in **Fig. 4-46.**

Mode 0

Mode 0 is the unidirectional 8-bit I/O mode. The label "unidirectional" means that the data-transfer direction over the data lines is not changing dynamically, but remains as the processor has programmed them.

In this mode, Ports A and B are programmed and operate independently. Submode 00 is called the 8-bit, double-buffered input mode. It is called sub-

mode 00 because the two submode bits in the port control register are both set to "0." The input function is indicated by the large arrow in the figure pointing into the port. Note, however, the smaller solid arrow pointing out of the port. This indicates that even though mode 0, submode 0, is considered an input configuration, some of the port data lines may be used as outputs.

This trick is performed by using the port's associated data-direction register. If a port data pin is defined as an output, that pin will assume the logic level of the associated bit in the port data register when the port is written to by the microprocessor.

Handshake lines are used to tell the PIT when information on the port data lines should be accepted. Handshake lines H1 and H2 are associated with Port A, and handshake lines H3 and H4 are associated with Port B. The H1 and H3 input handshake pins are programmable. They can be asserted either by the rising or falling edge of a signal. Whichever is programmed into the PIT, when H1 or H3 is asserted, information on the data lines is latched in the proper port data-input latch.

At the same time, the operation of H2 (or H4) is programmable. H2 (or H4) can be programmed to:

1. Act as an auxiliary input-handshake pin with programmable assertion on a rising or falling edge. This can be useful for three-wire handshake protocols.
2. Act as an output that is always low.
3. Act as an output that is always high.
4. Act as an interlocked handshake pin. In this configuration, H2 (or H4) is asserted when the PIT can accept another byte and is negated when the byte is latched into the data register by H1 (or H3).
5. Act as a pulsed handshake pin. In this configuration, H2 (or H4) is asserted when the PIT is able to accept another data byte as in 4, but the signal does not remain asserted. In less than four PIT clock cycles, the output-handshake pin will be negated.

In configurations 4 and 5, the level of the output-handshake pin during assertion is program-

187

REGISTER SELECT BITS

5	4	3	2	1	7	6	5	4	3	2	1	0	Register
0	0	0	0	0	PORT MODE CONTROL		H34 ENABLE	H12 ENABLE	H4 SENSE	H3 SENSE	H2 SENSE	H1 SENSE	PORT GENERAL CONTROL REGISTER
0	0	0	0	1	*	SVCRQ SELECT		INTERRUPT PFS		PORT INTERRUPT PRIORITY CONTROL			PORT SERVICE REQUEST REGISTER
0	0	0	1	0	BIT 7	BIT 6	BIT 5	BIT 4	BIT 3	BIT 2	BIT 1	BIT 0	PORT A DATA DIRECTION REGISTER
0	0	0	1	1	BIT 7	BIT 6	BIT 5	BIT 4	BIT 3	BIT 2	BIT 1	BIT 0	PORT B DATA DIRECTION REGISTER
0	0	1	0	0	BIT 7	BIT 6	BIT 5	BIT 4	BIT 3	BIT 2	BIT 1	BIT 0	Port C Data Direction Register
0	0	1	0	1	INTERRUPT VECTOR NUMBER						*	*	PORT INTERRUPT VECTOR REGISTER
0	0	1	1	0	PORT A SUBMODE		H2 CONTROL			H2 INT ENABLE	H1 SVCRQ ENABLE	H1 STAT CTRL.	PORT A CONTROL REGISTER
0	0	1	1	1	PORT B SUBMODE		H4 CONTROL			H4 INT ENABLE	H3 SVCRQ ENABLE	H3 STAT CTRL.	PORT B CONTROL REGISTER
0	1	0	0	0	BIT 7	BIT 6	BIT 5	BIT 4	BIT 3	BIT 2	BIT 1	BIT 0	PORT A DATA REGISTER
0	1	0	0	1	BIT 7	BIT 6	BIT 5	BIT 4	BIT 3	BIT 2	BIT 1	BIT 0	PORT B DATA REGISTER
0	1	0	1	0	BIT 7	BIT 6	BIT 5	BIT 4	BIT 3	BIT 2	BIT 1	BIT 0	PORT A ALTERNATE REGISTER
0	1	0	1	1	BIT 7	BIT 6	BIT 5	BIT 4	BIT 3	BIT 2	BIT 1	BIT 0	PORT B ALTERNATE REGISTER
0	1	1	0	0	BIT 7	BIT 6	BIT 5	BIT 4	BIT 3	BIT 2	BIT 1	BIT 0	PORT C DATA REGISTER
0	1	1	0	1	H4 LEVEL	H3 LEVEL	H2 LEVEL	H1 LEVEL	H4S	H3S	H2S	H1S	PORT STATUS REGISTER
0	1	1	1	0	*	*	*	*	*	*	*	*	(NULL)
0	1	1	1	1	*	*	*	*	*	*	*	*	(NULL)
1	0	0	0	0	TOUT/TIACK CONTROL			Z D CTRL.	*	CLOCK CONTROL		TIMER ENABLE	TIMER CONTROL REGISTER
1	0	0	0	1	BIT 7	BIT 6	BIT 5	BIT 4	BIT 3	BIT 2	BIT 1	BIT 0	TIMER INTERRUPT VECTOR REGISTER
1	0	0	1	0	*	*	*	*	*	*	*	*	(NULL)
1	0	0	1	1	BIT 23	BIT 22	BIT 21	BIT 20	BIT 19	BIT 18	BIT 17	BIT 16	COUNTER PRELOAD REGISTER (HIGH)
1	0	1	0	0	BIT 15	BIT 14	BIT 13	BIT 12	BIT 11	BIT 10	BIT 9	BIT 8	(MID)
1	0	1	0	1	BIT 7	BIT 6	BIT 5	BIT 4	BIT 3	BIT 2	BIT 1	BIT 0	(LOW)
1	0	1	1	0	*	*	*	*	*	*	*	*	(NULL)
1	0	1	1	1	BIT 23	BIT 22	BIT 21	BIT 20	BIT 19	BIT 18	BIT 17	BIT 16	COUNT REGISTER (HIGH)
1	1	0	0	0	BIT 15	BIT 14	BIT 13	BIT 12	BIT 11	BIT 10	BIT 9	BIT 8	(MID)
1	1	0	0	1	BIT 7	BIT 6	BIT 5	BIT 4	BIT 3	BIT 2	BIT 1	BIT 0	(LOW)
1	1	0	1	0	*	*	*	*	*	*	*	ZDS	TIMER STATUS REGISTER
1	1	0	1	1	*	*	*	*	*	*	*	*	(NULL)
1	1	1	0	0	*	*	*	*	*	*	*	*	(NULL)
1	1	1	0	1	*	*	*	*	*	*	*	*	(NULL)
1	1	1	1	0	*	*	*	*	*	*	*	*	(NULL)
1	1	1	1	1	*	*	*	*	*	*	*	*	(NULL)

*Unused, read as zero

Fig. 4-45. Motorola MC68230 PIT register map. Reprinted with permission of Motorola, Inc.

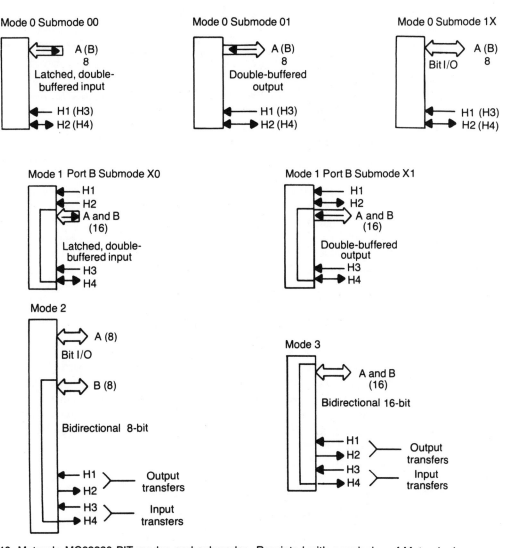

Fig. 4-46. Motorola MC68230 PIT modes and submodes. Reprinted with permission of Motorola, Inc.

mable. Thus either high- or low-true handshake signals can be directly obtained from the PIT. This can save a designer an inverter gate on these signal lines.

There is one other factor to take into consideration for mode 0, submode 00, as well as all of the other modes and submodes we will discuss in connection with the PIT. Data is double buffered. This means that the PIT can actually hold two bytes in the data latch. When the microprocessor reads the

data register, it will get the first byte latched in. On a subsequent read, the processor will get the next byte.

Double buffering reduces the time burden on a microprocessor. If the processor can transfer information at approximately the same rate as the peripheral can supply it, the operations of processor and peripheral transfers can be overlapped in time. This can result in quite a time savings.

If this advantage isn't clear, consider this. At

the same time the processor is removing a data byte from data latch number 1, the peripheral can be placing another byte in latch number 2. The PIT automatically moves the contents of latch number 2 into latch number 1 as soon as latch number 1 has been emptied. This sort of ''bucket brigading'' of data bytes can give the PIT a real performance advantage in higher-speed designs.

Moving on to mode 0, submode 01, we find a unidirectional 8-bit output configuration. There are many similarities between mode 0, submode 00, and mode 0, submode 01. Ports A and B are independent for both submodes. The handshake lines operate in nearly the same manner. The difference is that assertion of the H2 (or H4) output-handshake pin follows the microprocessor write of a byte into the port data register and the subsequent appearance of that byte on the port data lines.

The port is again double buffered so the processor may write a byte to the data port at the same time the peripheral is accepting a previously written byte. Output double buffering has the same performance advantages as input double buffering.

Although mode 0, submode 01 is defined as an output configuration, some of the port data lines may be used as inputs. This is again accomplished through the port data-direction register. Data pins defined as inputs have their output drivers disabled to prevent interference from data written to the port by the microprocessor.

The final mode 0 submode is called 1X. This means that submodes 11 and 10 are equivalent; the least significant bit is irrelevant. In this mode and submode, we find the data port operating in simple bit-I/O fashion. Data written to the port by the microprocessor is single buffered. A read of the data port produces the instantaneous value of the data pins.

In mode 0, submode 1X, the H1 (or H3) input is used to set a status bit in the port-control register and is not used for handshaking. H2 and H4 can be configured as similar status inputs or as an output which is always asserted or negated. H2 and H4 are also not used for handshaking in mode 0, submode 1X, and are available for other uses.

Mode 1

Mode 1 operation is similar to mode 0 operation in that the data ports are still considered to be operating in a unidirectional manner. Data Ports A and B are ganged together to form a 16-bit-wide data port. Two submodes are possible: X0 and X1. The X again means that ''X''ed bit is irrelevant. In this case, it is the most-significant bit, so mode 1, submodes 00 and 10 are equivalent, and mode 1, submodes 01 and 11 are also equivalent.

Mode 1 does not have a bit I/O submode, so the handshake lines are always used for handshaking. Only the H3 and H4 handshake lines are used, however, leaving H1 and H2 for other applications.

Though the PIT is an eight-bit device, the 68000 has a special MOVEP (move peripheral) instruction that will transfer a 16-bit word as two sequential bytes. This is the method Motorola intends for PIT mode 1 to be used. In order for this technique to work correctly, the circuit must be designed so that Port A is used to transfer the most significant byte.

Output and input submodes X0 and X1 work in a similar manner to mode 0, submode 00 and 01, respectively. The H3 and H4 handshake pins can be programmed for similar functions. The only difference is that the data port is now 16-bits wide instead of eight bits.

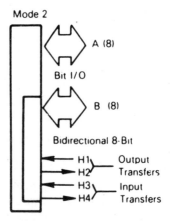

Fig. 4-47. Motorola MC68230 PIT Mode 2 port and pin definitions. Reprinted with permission of Motorola, Inc.

Since the handshake bits associated with Port B are being used for this mode, Port B should always be accessed last. For output operations, this means writing the high data byte to Port A first and then the low data byte to Port B. Access to Port B will activate the H4 handshake line. In a similar fashion, a read operation should read Port A first and then Port B, activating the H4 handshake line only on the second access. This is how the 68000 MOVEP instruction works.

Mode 2

Eight-bit, bidirectional, data transfers are possible using the 68230 PIT in mode 2. There are no submodes in this mode; all submode bits are ignored. In this mode, the H1, H2, H3, and H4 handshake lines are all dedicated to Port B.

This means that no handshake lines are available for Port A. As a result, Port A must be used in a bit I/O fashion. H1 and H2 are used as the output handshake pins, and H3 and H4 are the input handshake pins. Figure 4-47 illustrates the port and handshake pin definitions for mode-2 operation of the PIT.

There is only one difference in the handshake protocol for mode-2 operation. Since the data will be flowing in both directions over the Port-B data lines, some method is required to control the instantaneous data direction. H1 is used as the direction-control pin. When H1 is negated, the Port-B output buffers are enabled and the PIT drives the data lines. When H1 is asserted, the peripheral may drive the data lines. Bit settings in the Port-B data-direction register are ignored.

The sequence for the output handshake is supposed to work as follows:

1. The microprocessor outputs a byte to the 68230.
2. The 68230 asserts H2 to signal the availability of the data.
3. Up to this point, H1 has been negated so the Port-B data drivers are on and the data is available on the Port B pins. When the peripheral accepts the data, it asserts H1,

turning off the Port B data buffers and completing the handshake.

Clearly, for input transfers, H1 must be asserted to allow the peripheral to drive the data lines. Since H1 is asserted during both output and input transfers, it is important that the peripheral and the microprocessor remain synchronized. Otherwise, the peripheral may inadvertently cause an output transfer to complete during an input transfer.

If H1 is asserted when H2 is not asserted, no output transfer will take place, but the Port-B data buffers will be disabled. This will clear the data lines, allowing the peripheral to drive them with input data. However, if H2 is asserted when H1 is asserted, an output transfer will occur.

Thus, the microprocessor must not output a byte to the 68230 for an output transfer unless the peripheral will accept the data in a short period of time, or unless an input transfer is not likely to occur in the near future.

When the 68230 double buffering is added to this delicate sequencing of the H1 output-handshake/data-direction line, the problems associated with this mode become even more complex. The output latches must be empty by the time the peripheral decides to transfer data to the 68230, or H2 will be asserted and output transfers will take place in tandem with input transfers.

Mode 3

Mode-3 operation of the 68230 is similar to mode 2, except that the transfers are 16 bits wide instead of 8. Thus the 16-bit data-path descriptions of mode-1 operation and the handshake descriptions of mode-2 operation apply to mode 3. Both Port A and Port B are used as the data ports. All handshake lines are used for the bidirectional transfers. Figure 4-48 illustrates the port- and handshake-pin definitions for mode-3 operation.

Interrupts and the 68230

Interrupts are discussed in Chapter 8. They are signals used to quickly get the processor's at-

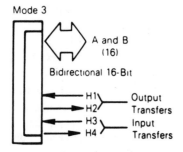

Fig. 4-48. Motorola MC68230 PIT Mode 3 port and pin definitions. Reprinted with permission of Motorola, Inc.

tention. One of the 68230 pins can be programmed as an interrupt pin for the parallel handshake pins. The interrupt can be programmed to occur when an input latch has received information and is ready to provide it to the microprocessor. Interrupts can also be programmed to occur when the peripheral takes data from an output latch, which means the processor can output another byte to the 68230 if it wishes. If you want more detailed information on interrupts and how they are used, look in Chapter 8.

DMA and the 68230

We have not yet discussed Direct Memory Access (DMA). We shall do so in Chapter 9. For now, it is sufficient to say that one of the Port C data lines can be programmed as a DMA request line. Such a signal is designed to be connected to a DMA controller and is used to sequence data transfers using the DMA protocols of that controller. The 68230 DMA request is pulsed and must be latched in most systems before being sent to a DMA controller.

The 68230 Timer

The "T" in PIT stands for timer. Within the 68230 is a versatile module called a timer/counter. It can be used to count input pulses, time events, generate pulse trains, and even kick the processor if it falls asleep. We are not going to cover the timer functions of the 68230 in this chapter. I'm saving that for Chapter 7, the chapter devoted to time interfacing.

TEXAS INSTRUMENTS 9914A GPIBA ADAPTER

The Texas Instruments 9914A General-Purpose Interface-Bus Adapter (GPIBA) implements the three entities of the IEEE-488 bus; talker, listener, and controller. With this chip, a system designer can readily build an IEEE-488 interface into a system.

Figure 4-49 is a "simplified" block diagram of the 9914A. The left side of the diagram is the microprocessor interface for the chip. It has an eight-bit data bus, three register-select lines, and a chip enable. Not shown in the diagram are the read and write control lines DBIN and $\overline{\text{WR}}$, the clock line, and the DMA handshake pins ACCRQ and $\overline{\text{ACCGR}}$. The 9914A has a negative-true write strobe ($\overline{\text{WR}}$) and a positive-true read strobe (DBIN).

The two DMA handshake pins are used with a DMA controller for the fastest possible data-transfer rate. ACCRQ (Access Request) is the DMA request pin which signals that the 9914A is ready to transfer another byte in the current transfer direction. ACCGR (Access Grant) is the acknowledge line from the DMA controller which signals when the next DMA transfer is taking place. DMA is covered in depth in Chapter 9. The clock may be any frequency up to 5 MHz.

At the right side of Fig. 4-49 is the interface between the 9914A and the IEEE-488 bus. This consists of the eight GPIB data lines, the three data-byte-transfer control lines, and the five interface-management lines. Thus, there are sixteen signals represented on the right side of the figure. Figure 4-50 is a pin diagram of the 9914A.

With three register selects, we would expect the 9914A to have no more than eight registers. Actually it has six read and seven write registers. Figure 4-51 lists the read registers, and Fig. 4-52 lists the write registers. Both figures show the required states of the register-select lines to access the various registers on the chip. All control of the 9914A by the microprocessor is performed by reading and writing these registers.

Starting with the read registers, we find two

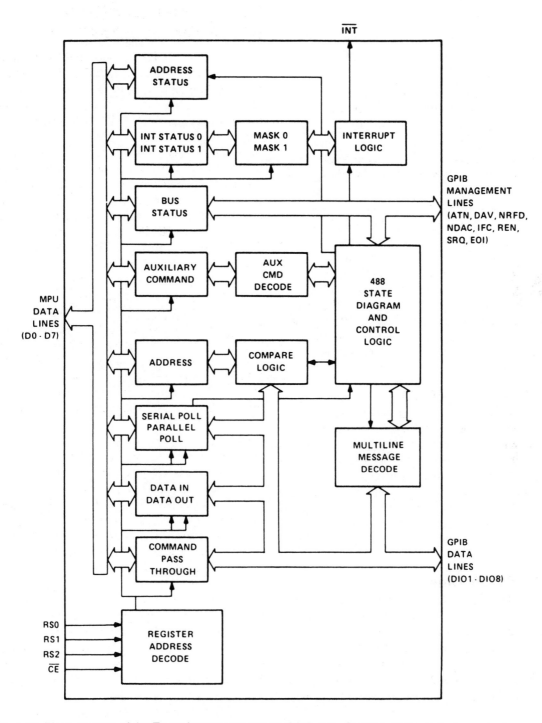

Fig. 4-49. Block diagram of the Texas Instruments 9914A GPIB chip. Courtesy of Texas Instruments, Inc.

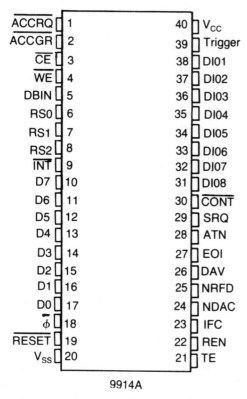

ACCRQ — 1   40 — V_CC
ACCGR — 2   39 — Trigger
CE — 3   38 — DIO1
WE — 4   37 — DIO2
DBIN — 5   36 — DIO3
RS0 — 6   35 — DIO4
RS1 — 7   34 — DIO5
RS2 — 8   33 — DIO6
INT — 9   32 — DIO7
D7 — 10   31 — DIO8
D6 — 11   30 — CONT
D5 — 12   29 — SRQ
D4 — 13   28 — ATN
D3 — 14   27 — EOI
D2 — 15   26 — DAV
D1 — 16   25 — NRFD
D0 — 17   24 — NDAC
ϕ — 18   23 — IFC
RESET — 19   22 — REN
V_SS — 20   21 — TE

9914A

Fig. 4-50. Pin diagram of the Texas Instruments 9914A GPIB chip. Courtesy of Texas Instruments, Inc.

interrupt status registers (interrupt status 1 and interrupt status 2), an address-status register, a bus-status register, an address-switch register, a command-pass-through register, and a data input register. All of these registers reside on the 9914A except for the address-switch register. This register must be externally implemented using switches and three-state buffers. Texas Instruments simply left a hole in their register-addressing scheme for the designer to use.

The data-input register allows the microprocessor to read information from the IEEE-488 bus. Reading the bus-status register gives the instantaneous state of the data-transfer control and interface-management lines. The bits in the register correspond to the following lines:

Bit 7: ATN (attention)
Bit 6: DAV (data valid)
Bit 5: NDAC (not data accepted)
Bit 4: NRFD (not ready for data)
Bit 3: EOI (end of identify)
Bit 2: SRQ (service request)
Bit 1: IFC (interface clear)
Bit 0: REN (remote enable)

ADDRESS			REGISTER	CONTENTS							
RS2	RS1	RS0	NAME	D0	D1	D2	D3	D4	D5	D6	D7
0	0	0	INT STATUS 0	INT0	INT1	BI	BO	END	SPAS	RLC	MAC
0	0	1	INT STATUS 1	GET	ERR	UCG	APT	DCAS	MA	SRQ	IFC
0	1	0	ADDRESS STATUS	REM	ATN	LLO	LPAS	TPAS	LADS	TADS	ulpa
0	1	1	BUS STATUS	ATN	DAV	NDAC	NRFD	EOI	SRQ	IFC	REN
1	0	0	ADDRESS SWITCH 1	edpa	dal	dat	A5	A4	A3	A2	A1
1	1	0	CMD PASS THRGH	DIO8	DIO7	DIO6	DIO5	DIO4	DIO3	DIO2	DIO1
1	1	1	DATA IN	DIO8	DIO7	DIO6	DIO5	DIO4	DIO3	DIO2	DIO1

Fig. 4-51. Read-register map of the Texas Instruments 9914A. Courtesy of Texas Instruments, Inc.

ADDRESS			REGISTER	CONTENTS							
RS2	RS1	RS0	NAME	D0	D1	D2	D3	D4	D5	D6	D7
0	0	0	INT MASK 0	X	X	BI	BO	END	SPAS	RLC	MAC
0	0	1	INT MASK 1	GET	ERR	UCG	APT	DCAS	MA	SRQ	IFC
0	1	1	AUXILIARY CMD	C/S	X	X	f4	f3	f2	f1	f0
1	0	0	ADDRESS REG	edpa	dal	dat	A5	A4	A3	A2	A1
1	0	1	SERIAL POLL	S8	RSV	S6	S5	S4	S3	S2	S1
1	1	0	PARALLEL POLL	PP8	PP7	PP6	PP5	PP4	PP3	PP2	PP1
1	1	1	DATA OUT	DIO8	DIO7	DIO6	DIO5	DIO4	DIO3	DIO2	DIO1

Fig. 4-52. Write-register map of the Texas Instruments 9914A. Courtesy of Texas Instruments, Inc.

194

As a parenthetical note, if you read the Texas Instruments data sheet for the 9914A, you will see that the bit assignments above are opposite those in the data sheet. This is because Texas Instruments numbers bits starting with the most-significant bit. Thus, the most-significant bit is bit 0 and the least-significant bit is bit 7 in Texas Instruments' data sheets. I have retained the numbering system used throughout this book so that bit 0 is always the least significant bit.

The address-status register provides the microprocessor with the current state of the 9914A. The bits in this register correspond to the following states:

Bit 7: REM (remote state)
Bit 6: LLO (local lockout, front panel disabled)
Bit 5: ATN (attention, command coming)
Bit 4: LPAS (listener primary addressed state)
Bit 3: TPAS (talker primary addressed state)
Bit 2: LADS (9914A is addressed to listen)
Bit 1: TADS (9914A is addressed to talk)
Bit 0: ulpa (lsb of last 9914A address)

All of the bit definitions listed in upper case correspond to states defined in the IEEE-488 standard. The ulpa bit is used for a special "dual primary addressing" mode. In this mode, the 9914A ignores the least-significant bit of addresses on the bus. The result is that the 9914A will recognize two addresses which differ only in the least significant bit. By reading the ulpa bit in the address status register, the microprocessor can determine which of the two addresses is currently active.

The command-pass-through register is needed for IEEE-488 commands which the 9914A does not recognize. It is also used in systems which implement secondary addressing. Secondary addressing allows subdevices within a primary address to be individually accessed. Since the 9914A does not know anything about subdevices implemented in the microprocessor system, it must pass the secondary addresses on to the microprocessor for further processing.

The two remaining read registers are the interrupt-status registers. Since each of these registers is eight-bits wide, there are sixteen conditions which can cause the 9914A to request an interrupt. The bit assignments for these registers are given in **Table 4-8**.

Bits 7 and 6 of interrupt status register 0 indicate which of the two interrupt-status registers contain the cause for the current interrupt. Bit 5 is the byte-input bit, signaling the receipt of a byte from the IEEE-488 bus, while bit 4 is the byte-output bit, signaling the readiness of the 9914A to accept another byte from the microprocessor to be output on the IEEE-488 bus. These bits are used for interrupt-driven data transfers. Bit 3 signals that the EOI line has been asserted during data transfers (as opposed to command transfers) which can be used to signal the last byte of a data transfer. SPAS, bit 2 of interrupt-status register 0, signals that a serial poll is taking place. This alerts the microprocessor to the need to send a status byte out onto the bus. The RLC bit signals a change from remote to local to remote status. Bit 0, MAC, is an interrupt if the bus address of the 9914A is changed.

Interrupt register 1, bit 7, is the GET bit and signals that a group-execute-trigger command has been received by the 9914A. This trigger is used to start several IEEE-488 devices together after each has been individually configured. Bit 6, ERR, is asserted when an incomplete handshake has occurred on the IEEE-488 bus. If the microprocessor connected to the 9914A is the system controller, it

Table 4-8. Interrupt-register Bit Assignments for the Texas Instruments 9914A.

| | BIT NUMBER | | | | | | | |
	7	6	5	4	3	2	1	0
INTERRUPT REGISTER 0	INT0	INT1	BI	BO	END	SPAS	RLC	MAC
INTERRUPT REGISTER 1	GET	ERR	UCG	APT	DCAS	MA	SRQ	IFC

may want to assert interface clear to abort any erroneous transfers in progress.

Bit 5, the UCG bit, signals the receipt of an unidentified command. This is where the command-pass-through register is used to allow the microprocessor to read in and interpret the command. In a similar manner, bit 4, APT, signals the receipt of a secondary address which the microprocessor must also interpret. DCAS, bit 3, signals a device clear. Bit 2, MA (my address), is asserted when the 9914A has been addressed to either talk or listen. SRQ (bit 1) indicates that a service request on the bus has occurred. SRQ will only be asserted if the 9914A is the controller currently in charge of the bus. IFC, bit 0, signals the receipt of an interface clear.

Clearly, with all of the interrupting conditions possible, the 9914A requires fairly sophisticated interrupt-service software. This complexity is much reduced, however, from what would be needed if the 9914A did not automatically handle the handshaking, major-command recognition, and primary-address recognition.

We start discussing the write registers with the two interrupt-mask registers. The bits in these registers directly correspond to the bits in the interrupt-status registers. When the bit in the interrupt-mask register is set to a 1, the corresponding condition is allowed to generate an interrupt if the condition occurs. If the GET, ERR, UCG, APT, DCAS, or MA interrupt conditions occur, the 9914A holds off completion of the bus handshake so that the microprocessor can intervene.

The data-out register is the path used by the microprocessor to output information to the IEEE-488 bus. It will do this when sending commands as a controller and when supplying information as a talker.

The address register allows the microprocessor to tell the 9914A which address to recognize. This address may be obtained from the off-chip address-switch register, or may be software controlled. The five least-significant bits of the address register determine the 9914A's bus address. Bit 5 is a disable for the 9914A's talk functions, and bit 6 disables the listen functions. If the system is a talk-only or listen-only device, these bits are used to inform the 9914A of that situation. This prevents the 9914A from being addressed to talk or listen when it isn't supposed to be capable of those functions. The most significant bit of the address register enables the dual primary-addressing capability of the 9914A as discussed above.

The parallel-poll and serial-poll registers are loaded by the microprocessor with the values for those polls. When the 9914A is polled by another controller, it automatically supplies the appropriate byte.

The last write register is the most complex. The auxiliary-command register is used to control the operation of the 9914A. Through this register, the microprocessor can send 24 commands to the 9914A. Table 4-9 lists these commands. The command number is sent to the auxiliary-command register on the five least-significant bits.

Some commands have a clear/set select bit which is sent on the most significant bit. If the clear/set bit is a 1 when the command is sent, the associated mode or function is selected or activated. If the clear/set bit is 0, the function is disabled. The auxiliary commands are:

swrst (software reset). This command causes the 9914A to be reset to a known, idle state. The parallel and serial poll registers are unchanged but all bus activity is halted. The software reset is activated when the microprocessor outputs the swrst command to the auxiliary command register with the clear/set bit equal to "1." The reset stays in effect until the processor sends the swrst command with the clear/set bit equal to a "0."

dacr (release DAC holdoff). This command is needed to allow an IEEE-488 bus handshake to complete for unrecognized commands and secondary addresses. When these are sent to the 9914A by another IEEE-488 bus controller, the 9914A will not accept the command or address until the dacr command is written into the auxiliary-command register. The clear/set bit should be a "1" for unrecognized commands. For secondary addresses, the clear/set bit should be a "1" if the address is

Table 4-9. Texas Instruments 9914A Auxiliary Commands.

C/S	F4	F3	F2	F1	F0	MNEMONIC	FUNCTION
0/1	0	0	0	0	0	swrst	Chip reset
0/1	0	0	0	0	1	dacr	Release ACDS holdoff
na	0	0	0	1	0	rhdf	Release RFD holdoff
0/1	0	0	0	1	1	hdfa	Holdoff on all data
0/1	0	0	1	0	0	hdfe	Holdoff on EOI ONLY
na	0	0	1	0	1	nbaf	Set new byte available false
0/1	0	0	1	1	0	fget	Force group execute trigger
0/1	0	0	1	1	1	rtl	Return to local
na	0	1	0	0	0	feoi	Send EOI with next byte
0/1	0	1	0	0	1	lon	Listen only
0/1	0	1	0	1	0	ton	Talk only
na	0	1	0	1	1	gts	Go to standby
na	0	1	1	0	0	tca	Take control asynchronously
na	0	1	1	0	1	tcs	Take control synchronously
0/1	0	1	1	1	0	rpp	Request parallel poll
0/1	0	1	1	1	1	sic	Send interface clear
0/1	1	0	0	0	0	sre	Send remote enable
na	1	0	0	0	1	rqc	Request control
na	1	0	0	1	0	rlc	Release control
0/1	1	0	0	1	1	dai	Disable all interrupts
na	1	0	1	0	0	pts	Pass through next secondary
0/1	1	0	1	0	1	stdl	Set T1 delay
0/1	1	0	1	1	0	shdw	Shadow handshake

Courtesy of Texas Instruments, Inc.

valid and a "0" if the address is not valid. If the clear/set bit is a "1," the 9914A will become addressed.

rhdf (release ready for data holdoff). This command is used to release a ready-for-data holdoff caused by the hdfa or hdfe auxiliary commands.

hdfa (hold off on all data). This command causes each byte handshake to be held off by the 9914A until an rhdf command is written to the auxiliary command register. The command is activated by writing the command with the clear/set bit set and deactivated with the clear/set bit cleared.

hdfe (holdoff on end). This command allows the 9914A to complete all bus handshakes unless the EOI line is asserted. Then, an rhdf auxiliary command is required to release the holdoff.

nbaf (set new byte available false). This command allows a byte placed in the 9914A data output register to be discarded. An example of when this might be necessary is when a service request occurs which requires an abort of the current message.

fget (force group-execute trigger). When this command is issued, the trigger pin on the 9914A is asserted. If the clear/set bit is clear, the trigger pin will assert for five clock cycles. If the clear/set bit is clear, the trigger pin will be asserted until the fget auxiliary command is reissued with the clear/set bit cleared. The trigger pin can be used to synchronize various modules within the microprocessor system.

rtl (return to local). Resets the remote/local status bit in the address-status register and generates an interrupt to the microprocessor (if the interrupt is enabled) to tell the processor to respond to the system's front panel.

feoi (force end or identify). When issued, this command causes EOI bus line to be asserted with the next outgoing data byte.

lon (listen only). If the clear/set bit is set, the 9914A immediately becomes an active listener. If the clear/set bit is clear, the listener state is deactivated.

ton (talk only). If the clear/set bit is set, the 9914A immediately becomes an active talker. If the clear/set bit is clear, the talker state is deactivated.

gts (go to standby). This command is issued to the 9914A when it is the system controller and has just sent out commands to configure the bus. The ATN line is negated in response to this command, allowing any addressed talker to take over the bus-control lines.

tcs (take control synchronously). Instructs the 9914A to assume control of the bus at the end of the current byte transfer. If the 9914A is not currently an active listener, the shdw (shadow handshake) auxiliary command must first be issued to allow the 9914A to synchronize with the handshake lines.

tca (take control asynchronously). The 9914A will immediately assume control of the bus by asserting the ATN line. Any data transfer in progress may be disrupted and the data being transferred will probably be invalid.

rpp (request parallel poll). When sent with the clear/set bit set, the 9914A will request a parallel poll on the bus, if it is the active system controller. The returned poll byte is read in the command-pass-through register. Then, the rpp command is again sent to the 9914A with the clear/set bit cleared, causing the 9914A to withdraw the poll request on the bus.

sic (send interface clear). The IFC bus line is asserted when this command is sent to the 9914A with the clear/set bit equal to a "1." The IFC line must remain asserted for at least 100 microseconds. Then the sic command is sent to the 9914A with the clear/set bit cleared, which causes the 9914A to negate IFC.

sre (send remote enable). The REN bus line is asserted or negated depending on whether the clear/set bit is a "1" or "0" respectively.

rqc (request control). When the microprocessor receives the IEEE-488 take control (TCT) command as an unrecognized command through the 9914A command-pass-through register, it issues the rqc

command to the 9914A. Then, when ATN is negated by the system controller, the 9914A will become the active controller.

rlc (release control). When the microprocessor no longer wishes to be the active controller and has passed bus control to some other controller, it issues the rlc auxiliary command to the 9914A which will then negate ATN and release control to the bus.

dai (disable all interrupts). This command disables the 9914A's INT interrupt line when the clear/set bit is set, and enables the INT line when the clear/set bit is clear.

pts (pass through next secondary). In response to a parallel-poll-configure command, which the 9914A will not recognize, the microprocessor sends the 9914A the auxiliary command pts. This allows the next byte received to also be passed through instead of interpreted so that the microprocessor may use it to configure the parallel-poll byte.

stdl (set T1 delay). This command controls the T1 delay in the talker handshake. The T1 delay is the bus settling time between the assertion of the data lines and the assertion of data valid. On power up, the delay is 10 clock cycles. If the stdl command is sent with the clear/set bit equal to "1," the delay is changed to 6 clock cycles, allowing the handshake to run a bit faster. The 10-cycle delay is activated if the clear/set bit is a "0."

shdw (shadow handshake). If the clear/set bit is set, the 9914A will participate and monitor the bus handshake even though it is not performing data transfers. This allows a 9914A acting as a controller, but not as a listener, to synchronize with the handshaking on the bus. The lon (listen only) command must also be issued to the 9914A in conjunction with the shdw command.

vstdl (very short talk delay). This command reduces the T1 delay to 3 clock cycles when the clear/set bit is a "1." Otherwise, the stdl definitions are used.

As companion circuits to the 9914A, Texas Instruments offers the 75160 series of buffers. The 9914A does not have bus drivers built into it and requires buffering to drive the IEEE-488 bus. The 75160 is used to buffer the eight data lines while the 75161 and 75162 are used to buffer the data-transfer-control and interface-management lines. If you are building a single-controller system, where the 9914A will always control the bus, the 75161 will serve. The 75162 is for multiple-controller systems where only the active controller may control the control lines.

Figures 4-53, 4-54, and 4-55 are the pin diagrams for the 75160, 161, and 162 respectively. In each diagram, the pins on the left are connected to the 9914A while the pins on the right connect directly to the IEEE-488 bus. Figure 4-56 illustrates a complete IEEE-488 interface design using the 9914A, a 75160, and a 75162.

The 9914A is an extremely powerful I/O controller and qualifies as more than a parallel I/O chip. It implements the state diagrams of the IEEE-488 specification with greater speed than that possible with a software implementation. This improves system performance and speeds system development. The 9914A is a very good example of migration of interface intelligence from the microprocessor to the I/O chip.

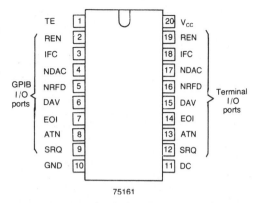

Fig. 4-54. Pin diagram of the Texas Instruments 75161. Courtesy of Texas Instruments, Inc.

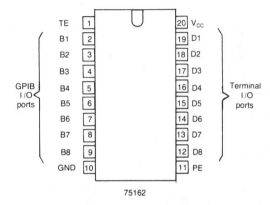

Fig. 4-55. Pin diagram of the Texas Instruments 75162. Courtesy of Texas Instruments, Inc.

THE NCR 5380 SCSI ADAPTER

As a final example of a parallel-I/O chip, let's look at the NCR 5380 SCSI interface device. This 40-pin device incorporates the handshaking logic and high-current bus drivers required for SCSI bus transfers plus interrupt and DMA (direct memory access) logic to help integrate the IC into a microprocessor system. The NCR 5380 can assume either the initiator or target roles.

A block diagram of the NCR 5380 appears in Fig. 4-57. Note the CPU interface at the top of the figure and the SCSI bus interface at the bottom. In between, we see a lot of registers. Figure 4-58 shows the pin diagram and Fig. 4-59 shows a functional diagram of the IC. The SCSI signals are on

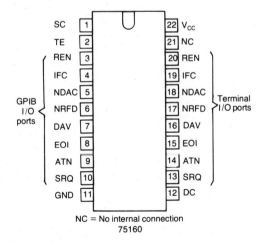

Fig. 4-53. Pin diagram of the Texas Instruments 75160. Courtesy of Texas Instruments, Inc.

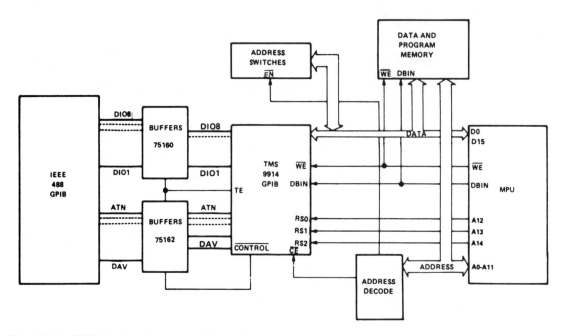

Fig. 4-56. A GPIB interface based on a Texas Instruments 9914A. Courtesy of Texas Instruments, Inc.

pins 1 through 20 and the microprocessor-bus signals are on pins 21 through 40.

The pins that connect the NCR 5380 to a microprocessor are fairly standard. Three address pins (A0, A1, and A2) in conjunction with the I/O read ($\overline{IOR}$) and I/O write ($\overline{IOW}$) pins allow a microprocessor to address the 16 individual registers (8 read and 8 write) in the chip. Asserting the chip select ($\overline{CS}$) activates the chip for microprocessor-bus communications. The read and write pins ($\overline{IOR}$ and $\overline{IOW}$) signal the NCR 5380's Intel-style microprocessor bus orientation. The $\overline{RESET}$ signal puts the IC into a known, stable state and the data lines (D0 through D7) form the IC's data port.

The remaining NCR 5380 microprocessor-bus signal lines enhance the IC's ability to perform interrupt- and DMA-driven I/O. IRQ is the chip's interrupt request and can signal an error condition or the completion of a command. Likewise, DRQ is the chip's DMA request. When asserted, DRQ signals that an internal data register needs to be read or written to continue a SCSI data transfer. The DACK input provides a path for the DMA con-

troller's response to DMA requests generated by the 5380. Assertion of DACK directly accesses the IC's data registers without the need to use the address lines.

Two other DMA-related signals further enhance the 5380's DMA capabilities. The EOP input allows a DMA controller to tell the NCR 5380 that the current transfer cycle on the microprocessor bus is the last data transfer in a block. READY allows the 5380 to control the rate at which the DMA controller moves data to and from the IC. READY simply signals when the 5380 is ready for another transfer, based on the transactions occurring on the SCSI bus. The READY signal is used in conjunction with DRQ for block-mode DMA transfers when the DMA controller is programmed to retain control of the microprocessor bus for a certain number of transfers.

A register map for the 5380 appears in **Fig. 4-60**. There are eight readable registers and eight writable registers. Register 0 (both read and write) and Register 6 (read) provide access to the SCSI data lines. The data registers are used to transfer

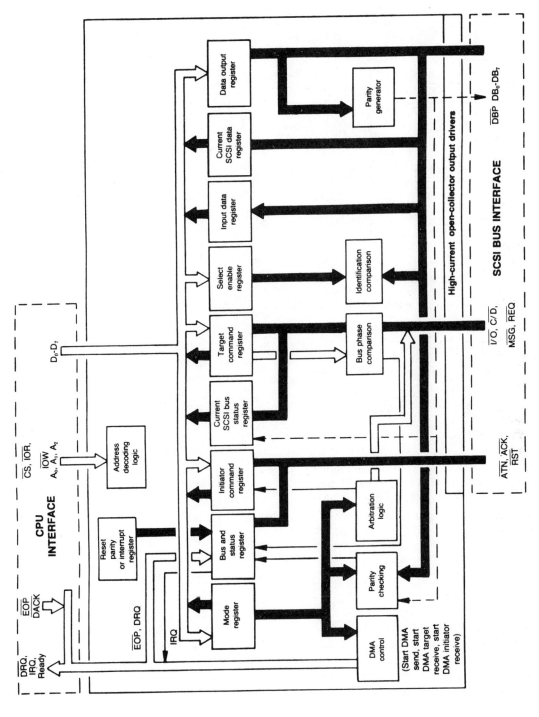

Fig. 4-57. Block diagram of the NCR 5380 SCSI adapter chip. Courtesy of NCR Corp.

201

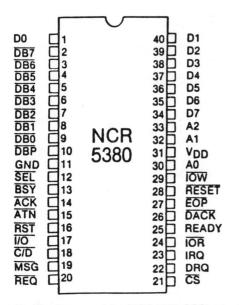

Fig. 4-58. Pin diagram of the NCR 5380 SCSI adapter chip. Courtesy of NCR Corp.

SCSI commands, data, status, and message bytes between the microprocessor data bus and the SCSI data bus.

Register 0 (read) acts as a transparent input port and provides the current state of the SCSI data lines. The register is not latched so that a microprocessor can peek at the data lines whenever

necessary. A microprocessor reads Register 0 when it wants to accept a data byte from the SCSI bus using programmed I/O data transfers or when it wants to check for asserted ID codes during a SCSI arbitration.

Register 0 (write) is the output data register that latches one byte so that the NCR 5380 can place that byte on the SCSI bus. This register is used for programmed I/O data transfers, for DMA transfers, and to assert ID bits on the SCSI data lines during the arbitration and selection phases. Register 6 (read) is used for incoming data transfers using DMA.

Register 1 (read and write) is the initiator command register. Many of the bits are the same between the read and write versions of this register but some bits differ. The pin definitions are as follows:

Bit 0 (assert data bus): Setting this bit causes the NCR 5380 to take the contents of Register 0 (write) and place them on the SCSI data lines. The NCR 5380 also generates a parity bit from the data on the SCSI data lines and places that bit on the DBP (data bus parity) pin.

Bit 1 (assert -ATN): Setting this bit causes the NCR 5380 to assert the -ATN line on the SCSI bus. Reading this bit gives the current status of the SCSI -ATN line.

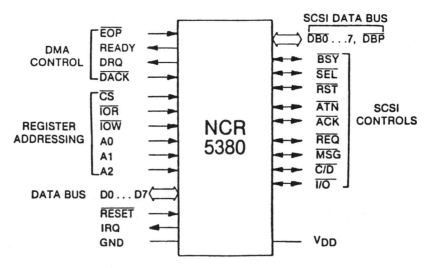

Fig. 4-59. Functional diagram of the NCR 5380 SCSI adapter chip. Courtesy of NCR Corp.

READ

CURRENT SCSI DATA (00)

7 6 5 4 3 2 1 0

$\overline{DB7}\ldots\overline{DB0}$

INITIATOR COMMAND REGISTER (01)

7 6 5 4 3 2 1 0

Assert Data Bus
Assert ATN
Assert SEL
Assert BSY
Assert ACK
Lost Arbitration
Arbitration in Progress
Assert RST

MODE REGISTER (02)

7 6 5 4 3 2 1 0

Arbitration
DMA Mode
Monitor BSY
Enable EOP interrupt
Enable Parity Interrupt
Enable Parity Checking
Target Mode
Block Mode DMA

TARGET COMMAND REGISTER (03)

7 6 5 4 3 2 1 0

| 0 | 0 | 0 | 0 | | | | |

Assert I/O
Assert C/D
Assert MSG
Assert REQ

CURRENT SCSI BUS STATUS (04)

7 6 5 4 3 2 1 0

DBP
SEL
I/O
C/D
MSG
REQ
BSY
RST

BUS & STATUS REGISTER (05)

7 6 5 4 3 2 1 0

ACK
ATN
Busy Error
Phase Match
Interrupt Request
Parity Error
DMA Request
End of DMA

INPUT DATA REGISTER (06)

7 6 5 4 3 2 1 0

$\overline{DB7}\ldots\overline{DB0}$

RESET PARITY/INTERRUPT (07)

7 6 5 4 3 2 1 0

| X | X | X | X | X | X | X | X |

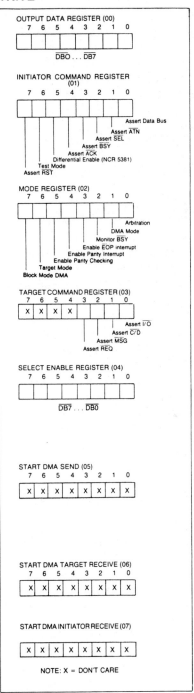

WRITE

OUTPUT DATA REGISTER (00)

7 6 5 4 3 2 1 0

DB0 ... DB7

INITIATOR COMMAND REGISTER (01)

7 6 5 4 3 2 1 0

Assert Data Bus
Assert ATN
Assert SEL
Assert BSY
Assert ACK
Differential Enable (NCR 5381)
Test Mode
Assert RST

MODE REGISTER (02)

7 6 5 4 3 2 1 0

Arbitration
DMA Mode
Monitor BSY
Enable EOP interrupt
Enable Parity Interrupt
Enable Parity Checking
Target Mode
Block Mode DMA

TARGET COMMAND REGISTER (03)

7 6 5 4 3 2 1 0

| X | X | X | X | | | | |

Assert I/O
Assert C/D
Assert MSG
Assert REQ

SELECT ENABLE REGISTER (04)

7 6 5 4 3 2 1 0

$\overline{DB7}\ldots\overline{DB0}$

START DMA SEND (05)

7 6 5 4 3 2 1 0

| X | X | X | X | X | X | X | X |

START DMA TARGET RECEIVE (06)

7 6 5 4 3 2 1 0

| X | X | X | X | X | X | X | X |

START DMA INITIATOR RECEIVE (07)

| X | X | X | X | X | X | X | X |

NOTE: X = DON'T CARE

Fig. 4-60. Read- and write-register map of the NCR 5380 SCSI adapter chip. Courtesy of NCR Corp.

Bit 2 (assert -SEL): Setting this bit causes the NCR 5380 to assert the -SEL line on the SCSI bus. Reading this bit gives the current status of the SCSI -SEL line.

Bit 3 (assert -BSY): Setting this bit causes the NCR 5380 to assert the -BSY line on the SCSI bus. Reading this bit gives the current status of the SCSI -BSY line.

Bit 4 (assert -ACK): Setting this bit causes the NCR 5380 to assert the -ACK line on the SCSI bus. Reading this bit gives the current status of the SCSI -ACK line.

Bit 5 write (differential enable): This bit is unused in the NCR 5380. It is used in the company's NCR 5381, a SCSI controller that supports the differential version of the SCSI bus.

Bit 5 read (lost arbitration): The NCR 5380 asserts this bit after it has detected a bus-free phase, arbitrated for use of the SCSI bus, and lost the arbitration.

Bit 6 write (test mode): Setting this bit disables all of the NCR 5380's SCSI output drivers, effectively disconnecting the IC from the SCSI bus.

Bit 6 read (arbitration in progress): When set, this bit indicates that the NCR 5380 is currently arbitrating for control of the SCSI bus.

Bit 7 (assert -RST): Setting this bit causes the NCR 5380 to assert the -RST line on the SCSI bus. Reading this bit gives the current status of the SCSI -RST line.

Register 2, the mode register, controls the overall operation of the NCR 5380. It determines whether the chip assumes the target or initiator role, whether data transfers use programmed I/O or DMA, and what conditions will generate an interrupt. The bit definitions are as follows:

Bit 0 (arbitrate): When set, this bit tells the NCR 5380 to arbitrate for control of the SCSI bus the next time it observes a bus-free phase. Prior to setting this bit, a microprocessor should also set the proper ID bit in Register 0 (write) so that when the NCR 5380 starts the arbitration sequence, it can assert the proper ID code on the SCSI data bus.

Bit 1 (DMA mode): When set, this bit tells the NCR 5380 to use its DMA pins for data transfers.

Bit 2 (monitor -BSY): When set, this bit tells the NCR 5380 to generate an interrupt if the -BSY line becomes negated. This interrupt could be used to alert a system that a target has just disconnected from the bus.

Bit 3 (enable EOP interrupt): This bit is used in conjunction with a DMA controller and DMA transfers. When set, the NCR 5380 will generate an interrupt when its EOP (end of process) pin is asserted. A DMA controller would generally assert this pin when it completes the transfer of a data block. The subsequent interrupt would then allow a microprocessor to either start another block transfer or to instruct the NCR 5380 to release the SCSI bus.

Bit 4 (enable parity interrupt): When set, this bit instructs the NCR 5380 to generate an interrupt if it detects a parity error during a SCSI bus data transfer. To use this feature, you must also set bit 5 in this register to enable parity checking.

Bit 5 (enable parity checking): When set, this bit enables the NCR 5380's internal parity checker. If a parity error occurs, the NCR 5380 sets the parity-error latch (Register 5, read, bit 5).

Bit 6 (target mode): When set, this bit instructs the NCR 5380 to operate as a SCSI target device. When clear, this bit instructs the NCR 5380 to operate as an initiator.

Bit 7 (block mode DMA): This bit controls the type of handshake mechanism the NCR 5380 uses for DMA transfers. When this bit is a 0, the chip uses the DRQ (data request) and DACK (data acknowledge) pins in an interlocked handshake sequence. When this bit is set, the chip uses the DRQ and the IOW or IOR pins in an interlocked handshake sequence while the DACK pin remains asserted during the entire block transfer.

Register 3, the target command register, contains only four active bits. These bits give a microprocessor control over the four data-transfer control lines -REQ, -MSG, -C/D, and -I/O. The bit definitions are as follows:

Bit 0: Assert -I/O
Bit 1: Assert -C/D
Bit 2: Assert -MSG
Bit 3: Assert -REQ

Using these lines, the NCR 5380 can perform all of the SCSI information-transfer phase data transfers. The various phases defined by the SCSI specification are:

Bus Phase	Assert -I/O	Assert -C/D	Assert -MSG
DATA OUT	0	0	0
COMMAND	0	1	0
MESSAGE OUT	0	1	1
DATA IN	1	0	0
STATUS	1	1	0
MESSAGE IN	1	1	1

Register 4 (read) provides a transparent port that gives the current state of seven SCSI bus control lines. The bit definitions are:

Bit 0: -DBP (data bus parity)
Bit 1: -SEL (select)
Bit 2: -I/O (input/output)
Bit 3: -C/D (command/data)
Bit 4: -MSG (message)
Bit 5: -REQ (request)
Bit 6: -BSY (busy)
Bit 7: -RST (reset)

A microprocessor can use this register to identify the cause of an interrupt.

Register 4 (write) is the select-enable register and allows the NCR 5380 to automatically monitor the SCSI bus for the assertion of a specific ID code during a SCSI selection phase. By setting a single bit in this register, a microprocessor enables the NCR 5380 to generate an interrupt when the correct ID code is present on the SCSI data lines, when -SEL is asserted, and when -BSY is not asserted. Thus, this interrupt alerts a system acting as a SCSI target device when it is being selected by an initiator during a selection phase.

Register 5 (read) is the bus and status register that allows a microprocessor to look at the remaining SCSI bus lines not handled by the current SCSI bus status register (Register 4, read) and to determine certain bus conditions. The bit definitions for this register are:

Bit 0: -ACK (acknowledge)

Bit 1: -ATN (attention)

Bit 2: (Busy error) The NCR 5380 sets this bit if the -BSY signal suddenly becomes negated.

Bit 3: (Phase match) The -MSG, -I/O, and -C/D SCSI signals define the bus transfer phase. If the states of these signal lines matches the corresponding bits in the NCR 5380's target command register (Register 3), the NCR 5380 will set this bit. The NCR 5380 requires that the phase on the SCSI bus must match the bits in Register 3 before it will perform data transfers.

Bit 4: (Interrupt request active) This bit echoes the state of the NCR's 5380 interrupt pin. Thus systems that do not use hardware interrupts or the chip's interrupt output line can periodically read this bit to perform a sort of polled-interrupt operation.

Bit 5: (Parity error) The NCR 5380 sets this bit when it detects a parity error during a data transfer, if Register 2, bit 5 is set to enable parity checking.

Bit 6: (DMA Request) This bit echoes the state of the NCR 5380's DMA request pin (DRQ). Because the DRQ pin will usually be connected directly to the DMA controller, bypassing the microprocessor, this bit allows a microprocessor to snoop on the NCR 5380's DMA activity.

Bit 7: (End of DMA transfer) The NCR 5380 asserts this bit when EOP, DACK, and either IOR or IOW are all asserted simultaneously for at least 100 nanoseconds. This condition signifies the last byte transfer in a block transfer is currently taking place.

Chapter 5

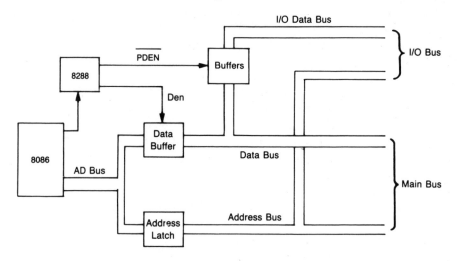

Serial Interfacing

The fact that the computer represents a relatively new technology may lead you to believe that digital I/O technology does also. The first electronic computers appeared in the 1940s, and serious work in computer data communications did not start until the next decade. But when engineers did begin to connect computers to other devices, they used a technology that originated in the previous century, serial I/O.

The first electrical device used extensively for communications was the telegraph. Samuel Morse improved the telegraph mechanically from an idea originated by Andre Ampere. More important, he devised the Morse code. This was the first really practical encoding of communications symbols into a machine-transmittable form. The key feature of interest to us is the technique of serial transmission.

Symbols are represented in the code by a series of dots and dashes, each character having its unique representation. The dots and dashes may be considered the predecessors to the ones and zeroes of the modern character codes we use in computer

data communications today. Improvements in the telegraph led to printing telegraphs that required no human operator to decipher the codes. New codes and more advanced machines were devised, culminating with the teletypewriter.

By the time the teletypewriter was introduced, the dots and dashes had become binary ones and zeroes. The Morse code was discarded in favor of codes that assign the same number of bits to each character. This made it much easier for a machine to decode a transmission. By the time the electronic computer came into being, there already existed a wealth of technology for electronic data communications.

At first, teletypewriters served as I/O devices between people and computers. The keyboard and printer of the teletypewriter provided a low-cost data entry and display mechanism. As technology progressed, CRT terminals and faster printers replaced the teletypewriter, but the serial interfacing was retained.

Computer time-sharing was born when computers became sufficiently powerful to handle several tasks simultaneously. Since computers were still very expensive, it was necessary to spread their cost over many users.

The problem then was how to connect users at several locations to the central computing facility. Stringing wires to each location was too expensive. Fortunately, such communications lines already existed. They belonged to the telephone system.

Unfortunately, many of the links in the telephone system are not wires. They can just as easily be satellite or land-based microwave links, since these also make up the phone system. All of these links are designed to carry only voice, not computer data.

In addition, the phone companies were extremely unhappy at the prospect of finding all kinds of strange signals in their networks. Teletypewriters did not have standardized interfacing requirements—the voltages involved could range anywhere from 6 to 140 volts. A standard was required.

The Electronic Industries Association (EIA) standard RS-232C resulted. This standard was specifically designed to do one thing: It defines the electrical characteristics for an interface between a piece of data terminal equipment (DTE) and a piece of data communications equipment (DCE). The DTE is the terminal for the timeshare user, while the DCE is a modulator-demodulator (modem) that encodes computer data into signals that are compatible with the phone system.

RS-232C is now the most common electrical specification used for serial interfacing, whether telephone lines are involved or not. In addition, RS-232C is the dominant interface used to connect microcomputers to peripherals. We will look at the RS-232C standard shortly, but first we start with the basics.

TRANSMITTING OVER ONE WIRE

The basis for serial data communications is the transmission of information over one wire. The interfacing techniques discussed in Chapter 4 have all relied on several parallel wires to carry information between devices. Each wire carries a single bit of a character composed of multiple bits.

When long distances are involved between a computer and its peripheral, the cost of running several wires in parallel becomes prohibitive. Serial interfacing provides a solution at much lower cost.

There are three basic modes of serial transmission: simplex, half-duplex and full duplex. Simplex operation is always unidirectional, and the direction is never changed. **Figure 5-1** illustrates a simplex connection. Device 1 always transmits and device 2 always receives. **Figure 5-2** illustrates a half-duplex connection. Device 1 may transmit to device 2 and device 2 may transmit to device 1. Only one of the devices may transmit at any given time. **Figure 5-3** illustrates a full duplex connection: both devices may transmit at the same time.

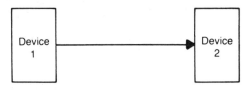

Fig. 5-1. A simplex serial connection.

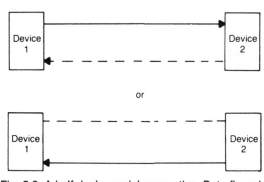

Fig. 5-2. A half-duplex serial connection. Data flows in only one direction at a time.

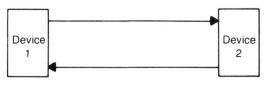

Fig. 5-3. A full-duplex serial connection. Data may flow in both directions at once.

The reason for simplex is that there are some devices which never need to transmit, such as some printers. A computer simply sends the printer characters to print and does not need to get any information back. Also, some communications channels, such as one-way radio transmission, are inherently simplex channels.

A half-duplex connection is used when there is not sufficient bandwidth in the communications channel to support simultaneous, bidirectional communications. Telephone lines can only support data rates up to about 2400 bits per second if used in both directions at the same time. Higher data rates require half-duplex operation.

Full duplex operation requires communications channels with good bandwidth. Cables and radio transmissions are good examples of high-bandwidth channels. Also, for lower data rates, telephone lines can be used in a full duplex mode.

SERIAL PROTOCOLS

The EIA RS-232C standard is a hardware specification. No mention is made as to how data is to be transmitted on the transmitted-data pin. That specification falls within the realm of the serial protocol.

There are two basic types of serial transmission: asynchronous and synchronous. Both transmission types use the concept of the bit time. Since bits are being transmitted over the serial link one at a time, some technique is needed to identify where one bit stops and the next begins. The technique used is to define the period of time when a bit is present on the line. This period is called a bit time.

Asynchronous transmission is called that because each character is transmitted without any fixed time between it and the preceding and succeeding characters. Since there is no timing information between characters, each character must have timing bits appended to it.

A start bit precedes each character transmitted in asynchronous format. This alerts the receiver that a character is coming. The character is followed by one or more stop bits which allow the receiver a rest period before the next character is transmit-

ted. No clock or other synchronizing signal is sent with the data. The transmitter and receiver have internal clocks and the start bit is used to synchronize them.

Synchronous transmission is block oriented. While synchronization information is included with each character in asynchronous transmission by adding start and stop bits, multiple-character messages are synchronized in synchronous transmission by adding characters to the beginning of the message. One or more synchronization (or sync) characters are appended to the front of the message. These sync characters serve to synchronize the receiver with the transmitter. They provide a sort of running start at the message.

Unlike asynchronous transmission, synchronous transmitters and receivers share a common clock. Either the transmitter or the receiver must send a clock bit to the other device. Thus, no start bit is needed because the synchronous transmitter and receiver are always in bit synchronization. Sync characters are used to allow the receiver and transmitter to synchronize on character or message boundaries.

Since synchronous transmission is block oriented, sophisticated methods of error detection can be used to ensure message integrity. The most popular error-detection technique used in synchronous transmission schemes is called cyclic redundancy checking (CRC).

There are two types of synchronous transmission. The older is called the byte-control protocol or BCP. Synchronous BCP transmission is strictly concerned with transmitting bytes of information. Sync characters come in byte sizes and the error checking is done at a byte level.

The other type of synchronous transmission is called the bit-oriented protocol or BOP. Bit-oriented protocols are more flexible than BCP protocols because they can transmit information as bits. Thus BOPs can be used to send odd-length data formats, such as 17 bits, although this is not usually done. We will study synchronous transmission and CRC later in this chapter, but first let's take a closer look at asynchronous communications.

ASYNCHRONOUS TRANSMISSION

Because the bits of a serially transmitted character are separated by time, a waveform is produced on the data line when a character is transmitted. Such a waveform for the transmission of the ASCII character "E" in asynchronous format is shown in **Fig. 5-4**. The ASCII code for "E" is 1000101 in binary and is transmitted least-significant-bit first. The data line idles in the logic-one state, and the waveform of **Fig. 5-4** is read from left to right.

For asynchronous serial data communications, a start bit is always sent first to mark the beginning of the character. Following the start bit are the data bits in the character, sent in order from least significant to most. Each bit is held on the data line for a precisely controlled length of time. This time is the bit time.

The receiver is alerted to the incoming character by the start bit. It then times the incoming signal, sampling each bit as near to the center of the bit time as possible. Naturally, both the transmitter and receiver must agree on the length of time a bit

will be held on the data line or the transmission will be garbled by samples made at incorrect times.

A bit time determines the maximum rate at which characters may be transmitted and thus defines the *bit rate* at which a particular interface is running. Standardized bit rates for asynchronous communications are 50, 75, 110, 134.5, 150, 300, 600, 1200, 2400, 3600, 4800, and 9600 bits per second.

Following the data bits, there may be a parity bit which is used for error detection. If a noise pulse should affect the data line at the wrong time, a bit in the transmission may be misread.

The transmitter keeps track of the number of ones in the character being transmitted so it can set the parity bit, making the total number of bits in a character always even (for even parity) or odd (for odd parity). The receiver can also keep track and use the parity bit to determine whether the transmission was received in error. Start and stop bits are not included in the parity-generated and detection scheme.

The last bits to be transmitted are the stop bits. These are not really bits since they contain no information. Stop bits allow the receiver sufficient

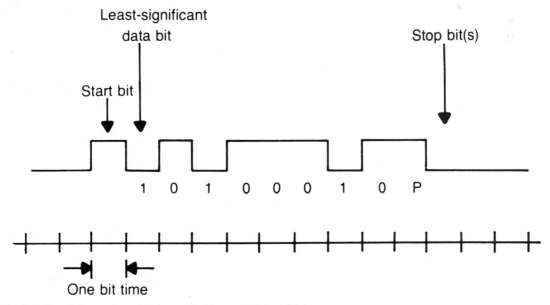

Fig. 5-4. A serial waveform for the capital letter "E" in ASCII.

time to assemble the serial bits just received, send the assembled character on, and prepare for the next character. There may be 1, 1.5, or 2 bit times allowed for stop bits. Since this is a rest period, fractional bits are allowed.

Commonly, 7-bit characters are transmitted using the asynchronous serial protocol. The most widely used character set associated with asynchronous transmissions is the ASCII character set. Even so, 5-, 6-, and 8-bit character sets may also be transmitted using the asynchronous format.

BYTE-CONTROL PROTOCOLS

Message transmission for the synchronous byte-control protocols is based on a block of characters. To the front of this block, several sync characters, a header, and a message separator are added. Another message separator and error-checking information are usually added to the end of the message. The entire block is called a message frame. Byte control protocols use special characters in the character set, such as the sync character and message separators, to control the operation of the communications link.

The sync characters serve to alert the receiver that a message is arriving, and allow the receiver to synchronize with the transmitter. The header generally contains control information that will help the receiver determine what to do with the message. A count of the total number of bytes in the frame is usually included in the header.

Following the block of characters in the message, there is a message separator and then a cyclic redundancy check (CRC) sequence. The CRC is used to determine if the frame has been received correctly. **Figure 5-5** illustrates a typical BCP frame. IBM's "Bisync" is the most popular byte-control protocol. It is called Bisync because two sync characters are used to start the frame.

BIT-ORIENTED PROTOCOLS

Bisync, and the other byte-control protocols, have limitations which prompted computer manufacturers to seek a more powerful synchronous-transmission format. This search resulted in the creation of the bit-oriented protocols, or BOPs.

Bit-oriented protocols are by definition not byte oriented. Messages are combined with control and error-checking information to create frames, but the synchronization, header, and error sections are not necessarily composed of characters from a character set. More frequently, the header and error sections are coded in binary.

Figure 5-6 illustrates a message frame of a bit-oriented protocol. At the start of the frame is a sequence of bits called a flag. This is a special sequence which uniquely identifies the start of the message. Usually, flags are the binary sequence 01111110. Flags serve as the sync character of a bit-oriented protocol.

Since they are so important, flags are the only characters allowed to have more than five "1" bits in a row. It is possible that certain bit sequences in the information portion of the frame may also have more than five "1" bits in a row. If that should happen, "bit stuffing" is used to prevent the receiver from mistaking such data as a flag character.

Bit stuffing occurs at the transmitter. When the transmitter sends five "1" bits in a row, it automatically inserts a "0" bit. The receiver detects the five "1" bits in a row and then makes a decision on the next incoming bit. If the next bit is a "1," then a flag has been received. If a "0" is received, it must have been stuffed into the data stream, so the receiver discards the "0." Thus, bit stuffing ensures that flag characters are truly unique and do not ever appear inside a frame.

More than five "1" bits in a row can be received in one other case. If eight or more "1"s are

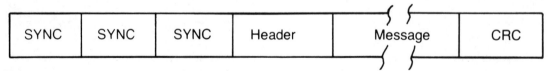

Fig. 5-5. A byte-control protocol (BCP) frame.

210

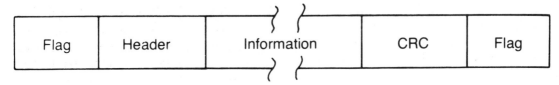

| Flag | Header | Information | CRC | Flag |

Fig. 5-6. A bit-oriented protocol (BOP) frame.

received sequentially, it is called an abort and the receiver disregards the message. Aborts can be caused by loss of the communications link or catastrophic failure of the transmitter.

There are several competing bit-oriented protocols. Generally, however, synchronous protocols are not used with microcomputers. Therefore, we will limit the rest of the chapter to discussions of asynchronous topics.

THE RS-232C STANDARD

The most common electrical specification used for asynchronous serial data communications is the Electronic Industry Association's (EIA) RS-232C standard. The standard was introduced in 1962 as RS-232, and the latest version, introduced in 1969, is the one presently in use, RS-232C. **Figure 5-7** is a picture of the connector used with the RS-232C standard, and **Fig. 5-8** illustrates the pin designations of the connector. The connector is called a 25-pin "D." Of the 25 pins, 20 are assigned to

RS-232C signals, three are reserved, and the remaining two are unassigned.

RS-232C was developed long before TTL integrated circuits existed. It therefore shouldn't surprise you that signal levels on the RS-232C pins do not use the 5-volt and ground logic levels. Instead, a high signal level for RS-232C is somewhere between +5 and +15 volts, while a low signal level is between −5 and −15 volts. In addition, RS-232C receivers must withstand signal levels of up to +/− 25 volts. This requirement assures compatibility with the older RS-232B standard. Clearly, the connection of an RS-232C driver to a TTL gate can result in destruction of the receiver!

Note that there is really more than one wire involved with this interface even though it is used for serial transmission. Pins 2 and 3 are the data-carrying wires, called transmitted and received data. Pin 7 is a signal ground and serves as a current-return path between the data communications equipment (DCE) and the data terminal equipment (DTE).

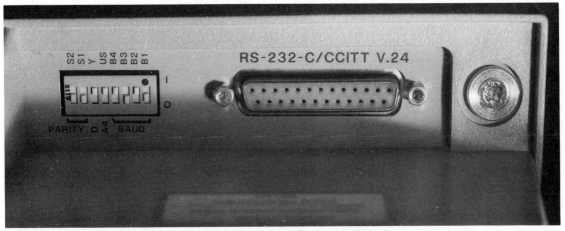

Fig. 5-7. An RS-232C connector on the back of a Hewlett-Packard 7470A plotter.

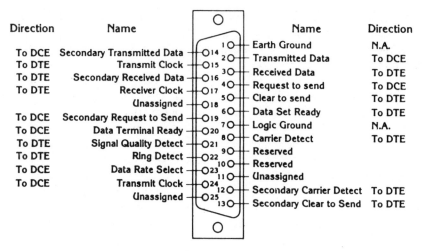

Direction	Name		Name	Direction
To DCE	Secondary Transmitted Data — O14	1 O —	Earth Ground	N.A.
To DTE	Transmit Clock — O15	2 O —	Transmitted Data	To DCE
To DTE	Secondary Received Data — O16	3 O —	Received Data	To DTE
To DTE	Receiver Clock — O17	4 O —	Request to send	To DCE
	Unassigned — O18	5 O —	Clear to send	To DTE
To DCE	Secondary Request to Send — O19	6 O —	Data Set Ready	To DTE
To DCE	Data Terminal Ready — O20	7 O —	Logic Ground	N.A.
To DTE	Signal Quality Detect — O21	8 O —	Carrier Detect	To DTE
To DTE	Ring Detect — O22	9 O —	Reserved	
To DCE	Data Rate Select — O23	10 O —	Reserved	
To DCE	Transmit Clock — O24	11 O —	Unassigned	
	Unassigned — O25	12 O —	Secondary Carrier Detect	To DTE
		13 O —	Secondary Clear to Send	To DTE

Fig. 5-8. Pin diagram and signal names for the RS-232C connector.

These three wires are sufficient for bidirectional communications between the DCE and DTE.

What are the other wires for then? They serve as control wires between the DCE and DTE and are there merely to establish and maintain a communication link with the computer. Let's ignore them for now.

First, we'll examine the data lines more closely. Information is sent out on the transmitted-data line and received on the received-data line. Nothing could be simpler, right?

Wrong! Which device transmits on the tramsmitted-data line, the DTE or DCE? Both cannot transmit on pin 2 and receive on pin 3. If the DTE transmits on one wire, the DCE must have a receiver on that same wire or there is no communication.

Note the difference between serial I/O and IEEE-488. The IEEE-488 standard specifies bidirectional data lines. Data may flow over those data lines in either direction. RS-232C is an older standard, and bidirectionality was not possible with the technology. Also, with just two data lines, it was not needed.

So who does transmit on the transmitted-data line? All signal names in the RS-232C standard are from the perspective of the DTE. It is the DTE that transmits on pin 2 and receives on pin 3. The DCE

transmits on pin 3 and receives on pin 2. Figure 5-9 should clear up any confusion about this.

Now to get confused again. Suppose we are going to connect a computer to a printer through the "standard RS-232C" port. Which device is a DTE and which is a DCE? More specifically, which is going to transmit on pin 2 of the RS-232C connector and which will transmit on pin 3? Neither the computer nor the printer is a terminal or a modem.

The manufacturers of these devices may offer cables which allow their equipment to look like either a DTE or a DCE. More often, however, the RS-232C connector is bolted to the back of the device and no choice is possible. The manufacturer had to make an arbitrary decision that will be wrong 50 percent of the time.

In the case of two devices of the same type, DTE or DCE, a "haywire" cable will have to be assembled to get signals onto the correct wires. Usually, this task falls to the user.

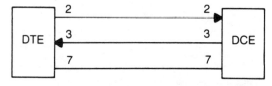

Fig. 5-9. The minimum RS-232C connection for full-duplex operation.

We have just jumped the first hurdle in connecting RS-232C equipment: physical plug-to-plug incompatibility on the data lines. There are many more potential problems related to the data signal itself.

First, signal levels are not like those of the other interfaces as discussed earlier. RS-232C does not use TTL signals because TTL didn't exist when the standard was written. A positive voltage between 5 and 15 volts is used to represent a logic-zero level on the data line in RS-232C. A negative voltage between -5 and -15 volts represents a logic-one level.

These levels are valid only for the data lines on pins 2 and 3. The data lines are therefore negative-true. All other signals in RS-232C are positive-true, so a positive voltage represents a logic one and a negative voltage represents a logic zero.

Now, given the format of the data transmission, what could possibly go wrong? First, there are several parameters on which the transmitter and receiver must agree. The bit rate has been mentioned already. In addition, the parity (odd, even, or none) and the number of stop bits must be set the same in both transmitter and receiver.

Character codes must also be considered. Our example uses the ASCII character set with seven bits per character. ASCII is the most popular code in use today, but not the only one. There are 5-bit codes (Baudot and Murray), 6-bit codes (IBM Correspondence Code) and 8-bit codes (IBM EBCDIC). The RS-232C standard does not restrict the number of bits per character.

Now that we have our computer and printer connected so that they use the proper wires and agree on bit rate, parity, number of stop bits, and character code to be used, you may feel we have this interface licked. Not so.

Let's say the printer is set up for ASCII seven-bit characters, odd parity, and one stop bit. In addition, the bit rate is set to 9600 bits per second (sometimes called baud). We have set the bit rate to the fastest rate so our equipment doesn't waste a lot of time sending characters and the printer will be used at its maximum efficiency. Assume that the

computer side of the interface has been set compatibly.

Now we write a program on the computer to send one line of text to the printer to be printed. We run the program and it works! Finally we list the program on the printer so that we have a record of our triumph. Unfortunately, several characters seem to be lost in the transmission. We try again with equally dismal results. Running the program meets again with success and listing again fails. Now what do you think is going on?

Consider the data rate at which the computer is sending characters. We are using ASCII, so that's seven bits, plus one for the parity bit, one for the stop bit, and a start bit, for a total of ten bits per character. We are sending 9600 bits per second which is equivalent to 960 characters per second.

A quick look at the printer specifications indicates the source of the problem. The printer can only print a maximum of 175 characters per second. We are sending data to the printer five times faster than it can print! Most printers have buffers and can tolerate this mismatched data rate for a limited period of time, but then the buffer fills. After that, any subsequent characters transmitted will "fall on the floor."

When we ran the program, less than a buffer-full of characters were transmitted. The buffer didn't overflow and there was no problem. Listing the program on the printer overflowed the buffer because more characters were sent to be printed. When the buffer overflowed, characters were lost.

The parallel interfaces described earlier had handshake mechanisms to prevent data transmitters from going too fast for their receivers. Surely, RS-232C must also have a handshake mechanism to prevent this problem? No it does not. Returning to **Fig. 5-8**, let's now consider the other RS-232C signals and try to find some to use as a handshake mechanism. We are looking in particular for two sets of handshake lines: one for the transmitted data line and the other for the receive data line.

Aha! pins 4 and 5 are called *request to send* and *clear to send*. These look like prime contenders for handshake lines. Unfortunately, many printer manufacturers have fallen into this trap. The names of the signals on pins 4 and 5 do indeed lead you to believe they form a data-handshake mechanism.

According to the strict RS-232C definition, the DTE asserts request to send when it has data to transmit. It then waits for the DCE to assert clear to send before transmitting. That is one half of the traditional handshake. The problem is that the DCE is not allowed to drop clear to send until the DTE drops request to send.

This situation is similar to taking a drink from a garden hose with a friend controlling the spigot. It's easy to start the flow, but you had better be prepared to take a long drink or a short shower.

The DTE and DCE signals on pins 4 and 5 were intended as a handshake between the terminal and the modem (remember those?) to allow the terminal to request control of the communications link from the modem. They also make it possible for the modem to tell the terminal when the link has been acquired. The terminal is then allowed to assume that it will keep the link as long as it wishes. Thus, the DCE cannot arbitrarily drop clear to send when it wishes.

Some manufacturers have ignored the strict definition of pins 4 and 5 and use them for a data handshake anyway. Others avoid the conflict by using the *data terminal ready* or *data set ready* lines (depending on whether they are pretending to be a terminal or a modem). None of these lines was intended to be used for data handshaking. Use of any RS-232C line for handshaking does not guarantee recognition of the handshake by the device at the other end of the cable.

Consider other possibilities of use of clear to send as a handshake line. If a device drops clear to send in the middle of a character transmission, what does that mean? If the transmitter stops immediately, in the middle of the character, that character is sure to be garbled. If the transmitter waits until that character transmission is complete and then stops, there may be no room in the receiver's buffer for that last character transmitted.

Because this possibility is not considered in the standard, the result of implementing a handshake mechanism is an RS-232C interface cannot be determined without studying interfacing manuals for both of the involved devices.

Now that we have looked at all the ways to misuse the RS-232C control lines, let's look at their intended purpose. Table 5-1 lists all of the RS-232C signals with the connector pin they are found on, and their use.

Note that the RS-232C connector actually can handle two simultaneous channels; a primary channel and a secondary channel. The secondary channel is not commonly used for asynchronous communications, but is more common in synchronous applications.

With 20 signals on the RS-232C connector, you certainly may be feeling a little confused. Relax and let me introduce you to the "basic eight" RS-232C signals. They reside on pins 2 through 8 and pin 20. These eight pins are all that are used for well over 90 percent of the connections using the RS-232C standard.

Start with the data lines, transmitted data and received data, on connector pins 2 and 3. These are obviously always needed for communications. Only one is required for a simplex connection, but both are generally used. Pin 4, request to send, and pin 5, clear to send, make up the primary modem handshake and are also frequently used as device handshake lines as we have already discussed.

Pin 6, data set ready, is paired with pin 20, data terminal ready. Normally, these pins assume asserted levels when a system is powered on, and never change. Frequently, one or both of these pins must be asserted for the interface to function properly. A piece of hardware, or some software test, may require a true indication on either pin before the transmitter is allowed to operate.

The logic ground is found on pin 7, and this is about the only pin you can depend on to be connected properly in all the RS-232C interfaces you will encounter. Finally, pin 8, data carrier detect, is frequently used in systems that actually are connected to DCEs so that some indication of an operable communications link is available.

Usually, if a computer or peripheral manufacturer misuses the RS-232C signals to implement handshaking or other "badly needed" functions, you

Table 5-1. RS-232C Signals and Their Definitions.

PIN	NAME	PURPOSE
1	Frame Ground	Earth ground for safety
2	Transmitted Data	Data line from DTE to DCE
3	Received Data	Data line from DCE to DTE
4	Request to Send	Asserted by the DTE when it is desired to send information over the communications link. The DCE responds by acquiring control of the link if it does not have it already.
5	Clear to Send	Asserted by the DCE when it has control of the communications link.
6	Data Set Ready	Asserted by the DCE when it is powered on and functioning properly.
7	Signal Ground	Logic ground for the interface
8	Data Carrier Detect	Asserted by the DCE when it is receiving a carrier over the communications link.
9	Reserved	
10	Reserved	
11	Unassigned	
12	Secondary Data Carrier Detect	Same as Data Carrier Detect but for a secondary channel
13	Secondary Clear to Send	Same as Clear to Send but for a secondary channel
14	Secondary Transmitted Data	Same as Transmitted Data but for a secondary channel
15	Transmit Clock	A clock frequency for the transmitter usually used for synchronous communications. This signal is supplied by the DCE to the DTE.
16	Secondary Received Data	Same as Received Data but for a secondary channel
17	Receiver Clock	A clock frequency for the receiver usually used for synchronous communications This signal is supplied to the DCE from the DTE.
18	Unassigned	
19	Secondary Request to Send	Same as Request to Send but for a secondary channel
20	Data Terminal Ready	Asserted by the DTE when it is powered up and functioning properly.
21	Signal Quality Detect	Asserted by the DCE when the communications channel is operating reliably. If negated, the DTE may wish to change the bit rate by changing the level on pin 23, Data Rate Select.
22	Ring Indicator	Asserted by the DCE when something on the communication channel is attempting to contact the DCE
23	Data Rate Select	Used to select the bit rate of the DCE. May be changed in response to a change of pin 21, Signal Quality Detect.
24	External Transmit Clock	A transmitter clock supplied by the DTE to the DCE.
25	Unassigned	

will be able to read about that misapplication somewhere in the manual. It may not be easy to find but it will probably be there.

What might you find on an RS-232C connector beside handshaking signals? I have found bit-rate-select pins, where the bit rate of the interface is determined by which pin(s) you connect to ground or to each other. Another favorite is to bring the power supply lines for a peripheral over some of the signal pins. That is usually not too bad if the power supply is 5 or 12 volts but I have also seen 110 volts from the wall socket! Current-loop signal pins are also frequently placed on the reserved or unassigned pins.

To bring this discussion of RS-232C to an end, and to introduce the next section on the newer EIA standards, I would like to cover two limitations of the RS-232C standard. The first is a data-rate limitation. RS-232C specifies that the "slew" rate of RS-232C signals be no greater than 30 volts per microsecond. Practically, this limits RS-232C to about 20,000 bits per second. Although that data rate is a very good match to asynchronous transmissions, which are usually limited to 19,200 bits per second or less, it hampers some synchronous systems.

The second limitation is one of distance. According to the RS-232C standard, cables between devices are to be limited to 50 feet. That may seem like quite a bit for a microcomputer system, but office wiring is another story. By the time a cable is run from a computer room, into the wall, up to the ceiling, over to the intended office, down the wall and over to the terminal, the 50-foot limit seems far too short. As a practical matter, RS-232C signals are routinely run for 100 or 200 feet without problem. The installations just don't meet the standard but it doesn't seem to bother the users.

RS-422, RS-423, AND RS-449

Since RS-232C has limitations and was getting on in years, some thought was given to generating a new standard for serial communications. In keeping with the "bigger and better" philosophy of progress, the EIA produced not one but three new standards to replace RS-232C. They are EIA standards RS-422, RS-423, and RS-449. The EIA adopted RS-449 in 1977 and it became a US Federal standard in 1980.

RS-449 defines a complete set of signals which can be used to establish, maintain, and break a communications link between two devices. Since this is an "all new" standard, many signals with functions previously found in the RS-232C standard were given "all new" names. Thus the old RS-232C transmitted-data signal is the RS-449 send-data signal. Only some of the signals were renamed, however, and the RS-232C received-data signal is easily recognized as the RS-449 received-data signal.

Table 5-2 lists all of the RS-449 signals and gives the RS-232C counterparts where applicable. Note that there are now 10 more signals, which means that RS-449 won't fit on a 25-pin "D" connector. The ten new signals and their use are:

Send Common. An extra signal return (logic ground) for the signal line used by the DTE to transmit data.

Receive Common. An extra signal return (logic ground) for the signal line used by the DCE to transmit data.

Terminal in Service. Asserted by the DTE to indicate that it is not only turned on but operational. This differs from the RS-232C signal data terminal ready which usually just indicated that the DTE was turned on. Today's smart and intelligent terminals may be turned on but not activated.

New Signal. Asserted by the DTE when it wants the DTE to prepare to acquire the communications line. This line can be used in a multiple-terminal network where a computer polls each terminal. As soon as a terminal is polled but before the poll response is generated, the DTE can assert new signal, telling the DCE to get control of the communications link in preparation for a transmission.

Select Frequency. Allows the DTE to select one of two frequency bands for the DCE to operate on. Full-duplex communications channels often use

Table 5-2. RS-449 Signals and Their Definitions.

FUNCTION	EIA RS-449 NAME	EIA RS-232C EQUIVALENT
Common	Signal Ground	Signal Ground
	Send Common	---
	Receive Common	---
Control	Terminal In Service	---
	Incoming Call	Ring Indicator
	Terminal Ready	Data Terminal Ready
	Data Mode	Data Set Ready
Primary Channel:		
Data	Send Data	Transmitted Data
	Received Data	Received Data
Timing	Terminal Timing	External Transmit Clock
	Send Timing	Transmit Clock
	Receive Timing	Receive Clock
Control	Request to Send	Request to Send
	Clear to Send	Clear to Send
	Receiver Ready	Data Carrier Detect
	Signal Quality	Signal Quality Detect
	New Signal	---
	Select Frequency	---
	Signaling Rate Selector	Signal Rate Select *
	Signaling Rate Indicator	Signal Rate Select *
Secondary Channel:		
Data	Secondary Send Data	Secondary Transmitted Data
	Secondary Received Data	Secondary Received Data
Control	Secondary Request to Send	Secondary Request to Send
	Secondary Clear to Send	Secondary Clear to Send
	Secondary Receiver Ready	Secondary Carrier Detect
Other:		
Control	Local Loopback	---
	Remote Loopback	---
	Test Mode	---
	Select Standby	---
	Standby Indicator	---

* The RS-232C signal Data-Rate Select could be either supplied to or generated by the DTE. RS-449 has two signals, one for each direction.

frequency-division multiplexing where one transmitter operates at a lower frequency and the other at a higher frequency. In telephone communications, these are sometimes called the ''answer'' and ''originate'' tones. ''Select frequency'' is not like data-rate select because it only affects the communications channel and not the rate of information flowing through the channel.

Local Loopback. When asserted by the DTE, this signal causes the DCE to connect the transmitter with the receiver at the interface to the communications channel. Thus the DTE can test the DCE by sending data and checking for a duplicate received message.

Remote Loopback. When asserted by the DTE, this signal requests that the DCE at the other end of the communications link connect the send data and received data lines together. This creates a large loop which can be verified for proper operation by sending data and checking for a duplicate received message.

Test Mode. Indicates to the DTE and the DCE is

in a test mode and is not using the communications channel for data transmission.

Select Standby. When asserted by the DTE, it issues a request that a standby means of communication be used. This signal is only useful where redundant communications hardware is available.

Standby Indicator. Indicates to the DTE when standby facilities are being used for communications.

With the extra signals, RS-449 won't fit on the RS-232C 25-pin "D" connector. Instead, RS-449 is implemented on one or two connectors. A 37-pin "D" connector is used for the overall-control and primary-channel signals, while a 9-pin "D" connector is used for the secondary-channel signals.

The reason RS-449 requires 46 pins relates to the limitations of the RS-232C specification discussed at the end of the previous section. Data rates and cable lengths are restricted in the RS-232C standard because the potentially large signal swings (30 volts peak-to-peak), and the rapid rise and fall times of the signals, can cause crosstalk problems in the cable.

Also, there is but a single signal-return conductor (logic ground) in the RS-232C standard, which contributes to noise susceptibility. Restricting the data rate reduces noise generation, while restricting cable length reduces coupling between conductors in the cable.

RS-449 combats the noise generation problem by limiting signal swings to 12 volts peak-to-peak, by placing more stringent restrictions on the rates at which signals may change, and by adding extra signal-return wires for critical signals. That is why a send common and a receive common were added.

The new signal specifications are RS-422A and RS-423A. There are two specifications because there are two implementations of RS-449. The RS-422A standard is a balanced line specification. A balanced-line is one where two wires are used to send a signal. If one line is in the logic "1" state, the other is in the logic "0" state and vice versa. This technique greatly improves the signal because

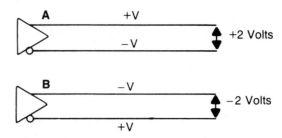

Fig. 5-10. Differential RS-422A drivers in both positive and negative output states.

the voltage swing is effectively doubled (see **Fig. 5-10**).

When one output of the balanced transmitter is at $+V$ volts, the other output is at $-V$ volts, making the difference between the two outputs $+2V$ volts, referenced to the bottom output pin as shown in **Fig. 5-10A**. If the input to the transmitter changes logic levels, the output pin which was at $+V$ volts changes to $-V$ volts, while the other output changes to $+V$ volts from $-V$ volts. The difference between the output pins is now $-2V$ volts, referenced once again to the bottom output pin of the transmitter. RS-422A requires a minimum voltage differential of 2 volts.

RS-423A specifies a single-ended line much like, and compatible with, the RS-232C specification. The signal is referenced to ground. RS-423A calls for a positive signal voltage of between $+200$ millivolts and $+6$ volts, and a negative voltage of between -200 millivolts and -6 volts. The maximum data rate for RS-423A drivers is 100,000 bits per second, which is possible on cables of up to 300 feet in length. If the data rate is reduced to 1,000 bits per second, a 4,000-foot cable is allowed. RS-423A is compatible with RS-232C. The 6-volt signal levels will work with RS-232C receivers. When operated with RS-232C devices, RS-423A is limited to 20,000 bit-per-second data rates and 50-foot cables, to conform to the RS-232C standard.

The big advantage provided by RS-449 is when RS-422A drivers and receivers are used. The maximum transfer rate allowed using RS-422A drivers is 10-million bits per second. This is one hundred times the rate allowed by RS-232C. At this rate, cable lengths of up to 40 feet are allowed. If the data rate is limited to 100,000 bits per second, cable lengths of up to 4,000 feet are possible.

Another advantage of RS-422A and RS-423A is the number of receivers allowed on the transmission line. RS-232C only made allowance for a single receiver, although multiple receivers are routinely found in RS-232C systems. The newer RS-422A and RS-423A specifications allow up to 10 receivers.

Table 5-3 is a list of the RS-449 signals on the 37-pin connector, while **Table 5-4** is a list of the signals on the RS-449 nine-pin connector. Unfortunately, RS-449 has failed to catch on the way its creators had hoped. RS-232C is everywhere, well established, and not likely to disappear just because a new standard which is technologically superior arrives on the scene. When most RS-232C implementations only use between three and eight wires and do not require data rates above 20,000 bits per sec-

Table 5-3. RS-449 Connector Pinout - 37-pin Connector.

PIN NUMBER	SIGNAL NAME
1	Shield
2	Signal Rate Indicator
3	Spare
4	Send Data
5	Send Timing
6	Receive Data
7	Request to Send
8	Receive Timing
9	Clear to Send
10	Local Loopback
11	Data Mode
12	Terminal Ready
13	Receiver Ready
14	Remote Loopback
15	Incoming Call
16	Signal Rate Select/Select Frequency
17	Terminal Timing
18	Test Mode
19	Signal Ground
20	Receive Common
21	Spare
22	Send Data (common or differential)
23	Send Timing (common or differential)
24	Receive Data (common or differential)
25	Request to Send (common or differential)
26	Receive Timing (common or differential)
27	Clear to Send (common or differential)
28	Terminal in Service
29	Data Mode (common or differential)
30	Terminal Ready (common or differential)
31	Receiver Ready (common or differential)
32	Select Standby
33	Signal Quality
34	New Signal
35	Terminal Timing (common or differential)
36	Standby Indicator
37	Send Common

Note: The signals marked **common or differential** are commons for RS-423A and are one of the two differential wire pairs for RS-422A. Those signals which do not have two pins allocated to their function must be implemented with RS-423A drivers and receivers.

Table 5-4. RS-449 Connector
Pinout - 9 pin Connector.

PIN NUMBER	SIGNAL NAME
1	Shield
2	Secondary Receiver Ready
3	Secondary Send Data
4	Secondary Receive Data
5	Signal Ground
6	Receive Common (for secondary channel)
7	Secondary Request to Send
8	Secondary Clear to Send
9	Send Common (for secondary channel)

ond, who would consider a standard with a larger and thus more expensive connector?

CURRENT LOOP

The last major electrical technique used for serial interfacing which I want to discuss is the method that started digital-serial communications. It is called current loop. Teletypewriters used current loop long before RS-232C was developed.

Current-loop operation is very simple. Look at Fig. 5-11 which is a simple illustration of a current loop circuit. When the switch is open, no current flows so the relay is open. This zero-current situation is considered a logic "0." When the switch is closed, current flows in the loop, limited by the resistor in the loop. The current flow causes the relay to activate, which is a logic "1."

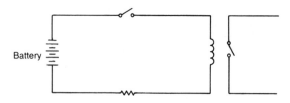

Fig. 5-11. A current-loop circuit.

Two types of current loops are in use: 20 milliampere and 60 milliampere loops. Both consider low or no current as a logic "0" and the maximum current as a logic "1."

Figure 5-12 illustrates a simple current-loop driver while Fig. 5-13 is a simple receiver. The driver will output current when the output of the logic gate is low. This turns on the pnp transistor and drives current out to the output conductor. The receiver is even less complex. The incoming current is converted to a voltage by the resistor, which controls the output state of the logic gate.

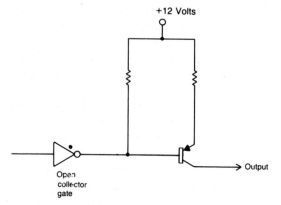

Fig. 5-12. A current-loop output driver.

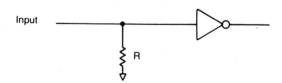

Fig. 5-13. A current-loop input receiver.

Current loop has one major advantage over RS-232C—distance. Current-loop connections may be wired up to 1,000 feet or more, depending on the driving voltage in the transmitter. This is because a constant current driven through a cable is not sensitive to cable resistance, as long as the maximum operating voltage of the current driver is sufficient to drive the proper current through the cable resistance.

Unfortunately, there are no standards as to maximum driver voltage, type of connector, or connector-pin assignments for the current loop. Except for teletypewriters, the current-loop interface is rarely seen anymore.

INTEGRATED CIRCUITS FOR SERIAL I/O

There are three basic types of integrated circuits used to build serial interfaces. The first type is the level converter, which transforms TTL signals to RS-232C, RS-422A, or RS-423A levels. The second type is the receiver/transmitter, and the third is the bit-rate generator.

Level converters are required because TTL levels commonly found in microprocessor systems are not directly compatible with voltage levels required by the serial-interfacing standards. Discrete transistor circuits can be used for level conversion, but integrated circuit drivers and receivers are more convenient and usually less expensive.

Receiver/transmitters perform the parallel-to-serial conversion required to generate, and the serial-to-parallel conversion required to receive, serial bit streams. Before receiver/transmitters were available in integrated form, shift registers were used to perform the same function. The newer and more advanced receiver/transmitters provide much more capability for similar expense. In fact, the availability of low-cost receiver/transmitter chips was a major factor in the widespread acceptance of serial interfacing as the major interfacing technique for microprocessors and microcomputer systems.

Bit-rate generators supply clock signals to the receiver/transmitter at precise, standardized frequencies. Often, a 16X or 64X bit-rate clock is required. Some of the newer receiver/transmitters have internal bit-rate generators. **Figure 5-14** illustrates how level converters, receiver/transmitters, and bit-rate generators are connected to a microprocessor system.

Level Converters The Motorola MC1488 AND MC1489

There are different level converter circuits for each of the serial interfacing standards. For RS-232C level conversion, the most popular circuits are the 1488 quad line driver and the 1489 quad line receiver. **Figure 5-15** is the pin diagram for the 1488 and **Fig. 5-16** is the pin diagram for the 1489.

The 1488 quad line driver provides the designer with three NAND gates and one inverter. The inputs of these gates are TTL compatible while the outputs are RS-232C compatible. A 1488 needs a positive power supply voltage of between 9 and 15 volts and a negative power supply voltage of between -9 and -15 volts in order to meet the RS-232C signal level specifications. Even though the part is TTL compatible, no 5-volt power is required.

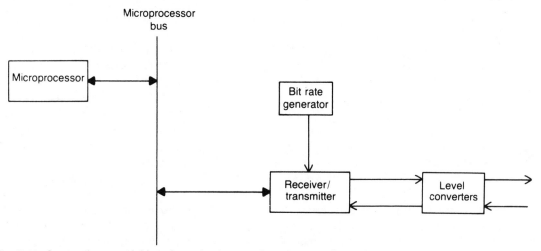

Fig. 5-14. Connecting a serial interface circuit to a microprocessor bus.

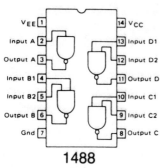

Fig. 5-15. Pin diagram for a Motorola MC1488. Reprinted with permission of Motorola, Inc.

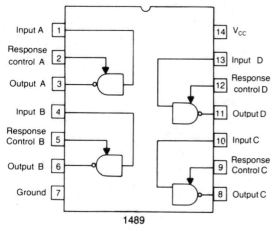

Fig. 5-16. Pin diagram for a Motorola MC1489. Reprinted with permission of Motorola, Inc.

In order to meet the 30-volt-per-microsecond slew rate requirement of the RS-232C standard, a 330 pF capacitor should be connected to the output of each gate of the 1488. In practice this is rarely done, with little or no consequences.

A 1488 is not only useful for converting TTL signals to RS-232C levels. It is frequently useful to be able to have logic levels which are either higher than TTL 5-volt signal swings or have negative voltage levels. The 1488 can be used as a voltage-level translator in these applications.

One characteristic of the 1488 to be careful of when building circuits with the part is to always be sure to ground the ground pin. Failure to do this will allow the inputs of the gates to rise to the level of the positive supply. This usually has catastrophic effects on the TTL circuitry driving the 1488.

A 1489 provides the designer with four gates, all inverters. The inputs are RS-232C compatible while the outputs supply TTL levels. Only a +5 volt power supply is required, even though up to + and −15 volt signals are being received.

In addition to an RS-232C compatible logic input and a TTL output, each 1489 gate has a response-control node. This pin can be left open for RS-232C operation, or it can be attached to an external voltage source to change the input threshold characteristics. A capacitor to ground can be connected to the response-control node to filter noise spikes from the input signal, but this is rarely done for RS-232C circuits.

THE MAXIM MAX230 SERIES

RS-232C continues to play a dominant role in microcomputer systems, despite the odd voltage levels employed. In fact, the newer serial interfacing standards haven't put much of a dent in RS-232's popularity. Even so, the 1488 and 1489 have remained the transceiver chips of choice and for many years, IC vendors ignored the RS-232C market.

But the 1488 and 1489 are not ideal solutions to the problem of designing an RS-232C interface. The parts use bipolar IC technology and consequently consume a fair amount of current. In addition, the 1488 driver requires +12V and −12V for operation. Most ICs in digital systems can run with just a +5V power supply except for the RS-232 drivers. Thus system designers sought a cure for the +12V and −12V required by an RS-232 interface.

A first cut at the solution involved the incorporation of dc-dc converter circuits that could boost the +5V power supply to +12V and then invert that voltage to produce −12V. These early dc-dc converters used transformers and cost quite a bit, so much that the cure was often worse than the disease.

System designers next tried charge-pump circuits. Charge pumps are sort of a poor man's dc-dc converter and use capacitors to move charge from one voltage level to another. Charge pumps work just fine but they can't supply very much current. So if a system incorporates several RS-232C drivers, it bogs a charge pump down and causes the interface voltage levels to drop. Thus if you add more drivers, you need additional charge pumps.

Recognizing that these solutions were all stopgap measures, Maxim Integrated products introduced a line of RS-232C drivers and receivers that integrated the necessary charge pumps right on the transceiver IC. Because each IC carries its own charge pump, adding extra drivers does not cause the RS-232 voltage levels to drop.

The first such integrated RS-232C/charge-pump ICs were the 10 members of the Maxim MAX230 series. In an attempt to satisfy every design requirement with a single IC, Maxim offered 10 different combinations of RS-232C drivers and receivers. Because the required charge-pump capacitors are fairly large (4.7 and 10 microfarads), they cannot be integrated onto the MAX230 ICs. However, two of the MAX230 family members are actually hybrid circuits and integrate the charge-pump capacitors into the IC's package.

Most of the MAX230 devices incorporate two charge pumps: one to boost the +5V power to +10V and one to invert the +10 power to produce −10V. Two of the MAX230 family members incorporate only one charge pump, that inverts a +12V (actually +7.5 to +13.2V) power supply obtained from elsewhere in the system into −12V power. Many microcomputer systems incorporate floppy and hard disk drives and thus already have the +12V available. These systems can make do with only a single charge pump. The members of the MAX230 family are listed in **Table 5-5. Figures 5-17** through 5-26 show the pin and functional diagrams of each member of the MAX230 family.

Since RS-422A and RS-423A have not existed for very long and have yet to become widely used, no particular line driver or receiver integrated circuit can be considered "most popular". Some RS-422A line driver part numbers are the Texas Instruments SN75172 and SN75174, the Advanced Micro Devices AM26LS31C, and the Motorola MC3487.

Some RS-422A line receivers are the Texas Instruments SN75173 and SN75175, the Advanced Micro Devices AM26LS32A, and the Motorola MC3486. An example of an RS-423A line driver is the Fairchild uA9637A. The RS-422A line receivers can also be used as RS-423A line receivers. Each of these line drivers and receivers supplies four converter circuits in one package.

RECEIVER/TRANSMITTER INTEGRATED CIRCUITS

Early serial interfaces used integrated-circuit shift registers for the parallel-to-serial and serial-to-

Table 5-5. The MAX230 Family of RS-232C Driver and Transceiver Chips.

PART NUMBER	POWER SUPPLIES	NUMBER OF DRIVERS	NUMBER OF RECEIVERS	ON-CHIP CAPACITORS
MAX230	+5V	5	0	NO
MAX231	+5V, +12V	2	2	NO
MAX232	+5V	2	2	NO
MAX233	+5V	2	2	YES
MAX234	+5V	4	0	NO
MAX235	+5V	5	5	YES
MAX236	+5V	4	3	NO
MAX237	+5V	5	3	NO
MAX238	+5V	4	4	NO
MAX239	+5V, +12V	3	5	NO

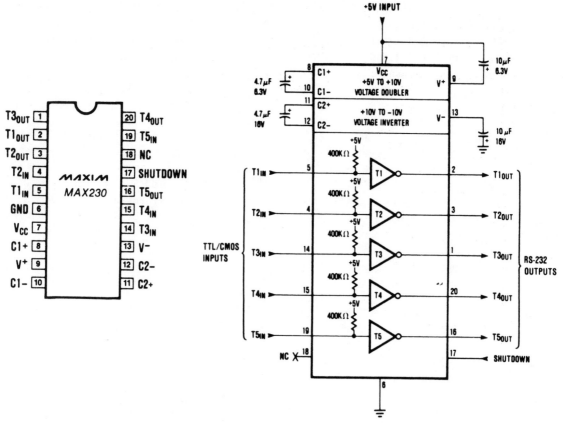

Fig. 5-17. Pin and functional diagrams of the Maxim MAX230 RS-232C driver IC. Courtesy of Maxim Integrated Products.

parallel conversions. Shift registers work well for synchronous transmission and reception because a clock is supplied to indicate when the next data bit is to be shifted in or out. They also work well for asynchronous transmission where the start and stop bits are loaded into the shift register and shifted out just like the data bits.

Shift registers don't work well for asynchronous reception unless a considerable amount of circuitry is added to synchronize the receiving shift register with the incoming bits. Fortunately, all this complexity is no longer required. Combination receiver/transmitters have been introduced and constantly improved during the 1970s to the point where a single integrated circuit supplies the system designer with two channels of asynchronous and synchronous receivers and transmitters with on-board

bit-rate generation, character buffering, extra modem control lines and status lines, interrupt, and DMA control lines.

We are going to look at a few of these receiver/trasmitter integrated circuits. There are so many that only a small percentage will fit in this chapter. The devices we will look at are the General Instruments AY-3-1015D UART, the Motorola 6850 ACIA, the National Semiconductor 8250 ACE, and the Intel 8251A USART. As an indication of the variety of receiver/transmitters available, take a closer look at the names of these chips:

UART   - Universal Asynchronous Receiver/Transmitter

ACIA   - Asynchronous Communications Interface Adapter

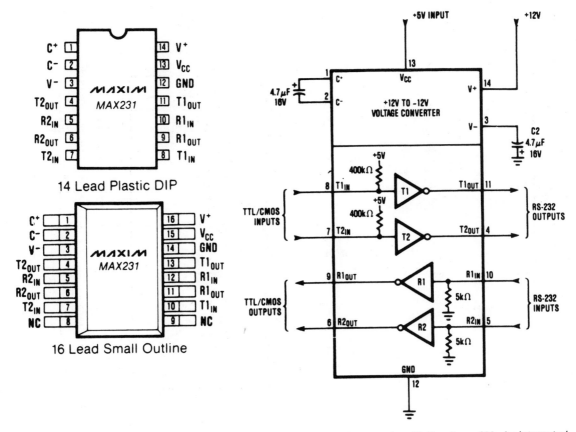

Fig. 5-18. Pin and functional diagrams of the Maxim MAX231 RS-232C transceiver IC. Courtesy of Maxim Integrated Products.

ACE   - Asynchronous Communi-
            cations Element
USART   - Universal/Synchronous/
            Asynchronous
            Receiver/Transmitter

Although each of these integrated circuits performs the same task, there are widely varying capabilities represented in this list, as well as varying approaches to operation.

THE MICROCHIP TECHNOLOGY AY-3-1015D UART

The first receiver/transmitter integrated circuit to see widespread use was the Universal Asynchro- nous Receiver/Transmitter or UART (pronounced you-art). It offered a degree of programmability and combined the transmitter and receiver shift registers with a few more features to make serial interfacing easier than ever before. This consistent performer is still available, and many companies manufacture pin-compatible versions of the UART.

Figure 5-27 is a block diagram of the UART. It is divided into two major sections, the receiver, which is shown on the bottom of the figure, and the transmitter, shown at the top. The transmitter and receiver operate independently but share control and status pins. Figure 5-28 is the pin diagram for the UART.

The UART can actually be considered as four independent registers, each with its own control pin.

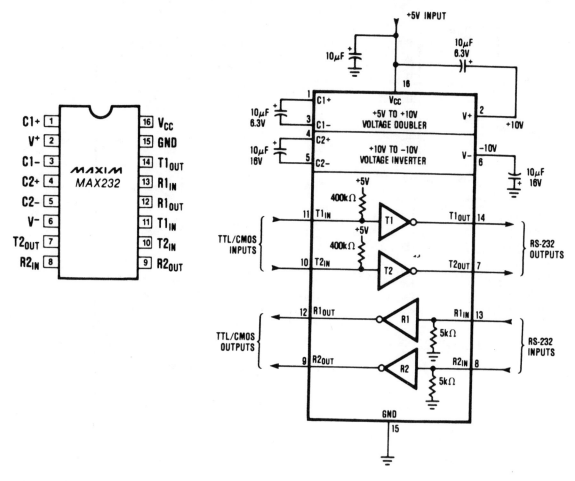

Fig. 5-19. Pin and functional diagrams of the Maxim MAX232 RS-232C transceiver IC. Courtesy of Maxim Integrated Products.

There are two writable registers (a transmit-buffer register and a control register), and two readable registers (a received-data buffer register and a status register). Each of these registers has its own data lines and control pin. The UART was not specifically designed with microprocessors in mind and therefore does not have a single data-bus port.

The transmit register can be loaded with a character to transmit by placing the appropriate levels on the TRANSMITTER DATA BIT lines and clocking them into the register with the DATA STROBE control line. When this is done, the END OF CHARACTER status line is negated until the character is transmitted, then it is asserted until another character is written to the transmitter register.

Control information is placed on the NO PARITY, NUMBER-OF-STOP-BITS, ODD/EVEN-PARITY-SELECT, and NUMBER-OF-DATA-BITS lines and clocking them in with the CONTROL STROBE line. Parity selection, the number of stop bits, and the number of bits per character are the same for both receiver and transmitter.

Table 5-6 lists the signals that must be applied to use the various control lines.

The status register can be read by driving the STATUS-WORD ENABLE control line low. This

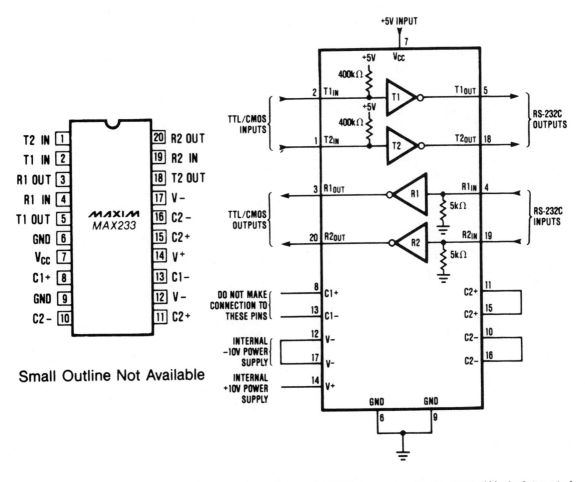

Fig. 5-20. Pin and functional diagrams of the Maxim MAX233 RS-232C transceiver IC. Courtesy of Maxim Integrated Products.

causes the contents of the status register to appear on the OVERRUN, FRAMING ERROR, PARITY ERROR, TRANSMITTER-BUFFER-EMPTY, and DATA AVAILABLE lines. An overrun occurs when a character is received before the previously received character is removed and the data-available bit in the status register is reset by assertion of the RESET DATA AVAILABLE control line. Framing error is asserted if the last character received had an invalid stop bit (not a "1"). Parity error will be asserted if the last received character had an incorrect parity bit, and will be asserted only if the UART

is operating with parity enabled. Once asserted, error bits in the status register can only be cleared by asserting the external reset pin.

The TRANSMITTER-BUFFER-EMPTY and DATA AVAILABLE status bits and status lines are the key to using the UART. When the microprocessor wishes to transmit a character, it must first check the TRANSMITTER-BUFFER-EMPTY bit. If the bit is asserted, there already is a character in the transmitter register and writing another character into the register would disrupt the transmission in progress. Thus the microprocessor must

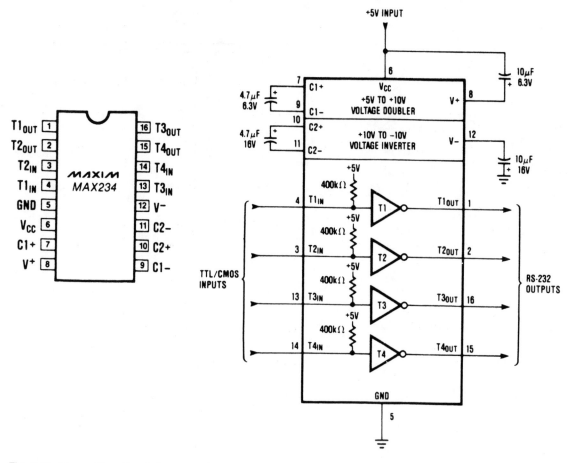

Fig. 5-21. Pin and functional diagrams of the Maxim MAX234 RS-232C driver IC. Courtesy of Maxim Integrated Products.

wait in a loop, reading the bit and waiting for it to be asserted before writing a character to the transmitter register.

In a similar manner, the microprocessor checks for the DATA AVAILABLE bit and status line to be asserted before reading a received character from the receiver register. If this is not done, the data obtained from the receiver register will either be the last character received and previously read by the microprocessor or it will be garbage if no character has been received since the UART was powered up.

A character can be read from the received data buffer by driving the RECEIVED-DATA-ENABLE line low. This makes the contents of the received-data register available on the RECEIVER DATA BITS lines. After the DATA AVAILABLE bit is asserted, the microprocessor should read the character and then assert the RESET-DATA-AVAILABLE pin on the UART to ready it for the next coming character.

When the STATUS-WORD-ENABLE and RECEIVER-DATA-ENABLE lines are not asserted, the associated output lines are three-stated. Thus they may be directly connected to a microprocessor bus with the enable pins driven by address-decoding circuitry. Similarly, the control and

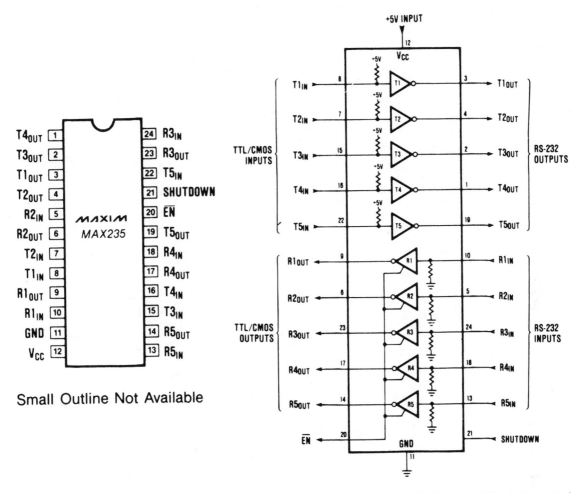

Fig. 5-22. Pin and functional diagrams of the Maxim MAX235 RS-232C transceiver IC. Courtesy of Maxim Integrated Products.

transmitter-data register inputs can be wired to the microprocessor data bus, and address decoding can generate the proper strobe signals. **Figure 5-29** illustrates this bus-oriented connection in a microprocessor.

In **Fig.** 5-30 an address decoder for an Intel 8080 or Zilog Z80 microprocessor is illustrated for the bus-oriented UART circuit. It is built from a 74LS139 dual 2-to-4 decoder integrated circuit. The two lowest address bits of the microprocessor address bus are combined with $\overline{RD}$ and $\overline{WR}$ to gener-

ate the five control signals required. An inverter is required for the CONTROL STROBE signal since it is high-true and the 74LS139 generates low-true outputs.

The circuit of **Fig.** 5-30 makes the UART appear to the microprocessor as two read and three write registers, as shown in **Table** 5-7. Note that reset-data-available is a write register and the DATA AVAILABLE bit of the status register will be reset no matter what is written to this "register." This technique of generating control signals other than

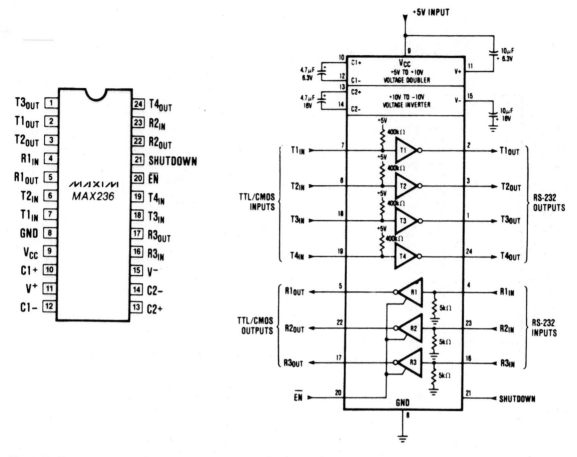

Fig. 5-23. Pin and functional diagrams of the Maxim MAX236 RS-232C transceiver IC. Courtesy of Maxim Integrated Products.

register strobes and enables is quite useful and requires a minimum of circuitry.

Two UART pins which we haven't discussed are the transmit (16 X T Clock) and receive (16 X R Clock) clock inputs. Both require a clock signal running at 16 times the desired bit rate. The higher frequency allows the UART receiver to divide each bit time into 16 periods. The UART samples the incoming-data line very close to the center of the bit time. This improves the UART's sensitivity to frequency errors. Since there is an independent bit-rate clock input for both the receiver and transmitter, the UART may be run with different bit rates for transmission and reception.

The Motorola 6850 ACIA

In the mid-1970s Motorola and Intel introduced their first major eight-bit microprocessors; the Motorola 6800 and the Intel 8080. Both manufacturers immediately started aggressive development programs to create companion lines of peripheral chips. They knew that microprocessors alone aren't worth much. Without support circuitry, the micros really can't perform.

The Motorola 6850 Asynchronous Communications Adapter (ACIA) is Motorola's serial I/O chip for the 6800 and its successors. Unlike the UART, the 6850 is specifically designed to be attached to a microprocessor bus. A detailed block diagram of

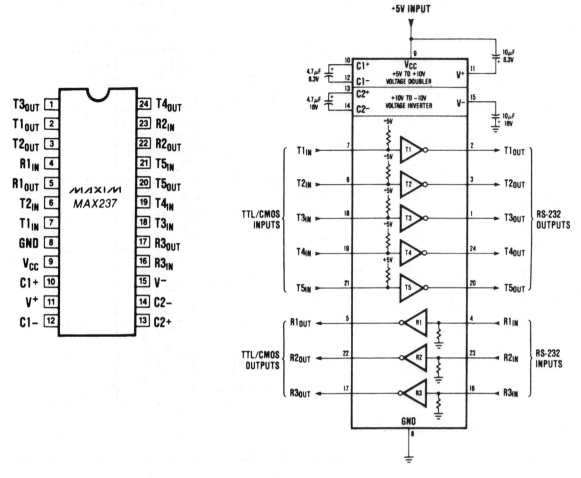

Fig. 5-24. Pin and functional diagrams of the Maxim MAX237 RS-232C transceiver IC. Courtesy of Maxim Integrated Products.

the 6850 is shown in **Fig. 5-31**. On the left side of the diagram are the microprocessor-bus interface lines and on the right are the pins for serial communications. Also on the right is an interrupt-request line intended for the micro-processor. **Figure 5-32** is the pin diagram for the ΛCIΛ.

We have already covered the function of the Motorola 6800 microprocessor bus in Chapter 2, and discussed the operation of the microprocessor bus interface in connection with the 6821 PIA in Chapter 4. The 6850 has a similar bus interface, and there is no need to cover old ground. There are three chip selects, one low-true, a read/write line, and the en-

able clock. In addition, there is a single register-select line. The 6850 has two read and two write registers.

The transmit clock and receive clock lines bring in frequencies which determine the bit rates that the transmitter and receiver sections will operate at. The transmit and receive clocks may either be at the desired bit-rate frequency, 16 times the bit rate, or 64 times the bit rate. If the receive clock is supplied at the bit-rate frequency, it must be externally synchronized with the incoming data.

Now look at the serial communications lines on the right side of **Fig. 5-31**. There are positive-

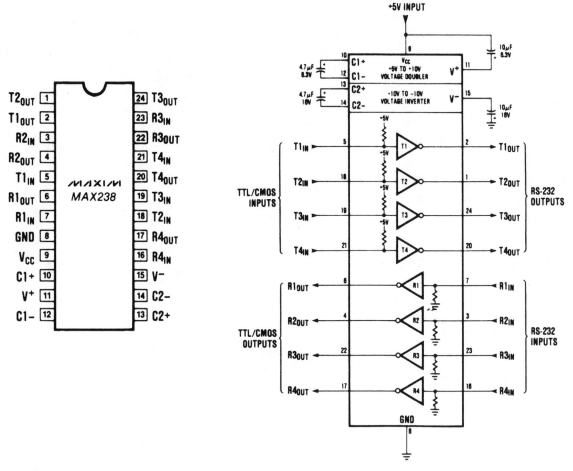

Fig. 5-25. Pin and functional diagrams of the Maxim MAX238 RS-232C transceiver IC. Courtesy of Maxim Integrated Products.

true transmit data and receive data pins. When connected to a 1488 driver and 1489 receiver, these signals will assume their proper, negative-true logic sense since both the 1488 and 1489 invert. Conversely, the low-true request-to-send, clear-to-send and data-carrier detect lines will become positive-true after passing through the 1488 and 1489. Motorola designers developed the ACIA with RS-232C line drivers and receivers in mind.

The four registers in the ACIA are shown in **Table 5-8**. To use the ACIA, the microprocessor system must first initialize it by writing a byte to the control register. Bit assignments for the ACIA control register are:

Bit	Assignment
7	Receive-Interrupt Enable
6	Transmit Control 2
5	Transmit Control 1
4	Word Select 3
3	Word Select 2
2	Word Select 1
1	Counter-Divide Select 2
0	Counter-Divide Select 1

Three control bit groups, transmit control, word select, and counter divide, govern the ACIA's operation. The receive-interrupt enable bit allows the

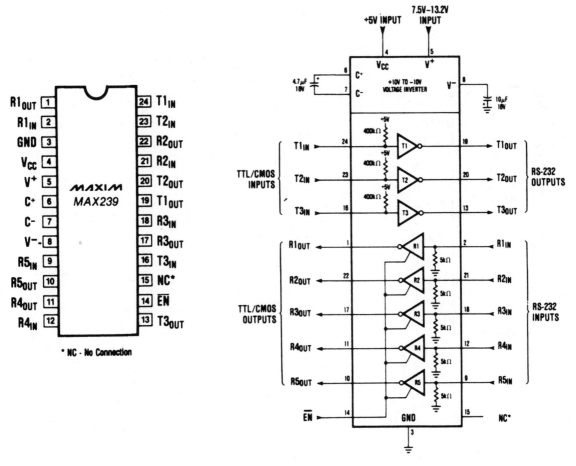

Fig. 5-26. Pin and functional diagrams of the Maxim MAX239 RS-232C transceiver IC. Courtesy of Maxim Integrated Products.

ACIA to assert the interrupt request line when a character is received.

The two transmit-control bits determine the operation of the request-to-send line and whether the ACIA may interrupt when the transmitter can accept a character for transmission. These bits are also used to force the ACIA to transmit a break, which is a constant "0." Normally, a serial line idles in the "1" state. The bits are encoded as shown in Table 5-9.

Note that the encoding of the bits does not allow request-to-send to be negated (high) and the transmitter interrupt to be enabled together and that the only way to send a break is with request-to-send asserted.

The three word-select bits determine the number of data bits per character, the number of stop bits, whether there will be parity and if there is, what type. The possibilities are shown in Table 5-10.

These definitions apply simultaneously to both the transmitter and receiver sections of the ACIA. Note that encoding of three characteristics into three bits reduces flexibility somewhat. For example, if you want eight data bits with two stop bits, it will not have parity.

The counter-divide bits determine the relation-

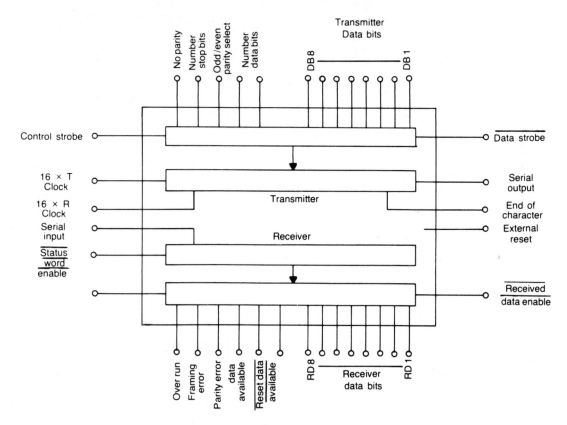

Fig. 5-27. Block diagram of a UART. This particular device is the Microchip Technology AY-3-1015D. Courtesy of Microchip Technology Inc.

ship between the transmit and receive clocks and the transmit and receive bit rates. These bits may also be used as a software reset to the ACIA. The bit encodings are shown in **Table 5-11**. The bit-rate definitions apply to both transmitter and receiver.

After the ACIA is configured through the control register, it may be used by checking the status register and then performing the desired data operations. The status register reports the conditions of various parts of the ACIA. Status-register bit definitions are:

Bit	Assignment
7	Interrupt Request
6	Parity Error
5	Receiver Overrun
4	Framing Error
3	Clear-to-Send
2	Data-Carrier Detect
1	Transmit Data Register Empty
0	Receive Data Register Full

Interrupt request indicates the status of the ACIA's interrupt request line. This bit is useful if several devices are all connected to a microprocessor's interrupt-request input. The interrupt-service software can interrogate the 6850 to determine if it is the device requesting the interrupt.

Parity error, receiver overrun, and framing error are all error bits indicating a problem in the reception of a character. Parity error indicates that the character in the receiver register was received with bad parity. This bit is negated when the offending character is read from the receive-data register.

TOP VIEW

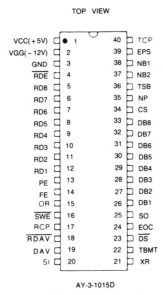

Fig. 5-28. Pin diagram of a Microchip Technology AY-3-1015D UART. Courtesy of Microchip Technology Inc.

The receiver overrun bit is set when a character is received and another character is already waiting to be read in the receive-data register. Since the ACIA has nowhere else to put this new character, it throws it away. To indicate this loss, the overrun-error bit is asserted the next time the ACIA is able

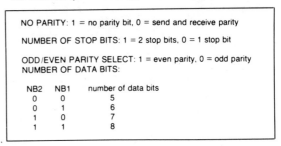

Table 5-6. Control Information on the Microchip Technology AY-3-1015D UART Lines.

NO PARITY: 1 = no parity bit, 0 = send and receive parity

NUMBER OF STOP BITS: 1 = 2 stop bits, 0 = 1 stop bit

ODD/EVEN PARITY SELECT: 1 = even parity, 0 = odd parity
NUMBER OF DATA BITS:

NB2	NB1	number of data bits
0	0	5
0	1	6
1	0	7
1	1	8

to put a received character in the receiver-data register. The overrun-error bit is cleared when this new character is read.

Framing error is asserted when a character is received without a stop bit in the expected place. This can happen when the number-of-bits-per-character setting for the ACIA is different from what is actually being received. It can also happen if the bit rate is not matched at both ends of the communications link or if a parity bit is not expected but is received. The framing-error status bit is updated with each character received.

The clear-to-send and data-carrier detect bits in the status register reflect the states of the ACIA pins with the same names. Note that these bits are low-true.

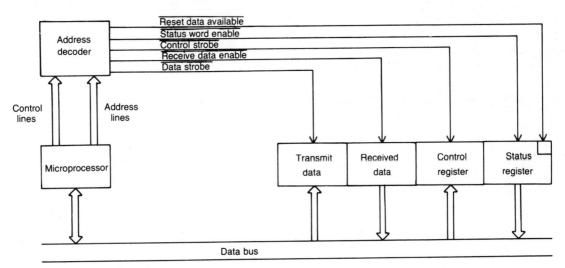

Fig. 5-29. Connection of a UART to a microprocessor bus.

235

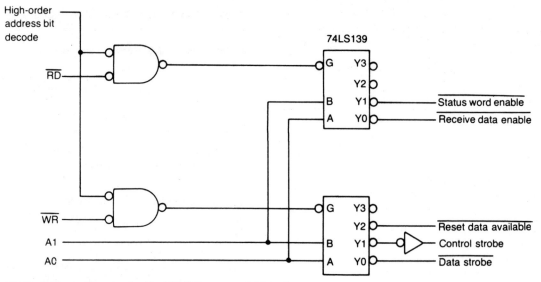

Fig. 5-30. Address decoder for the UART-based serial interface.

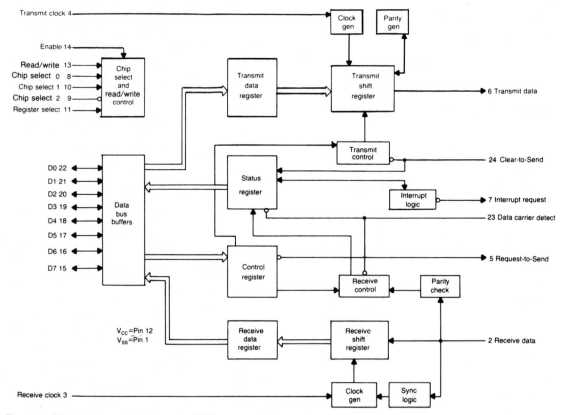

Fig. 5-31. Block diagram for a Motorola MC6850 Asynchronous Communications Interface Adapter (ACIA). Reprinted by permission of Motorola, Inc.

Table 5-7. Read and Write Registers
in the Microchip Technology AY-3-1015D UART.

A1	A0	READ ($\overline{RD}$=0)	Write ($\overline{WR}$=0)
0	0	Receive Data	Transmit Data
0	1	Status Register	Control Register
1	0	---	Reset Data Available
1	1	---	---

Table 5-8. Motorola MC6850 ACIA Registers.

Register Select	Read/$\overline{Write}$	Register Name
0	0	Control Register
0	1	Status Register
1	0	Transmit Data
1	1	Receive Data

Transmit-data-register empty and receive-data-register full are the bits used to indicate to the microprocessor when the transmitter and receiver sections of the ACIA require service. When the transmit-data-register-empty bit is asserted, the microprocessor may place another character in the transmit-data register to be transmitted.

If a character is placed in the transmit-data register without regard to the transmit-data-register-empty bit, a character which is already in the transmit-data register will be overwritten and never

Table 5-9. Motorola MC6850 ACIA
Transmit-control-bit Definitions.

TRANSMIT CONTROL		FUNCTION
Bit 2	Bit 1	
0	0	$\overline{\text{Request-to-send}}$ = low, Transmitter interrupt disabled
0	1	$\overline{\text{Request-to-send}}$ = low, Transmitter interrupt enabled
1	0	$\overline{\text{Request-to-Send}}$ = high, Transmitter interrupt disabled
1	1	$\overline{\text{Request-to-Send}}$ = low, Send break on Transmit Data, Transmitter interrupt disabled

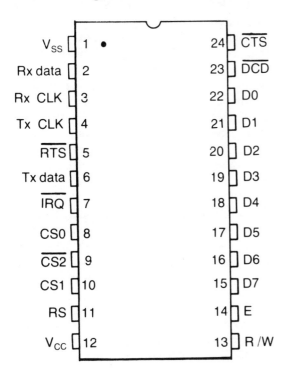

Fig. 5-32. Pin diagram for the Motorola MC6850 ACIA.
Reprinted by permission of Motorola, Inc.

Table 5-10. Motorola
MC6850 ACIA Word-select-bit Definitions.

WORD-SELECT BIT			FUNCTION
3	2	1	
0	0	0	7 bits/character, even parity, 2 stop bits
0	0	1	7 bits/character, odd parity, 2 stop bits
0	1	0	7 bits/character, even parity, 1 stop bit
0	1	1	7 bits/character, odd parity, 1 stop bit
1	0	0	8 bits/character, no parity, 2 stop bits
1	0	1	8 bits/character, no parity, 1 stop bit
1	1	0	8 bits/character, even parity, 1 stop bit
1	1	1	8 bits/character, odd parity, 1 stop bit

Table 5-11. Motorola MC6850
ACIA Clock-selection-bit Definitions.

WORD SELECT 2	WORD SELECT 1	FUNCITON
0	0	Bit Rate = Clock
0	1	Bit Rate = 1/16 Clock
1	0	Bit Rate = 1/64 Clock
1	1	Reset ACIA

transmitted. Transmit-data-register-empty is negated when a character is written to the transmit-data register, and asserted when the character is transferred to the transmit shift register.

The receive-data-register-full bit indicates when a character is ready in the receive-data register to be read by the microprocessor. The bit is asserted when the character is transferred from the receive-shift register to the receive-data register and negated when the microprocessor reads the character from the receive-data register.

The last two, the transmit-data and receive-data registers, are used to send and receive data through the ACIA. A character placed in the transmit-data register will be transmitted bit-by-bit out the TX-data pin. Bits received on the RX-data pin are assembled into characters and placed in the receive-data register to be read.

National Semiconductor 8250 ACE

The last asynchronous-only serial I/O chip we will look at is the National Semiconductor 8250 Asynchronous Communications Adapter (ACE). A very high degree of capability has been designed into the ACE. It not only performs the serial-to-parallel and parallel-to-serial conversion for asynchronous communications but also has a built in bit-rate generator and a complex interrupt structure.

A block diagram of the 8250 is shown in **Fig. 5-33** and a pin diagram in **Fig. 5-34**. The left side of **Fig. 5-33** is the microprocessor interface and the right side shows the serial-communications pins.

The microprocessor interface of the 8250 is quite involved. National has designed a very flexible interface with both high- and low-true control signals. This tends to minimize the number of extra gates ("glue" parts) required to connect the ACE to a microprocessor bus. The 8250 is an 8-bit part, as can be seen by the eight data lines (D7-D0) on the microprocessor side of the block diagram.

There are three chip selects; CS0, CS1 and $\overline{CS2}$. Two are high-true and one is low-true. All must be asserted to enable bus access to the 8250. When the 8250 is selected by assertion of all three of the chip select pins, the 8250 will assert the CSOUT (chip-select out) output pin.

There are three register select lines; A0, A1 and A2. This would lead us to believe that the 8250 has at most eight read and eight write registers. Instead there are nine. The extra registers are obtained by multiplexing access to four of the ten registers so that at some times one pair is accessible and at other times, the second pair is accessible. We will look at the registers in detail after all of the 8250's pins are covered.

An address strobe (ADS) is available to latch in the three-register-select lines. This is most useful for microprocessor systems with multiplexed address/data busses. When an address is on such a bus, there usually is an address strobe which is available for latching the address so that the bus may be switched to data mode. If the 8250 is being connected to a non-multiplexed bus, $\overline{ADS}$ may be tied to ground, permanently enabling the register-select lines.

The 8250 has four read/write control lines. Two are used for reading registers and two are used for writing. This may look similar to the UART at first glance; it, too, had two read and two write control lines. In the ACE's case, the two read lines serve the same purpose but one is high-true (data-input strobe or DISTR) and the other is low true ($\overline{DISTR}$). Similarly, the write control line is available as either a high-true (data-output strobe or DOSTR) or a low-true ($\overline{DOSTR}$) signal. Thus, the system designer can use all possible combinations of read and write control lines.

Only one of the input strobes and one of the output strobes need be used; the unused control lines can be permanently negated. Some interesting systems can be built where two devices in the system, say the processor and a DMA controller, can both access the ACE without gating required to combine control signals.

When a read operation is performed on the 8250, one of the data-input-strobe control lines will be asserted, while the chip is selected. This situation will cause the 8250 to negate the DDIS (driver disable) line. The low level on this output may then

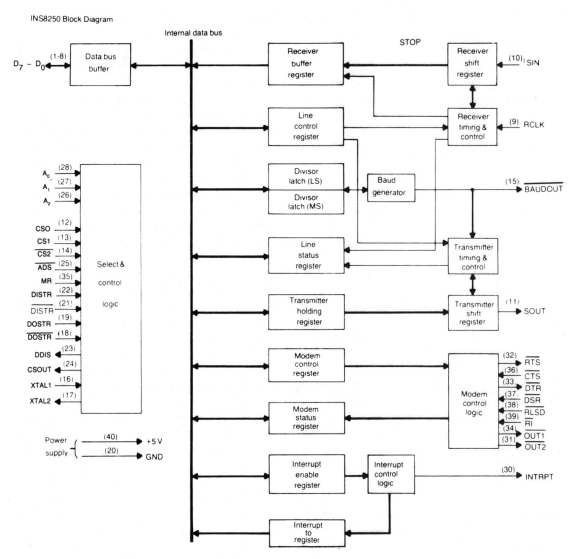

INS8250 Block Diagram

NOTE: APPLICABLE PINOUT NUMBERS ARE INCLUDED WITHIN PARENTHESES.

Fig. 5-33. Block diagram for the National Semiconductor INS8250 Asynchronous Communications Element (ACE). Copyright 1981 National Semiconductor Corporation.

be used to activate a data buffer which drives the processor data bus.

An interrupt output (INTRPT) is available for the microprocessor's interrupt circuitry. Interrupts can occur for errors in serial reception, data transfers, or if one or more of the serial-status lines change state.

The last 8250 control line on the microprocessor side is the master reset (MR). This pin, when asserted, clears most but not all of the registers in the 8250. Registers not cleared are the transmit and receive data registers and the bit-rate setting.

On the serial communications side, the 8250 has a transmit data (SOUT) and a receive data (SIN)

239

pin. Four status inputs and four control outputs are available for controlling the serial interface. The status inputs are clear-to-send (CTS), data-set ready (DSR), received-line-signal-detect (RLSD) and ring indicator (RI). The control outputs are data-terminal-ready (DTR), request-to-send (RTS), and two more general purpose outputs OUT1 and OUT2. Clearly, the names of the inputs and outputs imply connection to the RS-232C signals of the same name. Since all of these input and output pins are low-true, they are well matched to the inverting RS-232C drivers and receivers.

A clock input is required to make the ACE run. The ACE can use either a crystal or a clock frequency. If a crystal is used, it is connected between the XTAL1 and XTAL2 pins. If a clock frequency is supplied to the ACE, it is connected to XTAL1 and XTAL2 is left unconnected. The clock frequency runs the internal chip operations and serves as a master frequency reference for the internal bit-rate generator. The clock can be any frequency up to 3.1 MHz.

The internal bit-rate generator divides the clock frequency by the bit-rate divisor. A frequency output pin (BAUDOUT) is available which can be connected to the receiver-clock input. This receiver-clock input can also be connected to an external bit-rate source.

The 10 registers in the ACE are shown in Table 5-12.

DLAB is the indirect register pointer bit. It is the most significant bit of the line-control register. The processor must set this bit appropriately, de-

pending on what register pair it wishes to access. Typically, DLAB is set to a "1" during the initialization of the chip, for setting the bit rate divisor, and then cleared to a "0" and left there permanently unless a change in the bit rate is needed.

To use the 8250, it must first be configured. This involves setting the bit-rate divisor in the high and low bit-rate divisor registers, setting the communication format in the line-control register, and setting the levels of the serial-control-line outputs through the modem-control register. If interrupts are to be used, the interrupt-enable register will also need to be loaded. Let's look at each of these configuration registers first.

The bit rate is set by the bit-rate-divisor registers. The two bytes in these registers are combined into a 16-bit number which is used to divide the ACE's clock input. As a result, the ACE requires unusual clock frequencies that divide down to standard asynchronous bit rates. The divisor should be set to 16 times the desired bit rate. Table 5-13 lists divisors for standard asynchronous bit rates using a 1.8432-MHz master clock frequency, and Table 5-14 lists the divisors used for a 3.072-MHz master clock.

Since the master-clock frequency is being divided by an integer, some bit rate frequencies (110, 134.5, 1800, 2000, 3600, and 7200) are slightly off but the error for the values in the tables is always less than 1.5 percent, which is all that is needed for asynchronous communications.

The asynchronous communications-bit format is configured through the line-control register. Bits in

DLAB	A2	A1	A0	REGISTER
0	0	0	0	Received Data Register (read) or Transmit Data Register (write)
0	0	0	1	Interrupt Enable (read/write)
X	0	1	0	Interrupt Identification (read only)
X	0	1	1	Line Control Register (read/write)
X	1	0	0	Modem Control Register (read/write)
X	1	0	1	Line Status Register (read/write)
X	1	1	0	Modem Status Register (read write)
X	1	1	1	--
1	0	0	0	Bit Rate Divisor (low) (read/write)
1	0	0	1	Bit Rate Divisor (high) (read/write)

Table 5-12. National Semiconductor INS8250 ACE Register Definitions.

240

BIT RATE	DIVISOR (DECIMAL)	HIGH BYTE	LOW BYTE
		(DECIMAL)	
50	2304	9	0
75	1536	6	0
110	1047	4	23
134.5	857	3	89
150	768	3	0
300	384	1	128
600	192	0	192
1200	96	0	96
1800	64	0	64
2000	58	0	58
2400	48	0	48
3600	32	0	32
4800	24	0	24
7200	16	0	16
9600	12	0	12
19200	6	0	6

Table 5-13. National Semiconductor INS8250 ACE Bit-rate Divisors-1.8432-MHz Clock.

BIT RATE	DIVISOR (DECIMAL)	HIGH BYTE	LOW BYTE
		(DECIMAL)	
50	3840	15	0
75	2560	10	0
110	1745	6	209
134.5	1428	5	148
150	1280	5	0
300	640	2	128
600	320	1	64
1200	160	0	160
1800	107	0	107
2000	96	0	96
2400	80	0	80
3600	53	0	53
4800	40	0	40
7200	27	0	27
9600	20	0	20
19200	10	0	10

Table 5-14. National Semiconductor INS8250 ACE Bit-rate Divisors 3.072-MHz Clock.

the line-control register set the number of bits per character, the number of stop bits, and parity. Also in this register is a bit which can force the 8250 to send the break level, and a DLAB bit. The bit definitions for the line control register are:

Bit	Assignment
7	DLAB - The indirect register pointer
6	Send Break
5	Stick Parity
4	Odd/Even Parity Select
3	Parity Enable
2	Number of Stop Bits
1	WLSI - Word-Length Select 1
0	WLSO - Word-Length Select 0

Start with bits 0 and 1, the word-length-select bits. These bits determine how many data bits per character the ACE will transmit, and how many it will expect to receive. The possible word lengths

241

Table 5-15. National Semiconductor
INS8250 ACE Word-length Selection Bits.

WLS1 STATUS	WLSO STATUS	DATA BITS PER CHARACTER
0	0	5
0	1	6
1	0	7
1	1	8

are shown in **Table 5-15.** Bit 2 determines the number of stop bits which will be sent and how many will be expected. Since only a single bit is available for determining the number of stop bits, you may think that there are only two choices. That is almost true. There are two choices for each word-length setting but the choices change. The stop bit settings are shown in **Table 5-16.**

The only widely used device that has ever needed 1.5 stop bits is the IBM I/O Selectric™ electric typewriter, which also is the only widely used device that has ever required 5 data bits. Thus, the 5-bit word-length setting in the line-control register is the only setting which can have 1.5 stop bits.

Bits 3, 4, and 5 control the parity setting. Bit 3 is the parity enable; when the bit is a "1," a parity bit will be appended to all transmitted characters and parity will be tested on all incoming characters. Bit 4, when set to a "1," selects even parity. Odd parity is selected when bit 4 is a "0."

Line-control-register bit 5 modifies the definition of bit 4. When bit 5, the "stick parity" bit, is set, a parity bit will be transmitted but it will always be the same as bit 4. The ACE will also check for properly stuck parity bits on incoming information. Sticking the parity bit to always assume one logic level or the other effectively ruins the bit for error

detection, yet many large mainframes insist on using stuck parity.

Setting send break, bit 6, jams the SOUT line low. This creates a break condition on the line. Breaks should last at least 200 milliseconds for most mainframes to recognize the function. We have already discussed bit 7, DLAB. It is set to gain access to the divisor latches.

The modem control register has the following bit assignments.

Bit	Assignment
7	Not used, always reads 0
6	Not used, always reads 0
5	Not used, always reads 0
4	Local Loopback
3	$\overline{OUT2}$
2	$\overline{OUT1}$
1	Request to Send ($\overline{RTS}$)
0	Data Terminal Ready ($\overline{DTR}$)

Bits 0 through 3 control the four communications output lines of the ACE. When set to a "1," the associated low-true output is asserted, or driven low. When a bit is cleared, the associated output is driven high.

Bit 4 is a local loopback control. When asserted, SOUT is driven high and the 8250 receiver is disconnected from SIN and connected to the 8250 transmitter. Also, the four output-control lines and four input-status lines are disconnected and inter-

BIT 2	WLS1	WLS2	BITS/CHARACTER	NUMBER OF STOP BITS
0	X	X	5,6,7,8	1
1	0	0	5	1.5
1	0	1	6	2
1	1	0	7	2
1	1	1	8	2

Table 5-16. National Semiconductor
INS8250 ACE Stop-bit Settings.

nally connected together so that the processor may control the status bits in the modem-status register with the control bits in the modem-control register. This allows the microprocessor to test out the receiver/transmitter portion of the ACE and also the interrupt system, which can interrupt on any change in the input-status line.

The interrupt enable register has the following bit assignments:

Bit	Assignment
7	Not used, always reads 0
6	Not used, always reads 0
5	Not used, always reads 0
4	Not used, always reads 0
3	Enable Modem Status interrupts
2	Enable Receiver Line Status interrupts
1	Enable Transmitter Holding Register Empty interrupts
0	Enable Received Data Available interrupts

If all bits in the interrupt enable register are set to "0," the ACE will never assert the INTRPT output line. Received-data available and transmitter-holding-register-empty interrupts are used for interrupt-driven data transfers. The receiver-line-status contains three error bits for overrun, parity, and framing errors plus a break-detection indicator. If any of these bits in the receiver-line-status register becomes asserted due to received characters, they can cause an interrupt if bit 2 of the interrupt-enable register is asserted.

The modem-status register has four indicators that are set when one of the corresponding four status-input lines changes state. This condition can be used to generate an interrupt if bit 3 of the interrupt-enable register is set. This type of interrupt is most useful if the microprocessor is using the

8250's output-control lines to manage the communications channel and expects a change on the input-status lines for a change on the output-control lines. An example of this might be a response on clear-to-send to an assertion of request-to-send.

There are three status registers used to determine the ACE's state during I/O operations. These are the line-status, modem-status and interrupt-identification registers. The line-status register bit assignments are:

Bit	Assignment
7	Not used, always reads 0
6	Transmitter Shift Register Empty
5	Transmitter Holding Register Empty
4	Break Interrupt
3	Framing Error
2	Parity Error
1	Overrun Error
0	Data Ready

Bits 1 through 4 have already been covered. These four bits can be used to generate interrupts, or the microprocessor may check them after every received character without using interrupts. Reading the line-status register clears bits 1 through 4. Assertion of bit 0 indicates that a character has been received and should be read. This bit can be cleared either by reading the receive-buffer register or by writing a "0" to bit 0 of the line-status register. Bits 5 and 6 indicate the status of the transmitter. If bit 5 is asserted, a character may be in the process of being transmitted but there is room in the transmitter-holding register for another character to be transmitted. Bit 6 is asserted when the transmitter is idle. This is an indication that the transmitter has finished sending out all characters written to the ACE.

The modem-status-register bit assignments are:

Bit	Assignment
7	Received Line Signal Detect (RLSD)

6	Ring Indicator (RI)
5	Data Set Ready (DSR)
4	Clear-to-Send (CTS)
3	Delta Received Line Signal Detect
2	Delta Ring Indicator
1	Delta Data Set Ready
0	Delta Clear to Send

Bits 4 through 7 reflect the actual states of the 8250's input-status lines. In addition, if loopback is activated, these lines reflect the bit settings of the modem-control register for the control-output lines. If the associated low-true input-status line is asserted. Whenever a change occurs on one of the input status lines, the associated delta bit in the modem-status register is asserted.

If loopback is activated, the bits in the modem-status register reflect the states of the bits in the modem-control register as shown in **Table 5-17**.

When the appropriate bit in the modem-control register is set, it appears asserted in the modem-status register during loopback operation.

The interrupt-identification register allows the microprocessor to quickly determine why the 8250 is interrupting, and has the following bit assignments:

Bit Assignment

Bit	Assignment
7	Not used, always reads 0
6	Not used, always reads 0
5	Not used, always reads 0
4	Not used, always reads 0
3	Not used, always reads 0
2	Interrupt source, most significant bit
1	Interrupt source, least significant
0	Interrupt not pending

Bit 0 is used to determine if the 8250 is asserting INTRPT. If bit 0 is asserted, no interrupt is pending and bits 1 and 2 will be 0. This is useful if the 8250 is connected to the same interrupt line as other devices in the system. Bits 1 and 2 represent the encoded identity of the highest priority interrupting condition in the ACE. The interrupt codes are given in **Table 5-18**.

The last two registers in the ACE are the transmitter-holding register and the receiver-buffer register. Data to be transmitted is written to the transmitter-holding register. Incoming characters are read from the receiver-buffer register. The microprocessor can use the indicator bits in the line-status register or the ACE's interrupt system to alert the system software as to when these operations are required or permitted.

Intel 8251A USART

The last receiver/transmitter integrated circuit we will look at is the Intel 8251A Universal Synchronous/Asynchronous Receiver/Transmitter (USART). This part not only performs serial-to-parallel and parallel-to-serial conversion for asynchronous communications but also can output and input bit streams in a synchronous manner.

A block diagram of the 8251A appears in **Fig. 5-35** and a pin diagram is shown in **Fig. 5-36**. Again, the microprocessor interface is shown on the left side of the block diagram while the serial communications pins are shown on the right. Extra serial-control and status pins are shown in the lower left part of the diagram, labeled modem control.

The 8251A has as Intel type of interface, which should not be much of a surprise to you. There is a single, low-true chip select, a read strobe ($\overline{RD}$), a write strobe ($\overline{WR}$) and eight data lines. The pin

MODEM STATUS-REGISTER BIT	ASSOCIATED MODEM-CONTROL BIT
CTS (bit 4)	RTS (bit 1)
DSR (bit 5)	DTR (bit 0)
RI (bit 6)	OUT1 (bit 2)
RLSD (bit 7)	OUT2 (bit 3)

Table 5-17.
National Semiconductor
INS850 ACE Modem-status-register Bit Functions.

Table 5-18. National Semiconductor INS8250 ACE Interrupt Control Codes.

BIT 2	BIT 1	INTERRUPT TYPE	INTERRUPT SOURCE	PRIORITY
1	1	Receiver line status	Overrun error Framing error Parity error Break detect	Highest
1	0	Received data Available receiver		Second
0	1	Transmitter empty	Transmitter	Third
0	0	Modem status	Delta CTS Delta DSR Delta RI Delta RLSD	Lowest

labeled C/$\overline{\text{D}}$ is the control/data-select pin and is the 8251 register-select pin. It determines whether the processor will access the data port or the control/status port of the USART. As we shall see, there are actually several registers accessible through the control port. C/$\overline{\text{D}}$ is usually connected to the microprocessor's least-significant address line. Included as part of the microprocessor interface are a reset line and a clock input. The clock has a maximum input frequency of 3.125 MHz.

A modem-control section provides for two inputs and two outputs to the serial-communications circuits. The two outputs are $\overline{\text{DTR}}$ and $\overline{\text{RTS}}$. These correspond to the RS-232 signals data-terminal-ready and request-to-send, although they are really just general purpose outputs which can be used for any function. The two inputs are $\overline{\text{DSR}}$ and $\overline{\text{CTS}}$,

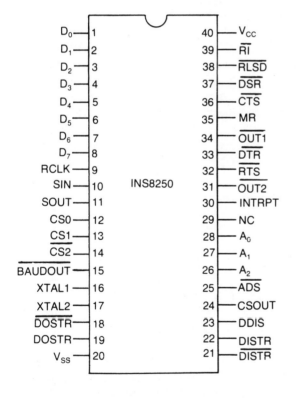

Fig. 5-34. Pin diagram for the National Semiconductor INS8250 ACE. Copyright 1981 National Semiconductor Corporation.

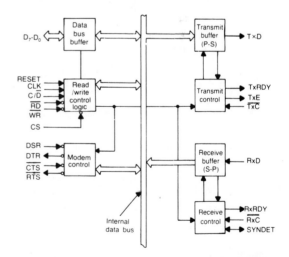

Fig. 5-35. Block diagram of the Intel 8251A Universal Synchronous/Asynchronous Receiver/Transmitter (USART). Reprinted by permission of Intel Corporation, Copyright 1983.

which correspond to the RS-232 signals data-set-ready and clear-to-send. $\overline{DSR}$ is a general purpose input, but $\overline{CTS}$ has a specific use. The USART cannot transmit unless $\overline{CTS}$ is asserted (meaning it is driven low).

The USART serial transmitter sends the serial bit stream out through the TxD line. The transmitter bit rate is determined by the clock frequency applied to the transmitter clock input $\overline{TxC}$. Two output pins indicate the status of the USART transmitter section. TxRDY indicates that the transmitter is ready to accept another character from the microprocessor. There may still be a character in the transmitter shift register but if there is space in the transmitter data-input register, TxRDY will be asserted. TxEMPTY indicates that the transmitter section has completed transmission of all characters written to the USART transmitter. TxRDY and TxEMPTY can be used as interrupt pins for interrupt-driven output software.

The USART receiver accepts a serial bit stream from the RxD input and assembles the bits into characters. Receiver bit rate is determined by the receiver clock applied to the $\overline{RxC}$ pin. When a character has been received, RxRDY is asserted. This pin may be used to drive an interrupt line to the microprocessor for interrupt-driven input software.

One other pin remains to be discussed. It is the triple function SYNDET/BRKDET pin. In asynchronous operation, the USART will assert this pin whenever a break lasting more than two character times is received. In a synchronous mode, this pin may be either an input or an output. Synchronous transmissions have no start or stop bits, therefore a special start character is used at the beginning of each message to allow the receiver to get into byte synchronization with the transmitter.

SYNDET, if defined as an output, will be asserted when the 8251A detects a SYNC character in the serial transmission. Recall that SYNC is the first character to be transmitted in a synchronous message, so the assertion of SYNDET by the 8251 also means "Start of Message."

If a special synchronous protocol is being used, internal SYNC detect may not be adequate. In this case, SYNDET may be defined as an input. Circuitry external to the USART is then responsible for detecting the start of the message and signaling to the USART when to start assembling characters from the incoming bit stream.

One last note about SYNDET/BRKDET. The original 8251 (not the ''A'' version) did not detect breaks. SYNDET/BRKDET on these older parts is only SYNDET.

As with the other receiver/transmitters we have studied in this chapter, the USART must first be configured by loading its registers with operational parameters. This is done by writing bytes to the control port (C/$\overline{D}$ = 1). In order to do this, you must first understand the control register structure of the 8251A. There is an internal pointer register in the 8251A that determines what register you will access when the control port is written to. The control port actually provides access to several registers.

When reset, the 8251A pointer register causes the USART mode register to be accessible through the control port. Bit definitions for this register differ depending on whether synchronous or asynchronous operation is chosen. The asynchronous bit definitions are:

Bit	Assignment
7	Number of stop bits, most significant bit
6	Number of stop bits, least significant bit
5	Even/Odd parity select
4	Parity Enable

Bit	Assignment
3	Character length, most significant bit
2	Character length, least significant bit
1	Bit-rate factor, most significant bit
0	Bit-rate factor, least significant bit

246

We start with the bit-rate factor, which sounds like a speed selector for the Starship Enterprise. The bit-rate factor determines the relationship between the receive and transmit clocks and the actual receive and transmit bit rates. The possible bit-rate factors are:

Bit 1	Bit 0	Bit-Rate Factor
0	0	Synchronous USART operation
0	1	Bit rate = Clock rate
1	0	Bit rate = Clock rate/16
1	1	Bit rate = Clock rate/64

From this, we see that there are three possible bit-rate factors. The 00 setting indicates to the USART that it is to operate in synchronous mode. In this mode, the mode-register-bit assignments for bits 2 through 7 listed above do not apply. The synchronous bit definitions will be covered shortly. It is an advantage to use as high a bit-rate factor as possible because higher bit-rate clocks allow the USART to more finely divide the bit time and more accurately identify the center of the bit time. This provides the USART with the best immunity to slight timing differences between a transmitting device and the receiver.

Conversely, a high bit-rate factor puts a lower ceiling on the maximum bit rate at which the USART can operate. This is because the transmit and receive clocks are limited to 615 kHz for the 64X bit-rate factor, which is a bit rate of roughly 9600 bits per second. The USART is limited to transmit and receive clocks of 310 kHz for a bit-rate factor of 16X, which is a bit rate of roughly 19,200 bits per second. Thus, a lower bit-rate factor permits the USART to run at a higher bit rate.

At the 1X bit-rate factor the USART can run at 64,000 bits per second. However, at the IX bit-rate factor, the USART cannot find the center of a character by itself and depends on external circuitry to center the rising edge of the receive clock in the middle of the bit time. This almost requires that the receive clock be connected to the clock of the transmitting device. Operating the serial interface in this mode is sometimes called Isochronous Serial Communications.

Character length in asynchronous operation is determined by the setting of bits 2 and 3 of the mode register. Character length settings are:

Bit 3	Bit 2	Bits Per Character
0	0	5
0	1	6
1	0	7
1	1	8

Parity is enabled when bit 4 of the mode register is asserted. The type of parity is determined by bit 5 of the mode register. If bit 5 is a "1," even parity is selected, otherwise bit 5 is a "0" and odd parity is selected.

The number of stop bits is determined by bits 6 and 7 of the mode register. The stop bit definitions are:

Bit 7	Bit 6	Number of Stop Bits
0	0	Not valid, don't use
0	1	1
1	0	1.5
1	1	2

Even though the USART transmitter may be set to operate at 1.5 or 2 stop bits per character, the USART receiver only requires 1 stop bit to operate.

Bit assignments in the mode register for synchronous operations are:

Bit	Assignment
7	One or Two SYNC Characters
6	Internal/External SYNC Detect
5	Even/Odd Parity Select

4	Parity Enable
3	Character length, most significant bit
2	Character length, least significant bit
1	Set to 0 for synchronous
0	Set to 0 for synchronous

Note that the definitions for bits 0 through 5 are the same as for the asynchronous mode register assignments. Bits 0 and 1 of the bit-rate factor must be set to 00 for synchronous operation.

Bit 6 determines whether the SYNDET pin is an input or an output. If bit 6 is set to a 1, SYNDET is an input, and external circuitry must synchronize the USART with the incoming message. Otherwise bit 6 is a 0, SYNDET is an output, and the USART will synchronize internally on the first SYNC character.

Bit 7 of the synchronous mode register indicates to the USART the number of SYNC characters at the start of a message. Some synchronous protocols, most notably IBM's Bisync, use two SYNC characters at the start of each message transmission. If bit 7 is set to a 1, the USART will start building characters after receiving the first SYNC. Otherwise, bit 7 is a 0, and the USART will expect two SYNC characters at the beginning of each message. SYNC characters which start a message are not passed on to the microprocessor but are simply used for synchronization and then discarded by the 8251A.

After the mode register has been initialized, the USART will change its internal-register pointer to another register. The mode register is no longer accessible unless another reset occurs. If the USART has been configured for aynchronous operation, the command register is now available for loading. If synchronous operation has been selected, the SYNC character register(s) become accessible next. The next byte the processor writes to the control port becomes the first SYNC character the USART will look for at the start of each message. If double SYNC operation has been chosen, the pointer will change to the second SYNC character register for the next output to the control port. Once the SYNC characters have been output to the USART, the pointer changes to point to the command register and stays there until a reset occurs.

Bit assignments for the command register are:

Bit	Assignment
7	Enter Hunt Mode (Synchronous Only)
6	Internal Reset
5	Request to Send
4	Error Reset
3	Send Break
2	Receive Enable
1	Data Terminal Ready
0	Transmit Enable

Starting with bit 0, we find a bit which allows the transmitter to operate. When this bit is asserted *and* the $\overline{CTS}$ pin is asserted (low), the transmitter can send out characters. If either bit 0 of the command register or $\overline{CTS}$ is not asserted, the transmitter is disabled.

Bit 1 controls the $\overline{DTR}$ output. When bit 1 is asserted, the USART asserts DTR by driving the pin low. Bit 2 is the receiver enable. Incoming bits will be converted to characters only if bit 2 is asserted.

Assertion of bit 3 forces the TxD pin low. This bit can be asserted for 200 milliseconds and then negated to send a break over the communications link.

Bit 4 resets the error-status bits in the status register which we will cover later. Bit 5 controls the $\overline{RTS}$ output. When bit 5 is asserted, the USART asserts the $\overline{RTS}$ pin by driving it low.

There exists a software method of resetting the USART's internal-pointer register. Software reset is accomplished by asserting bit 6 of the command register. This causes a complete reset of the USART, all internal operations are idled, and the pointer returns to point at the mode register.

Bit 7 is used in synchronous operation. When asserted, it causes the USART to enter a "hunt" mode and search for a SYNC character. Once found, the USART leaves the hunt mode and starts to assemble characters from the incoming bit stream.

When power is first applied to the USART, the pointer register setting is undefined. Intel recommends the following procedure to guarantee proper initialization of the USART: First, write three bytes of zero to the control port. This will account for a mode register and two SYNC bytes. At this time pointer is guaranteed to be pointing to the command register. Now write a 64 to the command register, causing a software reset. From here on, the mode register, SYNC register and command register can be written to in the normal sequence.

The USART status register is read by reading the control port. Bit definitions for the status register are:

Bit	Definition
7	Data Set Ready
6	SYNDET
5	Framing Error
4	Overrun Error
3	Parity Error
2	TxEMPTY
1	RxRDY
0	TxRDY

Bits 0, 1, 2, and 6 represent the same information as the USART pins of the same name. The three error bits (3, 4, and 5) should look familiar since they are the same errors we have seen throughout this chapter. These are the three bits which are reset by asserting bit 4 of the command register. This leaves data-set ready, a bit which lets the microprocessor read the state of the $\overline{DSR}$ input. If the input pin is being driven low, the DSR bit is asserted. The data sheet points out that it may take as many as 28 clock cycles for the status register to be updated with any changes.

In operation, the USART is quite simple to run. It has transmitter-ready and receiver-ready bits

in the status register which can be used by the software to send and receive characters in a straightforward manner. Modem control is possible through the control outputs and status inputs of the chip. Modem-control pins should not be changed until the USART indicates transmitter empty. Synchronous operation still requires quite a bit of software even though the synchronization is handled by the USART.

BIT-RATE GENERATORS

Although some receiver/transmitters have on-board bit-rate generators, many do not. There are two types of bit-rate generator integrated circuits available. The first takes a master-clock frequency, usually from a crystal, and divides it into several bit-rate frequencies. The various bit rates are accessible simultaneously on several of the bit-rate generator's pins. Usually, a bank of switches or jumpers

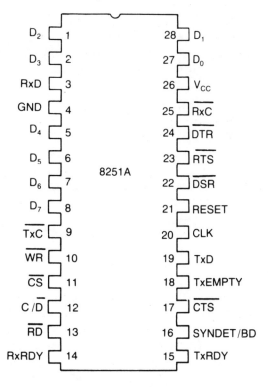

Fig. 5-36. Pin diagram of the 8251A. Reprinted by permission of Intel Corporation, Copyright 1983.

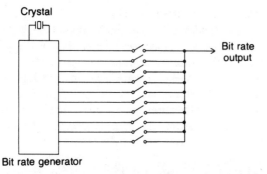

Fig. 5-37. A bit-rate generator with manually-switched selection of the bit rate. Each output pin of the generator carries a different frequency. The proper frequency is selected by closing the appropriate switch. All other switches must be left open.

is designed into the circuit so that one of the bit rates is supplied to the receiver/transmitter. **Figure 5-37** illustrates this type of generator. The Motorola MC14411 is an example of such a bit-rate generator.

The other type of bit-rate generator has an internal register which the microprocessor may write to. The value stored in the register selects a bit rate which is output on a frequency-output pin. This type of generator is better suited to programmable serial interfaces, and is shown in **Fig. 5-38**. The Western Digital BR1911 is an example of this type of part.

In between is the Fairchild 4702. This part has a single, switched, output but no register. It can be used in a system with switches, or an external latch may be added for a programmable system. An added feature of the 4702 is that, by adding a small 4-bit by 4-word RAM (74LS670) and an addressable latch (74LS259), the 4702 can supply four different bit rates simultaneously, each programmed by one of the 4-bit words in the RAM.

DEALING WITH SERIAL INTERFACES

There are some useful tools which you can build or buy to help you deal with serial interfaces. One item is called the Null Modem. This is simply a cable wired as shown in **Fig. 5-39**. With this cable, two devices pretending to be DTEs or DCEs can be connected together. Pin 2 of one connector is tied to pin 3 of the other connector and vice versa. This gets the data flowing out of and into the right pins. Pin 20 of each connector is tied to pins 5 and

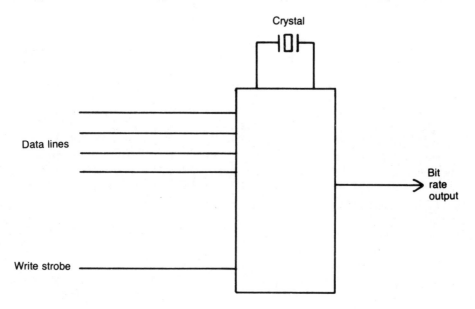

Fig. 5-38. A bit-rate generator with internally latched bit rate. The output frequency of the generator is selected by writing the appropriate value to the on-board latch.

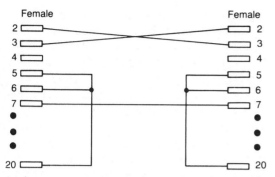

Fig. 5-39. Schematic for an RS-232C null modem cable. Each end plugs into a data terminal equipment (DTE) connector.

6 of the same connector. This way, the DTE or DCE asserts its own clear-to-send and data-set ready inputs by asserting the data-terminal-ready output. Both connectors should be female.

Another useful tool is a cable I call a "hermaphrodite." It is a foot-long piece of ribbon cable with two male and two female RS-232 connectors on it. With this cable, any combination of male and female connectors can be accommodated. This can come in handy when a peripheral manufacturer doesn't accurately predict which sex connector you need for your system. Figure 5-40 is a picture of

such a hermaphrodite cable.

The final tool, which is the most helpful, can also be the most expensive. It is called a "blue box," but it isn't the kind that helps you defraud the telephone companies. A blue box has male and female RS-232 connectors wired to 25 switches. Each of the 25 RS-232 lines can be independently broken with this arrangement. On each side of the switch is a tie point that will accept a jumper wire. Also, one side of the switch is usually connected to a row of light-emitting diodes (LEDs) to tell you the state of that line. Figure 5-41 illustrates the design of a blue box, and Fig. 5-42 shows a commercially available version.

The blue box helps you identify the pin requirements for any unknown RS-232 implementation. You can see with the LEDs which signals are asserted and which are not. With the switches and jumpers, you can break connections between the connectors and reconnect them as you wish.

If you are planning to do much connection to various RS-232 peripherals, a blue box is essential. Unfortunately, the cost of a blue box is between $100 and $200. However, with less than $50 of parts and some time, you can build one and it is well worth the effort.

Fig. 5-40. A hermaphrodite cable built by the author out of one foot of ribbon cable plus two male and female insulation-displacement connectors (IDCs).

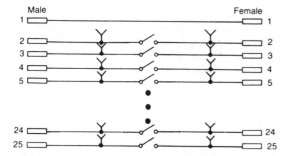

Fig. 5-41. Schematic for an RS-232C Blue box. The switches allow any circuit to be broken while the jacks allow two or more circuits to be interconnected.

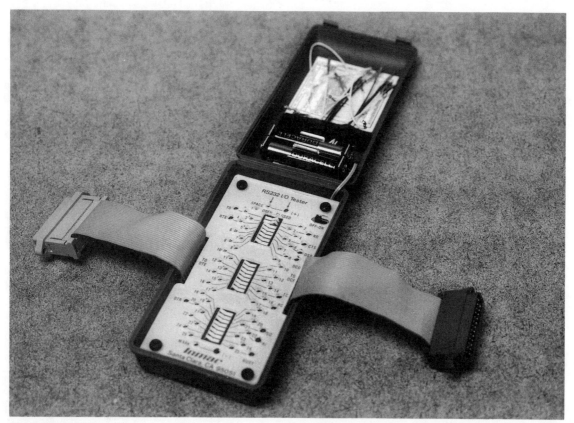

Fig. 5-42. A commercially available RS-232C Blue box. This one was offered by Inmac (2465 Augustine Drive, Santa Clara, CA 95054).

Chapter 6

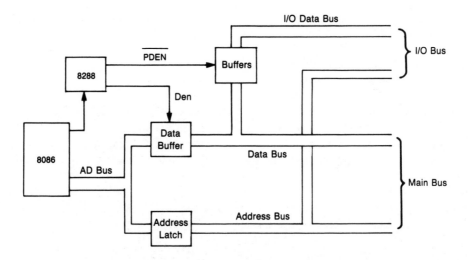

Interfacing to Analog Devices

People in the computer priesthood always refer to noncomputer topics as the "real world" as if computers don't reside in the same reality. The truth is that computers do exist in the same world as you and I, but it is difficult to make them take notice of it! That is what interfacing is all about.

Almost every electrical device used today for monitoring and controlling physical events was devised before digital technology became widespread. These devices use signals that vary continuously between two arbitrary extremes. Some devices use varying voltage levels while others use varying currents. Examples of analog signals in everyday use are those representing temperature (from thermocouples and thermistors), pressure (from pressure transducers and strain gauges), and light (from photocells, solar cells, photodiodes, and phototransistors).

In this chapter, we will consider several types of devices—D-to-A converters, A-to-D converters,

and analog multiplexers—but we will not consider any specific integrated circuits. There are two reasons for this. The first is that analog converters do not represent anything new as far as the interface between the microprocessor and the converter. Generally, the interface looks like one or two parallel input or output ports, and we have already studied these extensively.

The other reason is the lack of standardization among manufacturers of analog converter integrated circuits. Very few of the devices have multiple sources and, especially for A-to-D converters, there is wide diversity of conversion techniques. Instead of looking at specific devices therefore, I present the ideas behind these techniques in order to give you the tools to choose the parts and technologies best suited to your application.

Two leading integrated circuit analog converters manufacturers are Analog Devices and Burr-Brown. Both companies publish excellent catalogs containing device data sheets and applications notes. I highly recommend these data catalogs for further exploration into analog interfacing.

DIGITAL-TO-ANALOG CONVERSION

In order for computers to communicate with analog devices, analog input signals must be converted to a digital representation and digital output signals must be converted to analog. The first process is called Analog-to-Digital conversion, or A-to-D for short. The reverse process is called Digital-to-Analog conversion, or D-to-A. We will look at D-to-A converters first for two reasons; they are simpler, and some A-to-D converters use D-to-A converters as components.

Figure 6-1 is the schematic of a simple D-to-A converter (DAC), one that would really never be useful except as a learning tool. The triangle on the right side of the figure is called an operational amplifier (op amp). It is an analog, or linear, device and it is capable of amplifying analog signals.

When wired as shown in **Fig. 6-1**, the op amp will do its best to maintain its positive and negative inputs at the same voltage level. This is called negative feedback. Whatever signal we apply to the positive input, the op amp will apply an opposite signal so that the net effect of both signals is zero. Since the negative input is grounded, the op amp will make every effort to force the positive input to remain at near ground potential also. The positive op amp input is said to be at virtual ground. This will be very important for calculating voltages in the circuit.

The output of the op amp is connected to one end of a resistor. The other end of the resistor is connected to the op amp's positive input. This is the feedback resistor. The other four resistors are input resistors. If we assume that the positive input is at ground potential (a self-fulfilling prophecy, as we shall see), then the current through the feedback resistor can be calculated by dividing the op amp output voltage V_{OUT} by the resistance R. This results in the simple equation:

$$I1 = V_{OUT}/R$$

If no current is being supplied by the resistor network on the left of **Fig. 6-1**, then the op amp must also cause no current to flow in the circuit. It

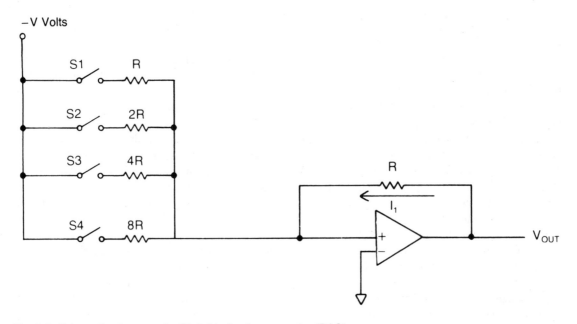

Fig. 6-1. Schematic diagram of a Digital-to-Analog converter (DAC).

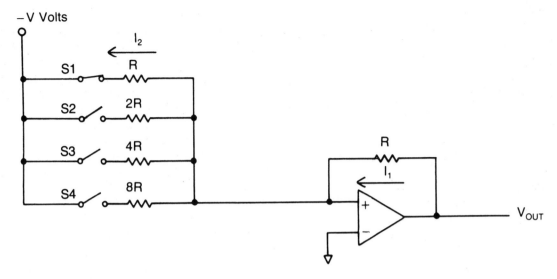

Fig. 6-2. DAC with switch S1 closed.

does this by forcing its output to zero volts. Thus, there is zero potential at both ends of the resistor and no current through it. With no current through the resistor, there is no voltage across it so the positive input must also be at zero volts.

Now let's induce a current in the circuit as shown in Fig. 6-2 by closing switch S1. This causes the resistor at the right, with resistance R, to have a differential voltage across it. Again we assume the op amp will maintain a zero potential at the negative input by whatever means possible.

The current, I2, through the resistor is − V/R (V is our reference voltage) which flows away from the negative op amp input because of the negative voltage. In order to maintain the negative input at zero volts, the op amp must inject exactly as much current into the negative input as is being extracted through S1. To do this, the op amp drives its output to V volts. This makes the current I1 equal to V/R which exactly counters current I2.

Since the currents into and out of the positive input are equal in magnitude but opposite in sign, the net current at the positive input is zero and the negative input remains at ground potential. Thus the op amp output is at V volts with switch S1 closed.

If we now open S1 and close S2 (Fig. 6-3), the current out of the negative op amp input will be − V/2R. To counter this, the op amp output must assume a level of V/2 volts. This makes the current through the feedback resistor V/2R, balancing the effect of closing S2. The output voltage will be V/2 volts, or half of the negative reference voltage − V. In a similar manner, closing switch S3 alone forces the op amp output to V/4 volts and closing switch S4 forces the output to V/8 volts.

The really interesting effects appear when more than one switch is closed at a time. The currents through the input resistors add. Thus we get sixteen voltage levels for the sixteen combinations of switch closures. These levels are shown in Table 6-1.

If you look carefully, you can see that the switch settings follow a binary code from 0000 to 1111 or from 0 to 15 decimal. The op amp output voltage steps in ⅛ V levels from 0 to 1⅞ V. Clearly, a four-bit number is being converted into one of sixteen voltage levels. This is the basis of the D-to-A converter.

D-to-A converters used for computer interfacing don't use mechanical switches for several rea-

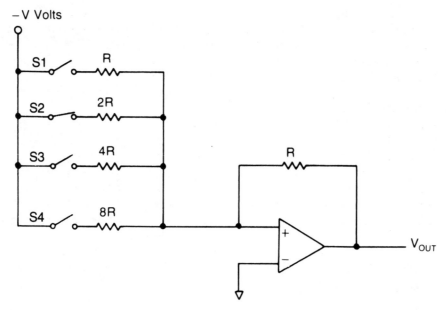

Fig. 6-3. DAC with switch S2 closed.

sons: Switches bounce, meaning that when they close, the contacts repeatedly make and break contact for several milliseconds after the switch is thrown. This is acceptable for turning on light bulbs, but microprocessors can execute hundreds of in-structions in that amount of time, therefore bounce cannot be tolerated.

Switches are also slow and, to be controlled by a computer, they must be in the form of relays, which consume relatively large amounts of power

Table 6-1. Switch Settings vs. Output Voltage for the R-2R-4R-8R DAC Resistor Network.

S1	S2	S3	S4	V_{OUT}
Open	Open	Open	Open	Zero
Open	Open	Open	Closed	⅛ V
Open	Open	Closed	Open	¼ V
Open	Open	Closed	Closed	⅜ V
Open	Closed	Open	Open	½ V
Open	Closed	Open	Closed	⅝ V
Open	Closed	Closed	Open	¾ V
Open	Closed	Closed	Closed	⅞ V
Closed	Open	Open	Open	V
Closed	Open	Open	Closed	1⅛ V
Closed	Open	Closed	Open	1¼ V
Closed	Open	Closed	Closed	1⅜ V
Closed	Closed	Open	Open	1½ V
Closed	Closed	Open	Closed	1⅝ V
Closed	Closed	Closed	Open	1¾ V
Closed	Closed	Closed	Closed	1⅞ V

compared to integrated circuits. In D-to-A converters used with microprocessors, the switches are built from transistors. Logic levels control the turning on and off of the transistors, producing appropriate voltages from the DAC.

The R-2R Ladder DAC

The DAC just discussed is called a Summing-Amplifier type DAC. This is because the various currents through the input resistors are summed to determine the current through the feedback resistor, and thus the output voltage.

If we were to build an 8-bit version of the Summing-Amplifier DAC, the input resistor on the least-significant bit would be 128 times larger than the one on the most-significant bit. Large-valued resistors make circuits more susceptible to noise and are more difficult to incorporate directly into integrated circuits.

In order to make the largest resistor a reasonable value, the smallest resistor would have to be quite small. For example, with a 1000-ohm value for the most-significant bit's input resistor R, the least-significant bit has an input resistor value of 128,000 ohms. All of these resistors in parallel appear as roughly a 540-ohm load on the reference voltage. Yet, if all switches but the least significant are off, the load is 127,000 ohms.

Such a varying load may cause the voltage reference to waver, decreasing accuracy. It isn't easy to build a precision-voltage reference that is really precise over a wide current-output range. Thus we have two basic design problems with the Summing-Amplifier DAC; high-valued resistors in the circuit and severe reference voltage loading.

Both of these problems are overcome by using a different DAC circuit, shown in **Fig. 6-4**. Only the input resistor network is shown. Generally, this network will be connected to a buffer amplifier to increase the output drive capability. For now, we ignore the buffer amplifier to make the analysis simpler.

Again we have four switches, S1 through S4. Each switch can be connected to either the reference voltage V, or ground. Clearly, if we place all switches in the grounded position, V_{OUT} is zero volts because there is no voltage source in the circuit. That is the easy part of the analysis.

Now, let's leave switches S2 through S4 grounded and place switch S1 in the position connected to the reference voltage. A very interesting situation develops. The circuit now appears as shown in **Fig. 6-5**. This circuit is extremely simple to analyze.

Starting at the left, the two 2R resistors in parallel form a resistance of R, so we replace them with a resistor of value R as shown in **Fig. 6-6**. We now have two resistors of resistance R on the left, which we combine to form a resistor of value 2R as shown in **Fig. 6-7**.

We can continue to collapse this resistor network by taking the two leftmost 2R resistors into a resistor of value R, leaving us with the circuit in **Fig. 6-8**, which ultimately reduces through **Figs. 6-9** and **6-10** to the simple voltage divider of **Fig. 6-11**. Since voltage V is applied to a series circuit of two equal value resistors, the voltage V_{OUT} between the resistors must be V/2.

Now let's try working with switch S2. It's a little more difficult, but not much. We start with the

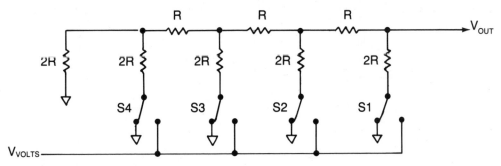

Fig. 6-4. An R-2R ladder network.

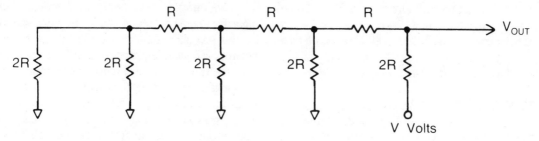

Fig. 6-5. R-2R ladder with switch S1 connected to V and all other switches grounded.

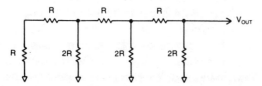

Fig. 6-6. Elimination of leftmost 2R resistors by parallel combination into a single resistor of resistance R.

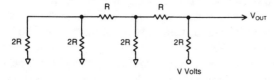

Fig. 6-7. Combining the leftmost two series resistors R produces a resistance 2R.

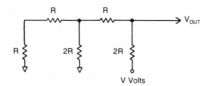

Fig. 6-8. Parallel combination again reduces the two leftmost 2R resistors to a single resistance R.

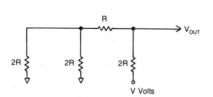

Fig. 6-9. Series resistors again combine to make a resistor of resistance 2R.

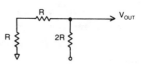

Fig. 6-10. Parallel resistances reduce to a resistor of resistance R.

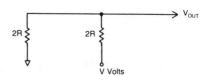

Fig. 6-11. Series resistances again combine to form a resistor of resistance 2R. This leaves a simple voltage divider which takes the voltage V and divides it in half.

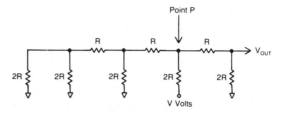

Fig. 6-12. R-2R Network with switch S2 connected to V and all other switches grounded.

258

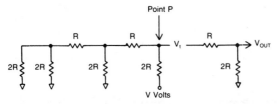

Fig. 6-13. Circuit of 6-12 is simplified by breaking it in two at point P which is at voltage V_t, a Thevinin-equivalent voltage.

circuit of **Fig. 6-12**. Thevenin's Equivalent analysis states that we may break off the rightmost R-2R resistor pair and discern the voltage at point P with an equivalent output impedance. This produces the circuit in **Fig. 6-13**. The output voltage at point P is called Vt for the Thevenin voltage. This quickly reduces to V/2 since the circuit is the same to the left of point P as the one shown in **Fig. 6-7**.

Thevenin's equivalent also allows us to determine the output impedance of this part of the circuit. The output impedance is the same as the impedance seen by shorting all internal voltages to ground and looking into the input terminal.

Using the same collapsing technique, and starting at the left of **Fig. 6-14**, we quickly conclude that the resistance is simply R. We do this by combining the two leftmost 2R resistors to form one resistor, R, which is in series with the leftmost resistor R, which forms a resistor of value 2R, etc.

This produces the Theveninized equivalent circuit of **Fig. 6-15**. This is truly a simple voltage divider. The Thevenin voltage V/2 flows through a voltage divider made of two resistors of value R and a 2R resistor, V_{OUT} must therefore be half of V/S, or V/4. Thus, switch S2 can cause the output of the original circuit in **Fig. 6-4** to reach a level of V/4 volts. Remember that switch S1 contributed V/2. In a similar manner, switch S3 can contribute V/8 and switch S4 can contribute V/16.

Using the electrical principle of superposition, we can add the contributions of the four switches to produce **Table 6-2**. Again we have sixteen output voltage possible with four switches although the voltages are different from those in **Table 6-1**.

The beauty of the R-2R ladder is that no matter how many bits are associated with the DAC, this R-2R collapsing technique is valid. Only two types of resistors are needed, and they can be selected to be of moderately high resistance to prevent reference-voltage loading while still low enough to make noise less of a problem.

The added complexity in the switches of an R-2R ladder DAC is not much of a problem for to-day's integrated-circuit design and processing techniques. Many packaged DACs are currently available for very little money. Radio Shack listed an 8-bit DAC for $4.49 in their 1983 catalog and in 1988, many DACs cost less than $1. Because of their low

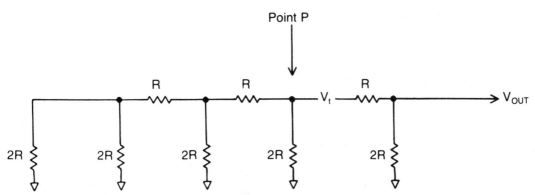

Fig. 6-14. Determining the equivalent output impedance of the left part of the circuit in Fig. 6-13.

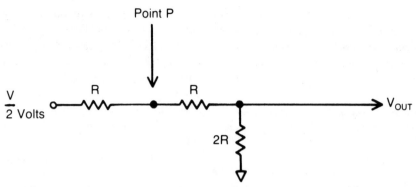

Fig. 6-15. Circuit of Fig. 6-12 with left side of circuit Thevenized.

cost, we won't study how to build DACs, only how to use them.

Using DACs

Now that you have seen how a DAC works, what can you do with one? Are there any applications for analog signals generated under microprocessor control? There are several. Waveform synthesis is possible. Since the DAC can output many voltage levels between an upper and lower limit, and since the microprocessor can be pro-grammed to change this output level every few microseconds, the DAC can be used to generate analog waveforms at frequencies up to 100 kHz or so.

The most common use for DACs, however, is as a part of an Analog to-Digital converter. In the next section, on A-to-D conversion, we will give this application a closer look. Right now, however, is a good time to see how a DAC is interfaced to a microprocessor.

A very simple interface is built using a zero-

Table 6-2. Switch Settings vs. Output Voltage for the R-2R DAC Ladder Network.

S1	S2	S3	S4	V_{out}
GROUND	GROUND	GROUND	GROUND	ZERO
GROUND	GROUND	GROUND	V	$\frac{1}{16}V$
GROUND	GROUND	V	GROUND	$\frac{1}{8}V$
GROUND	GROUND	V	V	$\frac{3}{16}V$
GROUND	V	GROUND	GROUND	$\frac{1}{4}V$
GROUND	V	GROUND	V	$\frac{5}{16}V$
GROUND	V	V	GROUND	$\frac{3}{8}V$
GROUND	V	V	V	$\frac{7}{16}V$
V	GROUND	GROUND	GROUND	$\frac{1}{2}V$
V	GROUND	V	V	$\frac{9}{16}V$
V	GROUND	GROUND	GROUND	$\frac{5}{8}V$
V	GROUND	V	V	$\frac{11}{16}V$
V	V	GROUND	GROUND	$\frac{3}{4}V$
V	V	GROUND	V	$\frac{13}{16}V$
V	V	V	GROUND	$\frac{7}{8}V$
V	V	V	V	$\frac{15}{16}V$

wire-handshake parallel interface as shown in **Fig. 6-16**. The microprocessor writes a byte to the parallel interface and the digital outputs of the interface drive the digital inputs of the DAC. This allows the microprocessor to specify the output voltage by the value written to the parallel port.

Some DACs are designed specifically for microprocessor use. These devices have latches built in so that the microprocessor can directly output binary information to the DAC. Such a DAC is called a "Registered DAC" since it has the data register on board. **Figure 6-17** is an illustration of a registered DAC.

There are three major considerations when designing a DAC into a microcomputer system. The first is the matter of power-supply voltages. Many DACs require both positive and negative power supplies, and some only operate within very specific supply-voltage limits.

Power-supply voltages available in microcomputer systems vary to a large extent. Some microprocessor busses have only +5 volts available. This will narrow the choice of DACs quite a bit. Other busses have +12 and −12 volts available. However, the standard supply voltages in the analog world are +15 and −15 volts, which your system just may not have.

The second consideration is the logic-level compatibility of the DAC. Are the digital inputs TTL compatible? If not, what logic levels are required and can your system supply them?

Finally, DACs have limited speed capabilities. Some DAC outputs switch in less than a microsecond, and they are expensive. Other DACs work more slowly and cost much less. Your application requirements determine how much speed you need in a DAC and thus how much you will pay for the part.

Other factors to consider are:

- Does the DAC have an internal voltage reference? If it does not, you will have to supply one with the accuracy required.
- How many bits of resolution does the application require? If it is wider than the data bus of the microprocessor, some special circuitry will be needed to allow the microprocessor to write to the DAC with two or more operations.
- What overall system accuracy is required?
- How much output drive capability is required? If the DAC isn't capable of driving the intended load, a buffer amplifier is required which will have an adverse effect on accuracy.

All of these questions affect what part you buy. As usual, interface design turns out to be an exercise

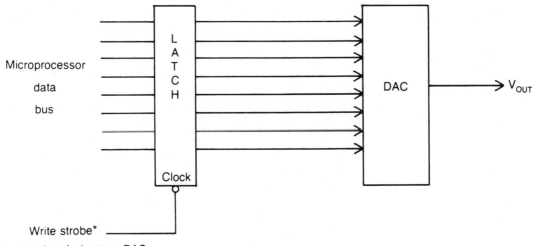

Fig. 6-16. Interfacing to a DAC.

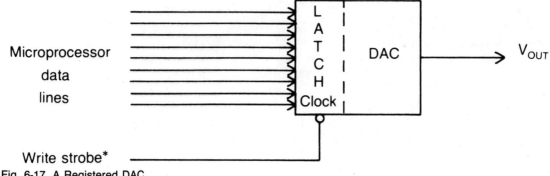

Fig. 6-17. A Registered DAC.

in compromise and a thorough study of specifications.

ANALOG-TO-DIGITAL CONVERSION

The conversion of analog signals to digital representation is called Analog-to-Digital conversion, or simply AD. This process is useful for converting existing analog signals to a form which can be manipulated by a microcomputer system.

There are several techniques for AD conversion. Some techniques are very fast but require a large number of electronic components for the conversion. Other techniques are clever in the way that components are used, reducing the hardware cost but increasing the time required for conversion. We will study the major AD techniques in the remaining sections of this chapter.

The Flash AD Converter

Flash AD conversion is a brute-force technique which also happens to be the fastest method for converting analog signals to a digital form. The name "flash" comes from the speed at which the conversion is done, "in a flash." A flash converter is shown in Fig. 6-18.

The analog input signal is applied to the positive inputs of a number of comparators. The negative input of each comparator is connected to a voltage divider which in turn is connected to a refer-

ence voltage. If, for example, four comparators were used in the flash converter, the negative input of the top converter would be connected to the reference voltage V, the next to 0.75 V, the next to 0.5 V, and the last input would be connected to 0.25 V.

When the input signal is applied, the outputs of all the comparators whose negative inputs are at a lower potential than the input signal go high, while the outputs of the rest of the comparators are low. A priority encoder determines the lowest output that is low, and generates a digital representation for that comparator position.

Flash converters look simple but tend to be complex when built. Since each voltage step requires a separate comparator, 2^n-1 comparators are required for an "n"-bit AD converter. If we want to build an 8-bit flash converter, we need 255 comparators, and the voltage divider will be made of 255 separate resistors. Also, the priority encoder requires 255 input pins. Most flash converters are integrated onto a single integrated circuit due to the interconnection complexity.

Since the time required to generate the digital output is the time through a comparator and the priority encoder, the conversion takes place rapidly. Flash converters are available that can perform several tens of millions of conversions per second, far faster than can be practically used by a microprocessor. For this reason, most microcomputer applications for AD converters do not use flash converters.

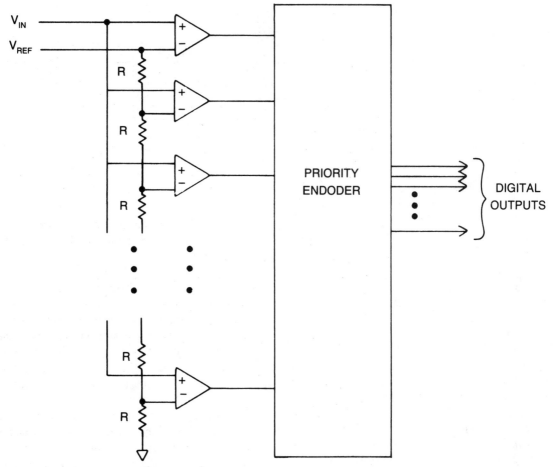

Fig. 6-18. A Flash A-to-D Converter (ADC).

INTEGRATING CONVERTERS

We now move from one extreme to the other. Flash converters are the fastest ADs, and integrating converters are the slowest. An integrating technique converts an analog input voltage into a period of time. Generally, the bigger the input voltage, the longer the time. The microprocessor is supplied a digital representation of the time required for the conversion, which is directly proportional to the magnitude of the input voltage.

Ramp AD Converter

A simple AD converter can be built from an integrator and a comparator as shown in Fig. 6-19.

The integrator is capable of integrating the negative reference voltage – V with a time constant of RC. The output of the integrator is connected to the input of a comparator, and the input voltage to the converter (V_{IN}) is applied to the other comparator input.

Conversion is initiated by zeroing the integrator. Any charge on the capacitor C is bled off by closing switch S2 for a short period of time. This forces the output of the integrator to ground since the junction of the resistor R and capacitor C is a virtual ground. After nulling the integrator, S2 is opened and S1 is closed, applying the reference voltage – V to the integrator input.

263

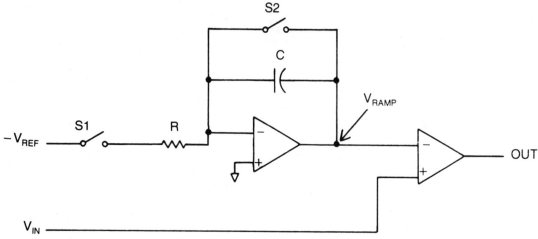

Fig. 6-19. A ramp ADC circuit.

Application of the reference voltage to the integrator input causes a current to flow through the input resistor R. The direction of current flow is out of the integrator input because the reference voltage is negative. To counter that current, the op amp must force current into the resistor-capacitor junction. The capacitor blocks direct current (dc) from the op amp output so the op amp must apply a constantly increasing voltage to the capacitor in order to obtain a current balance. This appears as a voltage ramp at the negative-comparator input. The slope of the ramp is determined by the timing components in the integrator (R and C) and the reference voltage $-V$.

Eventually, the ramp will reach the same voltage as the analog input voltage V_{IN}. At this point the output of the comparator will change state. This signals that the ramp voltage has matched the voltage being converted.

Thus, the input voltage, V_{IN}, is converted into a time T by the integrator-comparator combination, see **Fig. 6-20.** If the microprocessor is controlling switches S1 and S2, it will know when the conversion is started. Similarly, by monitoring the comparator output, the microprocessor knows when the conversion ends. The greater V_{IN} is, the longer it will take for the ramp voltage to reach equal potential. Therefore, greater input voltages take longer conversion times.

Lack of accuracy is the major disadvantage of the ramp AD converter. The accuracy of the conversion depends on four components; the resistor R, the capacitor C, the reference voltage $-V$, and

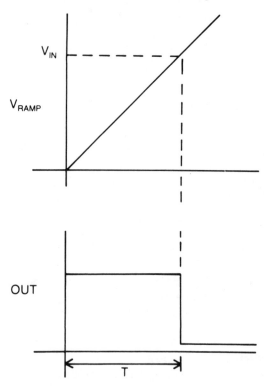

Fig. 6-20. Timing diagram for a ramp ADC.

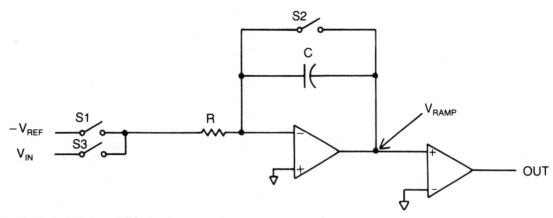

Fig. 6-21. A dual-slope ADC circuit.

the device timing the process. Usually, it is the microprocessor's crystal-controlled clock that does the timing. Crystal clocks tend to be fairly accurate. Also, it is now quite easy to purchase integrated voltage references which have good accuracy. However, resistors and capacitors are not especially accurate. They can be accurately trimmed, but their values tend to drift over time and are sensitive to temperature. For this reason, ramp converters, also called single-slope converters, are rarely used.

Dual-Slope AD Converters

Dual-slope AD conversion reduces the accuracy problem by nulling out the effect of the resistor and capacitor. This is done by first integrating the reference voltage for a known period of time, causing the integrator output to ramp up, and then integrating the unknown input voltage, causing the integrator output to ramp down until the output is zero again.

Figure 6-21 illustrates a dual-slope converter. The analog input voltage V_{IN} has been connected to a third switch S3 which can connect the input voltage to the integrator input. S2 is again used to drain the charge from the capacitor at the beginning of the cycle. Then S1 is closed for a controlled period of time. Let's call that time T1. The output of the integrator ramps up and reaches a voltage equal to $(V_{REF}/RC)*T1$. This formula comes from basic electronic theory.

Then the reference voltage is removed and the input voltage V_{IN} is applied. This causes the integrator output to ramp down. Eventually, the output of the integrator reaches zero and the comparator output switches, signaling the end of conversion. A diagram of the signals is shown in Fig. 6-22.

The time required for the downward ramp to reach zero is dependent on V_{IN}, R, C, and the voltage the downward ramp started with. Let's call that time T2. The end result is the equation:

$$(V_{REF}/RC) * T1 = (V_{in}/RC) * T2$$

This is true because the application of V_{IN} for time T2 exactly canceled the application of - V for T1. By multiplying both sides by RC we get:

$$V_{REF} * T1 = V_{in} * T2$$

A little further juggling produces:

$$V_{IN}/V_{REF} = T1/T2$$

Thus the voltages are inversely proportional to the time. Note that resistor R and capacitor C aren't in the final equation at all. Their effects have been nulled out by the dual-slope conversion technique.

Both V_{REF} and T1 are known quantities. V_{REF} is the reference voltage and T1 is a controlled charg-

265

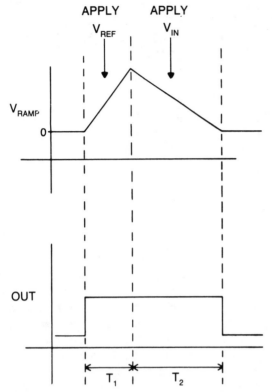

APPLY V$_{REF}$ APPLY V$_{IN}$

V$_{RAMP}$

0

OUT

$\overset{\longleftrightarrow}{\text{T}_1}$ $\overset{\longleftrightarrow}{\text{T}_2}$

Fig. 6-22. Timing diagram for the dual-slope ADC.

ing time. By measuring T2, the microprocessor can calculate V$_{IN}$ with the equation:

$$V_{IN} = V_{REF} * (T1/T2)$$

V$_{IN}$ is inversely proportional to T2. This is intuitively correct. If V$_{IN}$ is small, it will take a long time for the integrator to ramp down to zero and if V$_{IN}$ is large, the time will be short.

Practically, it is more convenient to invert V$_{IN}$ and use a positive reference voltage. Then by applying $-$V$_{IN}$ to the integrator first and then V$_{ref}$ to bring the output back to zero, the equations are:

$$(V_{IN}/RC) * T1 = (V_{REF}/RC) * T2$$

$$V_{IN} * T1 = V_{REF} * T2$$

$$V_{IN}/V_{REF} = T2/T1$$

V$_{IN}$ will be directly instead of inversely proportional to T2. Again this is intuitively correct. If V$_{IN}$ is large, the integrator will ramp to a high level and the ramp down will take longer. Conversely, if V$_{IN}$ is small, the ramp will not reach a high voltage and the downward ramp will quickly reach zero.

The reason that this second dual-slope alternative is more practical is that by making T2 directly proportional to V$_{IN}$, a simple counting technique can be used to determine the magnitude of V$_{IN}$. This is easier than calculation of V$_{IN}$ from an inverse proportion. In fact, several dual-slope AD converters are commercially available which have built in counters. They are merely started by the microprocessor and then signal when the conversion is finished. The processor may then obtain a digital value directly from the converter.

Accuracy is greatly improved for the dual-slope converter over the single-slope technique. The tradeoff is time. It takes longer to ramp up and then down instead of simply ramping up. Also, dual-slope conversion is not the last word in integrating AD converters.

Analog Devices, a company specializing in the manufacture of DA and AD converters, has patented a quadruple-slope conversion technique. Though the dual-slope technique nulls out the effect of R and C, the integrator and comparator have small offset voltages which affect accuracy. The quadruple-slope technique also nulls out the effect of these offsets. As you might expect, quadruple-slope conversion takes even longer than dual-slope conversion and is used when extremely high accuracy is desired.

AD CONVERTERS USING DA CONVERTERS

Somewhere between the flash converter and the integrating converters are the AD converters which incorporate DACs as part of their design. These converters use the DAC as a controlled analog signal source which is compared to the input analog voltage. When the controlled source is equal to the unknown input, the value of the input is known.

Figure 6-23 illustrates an approach for using

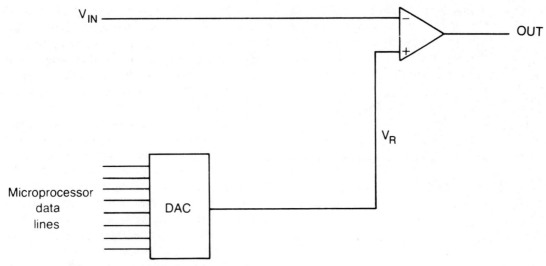

Fig. 6-23. A DAC used in an ADC circuit.

a DAC in an A-to-D converter. The DAC is connected to one input of a comparator and the input voltage V_{IN} is connected to the other. The two signals are compared and the OUT signal indicates which voltage, V_{IN} or the DAC output is greater.

A simple conversion technique using this hardware is to start the DAC at zero output and increment the value until the DAC output voltage matches and slightly exceeds the input voltage. This technique causes the DAC output voltage to resemble a staircase, as shown in Fig. 6-24.

A simple routine in the microprocessor can output a value to the DAC and then check the comparator output to see if the voltage generated by the which voltage, V_{IN} or the DAC output is greater. increments the value sent to the DAC and then outputs the new value to the DAC.

This simple scheme essentially is a counter which increments until the input voltage is matched. Alternatively, a real hardware counter can be used to relieve the microprocessor of almost all of the work. The microprocessor simply starts the counter. When the DAC output level exceeds V_{IN}, the comparator output changes state, stopping the counter and alerting the microprocessor that the conversion is complete.

A major drawback to this approach is that the

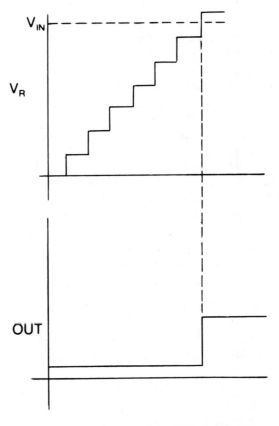

Fig. 6-24. Timing diagram for the DAC-based ADC.

average conversion time is half of the number of states possible. For an 8-bit DAC, 256 states are possible, so the average conversion will require 128 counts. Also, the conversion takes a variable amount of time, depending on the input voltage being converted. There is another approach which applies some clever logic to reduce the number of states to the number of bits of resolution of the DAC. It is called "successive approximation."

SUCCESSIVE-APPROXIMATION AD CONVERSION

We return to the picture of the DAC-based AD in Fig. 6-23. If the DAC is connected to a parallel port of the microprocessor instead of a counter or has a built in latch so that the DAC appears like a parallel port, there is no reason to output any specific sequence of bytes to it. The microprocessor can output 0, then 128, then 64 and then whatever. If a counter were actually used, this would not be true.

Successive approximation is the application of a computer technique called binary search to analog conversion. Binary searches look at the entire range of possible values, take the middle value and try it. For instance, if we have eight bits, the range of possible values is from 0 to 255. The middle of this range is roughly 128, which is simply the most significant of the eight bits.

If the initial try does not succeed, the binary search determines whether the target is above or below the first try. Whichever is true, the possible range is again split in half and the new value is tried. For example, if 128 wasn't correct and the actual value was determined to be lower than 128, the difference between 128 and 0 would be split, to get 64. That would be the new value to try.

As the technique is repeatedly applied, the range becomes rapidly smaller until the desired value is found. This technique does not require you to know the exact value you are searching for, only whether it is above or below the value you presently have. The number of tries required is simply the number of bits required to represent the largest possible value.

Successive approximation uses this technique with a DAC-based AD to quickly convert an analog voltage to a digital representation. First, a value with only the most significant bit is output to the DAC. The comparator output provides a determination as to whether this value is greater than or less than V_{IN}. If it is greater than V_{IN}, the most significant bit is too large for the digital value and it is cleared. If the value is too small, then a larger value is needed and the most significant bit will remain set throughout the conversion.

The next-to-most-significant bit is tried next. It is combined with the proper value of the most significant bit determined in the previous step and output to the DAC. A greater/less than determination is again made and the process is repeated. When all bits have been tried, the resulting digital representation is the converted representation of V_{IN}. Each conversion takes exactly eight tries. This is considerably better than the average of 128 tries for an eight-bit conversion encountered with the staircase method.

Complete A-to-Ds with successive approximation circuitry in them are commercially available. Again the microprocessor can be relieved of much of the overhead required to perform the conversion. In fact, the hardware successive approximation converters can perform the AD conversion much faster than the microprocessor. Some can perform the conversion in the time the microprocessor requires to execute a single instruction. These fast ADs reduce the microprocessor's job to starting the conversion with one instruction and reading the converted value with the next.

INTERFACING TO CONVERTERS

Most DA and AD converters have parallel interfaces similar to those discussed in Chapter 4. Some have BCD inputs or outputs and require BCD interfaces to the microprocessor. Zero-wire handshakes are common for DACs while two-wire handshakes are most common for AD converters. ADs have an initiate conversion input and a conversion complete output.

It is also possible to interface a class of AD converter which is designed for digital panel meters

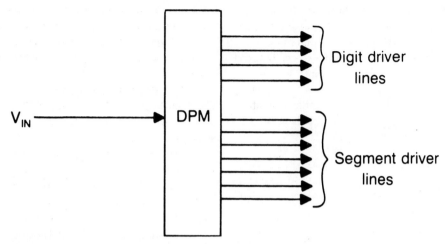

Fig. 6-25. A digital panel meter (DPM) circuit.

(DPMs). These integrated circuits are actually designed to drive seven-segment displays, but they are also inexpensive AD converters with good resolution and accuracy. They generally have seven outputs for segment drivers and other outputs for digit drivers. Such a chip is shown in **Fig. 6-25.**

The digit-driver lines are energized sequentially and are intended to activate a single digit in the display. At the same time, a 7-segment representation of the numeral to be displayed is output to the segment driver lines. A microprocessor routine can be written to first read the digit infor-

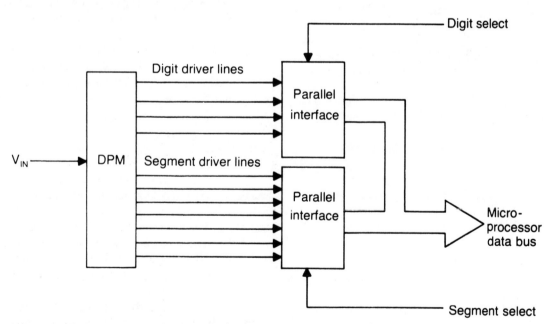

Fig. 6-26. Interfacing a DPM chip to a microprocessor bus.

269

mation, and then the segment information associated with that digit. Figure 6-26 illustrates a design for interfacing a DPM integrated circuit to a microprocessor. A simple lookup table can be used to convert 7-segment information into binary.

DETERMINING YOUR CONVERTER NEEDS

There are no standard analog interfaces to guide you in selecting a DA or AD converter. Each application is unique. Therefore, I present the following guidelines to help you determine what will best fit your application.

Resolution. This specification determines how many bits the DAC or ADC has. Common values are 4, 6, 8, 10, 12, and 16 bits for binary converters and 3, 3½, 4, 4½, 5, 5½, and 6 digits for BCD converters. The fractional digit specifications can be misleading. A half-digit is considered to be one count in the most significant digit. Thus a BCD converter which has a maximum output of 1999 is a 3½ digit converter.

There are also converters with ¾ digit resolution, such as a 3¾ digit converter. An example of such a converter is one with a maximum value of 4999. These conventions for specifying resolution are at best confusing and are not even standard among manufacturers. You really need to consult the data sheets for the parts you are considering.

Accuracy. This specification is hard to pin down. There may be disclaimers as to when the specified accuracy is really achieved. Also, for those converters where the reference voltage is supplied to the converter from an external device, accuracy depends not only on the accuracy of the converter but on the accuracy of the reference voltage.

It is important to make sure the accuracy is better than the resolution of the converter. For instance, 1 percent accuracy on an 8-bit converter means that the least significant bit is worthless but you are paying for that extra bit anyway.

Power Supplies. This is a critical specification for any device you put into your system, but is most critical for analog components since they tend to be the most sensitive to power-supply problems. Many analog components need bipolar power supplies, +15 and −15 volt requirements being the most common.

Several converter manufacturers have recognized that most microprocessor systems don't have 15-volt supplies available and have started supplying 12-volt versions of their most popular products while maintaining a +/− 10 volt conversion range. Also, some converters are available with +5 and −5 volt power supply requirements.

Input Range. You need to consider the nature of the signal you are converting. Though most A-to-D converters require +15 and −15 volt power supplies, they can only accommodate analog inputs between +10 and −10 volts. Converters with lower voltage power supplies have smaller input signal capabilities. If you need large analog signal swings, chances are there won't be a converter to exactly meet your requirements.

The same is true if you need extremely small signal swings, such as for thermocouples. In both of these cases, analog conditioning will be needed to convert the analog signals from what they are to levels compatible with available converters.

Conversion Speed. Only you can determine how fast you need the conversion to take place. If relatively slow signals such as temperature are being converted, the speed specification is not so critical. Speed and converter cost are directly related. Extremely fast converters sell for premium prices. Therefore, it is important that you only buy as much converter as you need.

For AD converters, required conversion speed will be determined by the maximum input frequency of the signal being converted. The Nyquist Criterion states that a signal must be sampled with at least twice the maximum frequency of the signal itself. Practically, sampling must take place considerably more often than that to get a good picture of the waveform being converted.

Table 6-3 shows the speeds you can expect from the different AD conversion techniques.

Table 6-3. Speed Comparison of Various ADC Types.

CONVERTER TYPE	CONVERSION SPEED	NUMBER OF BITS
Flash	0.001 to 1 microsecond	3 to 8
Successive Approximation	0.1 to 100 microseconds	8 to 16
Ramp Converter	10 to 1000 microseconds	8 to 16
Dual Slope Converter	1 to 1000 milliseconds	3 to 6 Digits
		8 to 16 Bits

ANALOG MULTIPLEXERS

Another important factor in microprocessor-based analog conversion systems is the ability to accept more than one analog signal into an AD converter. This is called multiplexing. There are two ways to multiplex a microprocessor system for analog conversion. One way is to simply connect several ADCs to the microprocessor, each connected to and converting its own signal. This approach is called digital multiplexing (Fig. 6-27) because the multiplexing is actually taking place on the digital side of the AD converters.

A major disadvantage of digital multiplexing is cost. A separate converter is required for each analog signal to be converted. If there are twenty or thirty signals of interest, the cost will be excessive.

An alternative to digital multiplexing is analog multiplexing. In this approach, a device that acts as a rotary switch is connected to the input of the ADC. Any one of several analog signals can be connected

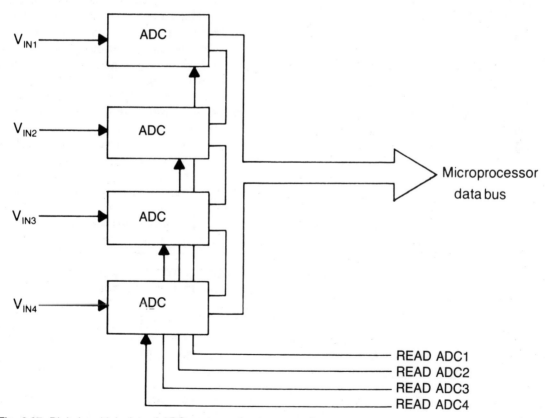

Fig. 6-27. Digital multiplexing of ADCs onto a microprocessor bus.

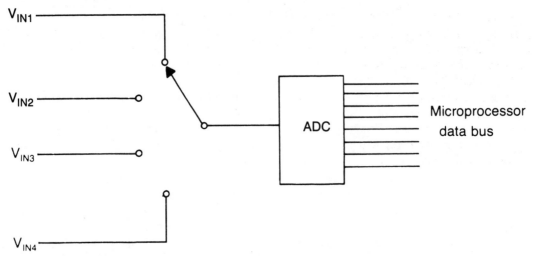

Fig. 6-28. Analog multiplexing of an ADC, conceptual diagram.

to the analog input through this switch, which is under microprocessor control. A conceptual model of an analog multiplexer is shown in Fig. 6-28 while the block diagram of an analog multiplexer is shown in Fig. 6-29.

The two inputs, M0 and M1, at the bottom of the block diagram specify which input is to be connected to the multiplexer output. Some analog multiplexers have independent enables for each input. In this case, an external digital selector may be required.

Generally, analog multiplexers do not have internal latches for the selection lines. The state of the selection inputs specify which analog input is passed through to the analog output. Since we want to use this multiplexer in a microprocessor system, we will need a zero-wire handshake parallel interface to latch the proper select line states.

Four important factors in choosing an analog multiplexer are power supply requirements, switching speed, signal handling capability, and channel crosstalk. Power requirements tend to match those

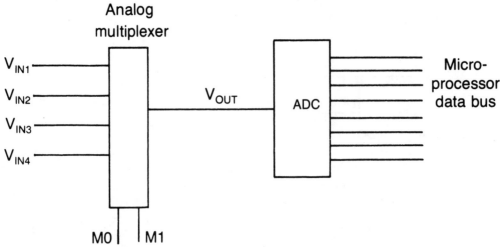

Fig. 6-29. An analog multiplexer.

of the converters. The +15 and −15 volt power supplies are again common. Switching speeds range from a few microseconds for the slower devices to tens of nanoseconds for the fastest ones.

Signal handling ability ranges widely. Some multiplexers can handle input signals very close to the power supply voltages. Others can't handle signals within one or two volts of the power supplies.

Channel crosstalk relates to the leakage of signal between multiplexer channels. It is usually rated in decibels or in leakage current. Crosstalk is also directly related to the frequencies of the signals being multiplexed, caused by capacitive coupling in the multiplexer.

As with the selection of analog converters, the selection of analog multiplexers requires a careful matching of needs versus capabilities as stated on the manufacturers data sheets. Be wary of specifications with special conditions attached. The conditions may not match your planned application.

Chapter 7

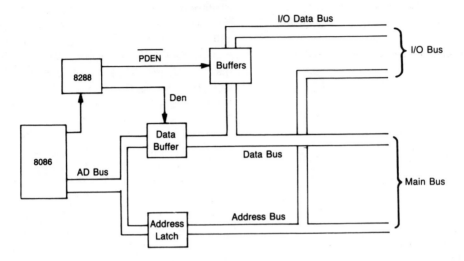

Time

How can you interface a microprocessor to time? Why would you do such a thing? These are valid and interesting questions.

There is no way to electrically connect to time. No standards organization has yet defined a connector or interface that will let a designer plug into time. Despite these minor inconveniences, time is one of the most important of the physical phenomena, and often it is important to be able to connect a microprocessor to some means of telling the time.

Microprocessors require information about two types of time: relative and absolute. *Relative time* marks intervals between events. An example of this would be the changing of a display every second. When dealing with relative time, the microprocessor is not concerned with when an event happens but with how long it has been since a previous event happened.

Absolute time is the type of time we are more familiar with. "It is 5:14 P.M. on July 22, 1982" is a statement of absolute time. All points on the absolute-time line are unique, they will never occur again. Absolute-time information is used in microprocessor systems for marking files with the time and date and for synchronizing the microprocessor with events in the "real" world.

TIMEKEEPING CIRCUITS

Most circuits used to keep time incorporate counters. A precise frequency is generated somewhere in the system, usually with a crystal-controlled oscillator. A counter is then used to count the oscillations. If we use the counter to interrupt the microprocessor whenever a certain number of oscillations have occurred, we have a relative timekeeping circuit. Such a circuit is shown in **Fig. 7-1**.

The circuit generates a signal every time the counter reaches its maximum count, then the count wraps around to zero and starts over. The signal is used to generate an interrupt to the microprocessor.

As an example, assume the oscillator is running at 4 MHz, and the counter can count up to 1000.

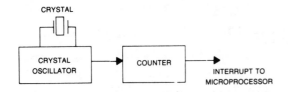

Fig. 7-1. A circuit for keeping track of relative time.

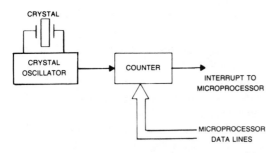

Fig. 7-2. A programmable timer used for variable-rate interrupt generation.

That means the circuit in **Fig. 7-1** will interrupt the microprocessor every 2.5 milliseconds. The microprocessor can then be forced to do something every 2.5 milliseconds. This could be used for scanning a keyboard, checking a floppy disk to see if it is up to proper speed, or checking to see if the yard has gotten enough water.

Note that all of these applications relate to some sort of I/O process. Time is used to help a processor to relate to outside events, which implies some sort of I/O application.

Using the circuit in **Fig. 7-1**, we can make the counter programmable. This allows the time interval between interrupts to be controlled by the microprocessor. The processor and its program can determine when and how often the interval timer will interrupt. Such a circuit is shown in **Fig. 7-2**. This type of time interface is useful when differing intervals are needed by a system at different times.

Taking the circuit in **Fig. 7-1** and changing it yet another way produces the circuit in **Fig. 7-3**. The oscillator drives a counter which is now labeled "prescaler." The prescaler is a counter that takes the frequency output of the crystal oscillator and divides it down to one pulse per second. This signal is fed to a series of counters which divide by the ratios required by our system of keeping time.

The first pair of divide-by-10 and divide-by-6 counters keeps track of the seconds by counting the one pulse-per-second signal from the prescaler. The output from this first counter pair is a one pulse-per-

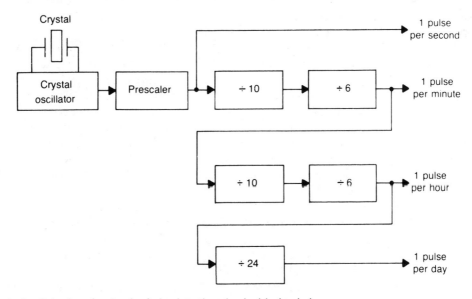

Fig. 7-3. A circuit for keeping track of absolute time (a clock/calendar).

minute signal which is used for counting minutes by the second counter pair. A divide-by-24 counter then counts the hours from the signal received from the minutes counter.

There are four interval signals generated by the circuit of **Fig. 7-3**; 1 pulse per second, 1 pulse per minute, 1 pulse per hour and 1 pulse per day. Usually, these signals are too slow to be of much use to the microprocessor.

The other and much more important application for this circuit involves the contents of the counters. If the counters are preset to the time of day at some point, they will keep the absolute time as long as power is applied. At any point, the microprocessor may find out what time it is by reading the counters. This circuit is the basis for time-of-day integrated circuits. We will look at some of these later in the chapter.

THE INTEL 8253 PROGRAMMABLE INTERVAL TIMER

Recognizing the need for timekeeping in microprocessor systems, the integrated-circuit manufacturers applied their silicon prowess to the task. They have produced a good assortment of chips to solve many of the problems we have talked about.

Intel's solution is the 8253 Programmable Interval Timer. It has three 16-bit programmable counters in it. A block diagram of the chip is shown in **Fig. 7-4** and a pin diagram appears in **Fig. 7-5**. Note that the 8253 is built into a 24-pin package. This is due to the non-electrical nature of interfacing to time: no pins are required to connect to time.

The microprocessor interface of the 8253 is the standard Intel design which we have become fa-

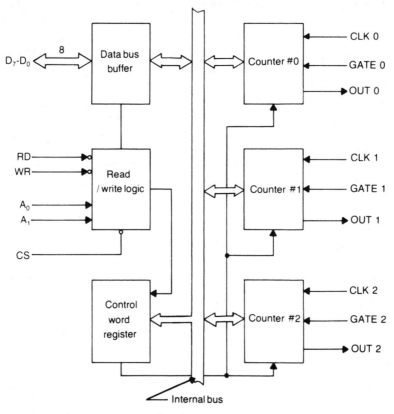

Fig. 7-4. Block diagram for the Intel 8253 Programmable Interval Timer chip. Reprinted by permission of Intel Corporation, Copyright 1983.

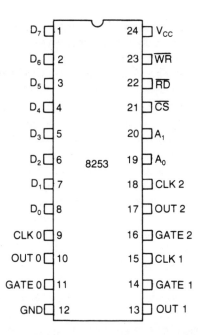

Fig. 7-5. Pin diagram of the Intel 8253. Reprinted by permission of Intel Corporation, Copyright 1983.

$\overline{CS}$	$\overline{RD}$	$\overline{WR}$	A_1	A_0	
0	1	0	0	0	Load Counter No. 0
0	1	0	0	1	Load Counter No. 1
0	1	0	1	0	Load Counter No. 2
0	1	0	1	1	Write Mode Word
0	0	1	0	0	Read Counter No. 0
0	0	1	0	1	Read Counter No. 1
0	0	1	1	0	Read Counter No. 2
0	0	1	1	1	No-Operation 3-State
1	X	X	X	X	Disable 3-State
0	1	1	X	X	No-Operation 3-State

Fig. 7-6. Register map of the Intel 8253. Reprinted by permission of Intel Corporation, Copyright 1983.

miliar with over the last few chapters. There are eight pins for a bidirectional data bus, a chip select ($\overline{CS}$), two address lines, and the read and write control signals $\overline{RD}$ and $\overline{WR}$.

Each counter has three pins associated with it; two inputs and an output. The inputs are for a clock to drive the counter and a gate to enable counting. The output may be used to interrupt the microprocessor or drive other circuitry.

Two address pins imply that the chip has a maximum of four read and four write registers. Actually the 8253 has three read and four write registers shown in Fig. 7-6. Each of the 16-bit counters has an eight-bit read and an eight-bit write register associated with it. A write-only mode register allows the processor to configure each of the three counters.

The mode register is used to independently set the mode of operation of each of the three counters. The bit definitions for the mode register are shown in Table 7-1.

The select-counter bits indicate which counter this particular mode word applies to. You may want to think of these bits as indicating which of three mode subregisters is to be accessed. SC1 and SC0 form a two-bit binary number indicating the affected counter. Bit patterns 00, 01 and 10 indicate counter 0, 1 and 2 respectively. Bit pattern 11 is illegal.

Each counter can be independently programmed with a maximum count. The counters are 16-bits wide but have only an 8-bit path to the microprocessor, thus all data transactions with the counter must be in byte-size chunks. The read/load bits indicate how the microprocessor will access the counter. Read/load definitions are given in **Table 7-2.**

Table 7-1. Intel 8253 Mode-register Bit Definitions.

BIT#	NAME	FUNCTION
7	SC1	Select Counter - Most significant bit
6	SC0	Select Counter - Least significant bit
5	RL1	Read/Load - Most significant bit
4	RL0	Read/Load - Least significant bit
3	M2	Mode - Most significant bit
2	M1	Mode - Middle bit
1	M0	Mode - Least significant bit
0	BCD	Binary/BCD mode bit

Table 7-2. Intel 8253 Read-load Bit Definitions.

RL1	RL0	OPERATION SPECIFIED
0	0	Latch current count
0	1	Read/Load most-significant byte only
1	0	Read/Load least-significant byte only
1	1	Read/Load least-significant byte first, then most-significant byte.

The 00 function is special and we will defer discussing it for a short time. Functions 01 and 10 indicate that the microprocessor will only read or write half of the bits in the counter. Function 01 is used when the least significant byte of the counter will start at zero and the microprocessor will not need to be able to read the counter in the lower eight bits of the counter. Function 10 is used when the counter is to be treated strictly as an eight-bit counter.

Function 11 allows the microprocessor to read and write the full 16-bit counter value. Writing to the counter must be done least significant byte first and then most significant. When a read of the counter contents is performed, the counter will supply the least significant eight bits first, then the most significant eight bits. This sequence must be followed with no exceptions or the 8253 may lose synchronization with the program.

While the counter is counting, a read of a counter value may not result in obtaining the actual count. This is because of ripple delays through the counter. The counter could be changing just as the read takes place. Read/load function 00 is used to avoid this problem.

By writing a mode word to the 8253 with read/load function 00, the microprocessor causes the 8253 to latch the current count in a special holding register. This may then be safely read in the same manner as reading the counter. The alternative to using read/load function 00 is to inhibit counting during a read by means of external circuitry on the clock or gate inputs.

The three mode bits are used to select one of five operating modes for each counter, see **Table 7-3.**

Mode 0, interrupt on terminal count, applies the counter as an interval timer which operates once and then stops. The counter output goes low when the mode word is written to the 8253. When the initial count is written to the counter, it starts to count down. Upon reaching 0 the counter asserts its output and the counting stops. The output will go low again when the microprocessor writes a new mode byte or reinitializes the count.

This mode is used when the microprocessor needs to be alerted after a certain amount of time elapses. The processor starts the counter and then goes off to do other tasks. When the counter reaches zero it will interrupt the processor, alerting it that time has run out.

Mode 0 is also useful as a watchdog timer, which is a device used to monitor the operation of the microprocessor. A watchdog is usually connected to the reset input of the microprocessor. The processor must tell the watchdog that it is functioning properly every so often or the watchdog assumes that something has gone wrong and resets the processor.

A watchdog is useful for process controllers where the microprocessor system is monitoring and controlling some industrial process. If noise, or some other external factor, causes the microprocessor to lose its place in the program, it could start executing sections of memory which aren't really program. This condition is variously called "lost in space" or "out to lunch." Should this happen, the processor will fail to control the process and will also stop communicating with the watchdog timer, which will even-

Table 7-3. Intel 8253
Operating-mode selection Bit Definitions.

M2	M1	M0	MODE
0	0	0	Mode 0: Interrupt on terminal count
0	0	1	Mode 1: Programmable one shot
X	1	0	Mode 2: Rate generator
X	1	1	Mode 3: Square wave generator
1	0	0	Mode 4: Software-triggered strobe
1	0	1	Mode 5: Hardware-triggered strobe

tually time out, reset the processor, and bring things back in line.

The 8253 mode 0 operation lends itself well to use as a watchdog. When the processor writes the first byte of the count to a counter running in mode 0, it stops counting. Then, when the second byte is written, the counter is reinitialized and starts counting down again.

When the 8253 is used as a watchdog timer, a routine in the software that tells the watchdog that everything is running well is required. Periodically, the program should call this routine which merely has to write two bytes to the 8253 to prevent the watchdog from asserting reset. Often, this routine is located in or called from the program's main loop. If the program has a large loop, there may have to be several watchdog-routine calls scattered in the program.

Mode 1, the programmable one-shot mode, can be used to generate precise pulses. In this mode, the counter output is initially high and the counter is idle. The output is driven low and the counter is started following a low-to-high transition of the counter's gate input. The counter output will then stay low until the counter reaches 0 and then return to a high level. If another low-to-high transition occurs on the gate input while the counter output is low, the count starts again. This makes the one-shot action retriggerable.

Mode 2, the rate generator, can be used to generate pulses at precise intervals. The counter continually counts down, reaches zero, and then reinitializes. While the counter is at 0, the counter output is driven low. At all other times the output is high. Mode-2 operation produces a series of short, low-true pulses. Driving the gate input low will cause the counter to reinitialize and stop counting. When the gate input returns high, counting resumes. This allows the count to be synchronized with external circuitry. Mode 3, the square-wave rate generator, operation is similar to that for mode 2 except that the counter output is high for the first half of the count and then is driven low for the remainder.

Mode 4 produces a software-triggered strobe. A pulse is generated after a programmed number of counts occurs. The counting starts when the

microprocessor loads the count into the counter. The pulse is produced for one clock pulse when the counter reaches 0. This mode is similar to mode 0 except that the output is low for only a single count pulse.

Mode 5 produces a hardware-triggered strobe. After the counter is initialized, a low-to-high transition on the gate input causes the counter to start counting. After the programmed number of counts, the counter reaches 0 and the counter output pin is driven low for a single count. This sequence can be retriggered by the gate input. If a second trigger occurs before the counter reaches zero, the counter is reinitialized and the sequence is restarted. Mode 5 can also be used as a watchdog timer in some applications.

The BCD/Binary bit in the mode register controls the counter operation as either a binary or BCD counter. If the bit is 0 the counter operates as a 16-bit binary counter. If the bit is a 1, the counter operates as a 4-digit BCD counter. The maximum count in the binary mode is 65536 and it is 10000 in the BCD mode.

MOTOROLA 6840 PROGRAMMABLE TIMER MODULE

Motorola has a counter/timer integrated circuit for its microprocessors. Called the 6840 Programmable Timer Module (PTM), the chip offers system designers three 16-bit counters, each with its own control register. A block diagram of the PTM appears in Fig. 7-7 and a pin diagram is shown in Fig. 7-8.

The microprocessor interface of the 6840 is the standard 6800-type interface. There are eight data lines, two chip selects, a Read/Write line, and an Enable clock. There is also an interrupt request pin (IRQ), and a reset pin.

The chip has three register-select lines, implying eight write and eight read registers. Actually the PTM has nine write and seven read registers. The extra write register is accessed by using an indirect-pointer bit in control register 2. All of the registers are illustrated in Fig. 7-9.

Each counter has a clock input, a gate input, and an output. The three counters are similar but

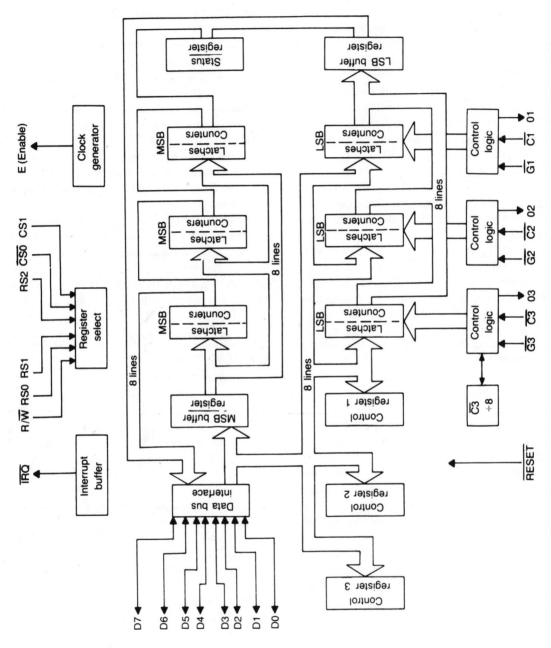

Fig. 7-7. Block diagram of the Motorola MC6840 Programmable Timer Module (PTM). Reprinted by permission of Motorola, Inc.

280

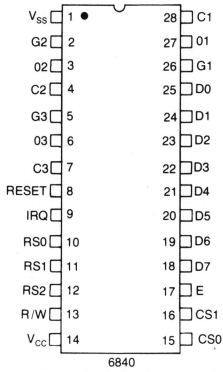

Vss ☐ 1 ● 28 ☐ C1
G2 ☐ 2 27 ☐ 01
02 ☐ 3 26 ☐ G1
C2 ☐ 4 25 ☐ D0
G3 ☐ 5 24 ☐ D1
03 ☐ 6 23 ☐ D2
C3 ☐ 7 22 ☐ D3
RESET ☐ 8 21 ☐ D4
IRQ ☐ 9 20 ☐ D5
RS0 ☐ 10 19 ☐ D6
RS1 ☐ 11 18 ☐ D7
RS2 ☐ 12 17 ☐ E
R/W ☐ 13 16 ☐ CS1
Vcc ☐ 14 15 ☐ CS0

6840

Fig. 7-8. Pin diagram of the Motorola
MC6840. Reprinted by permission of Motorola, Inc.

not identical, due to differences in bit 0 of the control registers for each counter. Bit 0 of control-register 2 is used to indicate whether control-register 1 (control-register 2, bit 0 = 1) or control-register 3 (control-register 2, bit 0 = 0) may be accessed. Control-register 1, bit 0 is a software reset bit for the 6840. When asserted, it inhibits counting in all registers. Bit 0 of control-register 3 controls a special divide-by-8 prescaler attached to the clock input of counter 3. When asserted, the prescaler is placed in operation, and clock to counter 3 is divided by eight.

The other seven bits of the three control registers all have the same functional definitions for their respective counters as shown in Fig. 7-10. Bit 1 determines the source of clock pulses to the counter. If bit 1 is 0, the external-clock-input pin is used to supply clock pulses to the counter. If bit 1 is 1, then the microprocessor-enable clock is used. Recall that the enable clock is the master system clock in 6800 systems. External-clock sources are internally synchronized with the enable clock by the 6840. Therefore, external clocks are limited to frequencies somewhat below the enable-clock frequency.

Register select inputs			Operations	
RS2	RS1	RS0	R/$\overline{W}$ = 0	R/$\overline{W}$ = 1
0	0	0	CR20 =0 Write Control Register#3	No Operation
			CR20 =1 Write Control Register #1	
0	0	1	Write Control Register #2	Read Status Register
0	1	0	Write MSB Buffer Register	Read Timer #1 Counter
0	1	1	Write Timer #1 Latches	Read LSB Buffer Register
1	0	0	Write MSB Buffer Register	Read Timer #2 Counter
1	0	1	Write Timer #2 Latches	Read LSB Buffer Register
1	1	0	Write MSB Buffer Register	Read Timer #3 Counter
1	1	1	Write Timer #3 Latches	Read LSB Buffer Register

Fig. 7-9. Register Map of the Motorola MC6840. Reprinted by permission of Motorola, Inc.

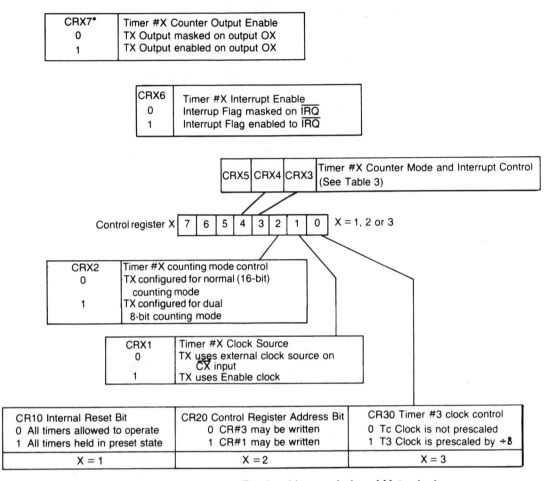

CRX7*	Timer #X Counter Output Enable
0	TX Output masked on output OX
1	TX Output enabled on output OX

CRX6	Timer #X Interrupt Enable
0	Interrup Flag masked on $\overline{IRQ}$
1	Interrupt Flag enabled to $\overline{IRQ}$

CRX5	CRX4	CRX3	Timer #X Counter Mode and Interrupt Control (See Table 3)

Control register X | 7 | 6 | 5 | 4 | 3 | 2 | 1 | 0 | X = 1, 2 or 3

CRX2	Timer #X counting mode control
0	TX configured for normal (16-bit) counting mode
1	TX configured for dual 8-bit counting mode

CRX1	Timer #X Clock Source
0	TX uses external clock source on $\overline{CX}$ input
1	TX uses Enable clock

CR10 Internal Reset Bit	CR20 Control Register Address Bit	CR30 Timer #3 clock control
0 All timers allowed to operate	0 CR#3 may be written	0 Tc Clock is not prescaled
1 All timers held in preset state	1 CR#1 may be written	1 T3 Clock is prescaled by ÷8
X = 1	X = 2	X = 3

Fig. 7-10. The Motorola MC6840 control register. Reprinted by permission of Motorola, Inc.

Bit 2 determines the configuration mode of the counter. When bit 2 is 0 the counter is configured as a 16-bit binary counter. When bit 2 is 1, the counter is split into two 8-bit counters, with the clock fed to the least significant 8-bit counter. The output of the least-significant bit counter then feeds the input to the most significant 8-bit counter. This is called the dual 8-bit mode. Both modes have a maximum count of 65536, but the second configuration is useful in defining complex output waveforms, as we shall see.

Before discussing the other bits in the control registers, we need to look at the status register. The 6840 has a single status register and only the four least-significant bits in the register have meaning; the rest read as 0. Each counter has an interrupt-status bit in this register. Bit 0 is the status bit for counter 1, bit 1 is the status bit for counter 2 and bit 2 is the status bit for counter 3. Bit 3 is an inclusive-OR of the other three bits, and serves as an overall request bit for the 6840. The meaning of the interrupt status bit varies, depending on the operating mode of its respective counter.

Counter operating modes are determined by bits 3, 4, and 5 of the associated control register. There are four operating modes, listed in **Table 7-4.** Since three bits are used to specify the mode but there are only four modes to specify, there is always

Table 7-4. Motorola MC6840 Operating-mode Bit Definitions.

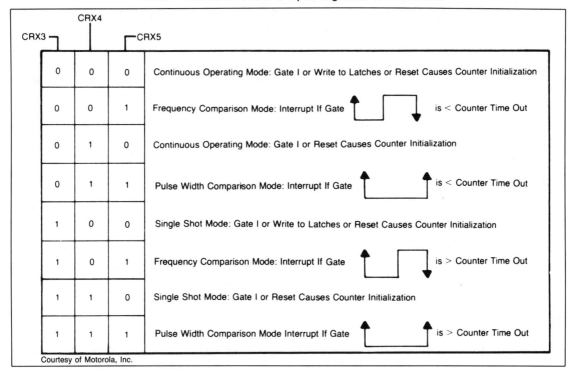

Courtesy of Motorola, Inc.

an extra bit for each mode selection. This extra bit is in a different position for the four modes and is marked in the table by an asterisk. The extra bit is used to further modify the mode of operation.

Continuous operation is simple. The microprocessor initializes the counter with an initial count. The counter will then count clock pulses as long as the gate input to the counter is asserted. When the counter reaches zero, a time out occurs, the appropriate interrupt status bit in the status register is asserted, the initial count is reloaded into the counter, and counting continues. This mode of operation allows the 6840 to interrupt the microprocessor at programmable intervals, providing that the interrupt-enable bit, bit 6 of the control register, is asserted.

The continuous operating mode may also be used to generate waveforms through the counter output pin. If control register bit 7 is asserted, the output pin of the associated counter is enabled. When the counter is operated as a simple binary

counter, a square wave will be output on this pin with a frequency equal to the clock input to the counter divided by the counter's initial value plus 1.

If the counter is configured in the dual 8-bit mode, the frequency of the waveform is somewhat more complex to calculate. If the lower 8-bit counter is initialized to L and the upper 8-bit counter is initialized to M, the total count will be

$$(M+1)*(L+1)$$

Thus, the counter will completely cycle with a frequency equal to the input clock divided by $(M+1)*(L+1)$. The output-pin waveform will be high for only L clock pulses. The frequency and duty cycle of the waveform can be specified by using the dual 8-bit mode of counting, and you are not limited to a square wave.

Single-shot operation resembles continuous operation with but three exceptions. First, the output pin will only generate one cycle. Second, the

283

counter is freerunning—it is not controlled by the gate input. Only the output pin is affected by the gate input pin. Third, the output is disabled when the counter reaches zero in either the binary or dual 8-bit modes.

This mode is used to generate a single pulse on the counter output pin. When the gate input to the counter is asserted, a cycle is started. After cycle initiation, the gate input does not have to remain asserted. When the counter reaches zero, the interrupt-status flag is asserted and the counter reinitializes and continues counting. The output waveform only cycles once, however, and remains negated until the microprocessor reinitializes either the counter's initial-count registers or the counter's mode register.

With both the continuous and single-shot operating modes, bit 4 of the control register determines whether the microprocessor can initialize the counter at any time. If bit 4 is a 0, the counter is initialized whenever the processor writes a value to the counter latches. The information must be written to the latches with the most significant byte of the 16-bit value first. This is because the 6840 buffers the most significant byte, and writes the full 16-bit initial count value when the processor supplies the least significant byte.

Only one buffer is actually built into the 6840 and it is shared by all three counters. This means you must always supply full 16-bit initial values when writing an initial count to the 6840, even when the count is less than 256, so that a previous most-significant-initialization byte, intended for one of the other counters, is not accidentally written into the counter currently being addressed.

Frequency comparison is a very useful operating mode of the 6840. With this mode, you can compare an input waveform with a clock period. The counter is started with the assertion of the gate input. When the counter reaches zero, the gate input is checked and the interrupt-status bit is set according to the gate input and the state of control register bit 5. If bit 5 is 1, the interrupt-status bit will be asserted if a second negative edge has not occurred on the gate input. This means that the frequency being applied to the gate input is lower than

that of the counter's cycle. If bit 5 of the control register is 0, the interrupt-status bit is set if the frequency applied to the gate input is higher than the counter cycle.

Pulse-width comparison is used to determine the length of a pulse. The pulse is defined as the length of time that the gate input is asserted. The counter is again started when the gate input is asserted, marking the start of the pulse. When the counter reaches zero, the gate input is checked and the interrupt-status bit is set according to the level on the gate input and bit 5 of the control register. The difference between pulse-width comparison and frequency comparison is that pulse-width comparison uses the level of the gate input for comparison while frequency comparison is edge-sensitive.

If bit 5 is 0 an interrupt is generated if the gate input is no longer asserted, meaning the pulse is smaller than the counter cycle. If bit 5 is 1, the interrupt status is set if the gate input is still asserted, meaning the pulse is longer than the counter cycle. In both frequency and pulse-width comparison modes, the counter cycles only once and then stops until the microprocessor reinitializes the counter.

MOTOROLA 68230 PIT

As I promised back in Chapter 4, we now return to finish the discussion on the Motorola 68230 Parallel Interface and Timer (PIT). In this section, we will concentrate on the timer/counter functions. To help refresh your memory, a pin diagram of the 68230 is shown in **Fig. 7-11**.

The timer section of the 68230 may be used to generate periodic interrupts, a single interrupt after a programmed period of time, or a square-wave output. In addition, the timer may be used as a watchdog.

A 24-bit counter forms the heart of the 68230 timer. Since the PIT has an 8-bit microprocessor interface, the initial count must be preset with three 8-bit writes to three preload registers in the chip. A clock signal may be obtained from an external signal supplied on the 68230 PC2/TIN line, or from the clock input which runs the 68230. A 5-bit prescaler that divides the timer-clock input by a factor of 32

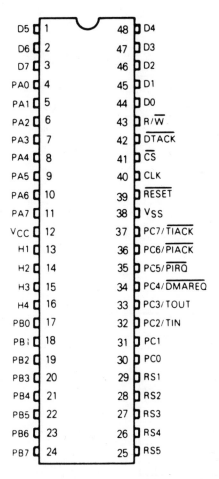

D5	1		48	D4
D6	2		47	D3
D7	3		46	D2
PA0	4		45	D1
PA1	5		44	D0
PA2	6		43	R/$\overline{W}$
PA3	7		42	$\overline{DTACK}$
PA4	8		41	$\overline{CS}$
PA5	9		40	CLK
PA6	10		39	$\overline{RESET}$
PA7	11		38	Vss
Vcc	12		37	PC7/$\overline{TIACK}$
H1	13		36	PC6/$\overline{PIACK}$
H2	14		35	PC5/$\overline{PIRQ}$
H3	15		34	PC4/$\overline{DMAREQ}$
H4	16		33	PC3/TOUT
PB0	17		32	PC2/TIN
PB1	18		31	PC1
PB2	19		30	PC0
PB3	20		29	RS1
PB4	21		28	RS2
PB5	22		27	RS3
PB6	23		26	RS4
PB7	24		25	RS5

Fig. 7-11. Pin diagram of the Motorola MC68230 Programmable Interface and Timer (PIT). Reprinted by Permission of Motorola, Inc.

may be optionally inserted between the clock source and the counter.

Figure 7-12 shows the 23 registers in the 68230. The timer uses registers with addresses between 10 Hex and 1A Hex. A timer event is signaled by the zero-detect bit in the timer-status register at address 1A Hex. Only the least-significant bit of this register has meaning. When the bit is set, the counter has reached zero. This bit may be used to generate an interrupt when set. The microprocessor may clear this bit by writing a 1 to address 1A Hex, which will also cause any interrupt to be cleared.

Operation of the 68230 Timer is controlled by writing to the timer-control register at location 10 Hex. This register controls the allocation of the three port-C pins PC2/TIN, PC3/TOUT, and PC7/$\overline{TIACK}$. The pins may be allocated either to the timer or the port-C parallel I/O port. Also controlled by the timer-control register are the operation of the timer when the counter reaches zero, the source of the counter's clock, the enabling of the prescaler, and the enabling of the timer itself.

Bits 7, 6, and 5 control the allocation of two of the three pins shared by the timer and Port C, see Table 7-5.

Bit 4 of the timer-control register is used to control the operation of the counter when the count reaches zero. If bit 4 is 0, the counter is preloaded from the counter-preload registers on the clock pulse following the zero count. If bit 4 is a 1, the counter will "roll over," meaning it will be loaded with all Fs. Bit 3 of the timer-control register is always 0.

Bits 2 and 1 of the timer-control register control the clock input to the timer and the operation of the PC2/TIN pin. The bit definitions are shown in Table 7-6.

The timer is enabled by asserting bit 0 of the timer-control register and disabled by clearing this bit.

Three timer-count-control-preload registers are used to hold the initial value of the counter. These registers are at addresses 13, 14, and 15 Hex and hold the high byte, middle byte, and low byte of the 24-bit value respectively. Any values loaded into the timer-count-preload registers will not be loaded into the counter when it is enabled to count.

The current value in the counter may be read through the Timer Count Registers at addresses 17, 18, and 19 Hex with location 17 supplying the most-significant byte, location 18 supplying the middle byte, and location 19 supplying the least-significant byte respectively. The 68230 will not update timer-count registers while they are being read by the microprocessor, so if it is necessary to read the counter contents, the timer should first be halted, or external circuitry must be used to stop the clock while the contents of the registers are being read. This second alternative is only valid if the PC2/TIN

5	4	3	2	1	7	6	5	4	3	2	1	0	
		Register Select Bits											
0	0	0	0	0	Port Mode Control	H34 Enable	H12 Enable	H4 Sense	H3 Sense	H2 Sense	H1 Sense		Port General Control Register
0	0	0	0	1	*	SVCRQ Select		Interrupt PFS		Port Interrupt Priority Control			Port Service Request Register
0	0	0	1	0	Bit 7	Bit 6	Bit 5	Bit 4	Bit 3	Bit 2	Bit 1	Bit 0	Port A Data Direction Register
0	0	0	1	1	Bit 7	Bit 6	Bit 5	Bit 4	Bit 3	Bit 2	Bit 1	Bit 0	Port B Data Direction Register
0	0	1	0	0	Bit 7	Bit 6	Bit 5	Bit 4	Bit 3	Bit 2	Bit 1	Bit 0	Port C Data Direction Register
0	0	1	0	1	Interrupt Vector Number						*	*	Port Interrupt Vector Register
0	0	1	1	0	Port A Submode	H2 Control				H2 Int Enable	H1 SVCRQ Enable	H1 Stat Ctrl.	Port A Control Register
0	0	1	1	1	Port B Submode	H4 Control				H4 Int Enable	H3 SVCRQ Enable	H3 Stat Ctrl.	Port B Control Register
0	1	0	0	0	Bit 7	Bit 6	Bit 5	Bit 4	Bit 3	Bit 2	Bit 1	Bit 0	Port A Data Register
0	1	0	0	1	Bit 7	Bit 6	Bit 5	Bit 4	Bit 3	Bit 2	Bit 1	Bit 0	Port B Data Register
0	1	0	1	0	Bit 7	Bit 6	Bit 5	Bit 4	Bit 3	Bit 2	Bit 1	Bit 0	Port A Alternate Register
0	1	0	1	1	Bit 7	Bit 6	Bit 5	Bit 4	Bit 3	Bit 2	Bit 1	Bit 0	Port B Alternate Register
0	1	1	0	0	Bit 7	Bit 6	Bit 5	Bit 4	Bit 3	Bit 2	Bit 1	Bit 0	Port C Data Register
0	1	1	0	1	H4 Level	H3 Level	H2 Level	H1 Level	H4S	H3S	H2S	H1S	Port Status Register
0	1	1	1	0	*	*	*	*	*	*	*	*	(null)
0	1	1	1	1	*	*	*	*	*	*	*	*	(null)
1	0	0	0	0	TOUT/TIACK Control			Z D Ctrl	*	Clock Control		Timer Enable	Timer Control Register
1	0	0	0	1	Bit 7	Bit 6	Bit 5	Bit 4	Bit 3	Bit 2	Bit 1	Bit 0	Timer Interrupt Vector Register
1	0	0	1	0	*	*	*	*	*	*	*	*	(null)
1	0	0	1	1	Bit 23	Bit 22	Bit 21	Bit 20	Bit 19	Bit 18	Bit 17	Bit 16	Counter Preload Register (High)
1	0	1	0	0	Bit 15	Bit 14	Bit 13	Bit 12	Bit 11	Bit 10	Bit 9	Bit 8	(Mid)
1	0	1	0	1	Bit 7	Bit 6	Bit 5	Bit 4	Bit 3	Bit 2	Bit 1	Bit 0	(Low)
1	0	1	1	0	*	*	*	*	*	*	*	*	(null)
1	0	1	1	1	Bit 23	Bit 22	Bit 21	Bit 20	Bit 19	Bit 18	Bit 17	Bit 16	Count Register (High)
1	1	0	0	0	Bit 15	Bit 14	Bit 13	Bit 12	Bit 11	Bit 10	Bit 9	Bit 8	(Mid)
1	1	0	0	1	Bit 7	Bit 6	Bit 5	Bit 4	Bit 3	Bit 2	Bit 1	Bit 0	(Low)
1	1	0	1	0	*	*	*	*	*	*	*	ZDS	Timer Status Register
1	1	0	1	1	*	*	*	*	*	*	*	*	(null)
1	1	1	0	0	*	*	*	*	*	*	*	*	(null)
1	1	1	0	1	*	*	*	*	*	*	*	*	(null)
1	1	1	1	0	*	*	*	*	*	*	*	*	(null)
1	1	1	1	1	*	*	*	*	*	*	*	*	(null)

*Unused, read as zero.

Fig. 7-12. Register map of the Motorola MC68230. Reprinted by permission of Motorola, Inc.

Table 7-5. Motorola MC68230 Port-C Control Bits.

7 6 5	PIN ALLOCATION
0 0 X	PC3/TOUT and PC7/TIACK are allocated to port C
0 1 X	PC3/TOUT is allocated to the timer, and PC7/TIACK is allocated to port C.
1 0 0	PC3/TOUT is allocated to the timer and is used as the timer-interrupt-request pin, but the interrupt request is disabled so the pin is never asserted. PC7/TIACK is also allocated to the timer and serves as an interrupt acknowledge. Since the interrupt will never occur in this mode, the acknowledge is not recognized either. This mode is useful only as a resting mode when using mode 101 for interrupts, and interrupts from the timer need to be temporarily disabled. A single bit change allows toggling between modes 100 and 101.
1 0 1	PC3/TOUT is the Timer interrupt request and PC7/TIACK is the Timer interrupt acknowledge.
1 1 0	PC3/TOUT is the Timer Interrupt Request but is disabled while PC7/TIACK is allocated to port C.
1 1 1	PC3/TOUT is allocated to the timer while PC7/TIACK is allocated to port C.

Courtesy of Motorola, Inc.

pin is being used as the clock because you can't stop the 68230 clock to read a register.

In order to use the 68230 timer as a counter, you must read and complement the timer-counter registers. This is because the timer always counts down. The timer-count-preload registers cannot be initialized to 0 according to the manufacturer's data sheet, so initialize the counter to FFFFFF Hex, which is –0 in ones-complement arithmetic. Since the timer counts down, by reading the timer-count registers and performing a binary complement on the number obtained, you can derive the positive

Table 7-6. Motorola MC68230 Timer-input-source-control Bit Definitions.

BIT 2 1	DEFINITION
0 0	PC2/TIN is allocated to port C, and the 68230 CLK pin is applied to the timer's counter through the prescaler. The timer is enabled by asserting bit 0 of the timer-control register.
0 1	PC2/TIN is used as a timer enable along with bit 0 of the timer-control register. The timer clock comes from the 68230 CLK pin, divided by the prescaler.
1 0	PC2/TIN serves as the clock to the timer, through the prescaler. The timer is enabled by bit 0 of the timer-control register.
1 1	PC2/TIN is directly used as the input to the timer, and bit 0 of the timer-control register enables the counter.

Courtesy of Motorola, Inc.

count. Thus, FFFFFF Hex becomes 000001, and so on.

Using the 68230 Timer as an interval, periodic-interrupt, or watchdog timer involves the use of the PC3/TOUT pin. This pin, although not labeled as such in the Motorola literature, is a low-true output. it is asserted when the zero-detect status bit is set in the timer-status register. This occurs when the counter reaches 0.

For periodic interrupts, or an interrupt after a programmed interval, the TOUT function is exactly what is required in the form of an interrupt signal. After it is asserted, it remains asserted until the microprocessor acknowledges the interrupt by writing a 1 to the timer-status register.

If bits 7 and 6 of the timer-control register are set to 0 and I respectively, the TOUT pin will generate a square wave instead of an interrupt signal. The period of the square wave is twice the time required to count down from the initial value to zero. This is because the TOUT pin is toggled for every zero crossing the counter makes.

ABSOLUTE TIME CLOCKS

In many applications, it is not sufficient to be able to simply mark the passage of time. It may also be important to allow the microprocessor system coordinate its operation by using the time of day. An example of this is an alarm clock.

It is fairly easy to use an interval timer in conjunction with a software routine to make an absolute-time or real-time clock. By counting the intervals, the processor marks the passage of time. One thousand, one-millisecond intervals makes one second, sixty seconds makes one minute and so on.

There are two problems associated with software time-of-day clocks. The first is that an appreciable amount of processor capability is spent keeping track of the time. If an interrupt routine is activated every millisecond and the time required to service the time of day function is 100 microseconds per activation, 10 percent of the microprocessor's time is spent counting seconds. If the timekeeping is fully implemented with day of the week, month, and year included in the timekeeping task, 100 microseconds may not be sufficient to

keep track of the time and more processor power will be required.

The second problem with software time-of-day implementations is that the time is lost whenever the system is turned off. Somehow, the time will have to be input to the computer system every time it is switched on. This may be difficult, depending on factors such as whether anyone is there to perform the task when the system comes on, what type of data-entry device is available for entering the time, and so on.

Once again, the integrated-circuit manufacturers have provided solutions to this problem, in the form of specially designed integrated circuits. What are the important features of these circuits? The first is that they are able to keep track of the time without help from the microprocessor. After all, the expense of placing them in the system has to be balanced by a reduced software burden on the processor or there is little point in designing the part.

Another important characteristic for a time-of-day integrated circuit to have is low power consumption. This is so that the device can be powered by a battery when the rest of the computer is turned off. Most time-of-day circuits are built from CMOS technology for this reason.

Other important features on many of these circuits are a convenient microprocessor bus interface; day, month, and year counters; as well as counters for seconds, minutes, and hours; automatic leap-year correction for February; and alarm functions.

NATIONAL MM58167 REAL-TIME CLOCK

National Semiconductor has two real-time-clock integrated circuits designed for microprocessor systems. The first we will look at is the MM58167. A pin diagram for this part appears in Fig. 7-13. This IC keeps track of milliseconds through months, and supports the Intel-style microprocessor-bus interface. It may also be programmed to interrupt every tenth of a second, once a second, once a minute, once an hour, once a day, once a week, and once a month. The MM58167 "knows" how many days are in each month except

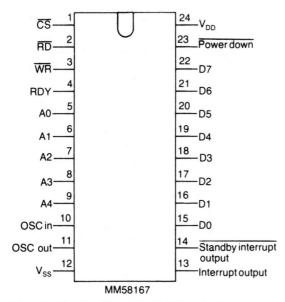

Fig. 7-13. Pin diagram of the National Semiconductor MM58167 real-time clock/calendar IC. Copyright 1980 National Semiconductor Corporation.

for February during a leap year, and that problem can be handled by software.

The standard Intel bus signals can be seen on the low numbered pins. A chip select, read, and write line give the processor access to the registers inside the MM58167. There are five address lines. The address lines may be set to any of 24 states, addressed 0 through 16 hex and address 1F hex. All other addresses are unused in the MM58167. The function for each of these addresses appears in **Table 7-7**.

An 8-bit interface links the MM58167 to the microprocessor. Most of the address locations in the part access two 4-bit counters. Definition for the data lines for each address is given in **Table 7-8**. Note that the table divides the eight address lines into two 4-bit nybbles. A notation of "0" in this table means the data line has no meaning. A notation of "I/O" means the data line is used for both read and write operations. Also listed in **Table 7-8** are the maximum values for each nybble.

Table 7-7. National Semiconductor MM58167 Reset Bit Definitions.

A4	A3	A2	A1	A0	FUNCTION
0	0	0	0	0	Counter—Thousandths of Seconds
0	0	0	0	1	Counter—Hundredths and Tenths of Seconds
0	0	0	1	0	Counter—Seconds
0	0	0	1	1	Counter—Minutes
0	0	1	0	0	Counter—Hours
0	0	1	0	1	Counter—Day of the Week
0	0	1	1	0	Counter—Day of the Month
0	0	1	1	1	Counter—Months
0	1	0	0	0	Latches—Thousandths of Seconds
0	1	0	0	1	Latches—Hundredths and Tenths of Seconds
0	1	0	1	0	Latches—Seconds
0	1	0	1	1	Latches—Minutes
0	1	1	0	0	Latches—Hours
0	1	1	0	1	Latches—Day of Week
0	1	1	1	0	Latches—Day of the Month
0	1	1	1	1	Latches—Months
1	0	0	0	0	Interrupt Status Register
1	0	0	0	1	Interrupt Control Register
1	0	0	1	0	Counter Reset
1	0	0	1	1	Latch Reset
1	0	1	0	0	Status Bit
1	0	1	0	1	"GO" Command
1	0	1	1	0	Standby Interrupt
1	1	1	1	1	Test Mode

All others unused.

Table 7-8. National Semiconductor MM58167 Register Map.

COUNTER ADDRESSED	UNITS				MAX USED BCD CODE	TENS				MAX USED BCD CODE
	D0	D1	D2	D3		D4	D5	D6	D7	
Ten Thousandths of a Second	0	0	0	0	0	I/O	I/O	I/O	I/O	9
Tenths and Hundredths of Seconds	I/O	I/O	I/O	I/O	9	I/O	I/O	I/O	I/O	9
Seconds	I/O	I/O	I/O	I/O	9	I/O	I/O	I/O	0	5
Minutes	I/O	I/O	I/O	I/O	9	I/O	I/O	I/O	0	5
Hours	I/O	I/O	I/O	I/O	9	I/O	I/O	0	0	2
Day of the Week	I/O	I/O	I/O	0	7	0	0	0	0	0
Day of the Month	I/O	I/O	I/O	I/O	9	I/O	I/O	0	0	3
Month	I/O	I/O	I/O	I/O	9	I/O	0	0	0	1

A separate 32,768-Hz crystal is generally used as the time reference for the MM58167. The separate crystal allows the MM58167 to be independent of the microprocessors clock, which will probably stop oscillating when the power is switched off. As long as the MM58167 has power it will continue to keep time.

Setting the MM58167 is very easy. First, the milliseconds through the seconds counters should be reset and stopped by writing an appropriate value to location 12 Hex. The value is determined by "OR"ing the bits shown in the reset chart listed in Table 7-9. The microprocessor then writes the correct time into all of the registers. It then issues a "GO" command with a write to location 15 Hex. From that point on, the internal oscillator keeps track of the time.

One problem arises here. There is a chance that the time could change in the middle of the register-read operation. That means the processor would not get the accurate time. In order to prevent this from being a problem, the MM58167 has a status bit which may be read in the least-significant position at location 14 Hex. This bit is set if the counters change during a read operation. The problem is solved if the processor checks this bit after every read to see if the last value obtained should be discarded. If the status bit is set, the processor should start the entire routine over again since the time has now changed from what it was.

The MM58167 interrupt capability is also easy to use. There is an 8-bit interrupt-control register at location 11 Hex. Periodic interrupts are enabled by setting the appropriate bits as follows:

Table 7-9. National Semiconductor MM58167 Reset Chart.

D0	D1	D2	D3	D4	D5	D6	D7	COUNTER OR LATCH RESET
1	0	0	0	0	0	0	0	Thousandths of Seconds
0	1	0	0	0	0	0	0	Hundredths and Tenths of Seconds
0	0	1	0	0	0	0	0	Seconds
0	0	0	1	0	0	0	0	Minutes
0	0	0	0	1	0	0	0	Hours
0	0	0	0	0	1	0	0	Days of the Week
0	0	0	0	0	0	1	0	Days of the Month
0	0	0	0	0	0	0	1	Months

FOR COUNTER RESET A4-A0 MUST BE 10010
FOR LATCH RESET A4-A0 MUST BE 10011

Bit	Period of Interrupt
7	Once per month
6	Once per week
5	Once per day
4	Once per hour
3	Once per minute
2	Once per second
1	Once per 1/10 second
0	Alarm comparator

Note that bit 0 is an alarm comparator. The MM58167 has latches corresponding to the counters of the clock. The processor sets these latches, using the same patterns as for the clock, but writing to locations 8 through F Hex. When the value in the counters is equal to the value in the latches, an alarm comparison interrupt will be generated if bit 0 of the interrupt-control register is set.

Multiple interrupt conditions may be enabled by setting more than 1 bit in the interrupt-control register. The technique to determine what the cause of the interrupt is, and for acknowledging the interrupt, is to read the interrupt-status register at location 10 Hex. Even if only one interrupt condition is enabled, this technique is used to tell the MM58167 to stop interrupting.

One point needs to be made about the microprocessor interface of the MM58167 which is true for most of the real-time-clock chips: It is slow. The nature of low-power parts is that they also tend to be slow. The MM58167 cycles in about 1 microsecond. A special ready (RDY) output is built into the chip in order to handshake with processors that have WAIT inputs or asynchronous busses. Most processors will have to be slowed down in some manner while accessing the MM58167 so that their bus-cycle time meets the specifications for access times to the real-time clock.

NATIONAL MM58174

National Semiconductor has a second integrated circuit designed to supply a microprocessor with real-time capabilities, the MM58174. A block diagram of the MM58174 appears in **Fig. 7-14**, and a pin diagram appears in **Fig. 7-15**. It, too, has an Intel-style microprocessor interface and requires a 32,768-Hz crystal. However, this part is different in several ways from the MM58167.

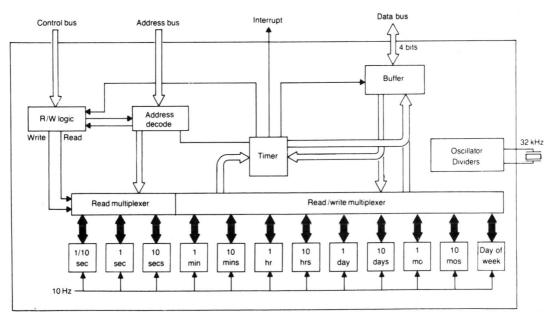

Fig. 7-14. Block diagram of the National Semiconductor MM58174 real-time clock/calendar IC. Copyright 1980 National Semiconductor Corporation.

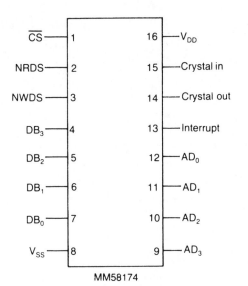

Fig. 7-15. Pin diagram of the National Semiconductor MM58174. Copyright 1980 National Semiconductor Corporation.

First, the part is faster, with a 600-nanosecond bus cycle instead of 1 microsecond. Since the device is faster, there is no output ready pin on the MM58174. The 600-nanosecond cycle is still not fast enough for some of the newer processors, and wait states will still be required to interface this device to them.

Another difference is the data path; it is four bits wide on the MM58174. This means that each counter has a separate address. Four address lines give the processor access to the sixteen locations in the MM58174. Most of these locations access the counters in the chip. Table 7-10 lists the registers and their corresponding addresses.

The MM58174 can adjust the number of days in February if the current year is a leap year. A code for the current year is written into the year register at address 13 (D Hex). The possible codes are listed in Table 7-11.

Setting the MM58174 is simple. The microprocessor first writes a 0 to address 14 (E Hex) which stops the counters. Then the time (minutes, hours, day, etc.) is written to the appropriate registers. The year code is also written but it cannot be read back as part of the time. Finally, the

clock is started by writing a 1 to location 14. Reading the time is simply a matter of reading the counters.

Interrupts are quite a bit different in the MM58174 as compared to the MM58167. Three interrupt sources can be selected; a .5-second interval, a 5-second interval and a 6-second interval. You may also program a single interrupt or a periodic interrupt.

When an interrupt occurs, bit 3 of the interrupt-status register will be asserted. By reading this bit, (address 15, or F Hex), the processor clears the MM58174 interrupt request.

Table 7-11. National
Semiconductor MM58174 Leap-year Settings.

OKI MSM5832

Another real-time-clock chip is available from OKI Semiconductor. It is the MSM5832 real-time clock/calendar. This part has a 4-bit data bus and an Intel-style microprocessor interface. It requires a 32,768-Hz crystal for operation. A block diagram of the MSM5832 is shown in **Fig. 7-16** and a pin diagram is shown in **Fig. 7-17**. The bus cycle for this part is very long—6 microseconds. As a result, many designs using the MSM5832 place a parallel-

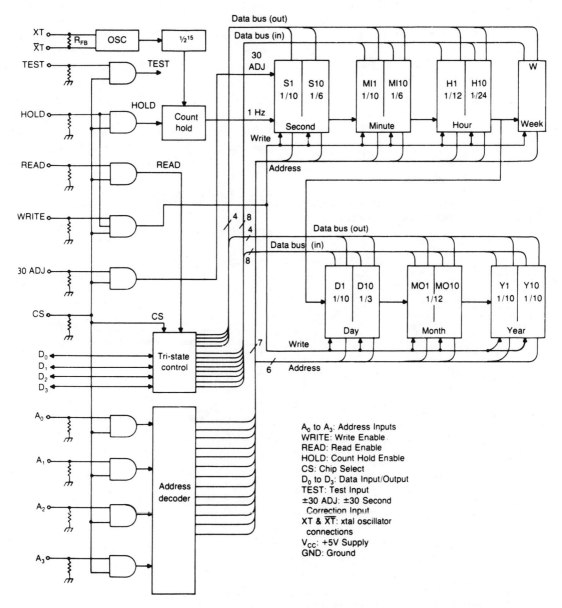

Fig. 7-16. Block diagram of the OKI Semiconductor MSM5832 real-time clock/calendar IC. Courtesy of OKI Semiconductor.

293

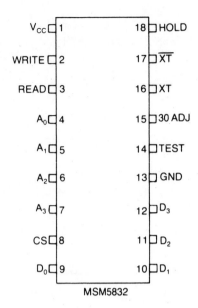

```
        ┌────────┐
 Vcc ☐ 1│        │18 ☐ HOLD
WRITE ☐ 2│        │17 ☐ XT̄
 READ ☐ 3│        │16 ☐ XT
   A₀ ☐ 4│        │15 ☐ 30 ADJ
   A₁ ☐ 5│        │14 ☐ TEST
   A₂ ☐ 6│        │13 ☐ GND
   A₃ ☐ 7│        │12 ☐ D₃
   CS ☐ 8│        │11 ☐ D₂
   D₀ ☐ 9│        │10 ☐ D₁
        └────────┘
         MSM5832
```

Fig. 7-17. Pin diagram of the OKI Semiconductor MSM5832 real-time clock/calendar IC. Courtesy of OKI Semiconductor.

interface chip, such as an 8255, between the microprocessor and the real time clock.

There are 13 read/write registers in the MSM5832, listed in **Table 7-12.** There is no recognition of leap year in this part, so the processor must handle February 29. Setting the time is a matter of writing it to the registers, and reading the time requires that the processor simply read the registers.

A hold input to the real-time clock allows external circuitry to stop the counters to synchronize the device with some outside event. Asserting the 30-second-adjust pin will reset the seconds counters, and, if the seconds counters had more than a 30 second count in them, advance the minute counter by 1. Both the hold and 30-second-adjust pins are high-true and have internal pull-down resistors to negate them if they are unconnected.

OKI MSM58321

OKI improved the design of the MSM5832 and named the new version of MSM58321. The part has

Table 7-12. Register Map of the OKI MSM5832.

ADDRESS INPUTS A₀ A₁ A₂ A₃				INTERNAL COUNTER	DATA I/O D₀ D₁ D₂ D₃				DATA LIMITS	NOTES
0	0	0	0	S 1	•	•	•	•	0 ~ 9	S₁ or S₁₀ are reset to zero irrespective of input data D₀~D₃ when write instruction is executed with address selection
1	0	0	0	S 10	•	•	•		0 ~ 5	
0	1	0	0	MI 1	•	•	•	•	0 ~ 9	
1	1	0	0	MI 10	•	•	•		0 ~ 5	
0	0	1	0	H 1	•	•	•	•	0 ~ 9	
1	0	1	0	H 10	•	•	†	†	0~1 / 0~2	D₂ = "1" for PM D₃ = "1" for 24 hour format D₂ = "0" for AM D₃ = "0" for 12 hour format
0	1	1	0	W	•	•	•		0 ~ 6	
1	1	1	0	D 1	•	•	•	•	0 ~ 9	
0	0	0	1	D 10	•	•	†		0 ~ 3	D₂ = "1" for 29 days in month 2 D₂ = "0" for 28 days in month 2 (2)
1	0	0	1	MO 1	•	•	•	•	0 ~ 9	
0	1	0	1	MO 10	•				0 ~ 1	
1	1	0	1	Y 1	•	•	•	•	0 ~ 9	
0	0	1	1	Y 10	•	•	•	•	0 ~ 9	

(1) *data valid as "0$CA or "1"
   blank does not exist (unrecognized during a write and held at "0" during a read)
   † data bits used for AM/PM, 12/24 HOUR and leap year
(2) If D₂ previously set to "1," upon completion of month 2 day 29, D₂ will be internally reset to "0"

Courtesy of OKI Semiconductor

been improved and significantly changed. The bus interface is different, although no faster, and a leap-year compensator has been built into the device. **Figure 7-18** is a block diagram of the MSM58321 and **Fig. 7-19** is a pin diagram.

The major change to the part is from separate address and data pins to a multiplexed address/data bus. This requires the address to be clocked into the device first, using the ADDRESS WRITE pin, followed by the data access using either the WRITE or READ pins. This multiplexing of address and data allowed OKI to put the MSM58321 in a 16-pin package instead of the 18-pin package used for the MSM5832.

Table 7-13 lists the registers and addresses for the MSM58321. In addition to all of the registers available in the MSM5832, some extra functions have been added. The leap year is set by appropriately writing the two most-significant bits of the tens-of-days register. Since there are never more than 31 days in a month, these bits were previously unused.

An address-write of Hex value D to the MSM58321 resets the counters between the

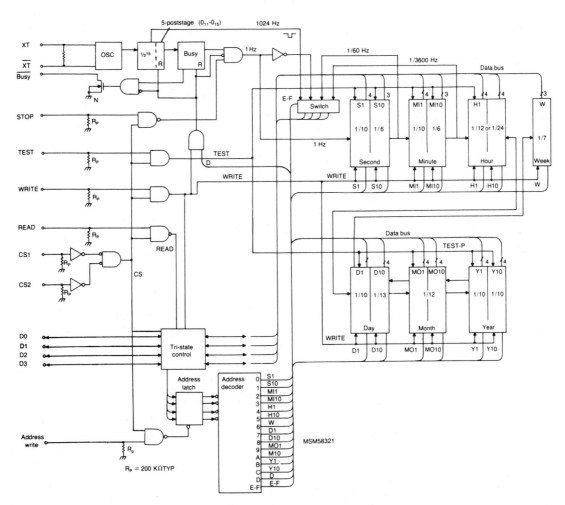

Fig. 7-18. Block diagram of the OKI Semiconductor MSM58321 real-time clock/calendar IC. Courtesy of OKI Semiconductor.

Table 7-13. Register Map of the OKI MSM58321.

HEX CODE	ADDRESS INPUT D_0 (A₀)	D_1 (A₁)	D_2 (A₂)	D_3 (A₃)	INTERNAL COUNTER	DATA INPUT/OUTPUT D_0 D_1 D_2 D_3	COUNT VALUE	REMARKS
0	L	L	L	L	S 1	· · · ·	0 ~ 9	
1	H	L	L	L	S 10	· · ·	0 ~ 5	
2	L	H	L	L	MI 1	· · · ·	0 ~ 9	
3	H	H	L	L	MI 10	· · ·	0 ~ 5	
4	L	L	H	L	H 1	· · · ·	0 ~ 9	
5	H	L	H	L	H 10	· · · ⊙	0 ~ 1 0 ~ 2	D2 = H specifies PM, D2 = L specifies AM, D3 = H specifies 24-hour timer, and D3 = L specifies 12-hour timer. When D3 = H is written, the D2 bit is reset internally.
6	L	H	H	L	W	· · ·	0 ~ 6	
7	H	H	H	L	D 1	· · · ·	0 ~ 9	
8	L	L	L	H	D 10	· · ⊕ ⊕	0 ~ 3	The D2 and D3 bits of D10 are used to select a leap year.
9	H	L	L	H	MO 1	· · · ·	0 ~ 9	Calendar D2 D3

A	L	H	L	H	MO 10	·	0 ~ 1	Gregorian L L 0
								 Showa H L 3
								           L H 2
								           H H

B	H	H	L	H	Y 1	· · · ·	0 ~ 9	*Remainder obtained by dividing
C	L	L	H	H	Y 10	· · · ·	0 ~ 9	the year number by 4.
D	H	L	H	H				A selector to reset 5 poststages in the ½¹⁵ frequency divider and the BUSY circuit. They are reset when this code is latched with ADDRESS LATCH and the WRITE input goes to the H level.
E-F	L/H	H	H	H				A selector to access the reference signal outputs. Reference signals are output to D0-D3 when this code is latched with ADDRESS LATCH and READ input goes to H.

NOTES:
1. ·Data valid as "0" or "1". Data does not exist in blank fields (unrecognized during a write and held at "0" during a read)
2. The bit marked ⊙ is used to select the 12/24-hour timer and the bits marked ⊕ are used to select a leap year. These three bits can be read or written.
3. When signals are input on bus lines D0-D3 and ADDRESS WRITE goes to the H level for address input, ADDRESS information is latched to an internal address decoder.

Courtesy of OKI Semiconductor

32,768-Hz oscillator and the seconds counter. This can be used to synchronize the real time clock to external events. The data access following the address write to this address performs the reset.

Setting the time in the MSM58321 is a matter of writing the appropriate values to the proper registers. Reading the time, however, is a slightly more complex process. A BUSY output indicates

296

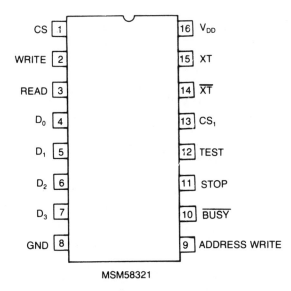

Fig. 7-19. Pin diagram of the OKI MSM58321. Courtesy of OKI Semiconductor.

when the device is changing the counters. This is a long process, taking 183 microseconds. BUSY is asserted 244 microseconds before the counters start to change. If the processor checks BUSY and sees that it is not asserted, it is guaranteed to have 244 microseconds to read the time.

When using the MSM58321 with battery backup, it is important to place pull-down resistors on the three control and four data lines. This will guarantee negation of the chip's inputs when the power is lost or turned off.

MOTOROLA MC146818

The major microprocessor semiconductor manufacturers ignored real-time clocks for years. There just didn't seem to be much profit in the devices because so few were used. Of course, with few devices to pick from, designers tended to not design real-time clocks into their systems. Those that did were often forced to use integrated circuits designed for wrist watches.

Motorola finally applied its considerable CMOS expertise to real-time clocks and developed the MC146818, a very powerful real-time clock/cal-

endar. This part has everything a designer could want and even includes some storage locations for the system software to use. These locations retain the information stored in them if the MC146818 is powered by a battery when the system is turned off.

Figure 7-20 is a block diagram of the MC146818, while Fig. 7-21 is a pin diagram of the part. Looking at the block diagram, we note a microprocessor-bus interface we have not yet seen, counters for the clock, registers for an alarm function, and a 50-byte general purpose RAM storage area.

Let's look at the microprocessor-bus interface first. Note the few pins involved; a bidirectional 8-bit data bus, an address strobe (AS), a data strobe (DS), a read/write line (R/W) and a chip select (CE). There are no address lines! This part has a multiplexed address/data bus, something that originally was quite unheard of in Motorola parts. The address of interest is strobed in over the data lines using the AS control line, and then the data is transferred using the other control lines.

In addition to the multiplexed address/data bus, the MC146818 employs the MOTEL (Motorola/Intel) circuit to automatically detect and use either Motorola-bus control lines or Intel control lines. The MOTEL circuit is shown in Fig. 7-22. The figure shows how to connect the MC146818 to either type of bus.

If you are trying to interface this device to a nonmultiplexed bus, you may feel that the address multiplexing on the part makes things difficult. It does not. There are two simple solutions. The first is to use a parallel-interface chip to drive the bus interface of the MC146818. This is practical, but possibly more costly than necessary.

The other alternative is to use two addresses for the part. When the processor writes to one address, the address decoder asserts the real-time clock's address strobe. When the other address is accessed, the data strobe is asserted. Then, access to registers on the chip is a two-step process, first writing the address of interest using one bus address, and then performing the data access using the other address.

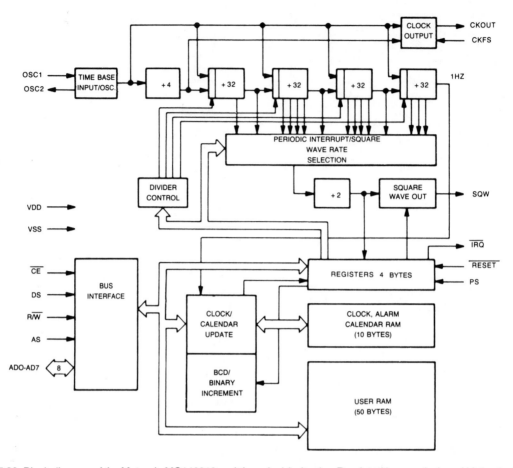

Fig. 7-20. Block diagram of the Motorola MC146818 real-time clock/calendar. Reprinted by permission of Motorola, Inc.

One of three clock frequencies may be used to drive the MC146818; 4.914304 MHz, 1.048576 MHz, or 32,768 Hz. The frequency is selected by writing the proper value to register A in the device. Register A is at location A Hex. A map of all of the MC146818 registers appears in Fig. 7-23.

The MC146818 has a real-time clock which keeps track of the seconds, minutes, hours, day of the week, day of the month, month, and year. It has an alarm function that monitors hours, minutes, and seconds. Each register handles two digits of time, and the MC146818 can accept and supply the time in either binary or BCD formats.

Besides the time and alarm registers, the MC146818 has four status and control registers, A

through D. Register A is used to select the time-base frequency and a periodic interrupt frequency. Also, in the most-significant bit of register A is an ''Update-In-Progress'' bit. This is a read-only bit which is asserted 244 microseconds before the real time counters start to change. This bit allows the processor to decide when it is safe to read the time from the MC146818.

Register B contains a counter-enable bit, interrupt-enable bits for the periodic-interval and alarm interrupts, the binary/BCD data-mode-select bit, and a 12/24 hour mode-select bit. In addition, there is a Daylight-Savings-Time-select bit. If this bit is asserted, the MC146818 will follow the proper rules for advancing and setting back the time in April

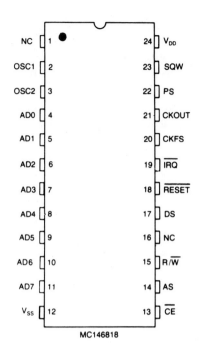

Fig. 7-21. Pin diagram of the Motorola MC146818. Reprinted by permission of Motorola, Inc.

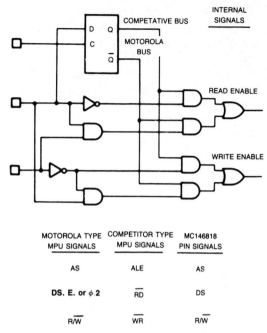

MOTOROLA TYPE MPU SIGNALS	COMPETITOR TYPE MPU SIGNALS	MC146818 PIN SIGNALS
AS	ALE	AS
DS. E. or ϕ.2	$\overline{RD}$	DS
R/$\overline{W}$	$\overline{WR}$	R/$\overline{W}$

Fig. 7-22. The MOTEL (Motorola/Intel) circuit incorporated into the bus interface of Motorola's MC146818. Reprinted by permission of Motorola, Inc.

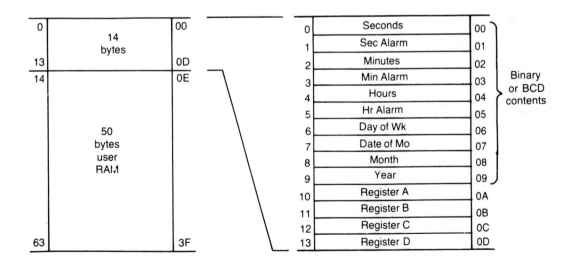

Fig. 7-23. Register map of the Motorola MC146818. Reprinted by permission of Motorola, Inc.

and October. This chip literally has everything but the kitchen sink! Leap year is automatically handled by the MC146818 simply by telling it the current year.

Register C is the interrupt-status register and can be used to determine the cause of an interrupt. Reading register C clears the interrupts. Register D contains only a single valid bit. Its job is to indicate whether the power to the MC146818 is suffi-cient to talk to the microprocessor. This is needed because the battery backup systems that are connected to real-time clocks generally run at lower voltages than the microprocessor power supply. Register D can be used as a power-failure indicator to prevent the microprocessor from accessing the time data when power is going down or just coming on.

Chapter 8

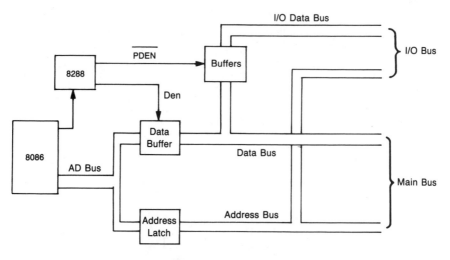

Interrupts

In our discussions about I/O hardware, we covered the needs of a wide range of peripheral devices. Some devices are much slower than computer internal processes, some are about the same speed, and some are faster than the computer can comfortably handle through normal means.

There are three types of I/O software driver associated with these three classes of peripheral. Slow devices are best handled by interrupt. Only when the device is ready for another data transfer is the processor interrupted so that it can service the peripheral. Medium-speed devices can interact with the processor directly since they will not degrade system performance. High-speed devices require special hardware for direct-memory access (DMA) because the processor alone is not fast enough to service them. DMA is covered in the next chapter.

Almost every commercial microprocessor supports some sort of interrupt capability; the function is that important. Interrupts are useful not only in adapting slower peripherals to microcomputers but also for getting the processors attention when something has gone wrong.

An interrupt is a hardware technique for making a subroutine-call in the program. That is really all there is to interrupts, even though this is a gross simplification of what happens. When external circuitry needs to generate an interrupt, it asserts the processor's interrupt pin(s). This causes the processor to stop executing the current sequence of instructions, save the point in the program where it has been interrupted, and start execution of a special sequence of instructions called the interrupt-service routine. Such a sequence of events is shown in Fig. 8-1.

This sequence is quite similar to what happens in a processor during a subroutine call. The difference is the interrupt service routine is initiated by a hardware interrupt signal rather than by executing a CALL instruction. Each processor manufacturer has an idea of what represents a good interrupt capability in a microprocessor. Thus, each microprocessor's interrupt facilities work somewhat

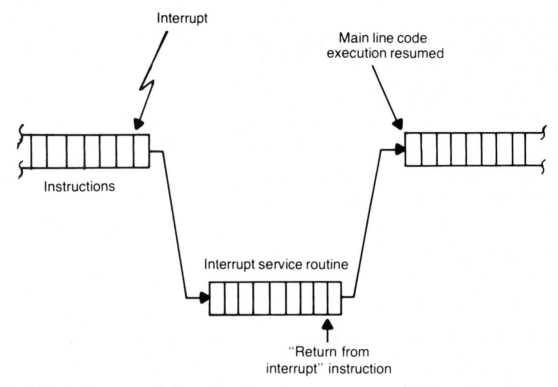

Main line code
execution resumed

Instructions

Interrupt service routine

"Return from
interrupt" instruction

Fig. 8-1. Instruction sequence during an interrupt.

differently. We look at some of these interrupt structures to get an idea of how interrupts work.

TYPES OF INTERRUPTS

There are several categories of interrupt: vectored and nonvectored, maskable and nonmaskable. A maskable interrupt can be turned off by the processor. Often, there are times when a critical piece of software cannot be interrupted. At these times, the processor may disable maskable interrupts. There is frequently a disable-interrupt instruction in the processor's machine-code instruction set to do this. A nonmaskable interrupt cannot be turned off. This type of interrupt is usually reserved for really important events such as a power failure.

When an interrupt occurs, how does the processor know where the interrupt service routine starts? Two techniques are used. The simplest is for the processor to branch to a set location when

servicing an interrupt. This location should contain the first instruction of the interrupt-service routine.

The second approach is a little more flexible. A certain location in the processor's memory space is reserved for the starting address of the service routine. When an interrupt occurs, the processor saves the program counter so that it can return to where it left off, and then fetches the address of the interrupt service routine from this reserved memory location. Circuits built into the processor always fetch the starting address of the interrupt service routine from this same memory location.

Often, a single interrupt service routine is not adequate for the application. Newer processors have several memory locations reserved for the addresses of many interrupt service routines. How is one picked over the other?

One way to do this is to have several interrupt lines built into the processor. Each interrupt line has an associated interrupt service routine and a memory location reserved for the routine's start address. There is no confusion as to which routine to use for an interrupt. This scheme is called a hardware-vectored interrupt because the proper start address or vector is automatically chosen by the hardware.

Another approach to having multiple interrupt service routines is to have the processor run a special interrupt acknowledge cycle. When this occurs, the interrupting hardware supplies additional information to help the processor pick a service routine. This is called a software-vectored interrupt.

Intel 8080 Interrupts

The Intel 8080 microprocessor has a single interrupt input called INT. There is also an interrupt enable output called INTE which is controlled by the Enable Interrupt (EI) and Disable Interrupt (DI) instructions. External circuitry is required to allow the INT input to be masked by the INTE output. In this way, Intel gives the system designer the choice as to whether the single interrupt input is maskable or nonmaskable. If INTE is used to gate the interrupt requests to the INT input, the interrupts are maskable. You may wish to refresh your memory as to 8080 machine and instruction cycles by going back to Chapter 2 before reading this section on interrupt cycles.

An interrupt request is not immediately recognized. A special interrupt latch in the 8080 microprocessor assumes the state of the interrupt in the T3 cycle of an instruction. Recall that the T3 cycle is the last machine cycle in an 8080 instruction cycle. This ensures the completion of the current instruction before an interrupt is recognized.

At the start of the next instruction cycle, the 8080 will assert the interrupt-acknowledge bit in the status byte while outputting an address and performing an instruction fetch. The address is bogus; it is not supposed to be used for anything. External circuitry must decode the interrupt-acknowledge status bit, prevent the rest of the system from driving the data lines and drive a single-byte instruction onto the data bus. This is a software-vectored interrupt.

The 8080 has a special group of instructions designed to be used with this interrupt scheme. They are the RESTART instructions. There are eight restart instructions; RESTART 0 through RESTART 7. Each causes the processor to start execution at a dedicated location in low memory. A RESTART 0 forces execution at location 0, a RESTART 1 forces it to location 1 and so on. The RESTART is treated as a subroutine call which causes the processor to put the program counter onto the stack. Thus, a RETURN instruction is all that is required to terminate the interrupt service routine and return to the interrupted program.

Each area dedicated to an interrupt service routine is eight bytes long. This is sufficient room to place a jump instruction to the actual routine, or it may even be large enough for a very small interrupt service routine. In either case, the 8080 does not pick up an address from the reserved area, it actually starts executing there.

RESTART instructions do not have to be used only in conjunction with interrupts. They are short, single-byte subroutine calls which are useful for other applications as well.

Motorola MC6800 Interrupts

The Motorola MC6800 processor has two interrupt input pins; a non-maskable interrupt ($\overline{\text{NMI}}$), and a maskable interrupt request ($\overline{\text{IRQ}}$). Each pin has an associated interrupt-vector location in memory.

If the interrupt-mask bit in the MC6800 condition-code register is not set, assertion of the $\overline{\text{IRQ}}$ pin will cause the processor to initiate an interrupt sequence at the start of the next instruction cycle. The first step the MC6800 takes during an interrupt sequence is to save the state of the processor. All registers except the stack pointer are saved on the stack. This includes the program counter, accumulators, index register, and the condition-code register.

After all of the registers are saved, the MC6800 fetches the 16-bit address of the interrupt service routine from memory locations FFF8 and FFF9 Hex. It then branches to the address stored in these locations. The interrupt service routine must end with a return from interrupt instruction (RTI) so that the registers will be restored before the interrupted program resumes execution.

There are only two functional differences in the operation of the MC6800 when it responds to the assertion of $\overline{\text{NMI}}$ instead of $\overline{\text{IRQ}}$. The first is that a nonmaskable request will always be serviced, regardless of the state of the condition-code register. The other difference is that the address for the interrupt service routine is fetched from locations FFFC and FFFD Hex for a non-maskable interrupt. All else is the same.

ZILOG Z80 Interrupts

The ZILOG Z80 microprocessor has two interrupt inputs, a maskable interrupt ($\overline{\text{INT}}$) and a nonmaskable interrupt ($\overline{\text{NMI}}$). The nonmaskable interrupt operates in a single mode but the maskable interrupt has three operating modes.

When the Z80 processor recognizes a nonmaskable interrupt, it completes the current instruction and then branches to memory location 66 Hex. It expects the interrupt service routine to be at this location. The software designer may choose, however, to put a jump to the actual interrupt service routine at this location instead.

The three operating modes for the maskable interrupt are modes 0, 1 and 2. A special interrupt mode instruction (IM) is used to set the current interrupt mode for the processor. Mode 0 interrupts are serviced in the same manner as the Intel 8080 processor. When an interrupt occurs, the Z80 processor signals an interrupt acknowledge. This is not done in the same manner as the Intel 8080 processor.

An interrupt acknowledge is signified by the assertion of $\overline{\text{IORQ}}$ (I/O request) during M1 instead of $\overline{\text{MREQ}}$ (memory request). This is the indication that an instruction fetch is not taking place. Instead, the processor expects a single-byte instruction, probably a RESTART, to be jammed onto the data bus. See Chapter 2 to refresh your memory about Z80 processor M1 cycles.

Mode-1 maskable interrupts work in a manner similar to the nonmaskable interrupt. The only difference is that the processor branches to location 38 Hex instead of location 66 Hex. Again, the interrupt service routine may be placed here, or a jump instruction to the interrupt service routine may be here.

Mode-2 maskable interrupts work in a more complex manner and also provide the programmer with the most flexibility. When the processor acknowledges the interrupt, it expects an 8-bit vector to be jammed onto the bus. This vector is treated as the lower byte of a 16-bit vector address.

The upper byte of the address is supplied by an internal Z80 processor register called the interrupt register. The mode-2 interrupt allows selection of interrupt service routines over a 256-byte range. Since a minimum of 3 bytes is required to at least build a jump table, up to 85 different interrupt service routines may exist. Zilog builds many of its I/O chips to directly support this mode-2 interrupt facility of the Z80 microprocessor.

Motorola MC68000 Interrupts

As a 16-bit processor, the Motorola MC68000 should be expected to have a more complex interrupt structure than the 8-bit processors. It does. To begin with, the MC68000 has three interrupt-input lines. These are not separate interrupt inputs, however. They are designed to have an encoded interrupt level driven onto them. Thus seven active interrupt levels are supported. When none of the interrupt inputs is driven low, there is no interrupt request. This seven-level interrupt scheme is hardware-interrupt vectoring.

When a level is driven onto the interrupt lines, the MC68000 compares it against a mask level in its status register. If the interrupt request is below the mask level, it is ignored. Interrupt-level 7 is nonmaskable. The interrupt levels are also prioritized, with level 7 having the highest priority. Lower-priority interrupt requests cannot interrupt higher-level interrupt service routines. This is because the mask level is automatically adjusted to the level of the interrupt being serviced. The mask is restored when the interrupt service routine returns to the main program with a return from exception (RTE) instruction.

An interrupt acknowledge is signaled by an

MC68000 bus cycle with all function-code bits asserted. Address bits A1 through A3 signal the level of interrupt being acknowledged. The external circuitry can then do one of two things. It can complete the bus cycle by placing an interrupt vector on the lower eight data bits and asserting the data transfer acknowledge $\overline{(\text{DTACK})}$ control line. This provides the MC68000 with one of 256 possible interrupt vectors and is an example of software-interrupt vectoring.

The other alternative is for the external circuitry to assert the MC68000 Valid Peripheral Address (VPA) input. This requests that the MC68000 use an auto vector. There are seven auto vectors in the MC68000 vector table, one for each interrupt level. When an auto vector is requested, the MC68000 selects the proper auto vector for the interrupt level being acknowledged and branches to the indicated location.

INTERRUPT SERVICE ROUTINES

When a microprocessor finally manages to reach an interrupt service routine, something had better happen because a lot of work went into getting to the routine. Usually, an interrupt branch occurs in response to an I/O request for service. The request may have happened for a variety of reasons. The three most frequent reasons are;

1. An output device is ready for another chunk of data to output.

2. An input device has just received a chunk of information from a peripheral.

3. Something has gone wrong with an I/O transfer.

The first two reasons form the core of interrupt-driven I/O software. As we said at the beginning of the chapter, the processor is much faster than the devices we are going to access using interrupt-driven I/O. In order to prevent the processor from wasting its time waiting for the device to get ready for the next transfer, we plan to use interrupts to signal this event.

Most good interrupt-driven I/O schemes use buffers to hold the information to be transferred. The interrupt service routine can be considerably simplified if buffer transfers are used. If an output transfer is under way, the routine merely gets the next piece of data from the buffer and sends it to the I/O device. If this action is not sufficient to satisfy the interrupt, the routine may have other housework to do. If an input transfer is taking place, the interrupt service routine gets the data from the interrupting I/O device and puts it into the next available position in the buffer.

When the output buffer empties or the input buffer fills, the interrupt service routine will also have to set a signal so that the main program can learn of the completed task. The complete scheme is for the main program to first create a buffer, then to fill it if it is an output buffer. Then the interrupts should be enabled. Often, the first-time interrupt programmer will blindly enable interrupts and find that the program isn't really ready to handle an interrupt because the buffer isn't set up yet. It is important to enable the interrupts last, when everything else is ready to go, because the first time an I/O chip is enabled for interrupt, it is likely to interrupt immediately.

An example where this is true is a serial I/O chip. The transmitters of these devices are generally designed to interrupt whenever they are ready for a character to transmit. Since the serial I/O chip was probably ready long before being enabled to interrupt, it will interrupt within nanoseconds after being enabled.

Interrupts can be enabled in one of several ways. First there may be an interrupt-enable facility in the processor, assuming we aren't dealing with non-maskable interrupts. Then, there is probably an interrupt enable in the I/O chip. There may also be several interrupt conditions to select from in the I/O chip. Finally, hardware between the I/O chip and the processor may contain interrupt enables.

HIGH-LEVEL INTERRUPTS

So far, the interrupts we have been considering are low- or machine-level interrupts. This type of interrupt is directly supported by the interrupt circuitry built into the processor. When a microcomputer is executing a program written in a high-level language such as BASIC or Pascal, low-level interrupts may have very little to do with program execution.

Let's consider why this might be true. During the execution of a single high-level-language statement, thousands of machine instructions are actually being executed. Variables are changing, stacks move up and down, the registers in the processor change frequently. All of a sudden, an interrupt comes in. What happens?

The interrupt may occur at a most inconvenient time in relation to where the high-level program is executing. Perhaps a large array of numbers is being filled and some of the numbers in the array will be modified by the interrupt service routine.

Because the connection between machine-level interrupts and a high-level language is difficult to define and implement, most microprocessor high-level languages simply do not support any sort of interrupt operation. Notable exceptions are the HPL and BASIC interpreters in Hewlett-Packard's desktop computers and the Microsoft BASIC found in the IBM PC. These high-level languages support some sort of user interrupt service routine or buffer-transfer capability.

High-level languages frequently have subroutine capability in them. In HPL (Hewlett-Packard's High Performance Language of the 9825A/B) subroutines are invoked with the "gsb" (go subroutine) statement, and the main program is returned using a "ret." BASIC uses the corresponding statements GOSUB and RETURN.

User interrupt service routines are a variation of the subroutine. After interrupts are enabled, the subroutine is invoked because a peripheral interrupts. The subroutine is written in the high-level language of the computer and is terminated with an interrupt return statement such as "iret" in HPL. The following HPL program fragment illustrates how user interrupt service routines are written:

```
10: 1→I
11: oni 6, "send"
12: eir 6
    •
    •
    •
87: "send": wtb 6,A$[I,I]
88: I+1−I;if I<len(A$);eir 6
89: iret
```

Line 10 sets a counter that points to individual characters in string A$. Line 11 directs the program to line 87, labeled "send," should an interrupt occur, and line 12 enables the interface hardware and software to accept interrupts. Line 87 sends a single character from string A$ each time the user interrupt service routine is called. Line 88 increments the counter I to the next character and reenables interrupts if there are more characters to transmit. Line 89 forces a branch back to the main program.

There are several things to note from this example. The "eir 6" enables the interface. The meaning of an interrupt is that the interface is not busy. The first interrupt will occur immediately after the computer executes line 12. Novices at interrupt routines are always bitten by this the first time they write one. If the interface has not been made busy by sending it a character before interrupts are enabled, the interrupt is immediate.

Note that a counter must be used by the program to keep track of where the next character will come from in A$. Also note that interrupts must be reenabled in the interrupt service routine if the transfer is not done. This is necessary because the "eir" is canceled when it is invoked. That prevents the interrupt service routine from being interrupted.

High-level language program lines are slow compared to the processor speed. Only low data rates can be supported using user interrupt service routines. Buffer transfers are a much better choice for data transfers, leaving user routines to service special situations.

Buffers are blocks of computer memory allocated for I/O. Data passes through the buffer on the way into or out of the computer. Enabling of interrupts and character counters are taken care of automatically and new features are available. Data transfers can be terminated on a count, as in the above example, or by a character match for buffered input.

The following example performs the same task as the first, but uses buffered I/O.

```
10: buf "OUT",100,1
11: wrt "OUT",A$
12: tfr "OUT",6
```

As you can see, this is much simpler. Line 10 creates a buffer of 100 characters, line 11 fills the buffer with the contents of string A$, and line 12 sends the data to the peripheral. The 1 at the end of line 10 specifies an interrupt buffer.

Why is this technique superior to simply writing out the data directly to the peripheral? Line 12 only initiates the data transfer. After that process is started, the program will continue with line 13. When the peripheral interrupts, it will automatically be given the next character. Meanwhile, the computer is executing the rest of the program.

Interrupt buffers are faster than user interrupt service routines for one primary reason: The only safe place to interrupt a high-level language program is at the end of a line. In the execution of a line of high-level-language code, temporary locations are set up, addresses are calculated, and a whirl of activity is taking place.

An interrupt routine must be able to return to where the program was interrupted after the interrupt is serviced. If the user routine accesses variables being used by the main program, or worse yet, changes them, there could be disastrous results. That is why high-level-language interrupts are restricted to the end of a line. Things are safe there.

Conversely, the routines used by the buffer-transfer interrupt service routines are in machine code and are very restricted in what they can do. Their effect on the system is well known because all they are allowed to do is transfer data.

Buffer interrupts are allowed any time they are enabled. Thus, interrupt-buffer transfers can be much faster than user interrupt service routines for data transfer. They are also easier to use.

INTERRUPT BUFFERS

There are two types of interrupt buffer: linear and circular. Linear buffers are good for output processes, and circular buffers are especially well suited for input buffers. A linear buffer is a block of memory locations designated as a buffer.

For output, the processor fills the buffer under programmed I/O and then starts the I/O transfer. The interrupt service routine then outputs the characters in the buffer until it is empty, at which time the main program is alerted. The main program may then choose to refill the buffer or do something else. Figure 8-2 illustrates a linear output buffer.

A linear buffer is used for input only when some terminating condition on the input process can be defined. Two terminating conditions are common; a terminal count and a terminating character. A terminal count defines the number of characters which will be received. After that number of characters is placed in the buffer, the input transfer is stopped and the main program is alerted that the buffer is full and needs to be read. If a terminating character is used, the transfer is stopped upon receipt of that character and its placement into the input buffer. Once the transfer terminates, the buffer must be read before it may be reused. Figure 8-3 illustrates a linear input buffer.

Circular buffers are useful for I/O processes which do not have any fixed termination condition.

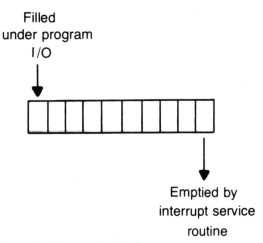

Fig. 8-2. A linear output buffer.

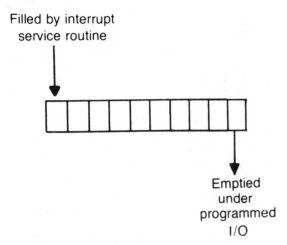

Filled by interrupt
service routine

Emptied
under
programmed
I/O

Fig. 8-3. A linear input buffer.

A very good example of such a process is serial asynchronous communications during the emulation of a video display terminal (VDT). Characters come in a continuous stream and are supposed to be printed on the screen as they are received. The process continues until the emulation is stopped.

If the emulation program is written in assembly language, interrupts may be used to handle incoming characters on a character-by-character basis. The time required to service an interrupt at this level is very short, on the order of 100 microseconds.

However, if the emulation has been written in a high-level language, and the interrupt service routine is also written in a high-level language, the time required to service each interrupt may take milliseconds. This is because high-level languages that support high-level interrupt service routines only allow the interrupt to occur at the end of a line. It's the only way to ensure orderly interruption of the program.

With an interrupt-service time of several milliseconds, a high-level VDT emulator could only support low bit rates on the asynchronous communications port, if the interrupt service routine handles one character at a time. By using circular buffers, however, the performance can be considerably enhanced. This is because the characters are brought in by a small machine-level routine just smart enough to fill a buffer, which can be fast. At its leisure, the high-level program can check the buffer to see if there are any characters to print. It can take all the characters in the buffer as a block, which is an efficient way for a high-level language to handle characters.

Naturally, an output process can also make use of a circular buffer. The same advantages are in effect. **Figure 8-4** shows a circular input buffer and **Fig. 8-5** illustrates a circular output buffer. Circular buffers use the same block of RAM as that used by

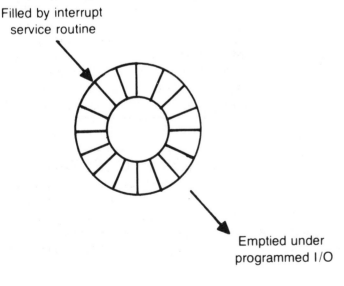

Filled by interrupt
service routine

Fig. 8-4. A circular input buffer.

Emptied under
programmed I/O

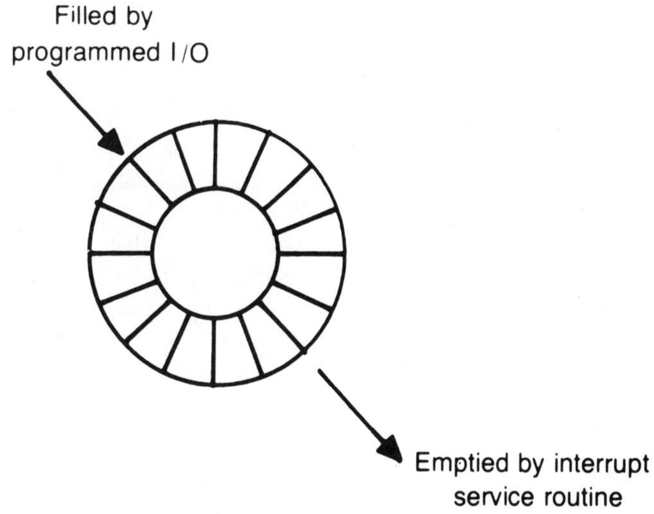

Filled by
programmed I/O

Fig. 8-5. A circular output buffer.

Emptied by interrupt
service routine

a linear buffer. The difference is in the way the programmed I/O and interrupt service routine keep their place in the buffer.

In both cases, the place in the buffer is remembered by some sort of software counter. For a linear buffer, the counter starts at the first address in the buffer and increments or decrements by one for each character put in or taken out. When the counter reaches the end of the buffer, it has either been emptied or filled, depending on whether the buffer is being used for input or output.

The counter works differently for a circular buffer. Again, it starts at the address which serves as the "beginning" of the buffer, and increments or decrements. However, when the counter reaches the end of the buffer, the counter is reset to the beginning again. This can only work if the process which empties the buffer is faster than the process which fills it.

Let's take a circular input buffer as our example again. The process filling the buffer is an interrupt service routine. An input device interrupts when it has a character ready to be placed in the buffer. This activates the interrupt service routine which takes the character and places it in the next available location in the buffer. At the same time, the main program periodically checks the status of the buffer to see if it needs to be emptied.

As soon as any characters are placed into the buffer by the interrupt service routine, it should be emptied by the main program. Otherwise, the circular buffer will continue to fill until it overflows. Data will be lost as older data in the buffer is overwritten by the newer data coming in.

Actually, circular buffers require that two counters be used. One is used by the process putting information into the buffer, and the other is used by the process taking the information out. The counter used by the filling process is called a fill pointer and the counter used by the emptying process is called the empty pointer.

Serial communications is not the only type of I/O which benefits from circular buffering. Keyboards frequently are serviced by a circular buffer routine. Any device which has unpredictable short-term I/O speed requirements, but an average requirement that can always be serviced, is a candidate for circular-interrupt buffering.

EXCEPTION PROCESSING

Interrupts are not used just to transfer data. Often, an interrupt is needed if something goes wrong, and the processor needs to be alerted when it does. Examples of such cases are loss of power to the system, or a read-error by a storage device.

In the case of power loss, we assume that the computer's power supply can maintain the system long enough after the loss of the main power to allow the processor to do something useful, such as saving important data in RAM with battery backup, or simply shutting down all I/O in an orderly fashion.

Interrupts based on something failing to happen as planned activate exception processing. What occurs during the exception processing is up to the programmer. If a nuclear reactor is going super-critical, the computer may drop the control rods to achieve a SCRAM. If a tape-read error occurs, nothing more than a printed error message may be produced. It really depends on what the system designer, programmer, and user need.

Exceptions aren't always caused by system problems, however. The real-time clocks we looked at in Chapter 7 were capable of generating periodic interrupts. These would also cause exception processing, although their function is a normal part of system operation.

Chapter 9

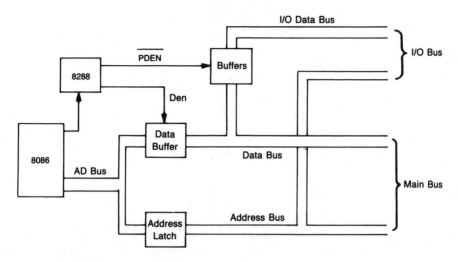

Direct-Memory-Access Interfacing

My previous discussions have all assumed that the microprocessor is in control of the data-transfer process. This situation is true for a large portion of the devices interfaced. The processor is usually fast enough that the peripheral device limits the data-transfer rate, but this is not always the case.

Some devices are too fast for processor-controlled I/O. These devices are capable of data rates approaching the speed of the computer memory, and require a different I/O technique. Such a technique for interfacing these fast peripherals is called direct-memory access (DMA).

WHAT IS DMA?

In order to discuss DMA and how it works, we must return to the model of the processor-memory-I/O system discussed in Chapter 1. Recall that the processor is linked to the memory via a set of lines called a bus, as illustrated in Fig. 9-1. The processor is required to generate address and control signals to synchronize the flow of data over the bus. Generally, an I/O task consists of taking infor-

mation from the interfaces and transmitting this information to the memory, or vice versa.

During this transfer, the processor is also using the memory and the bus to obtain machine instructions so that it knows how to perform the data transactions. If we assume that it takes only 10 bus cycles to perform one data transaction, we can see that the effective I/O throughput is only 10 percent of the rate that the memory could support. That is, for every 10 memory cycles, nine are used to instruct the processor and only one is used to place data for I/O. An example sequence for an input process with an 8-bit microprocessor might be:

1. Read the status of the interface (2 byte instruction plus an I/O cycle)
2. Is the interface ready? (2 byte instruction)
3. If not ready, go back to 1 (2 byte instruction)
4. Input a piece of data (2 byte instruction plus an I/O cycle)

In this example, ten bus cycles are executed. Eight are memory cycles, two are I/O cycles but

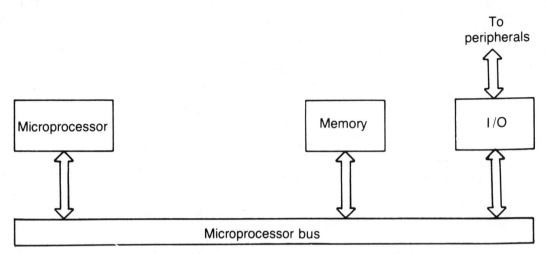

Fig. 9-1. Block diagram of a microcomputer system.

one I/O cycle is used to check the status of the interface. Only very simple data transactions can be performed with nine machine instructions. If formatting or code conversions are necessary, many more instructions are needed.

The only way to speed up the I/O process is to eliminate the slowest link in the data path. For high-speed peripherals, the slowest link is clearly the processor itself! How can we eliminate the processor when that is the component required for the generation of the signals that actually make the bus work? The answer is to build a specialized circuit that is designed to transfer data at the full memory speed.

Since the only function this circuitry must perform is data transfer, the transfer sequence can be hard-wired into the circuit. Instructions from memory are not needed and do not reduce the effective memory bandwidth.

If we place this specialized circuitry so that it too has the capability of generating the address and control signals required by the bus, then we have a machine that is capable of performing I/O at the full memory speed. This specialized circuitry is called a direct-memory access, or DMA, machine. **Figure 9-2** shows how a DMA controller can be added to a microprocessor system. All that remains is to select which device will have control of the busses— the processor or the DMA machine.

BUS AND DMA REQUESTS

Normally, the processor will have control of the bus because otherwise, no processing will be done. It is therefore necessary for the DMA machine to acquire control from the processor whenever DMA transfers are to take place. The processor can enable the DMA machine to request bus control, but it is the interface that must actually trigger the bus request by requesting service by the DMA machine. Only the interface knows when the peripheral it is attached to requires DMA service. Thus, we must add some signals between the interface and the DMA machine and between the DMA machine and the processor for the various requests.

The interface must have some means of requesting service from the DMA machine. A signal called DMA Request (DMAR) added to the collection of signal lines on our bus will be sufficient. Upon receipt of this request from an I/O device, the DMA machine must request bus control from the processor. The processor may decide that the timing of the request is not convenient and will temporarily ignore the request. This usually happens when the request is received in the middle of an instruction-fetch cycle. The processor cannot cut the bus cycle short without violating bus protocol, and so it postpones the granting of the bus request until it has finished with the bus. Eventually, though, the

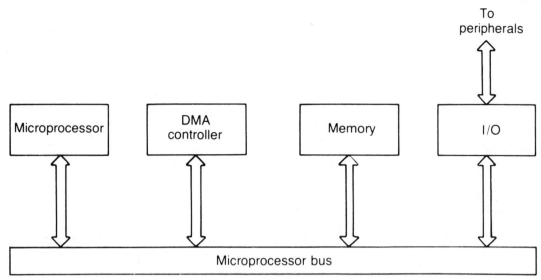

Fig. 9-2. Microcomputer system with DMA controller added.

processor will grant the request and allow the DMA controller to take over the bus.

We will create two handshake lines called Bus Request and Bus Grant. The DMA machine will ask for bus control with Bus Request, but will not actually take control until it receives a signal on Bus Grant. Thus, the processor can maintain control of the memory and address busses as long as required. When the processor does grant the bus to the DMA controller, the controller performs the transfer or transfers needed to satisfy the DMA request from the I/O device. It then returns control of the bus back to the processor. Figure 9-3 shows the new DMAR, Bus-Request, and Bus-Grant signals in a microcomputer system.

TYPES OF DMA TRANSFERS

There are two types of DMA transfer possible; burst and cycle-steal. Each has advantages and disadvantages. During a burst DMA transfer, the DMA controller performs multiple bus transfers each time it acquires the bus. Burst operation is well matched to block-transfer tasks such as the transfer of a sector of information from a disk, or a record from a magnetic-tape drive. Here, the data is physically blocked together and speeds are high

enough to require a quick burst transfer. Typically, the entire sector will be transferred in one burst. During a burst DMA transfer, the processor is idle.

If the entire bus bandwidth is not required to solve the high-speed I/O problem, the other type of DMA can be employed. Called cycle-steal DMA, the DMA machine alternates control of the bus with the processor, using every other memory cycle. Cycle-steal DMA allows the processor to operate at approximately 50 percent efficiency while still providing higher speed transfers than does programmed I/O.

In addition to burst and cycle-steal DMA, we must also consider how the data actually flows over the bus during a DMA transfer. With the signals we have created so far, there is no way for the DMA controller to make a transfer directly from the I/O to memory, or from memory to I/O.

This is because a microprocessor bus is designed to only access one device at a time. If memory is being addressed during a bus cycle, only memory will respond. If an I/O device is accessed, memory is idle. Bus transfers are always made assuming that the microprocessor is either the source or destination for the transfer, thus only the other device needs to be explicitly addressed.

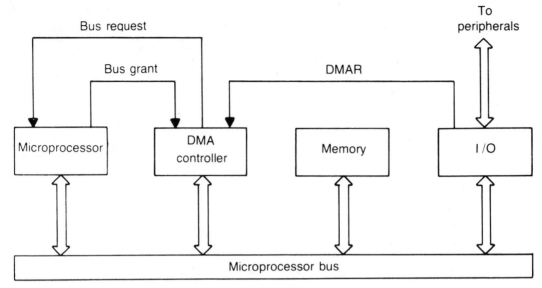

Fig. 9-3. Extra signals must be added to the system for DMA operation.

One solution to this problem is to have the data flow through the DMA controller. During one DMA transfer, the DMA controller accesses the source device and accepts one piece of information, storing it in an internal register. During the next DMA transfer, the DMA controller outputs the stored information to the destination device. Though this type of operation works well, it halves the maximum DMA transfer rate because two bus cycles are required for each transfer.

A better solution requires the addition of more signal lines. Not only is a DMA Request needed from each I/O device but a DMA Acknowledge (DACK) for each is used to signal when a transfer is taking place. The DMA Acknowledge is supplied to the I/O device by the DMA controller. It serves as an alternate addressing route to free up the address lines on the bus. This allows the DMA controller to always use the bus address lines to address memory, while using DMA Acknowledge lines to address I/O devices. One bus cycle can then transfer information directly from I/O to memory or from memory to I/O.

This is called a flyby transfer because the information flies by the DMA controller and never passes through it. **Figure 9-4** shows how this is

done. In addition to the signal lines shown, the DMA Controller and the four I/O devices are also connected to the microcomputer bus so that they can be accessed by the processor for initialization.

DMA CONTROLLERS

What is in a DMA controller? In addition to the circuitry needed to control a microcomputer bus, there are registers to regulate DMA controller operation. One register is needed to specify the address of the source device while another is needed to specify the address of the destination. A third register is needed to program the number of transfers to take place under DMA.

Also, various registers are required to more completely define the type of DMA which will take place. Will it be burst or cycle-steal, flyby or flowthrough? Other parameters are whether the source and destination address registers will be incremented, decremented, or left alone after each transfer. With the flexibility to specify these parameters, buffers can be created in memory in either direction. For transfers to an I/O device, the address will not change from one transfer to the next.

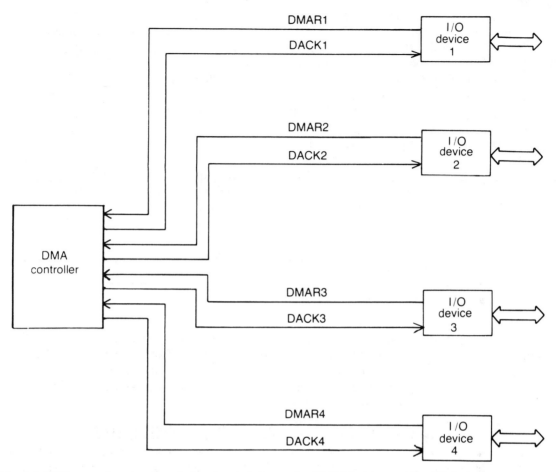

Fig. 9-4. DMA-request and -acknowledge signals between the DMA Machine and the I/O devices.

DMA controllers are designed to handle only a certain number of channels. Two- and four-channel controllers are common. Each channel must have its own source, destination, count, and configuration registers. This way, multiple DMA transfers may be active simultaneously, although only one is in control of the bus at any given time.

Each microprocessor usually has a DMA controller designed especially for it. This is because the controller becomes intimately connected to the processor bus. The controller must closely emulate the operation of the processor's bus-control lines in order to be compatible with the other devices on the bus. Other factors which need to match are the

type of bus handshake, the Bus Request and Bus Grant lines, and the number of address lines driven.

One big problem with the newer 16-bit processors is that 8-bit DMA controllers don't match the new bus structures. Considerable design effort and extra circuitry is required to adapt these controllers to processor busses which they weren't designed to be compatible with.

WHY DMA?

DMA controllers add a lot of complexity to the design of a microprocessor system. They should only be used when interrupt or programmed I/O cannot service a device fast enough to satisfy system requirements.

The most common I/O devices to require DMA operation are mass-storage devices such as tape and disk drives. These devices are fast, and when they require service, it cannot be withheld. When a disk sector is passing by a read head at 600 miles per hour, the electronics must be ready to accept or provide the information at the proper rate. Otherwise, data will be lost. DMA is the best way to assure the proper operation of these devices.

Another class of device which can work better under DMA is buffered peripherals. These devices have RAM buffers in them and can accept or provide data at a very high rate. DMA can be used to quickly fill or empty these buffers. Buffered devices don't always require DMA, however. Often, the buffering is designed into a device to smooth the flow of data between the processor and the device. In effect, the buffer takes the place of a DMA controller. As RAM prices have dropped, buffered devices have become more common. Many disks are now offered with sector buffers so that DMA operation isn't required. However, DMA can still be used to maximize performance with these peripherals.

Appendices

Appendix A
Number Base Calculator Program

The following program was written for the IBM Personal Computer. With minor changes it will run on most microcomputers that use Microsoft BASIC. Terms that may need to be changed include CLS, INKEY$, BEEP, and the symbol for exponentiation. Consult your BASIC manual if you have problems running the program on your machine.

    The program is designed to convert a number from any base between 2 and 16 to its binary, octal, decimal, hexadecimal, or ASCII code equivalent. It also enables you to perform simple one-function computations and will print the result in any of the five systems.

    To use the program, load BASIC and then enter or load the program and run it. You will first be asked what base you will be entering numbers in.

Enter a value between 2 and 16. Then you will be asked for a number or an equation. Valid inputs are

> <number> = (you may press the return or enter key instead of typing the equal sign.)

or

> <number> <function> <number> = (where function is +, −, * or /.)

    After either of the above lines is entered, the program prints the results. The messages on the screen are self-explanatory.

319

```
1000 REM ***********************************************************************
1010 REM *
1020 REM * NUMBER CONVERSION PROGRAM
1030 REM *
1040 REM *    THIS PROGRAM ACTS LIKE A TI PROGRAMMER CALCULATOR
1050 REM *    IT WILL TAKE NUMBERS IN ANY BASE BETWEEN 2 AND 16
1060 REM *    INCLUSIVE AND CALCULATE AN ANSWER.  LEGAL INPUTS ARE:
1070 REM *
1080 REM *    <NUMBER> =  THIS SIMPLY CONVERTS THE NUMBER FOR YOU
1090 REM *    <NUMBER><OPERATION><NUMBER> =
1100 REM *                    WHERE <OPERATION> IS +,-,* OR /
1110 REM *
1120 REM *
1130 REM * ANSWERS ARE PRINTED IN BINARY, OCTAL, DECIMAL, HEXADECIMAL
1140 REM * AND ASCII EQUIVALENT IF THE RESULT IS LESS THAN 255
1150 REM * DECIMAL.
1160 REM *
1170 REM ***********************************************************************
1180 DIM A$(1),O$(30),C9$(16),C$(3)
1190 C9$="0123456789ABCDEF"
1200 REM * IBM PC AND OTHER MICROSOFT BASICS USE CLS FOR CLEAR SCREEN
1210 REM START OF MAIN PROGRAM
1220 CLS
1230 REM POINT A
1240 INPUT "ENTER THE BASE YOU WILL BE ENTERING NUMBERS IN ",B1
1250 B1=INT(B1)
1260 IF B1>1 AND B1<17 THEN 1330
1270 PRINT "I CANNOT HANDLE BASES LESS THAN 2 OR GREATER THAN 16"
1280 PRINT "PLEASE RECONSIDER AND PRESS THE RETURN KEY WHEN YOU"
1290 PRINT "ARE READY.":BEEP
1300 GOSUB 2340
1310 CLS
1320 GOTO 1240
1330 REM INITIALIZE ALL VARIABLES
1340    N1=0:REM FIRST NUMBER TO BE ENTERED
1350    N2=0:REM SECOND NUMBER, IF ANY
1360    N=0:REM NUMERIC ENTRY VARIABLE
1370    F=0:REM ARITHMETIC FUNCTION CODE, ZERO IS NO FUNCTION
1380 CLS
1390 PRINT "ENTER YOUR NUMBER OR EQUATION NOW: "
1400 PRINT
1410 REM POINT C
1420 GOSUB 2340
1430 A=ASC(A$)
1440    IF (A)47 AND A<58) OR (A)64 AND A<71) THEN 1530
1450    IF A=43 OR A=45 OR A=42 OR A=47 THEN 1660
1460    IF A=61 THEN 1750
1470    IF A=13 THEN 1750
1480 PRINT
1490 PRINT "ILLEGAL KEY PRESSED, PLEASE PRESS RETURN AND WE WILL START"
1500 PRINT "AGAIN":BEEP
1510 GOSUB 2340
1520 GOTO 1210
1530 REM NUMERIC CALCULATION
1540    A=A-48:REM CONVERT THE NUMERALS 0 THROUGH 9
1550    IF A>9 THEN A=A-7:REM CONVERT THE HEX NUMERALS A THROUGH F
```

```
1560    IF A<B1 THEN 1630
1570      PRINT
1580      PRINT "NUMERAL IS NOT APPROPRIATE FOR YOUR NUMBER BASE."
1590      PRINT "PLEASE PRESS RETURN AND WE WILL START OVER."
1600      BEEP
1610      GOSUB 2340
1620      GOTO 1330
1630    N=N*B1+A:REM BUILD UP THE INPUT NUMBER
1640      PRINT A$;
1650      GOTO 1420
1660 REM FUNCTION CODE DETECTION
1670      IF A=43 THEN F=1
1680      IF A=45 THEN F=2
1690      IF A=42 THEN F=3
1700      IF A=47 THEN F=4
1710    N1=N:REM SAVE THE FIRST NUMBER
1720    N=0:REM RESET INPUT VARIABLE
1730      PRINT A$;:REM PRINT THE FUNCTION SYMBOL
1740      GOTO 1420
1750 REM CALCULATION OCCURS HERE
1760      PRINT "=";
1770      IF F=0 THEN 1860
1780      IF F<4 THEN 1860
1790      IF N<>0 THEN 1860
1800      PRINT
1810      PRINT "YOU HAVE TRIED TO DIVIDE BY ZERO, SORRY"
1820      PRINT "PRESS RETURN TO CONTINUE":BEEP
1830      GOSUB 2340
1840      GOTO 1330
1850 REM USE FUNCTION CODE TO DETERMINE THE OPERATION
1860      IF F=0 THEN N2=N
1870      IF F=1 THEN N2=N1+N
1880      IF F=2 THEN N2=N1-N
1890      IF F=3 THEN N2=N1*N
1900      IF F=4 THEN N2=N1/N
1910 REM PRINT THE ANSWERS
1920      PRINT
1930      D=N2
1940      B=2
1950      GOSUB 2460
1960      PRINT
1970      PRINT "ANSWER IN BINARY IS      ",O$
1980      D=N2
1990      B=8
2000      GOSUB 2460
2010      PRINT
2020      PRINT "ANSWER IN OCTAL IS       ",O$
2030      D=N2
2040      B=10
2050      GOSUB 2460
2060      PRINT
2070      PRINT "ANSWER IN DECIMAL IS     ",O$
2080      D=N2
2090      B=16
2100      GOSUB 2460
2110      PRINT
2120      PRINT "ANSWER IN HEXADECIMAL IS ",O$
```

```
2130     D=N2
2140     IF D<32 OR D>127 THEN 2180
2150     PRINT
2160     PRINT "ASCII EQUIVALENT OF THE NUMBER IS   ",CHR$(D)
2170   REM
2180     PRINT
2190     PRINT
2200     PRINT
2210     PRINT "PRESS RETURN WHEN YOU ARE READY FOR THE NEXT CALCULATION"
2220     GOSUB 2340
2230     GOTO 1330
2240 REM ***********************************************************************
2250 REM *
2260 REM * INPUT ROUTINE - tHIS ROUTINE GETS A CHARACTER FROM THE
2270 REM *                  KEYBOARD AND RETURNS IT IN A$, A ONE
2280 REM *                  BYTE STRING.  IT MUST WAIT FOR THE
2290 REM *                  CHARACTER AND NOT RETURN UNTIL A KEY
2300 REM *                  HAS BEEN PRESSED
2310 REM *
2320 REM ***********************************************************************
2330 REM
2340 A$=INKEY$:IF A$="" THEN 2340
2350 RETURN
2360 REM ***********************************************************************
2370 REM *
2380 REM * DECIMAL TO BASE CONVERSION ROUTINE
2390 REM *
2400 REM *                  THIS ROUTINE TAKES A DECIMAL NUMBER IN
2410 REM *                  D AND AN OUTPUT BASE IN B AND RETURNS A
2420 REM *                  CONVERTED NUMBER TO BE PRINTED IN
243. REM *                  STRING O$.
244. REM ***********************************************************************
2450 REM
2460 O$=""
2470     T1=INT(LOG(D)/LOG(B))
2480     FOR J=T1 TO 0 STEP -1
2490       T2=INT(B^J)
2500       T3=INT(D/T2)
2510       O$=O$+MID$(C9$,T3+1,1)
2520       D=INT(D-T3*T2)
2530     NEXT J
2540 RETURN
2550 END
```

Appendix B
Chips

PARALLEL PART#	MANUFACTURER	PORT 1 # BITS	PORT 2 # BITS	PORT 3 # BITS	PORT 4 # BITS	PACKAGE # PINS	COMMENTS
10696	ROCKWELL	4,4	4,4	4,4	4,4	42	
146823	MOTOROLA	8	8	8		40	CMOS
1851	RCA	8	8	4		40	CMOS FOR 1802
1852	RCA	8				24	CMOS FOR 1802
32B450A	SILICON SYS.	8				52/44	SCSI CONTROLLER
32C451	SILICON SYS.	8				52/44	SCSI CONTROLLER
5380	NCR	8				40	SCSI CONTROLLER
6103	INTERSIL	12	8			40	CMOS FOR 6100
6250	ADAPTEK	8				68	SCSI CONTROLLER
6520	COMMODORE	8+2H	8+2H			40	
6522	COMMODORE	8+2H	8+2H	SERIAL	16-BIT TIMER	40	
6523	COMMODORE	8	8	8		40	
6525	COMMODORE	8	8	8		40	
6526	COMMODORE	8	8	SERIAL		40	
6529	COMMODORE	8				20	
6821	MOTOROLA	8+2H	8+2H			40	
6822	MOTOROLA	8+2H	8+2H			40	6821 W/OPEN COLLECTOR
68230	MOTOROLA	8+2H	8+2H	8	24-BIT TIMER	48	
68488	MOTOROLA	8	8			40	IEEE-488 TALKER/LISTENER
7210	NEC	8				40	IEEE-488 TALKER/LISTENER/CON
82C11	SMC	8				40	CENTRONICS PRINTER PORT
8212	INTEL	8+1H				24	
8243	INTEL	4	4	4	4	24	8048 EXPANDER
82C43	INTERSIL	4	4	4	4	24	CMOS 8243
8254	NATIONAL	16				24	
8255A	INTEL	8	8	4	4	40	
8291A	INTEL	8	8			40	IEEE-488 TALKER/LISTENER
8292	INTEL	8	8			40	IEEE-488 CONTROLLER
8293	INTEL	8	8			40	IEEE-488 TRANSCEIVER
87030	FUJITSU	8 IN	8 OUT			88/100	SCSI CONTROLLER

PART #	MANUFACTURER					PACKAGE	COMMENTS
87033	FUJITSU	8				68	SCSI CONTROLLER
89351	FUJITSU	8 IN	8 OUT			64	SCSI CONTROLLER
89352	FUJITSU	8				48	SCSI CONTROLLER
8T31/8×31	SIGNETICS	8	8			24	FOR 8×300
8T32/8×32	SIGNETICS	8	8			24	FOR 8×300
8T36/8×36	SIGNETICS	8	8			24	FOR 8×300
8×42	SIGNETICS	8	8			24	FOR 8×300
8×320	SIGNETICS	8	8/16			40	FOR 8×300
9901	TEXAS INST.	9	7	6	CRU	40	FOR TI 9900
9914A	TEXAS INST.	8	8			40	IEEE-488 TALK/LIST/CNTRL
9960	TEXAS INST.	16				28	CRU SERIAL-PARALLEL CNV.
9965	TEXAS INST.	8	8			40	
HEF4738	SIGNETICS	8	8			40	IEEE-488 TALKER/LISTENER
NSC831	NATIONAL	8	8	4		40	FOR NSC800
TMS1024	TEXAS INST.	4	4	4	4	28	TMS1000 EXPANDER
TMS1025	TEXAS INST.	4,4	4,4	4,4	4,4	40	TMS1000 EXPANDER
Z80-PIO	ZILOG	8+2H	8+2H			40	ALSO MOSTEK 3881
Z8036	ZILOG	8	8	4		40	Z BUS 8536
Z8038	ZILOG	8+H	8+H			40	128×8 FIFO - Z BUS
Z8060	ZILOG	8+H	8+H			28	128×8 FIFO - GEN. BUS
Z84C20	ZILOG	8+2H	8+2H			40/44	FOR Z80
Z84C90	ZILOG	8+2H	8+2H	8		84/80	ALSO INCLUDES SERIAL PORT AN
Z8536	ZILOG	8	8	4		40	IEEE-488 HANDSHAKE

NOTE: H MEANS HANDSHAKE LINE

SERIAL

PART #	MANUFACTURER	MAX SPEED	ASYNC	BISYNC	SDLC	HDLC	ADCCP	PACKAGE	COMMENTS
1602	WEST. DIG.	800K	Y					40	UART
1671	WEST. DIG.	1M	Y	Y				40	
1854	RCA	250K	Y					40	CMOS UART
1933	WEST. DIG.	1.5M	N	N	Y	Y	Y	40	
1983	WEST. DIG.	20K	Y					28	ASYNC ONLY 8251
2123	WEST. DIG.	19.2K	Y					40	2 SERIAL PORTS
2601	SMC	250K	N	Y				40	
2651	SIGNETICS	19.2K	Y					28	
2651A	NATIONAL	19.2K	Y					28	IMPROVED 2651
2652	SIGNETICS	2M	N	Y	Y	Y	Y	40	
2661	SIGNETICS	38.4K	Y	Y				28	ENHANCED 2651
2681	SIGNETICS	38.4K	Y					40	2 PORTS, BIT RATE GEN.
2681	SIGNETICS	38.4K	Y					28	28-PIN 2681
2681	SIGNETICS	38.4K	Y					24	24-PIN 2681
2692	SIGNETICS	1M	Y					24/28/40	2 PORTS, BIT RATE GEN.
2698	SIGNETICS	1M	Y					48/84	8 PORTS, 4 TIMERS
5025	SMC	1.5M	N	Y	Y	Y	Y	40	
6402	INTERSIL	250K	Y					40	CMOS
6551	COMMODORE	19.2K	Y					28	
6850	MOTOROLA	500K	Y					24	
6854	MOTOROLA	2M	N		Y	Y	Y	28	
68681	SIGNETICS	38.4K	Y					40	2681 FOR 68000 BUS
68C681	EXAR	1M	Y					24/28/40	
78808	SMC	19.2K	Y					68	8 PORTS, 8 BIT RATE GEN.
82050	INTEL	10M	Y	Y				28	
8250	NATIONAL	56K	Y					40	W/BIT RATE GEN.
8251A	INTEL	64K	Y	Y				28	
82C51	INTEL	64K	Y	Y				28/44	
8273	INTEL	64K			Y			40	
8274	INTEL	1M	Y	Y	Y	Y	Y	40	
8868	FUJITSU	800K	Y					40	UART
88C681	EXAR	1M	Y					24/28/40	
9902	TEXAS INST.	250K	Y					18	CRU UART
9903	TEXAS INST.	500K		Y	Y	Y		20	CRU SYNCHRONOUS CHIP
CD180	CIRRUS LOGIC	38.4K	Y					84	8 PORTS
Z8030	ZILOG	1.67M	Y	Y	Y	Y		40	2 PORTS, BAUD RATE GEN.

Part #	Manufacturer	Speed					Pins	Comments
Z8470	ZILOG	500K	Y				40	2 PORTS, BAUD RATE GEN.
Z8449	ZILOG	800K	Y	Y	Y	Y	40	1-PORT 8470
Z8442	ZILOG	1.2M	Y	Y	Y	Y	40	2 PORTS
Z8530	ZILOG	1.67M	Y	Y	Y	Y	40	GENERAL Z8030

TIMERS

PART #	MANUFACTURER	TIMER 1 # BITS	TIMER 2 # BITS	TIMER 3 # BITS	TIMER 4 # BITS	PACKAGE # PINS	COMMENTS
1878	RCA	16	16			28	CMOS
2942	AMD	8	8			22	CASCADABLE
6840	MOTOROLA	16	16	16		28	
8253	INTEL	16	16	16		24	
8254	INTEL	16	16	16		24	IMPROVED 8253
9513	AMD	16	16	16	16,16	40	5 TIMERS
9964	TEXAS INST.	14				20	
Z8036	ZILOG	16	16	16		40	Z BUS TIMER
Z84C30	ZILOG	16	16	16	16	40	
Z8536	ZILOG	16	16	16		40	GENERAL Z8036

REAL-TIME CLOCKS

PART #	MANUFACTURER	H:M:S	D:M	Y	LEAP YEAR	ALARM	PULSE OUTPUT	PACKAGE # PINS	COMMENTS
1215	DALLAS SEMI	Y	Y	Y	Y	N	N	16	SERIAL INTERFACE
1216	DALLAS SEMI	Y	Y	Y	Y	N	N	28	CLOCK AND BATTERY IN IC SOCKET
146818	MOTOROLA	Y	Y	Y	Y	Y	Y	24	50 BYTES OF RAM
1879	RCA	Y	Y	N	N	Y	N	24	REAL TIME CLOCK
1990	NEC	Y	Y	N	N	N	N	14	SERIAL INTERFACE
58167A	NATIONAL	Y	Y	N	N	Y	Y	24	8-BIT PARALLEL I/O
58174A	NATIONAL	Y	Y	Y	Y	N	Y	16	4-BIT PARALLEL I/O
58274	NATIONAL	Y	Y	Y	Y	N	Y	16	IMPROVED 58174
5832	OKI	Y	Y	Y	N	N	N	18	4-BIT PARALLEL I/O
58321	OKI	Y	Y	Y	Y	N	Y	16	MULTIPLEXED ADDRESS/DATA
6242	OKI	Y	Y	Y	Y	N	Y	18	
68HC68T1	RCA	Y	Y	Y	Y	Y	Y	16	SERIAL INTERFACE
7170	INTERSIL	Y	Y	Y	Y	Y	Y	24	0.01-SEC RESOLUTION
8570	NATIONAL	Y	Y	Y	Y	Y	Y	28	33 BYTES OF RAM ON-CHIP
8571	NATIONAL	Y	Y	Y	Y	Y	Y	24	33 BYTES OF RAM ON-CHIP
CA01C50	CALMOS	Y	Y	Y	Y	Y	Y	24	

DMA CONTROLLERS

PART #	MANUFACTURER	BUS	# OF CHANNELS	MODES	PACKAGE
32104	AT&T	32000	4	CYCLE STEAL, BURST	133
32204	AT&T	32000	4	CYCLE STEAL, BURST	133
6844	MOTOROLA	6800	4	CYCLE STEAL, BURST	40
68430	SIGNETICS	68000	1	CYCLE STEAL, BURST	48
68440	MOTOROLA	68000	2	CYCLE STEAL, BURST	64/68
68442	MOTOROLA	68000	2	CYCLE STEAL, BURST	68
68450	HITACHI	68000	4	CYCLE STEAL, BURST	64
71071	NEC	8086	4	SINGLE, DEMAND, BLOCK	48/52
82257	SIEMENS	8086/286/386	4	32 SUBCHANNELS	68
82258	SIEMENS	8086/286/386	4	32 SUBCHANNELS	68
8237A	INTEL	8080	4	BLOCK DEMAND	40
82380	INTEL	80386	8	SINGLE, CHAINING	132
8257	INTEL	8080	4	READ/WRITE/VERIFY	40
9516A	AMD	Z8000	2	FLOWTHRU, BURST, CONTINUOUS	48
9517A	AMD	8080	4	BLOCK DEMAND	40
Z84C10	ZILOG	Z80	1	BURST, CONTINUOUS	40

ANALOG A-TO-D

PART #	MANUFACTURER	# OF BITS	CONVERSION TIME	CONVERSION TECHNIQUE	# OF PINS	COMMENTS
14443	MOTOROLA	8	300 US	SINGLE SLOPE	16	
14444	MOTOROLA	8	32 US	SUCC. APPROX.	40	
7109	INTERSIL	12	1-50 HZ	DUAL SLOPE	40	
8052	INTERSIL	3.5-4.5 DIG	3-30 HZ	DUAL SLOPE	40 OR 14	
8054	INTERSIL	12, 14, 16	VARIABLE	DUAL SLOPE	2 PKGS	
AD570	ANALOG DEV.	8	20 US	SUCC. APPROX.	16	
AD571	ANALOG DEV.	10	25 US	SUCC. APPROX.	18	
AD572	ANALOG DEV.	12	25 US	SUCC. APPROX.	32	
AD573	ANALOG DEV.	10	20 US	SUCC. APPROX.	20	
AD574	ANALOG DEV.	12	25 US	SUCC. APPROX.	28	
AD575	ANALOG DEV.	10	20 US	SUCC. APPROX.	14	SERIAL INTERFACE
AD578	ANALOG DEV.	12	3 US	SUCC. APPROX.	24	
AD579	ANALOG DEV.	10	1.8 US	SUCC. APPROX.	32	
AD673	ANALOG DEV.	8	20 US	SUCC. APPROX.	20	
AD5010	ANALOG DEV.	6	10 NS	FLASH	16	
AD5240	ANALOG DEV.	12	5 US	SUCC. APPROX.	32	
AD6020	ANALOG DEV.	6	20 NS	FLASH	16	
AD7550	ANALOG DEV.	13	40 MS	QUAD SLOPE	40	
AD7552	ANALOG DEV.	12	160 MS	QUAD SLOPE	40	
AD7571	ANALOG DEV.	10	80 US	SUCC. APPROX.	28	
AD7574	ANALOG DEV.	8	15 US	SUCC. APPROX.	16	
AD7581	ANALOG DEV.	8	80 US	SUCC. APPROX.	28	CMOS
AD9000	ANALOG DEV.	6	13 NS	FLASH	16	
ADC71	BURR-BROWN	16	50 US	SUCC. APPROX.	32	
ADC72	BURR-BROWN	16	50 US	SUCC. APPROX.	32	
ADC73	BURR-BROWN	16	170 US	SUCC. APPROX.	48	
ADC76	BURR-BROWN	16	15 US	SUCC. APPROX.	32	
ADC80	BURR-BROWN	12	25 US	SUCC. APPROX.	32	
ADC84	BURR-BROWN	12	10 US	SUCC. APPROX.	32	
ADC85	BURR-BROWN	12	10 US	SUCC. APPROX.	32	
ADC574	BURR-BROWN	12	25 US	SUCC. APPROX.	24	
ADC600K	BURR-BROWN	12	100 NS	SUBRANGING	40	
ADC674	BURR-BROWN	12	15 US	SUCC. APPROX.	24	
ADC803	BURR-BROWN	12	1.5 US	SUCC. APPROX.	32	
ADC804	BURR-BROWN	12	17 US	SUCC. APPROX.	32	
ADC0800	NATIONAL	8	50 US	SUCC. APPROX.	18	
ADC0801	NATIONAL	8	110 US	SUCC. APPROX.	20	DIFFERENTIAL INPUT
ADC0802	NATIONAL	8	110 US	SUCC. APPROX.	20	DIFFERENTIAL INPUT
ADC0803	NATIONAL	8	110 US	SUCC. APPROX.	20	DIFFERENTIAL INPUT
ADC0804	NATIONAL	8	110 US	SUCC. APPROX.	20	DIFFERENTIAL INPUT
ADC0805	NATIONAL	8	110 US	SUCC. APPROX.	20	DIFFERENTIAL INPUT
ADC0808	NATIONAL	8	100 US	SUCC. APPROX.	28	8 INPUT CHANNELS
ADC0811	NATIONAL	8	32 US	SUCC. APPROX.	20	11 INPUT CHANNELS, SERIAL OU
ADC0816	NATIONAL	8	100 US	SUCC. APPROX.	40	16 INPUT CHANNELS
ADC0820	NATIONAL	8	1.2 US	HALF-FLASH	20	
ADC0829	NATIONAL	8	100 US	SUCC. APPROX.	28	11 INPUT CHANNELS
ADC1001	NATIONAL	10	200 US	SUCC. APPROX.	20	
ADC1005	NATIONAL	10	200 US	SUCC. APPROX.	20	
ADC1021	NATIONAL	10	200 US	SUCC. APPROX.	24	
ADC1025	NATIONAL	10	200 US	SUCC. APPROX.	24	
ADC1205	NATIONAL	12	100 US	SUCC. APPROX.	24	
ADC1210	NATIONAL	12	200 US	SUCC. APPROX.	24	
ADC1211	NATIONAL	12	200 US	SUCC. APPROX.	24	
ADC1225	NATIONAL	12	100 US	SUCC. APPROX.	28	
ADC3511	NATIONAL	3.5 DIG.	200 MS	PULSE MODULATION	24	
ADC3711	NATIONAL	3.75 DIG.	400 MS	PULSE MODULATION	24	
ADC-908	PMI	8	6 US	SUCC. APPROX.	18	
ADC-910	PMI	10	6 US	SUCC. APPROX.	28	
ADC-9012	PMI	12	12 US	SUCC. APPROX.	24	
AM6108	AMD	8	1 US	SUCC. APPROX.	28	
HI5712	HARRIS	12	8 US	SUCC. APPROX.		
MAX133	MAXIM	3.75 DIG.	50 MS	RESIDUE MULT.	40	DIGITAL MULTIMETER CIRCUIT
MAX134	MAXIM	3.75 DIG.	50 MS	RESIDUE MULT.	40	DIGITAL MULTIMETER CIRCUIT
MAX136	MAXIM	35 DIG.	VARIABLE	DUAL SLOPE	40	

PART #	MANUFACTURER	# OF BITS			# OF PINS	COMMENTS
MAX150	MAXIM	8	1.34 US	HALF-FLASH	20	
MAX154	MAXIM	8	2.5 US	HALF-FLASH	24	4 INPUT CHANNELS
MAX158	MAXIM	8	2.5 US	HALF-FLASH	28	8 INPUT CHANNELS
MAX160	MAXIM	8	4 US	SUCC. APPROX.	18	
MAX161	MAXIM	8	20 US	SUCC. APPROX.	28	8 INPUT CHANNELS
MAX162	MAXIM	12	3 US	SUCC. APPROX.	24	
MAX172	MAXIM	12	10 US	SUCC. APPROX.	24	
NE5036	SIGNETICS	6	22 US	SUCC. APPROX.	8	
NE5037	SIGNETICS	6	9 US	SUCC. APPROX.	16	
NE5034	SIGNETICS	8	10 US	SUCC. APPROX.	18	
TDC1019J	TRW	9	50 NS	FLASH	64	
TDC1025J	TRW	8	16 NS	FLASH	64	

ANALOG, D-TO-A

PART #	MANUFACTURER	# OF BITS OR DIGITS	SETTLING TIME	PACKAGE # OF PINS	COMMENTS
AD390	ANALOG DEV.	12	8 US	28	QUAD 12-BIT DAC
AD558	ANALOG DEV.	8	1 US	16	TWO OUTPUT RANGES
AD561	ANALOG DEV.	10	250 NS	16	
AD562	ANALOG DEV.	12	1.5 US	24	
AD563	ANALOG DEV.	12	1.5 US	24	
AD565A	ANALOG DEV.	12	250 NS	24	
AD566A	ANALOG DEV.	12	350 NS	24	
AD567	ANALOG DEV.	12	500 NS	28	
AD569	ANALOG DEV.	16	6 US	28	
AD667	ANALOG DEV.	12	4 US	28	
AD1408	ANALOG DEV.	8	250 NS	16	MULTIPLYING DAC
AD3860	ANALOG DEV.	12	5 US	24	
AD6012	ANALOG DEV.	12	250 NS	20	
AD7110	ANALOG DEV.	6	20 KHZ	16	LOGARITHMIC, AUDIO DAC
AD7226	ANALOG DEV.	8	7 US	20	QUAD DAC
AD7240	ANALOG DEV.	12	550 NS	18	
AD7520	ANALOG DEV.	10	500 NS	16	
AD7521	ANALOG DEV.	12	500 NS	18	
AD7522	ANALOG DEV.	10	500 NS	28	
AD7523	ANALOG DEV.	8	100 NS	16	
AD7524	ANALOG DEV.	8	100 NS	16	ON-CHIP LATCH
AD7525	ANALOG DEV.	3.5 DIG.	1 US	18	BCD DAC
AD7528	ANALOG DEV.	8	500 NS	20	
AD7530	ANALOG DEV.	10	500 NS	16	
AD7531	ANALOG DEV.	12	500 NS	18	
AD7533	ANALOG DEV.	10	600 NS	16	
AD7541	ANALOG DEV.	12	1 US	18	
AD7542	ANALOG DEV.	12	2 US	16	
AD7543	ANALOG DEV.	12	2 US	16	SERIAL INPUT
AD7545	ANALOG DEV.	12	2 US	20	ON-CHIP LATCH
AD7546	ANALOG DEV.	16	4 US	40	ON-CHIP LATCH
AD7548	ANALOG DEV.	12	1.5 US	20	DUAL LATCHES FOR 8-BIT BUS
AD9768	ANALOG DEV.	8	5 NS	18	ECL INPUTS
DAC10HT	BURR-BROWN	12	300 NS	24	
DAC63	BURR-BROWN	12	30 NS	24	
DAC70	BURR-BROWN	16	10 US	24	
DAC71	BURR-BROWN	16	10 US	24	
DAC74	BURR-BROWN	16	50 US	94	SELF-CALIBRATING
DAC80	BURR-BROWN	12	4 US	24	
DAC82	BURR-BROWN	8	2.5 US	18	
DAC85	BURR-BROWN	12	300 NS	24	
DAC90	BURR-BROWN	8	200 NS	16	
DAC700	BURR-BROWN	16	8 US	24	
DAC705	BURR-BROWN	16	8 US	24/28	ON-CHIP LATCHES, SERIAL INPUT
DAC710	BURR-BROWN	16	8 US	24	
DAC800	BURR-BROWN	12	300 NS	24	
DAC811	BURR-BROWN	12	4 US	28	ON-CHIP LATCHES
DAC812	BURR-BROWN	12	55 NS	24	ON-CHIP LATCHES
DAC850	BURR-BROWN	12	5 US	24	
DAC1200	BURR-BROWN	12	7 US	24	
DAC1201	BURR-BROWN	12	7 US	24	ON-CHIP LATCHES

DAC1600	BURR-BROWN	16	10 US	24	
DAC0800	NATIONAL	8	100 NS	16	
DAC0801	NATIONAL	8	100 NS	16	
DAC0802	NATIONAL	8	100 NS	16	
DAC0806	NATIONAL	8	150 NS	16	
DAC0807	NATIONAL	8	150 NS	16	
DAC0808	NATIONAL	8	150 NS	16	
DAC0830	NATIONAL	8	1 US	20	ON-CHIP LATCH
DAC0831	NATIONAL	8	1 US	20	ON-CHIP LATCH
DAC0832	NATIONAL	8	1 US	20	ON-CHIP LATCH
DAC1000	NATIONAL	10	500 NS	24	ON-CHIP LATCH
DAC1001	NATIONAL	10	500 NS	24	ON-CHIP LATCH
DAC1002	NATIONAL	10	500 NS	24	ON-CHIP LATCH
DAC1006	NATIONAL	10	500 NS	24	ON-CHIP LATCH
DAC1007	NATIONAL	10	500 NS	24	ON-CHIP LATCH
DAC1008	NATIONAL	10	500 NS	24	ON-CHIP LATCH
DAC1020	NATIONAL	10	500 NS	16	
DAC1208	NATIONAL	12	1 US	24	CMOS
DAC1210	NATIONAL	12	1 US	24	CMOS
DAC1220	NATIONAŁ	12	500 NS	18	
DAC1230	NATIONAL	12	1 US	24	CMOS
DAC1231	NATIONAL	12	1 US	24	CMOS
DAC1232	NATIONAL	12	1 US	24	CMOS
HI562A	HARRIS	12	300 NS	24	
HI5610	HARRIS	10	85 NS	24	
HI5618A	HARRIS	8	45 NS	18	
ICL7134	INTERSIL	14	1 US	28	
NE5018	SIGNETICS	8	1.8 US	22	
NE5020	SIGNETICS	10	5 US	24	
NE5118	SIGNETICS	8	200 NS	22	

Appendix C
Integrated Circuit Manufacturers

Advanced Micro Devices (AMD)
901 Thompson Place
Sunnyvale, CA 94086
(408) 732-2400

Altera Semiconductor
3525 Monroe St
Santa Clara, CA 95051
(408) 984-2800

AT&T
555 Union Blvd
Allentown, PA 18103
(800) 372-CHIP

Analog Devices, Inc.
Box 280
Norwood, MA 02062
(617) 329-4700

Burr-Brown Corp.
Box 11400
Tucson, AZ 85734
(602) 746-1111

Calmos Semiconductor
20 Edgewater St
Kanata, Ontario
Canada K2L 1V8
(613) 836-1014

Cirrus Logic
1463 Centre Point Dr
Milpitas, CA 95035
(408) 945-8300

Commodore Semiconductor Products Group
950 Rittenhouse Rd
Norristown, PA 19403
(215) 666-7950

Dallas Semiconductor Corp
4350 Beltwood Pkwy
Dallas, TX 75244
(214) 450-0400

Exar-Excel
2222 Qume Dr
Box 49007
San Jose, CA 95161
(408) 434-6400

Fujitsu Microelectronics
3320 Scott Blvd
Santa Clara, CA 95054
(408) 562-1000

GE Solid State - Intersil
10600 Ridgeview Ct
Cupertino, CA 95014
(408) 996-5000

GE/RCA, Solid State Div
Rte 202
Somerville, NJ 08876
(201) 685-6420

Harris Semiconductor Products Div
Box 883
Melbourne, FL 32901
(305) 724-7800

Hitachi America Ltd.
Semiconductor and IC Div
2210 O'Toole Ave
San Jose, CA 95131
(408) 435-8300

Inmos
Box 16000
Colorado Springs, CO 80935
(303) 630-4000

Intel Corp.
3065 Bowers Ave
Santa Clara, CA 95051
(408) 987-8080

Lattice Semiconductor
555 N E Moore Ct
Hillsboro, OR 97124
(503) 681-0118

Linear Technology Corp
1630 McCarthy Blvd
Milpitas, CA 95035
(800) 637-5545

Logic Devices Inc
628 E Evelyn Ave
Sunnyvale, CA 94086
(408) 720-8630

Maxim Integrated Products
510 N Pastoria Ave
Sunnyvale, CA 94086
(408) 737-7600

Microchip Technology Inc
2355 W Chandler Blvd
Chandler, AZ 85224
(602) 963-7373

Mitsubishi Electronics America Inc
1050 Arques Ave
Sunnyvale, CA 94086
(408) 730-5900

Motorola, Inc
Box 52073
Phoenix, AZ 85072
(602) 962-2202

National Semiconductor Corp
2900 Semiconductor Drive
Box 58090
Santa Clara, CA 95052
(408) 721-5000

NCR Microelectronics
2001 Danfield Ct
Ft Collins, CO 80525
(800) 334-5454

NEC Microcomputer Div
1 Natick Executive Park
Natick, MA 01760
(617) 655-8833

OKI Semiconductor Inc
650 N Mary Ave
Sunnyvale, CA 94086
(408) 720-1900

Philips International BV
Box 218
5600 MD
Eindhoven
The Netherlands

Rockwell International
Microelectronics Devices Div
4311 Jamboree Rd
Newport Beach, CA 92660
(714) 833-4700

SGS Thomson Microelectronics
1000 E Bell Rd
Phoenix, AZ 85022
(602) 867-6100

Siemens Components
IC Standard Products Div
2191 Laurelwood Rd
Santa Clara, CA 95054
(408) 980-4500

Sierra Semiconductor
2075 N Capitol Ave
San Jose, CA 95123
(408) 263-9300

Signetics
811 E. Arques Avenue
Box 3409
Sunnyvale, CA 94088
(408) 991-2000

Silicon Systems
14351 Myford Rd
Tustin, CA 92680
(714) 731-7110

Siliconix
2201 Laurelwood Rd
Santa Clara, CA 95054
(408) 988-8000

Standard Microsystems Corp (SMC)
35 Marcus Blvd
Hauppauge, NY 11788
(516) 273-3100

Texas Instruments Inc
Semiconductor Group
Box 809066
Dallas, TX 75380
(800) 232-3200

Toshiba America Inc
2692 Dow Ave
Tustin, CA 92680
(714) 832-6300

TRW Electronic Components
Box 2472
La Jolla, CA 92038
(714) 578-5990

VLSI Technology
8375 S River Pkwy
Tempe, AZ 85284
(602) 752-8574

Western Design Center Inc
2166 E Brown Rd
Mesa, AZ 85203
(602) 962-4545

Western Digital Corp
2445 McCabe Way
Irvine, CA 92714
(714) 863-0102

Zilog, Inc
210 Hacienda Ave
Campbell, CA 95008
(408) 370-8000

Parts List

Index

status of, 134
timing for, 130
NUL, 22
number base calculator program, 319-322
number systems, 15-17

O

octal number system, 16
OKI MSM58321 clock, 294-297
one-wire handshaking, 149-152
one-wire serial interfaces, 207
open collector, 161
open collector output circuit, 14
OR, 3
output timing, Intel 8080 microprocessor, 45

P

parallel I/O integrated circuits, 169-171
  Intel 8255A , 172-179
  Motorola 6821, 179-185
  Motorola 68230, 185-192
  NCR 5380 SCSI adapter, 199-205
  Texas Instruments 9914A GPIBA, 192-199
parallel interface and timer (PIT), 284
parallel interfaces, 29, 144-205
  Centronics , 155-159
  classifications for, 144-145
  IEEE-488-1978 interface, 159-164
  Intel 8255A programmable peripheral interface, 172-179
  Motorola 6821 parallel interface adapter, 179-185
  Motorola 68230 parallel interface and timer, 185-192
  NCR 5380 SCSI adapter, 199-205
  one-wire handshaking, 149-152
  parallel I/O integrated circuits, 169-171
  small computer system interface (SCSI), 164-169
  Texas Instruments 9914A GPIBA, 192-199
  three-wire handshaking, 155
  two-wire handshaking, 152-155
  zero-wire handshaking in, 145-149
physical communication control characters, 22
pipelining, 25
polling, 164
positive true logic, 11
power supplies, converter, 270

processing, exception, 309
protocols
  bit-oriented, 210
  byte-control, 210
  component-level busses, 31
  serial interfaces, 208

R

R-2R ladder DAC, 257-260
ramp AD converter, 263
read cycle, 8-bit microprocessor, 37
receive common, 216
receiver/transmitter ICs for serial interfaces, 223
relative time, 274
remote loopback, 217
requests, bus and DMA, 312
resolution, 270
RS flip-flop, 7
RS-422, 216
RS-423, 216
RS-449, 216
RS232C standard, serial interfaces, 211-216

S

S100 bus, 98-105
  bus status for, 104
  bus timing for, 103
  physical description of, 104
  pins for, 99
select frequency, 216
select standby, 218
send common, 216
serial interfaces, 29
  asynchronous transmission in, 209
  bit-oriented protocols for, 210
  bit-rate generators for, 249
  byte-control protocols for, 210
  current loop for, 220
  integrated circuits for, 221
  Intel 8251A USART, 244-249
  level converters for, 221
  Maxim MAX230 series ICs for, 222
  Microchip Technology Ay-3-1015D UART, 225-230
  Motorola 6850 ACIA, 230-238
  Motorola MC1488/1489 level converters for, 221

Other Bestsellers From TAB